CLARA'S WHISPER

SALLY V. MCNICHOL

First Edition in 2025 by
Salvito Publishing, Perth, Australia

Copyright © 2024 Sally V McNichol
The right of Sally V McNichol to be identified as the author of the work has been asserted by her in accordance with the Copyright, Designs
and Patents Act 1988.

All rights reserved. This book is sold subject to the condition that no part of this book is to be reproduced, in any shape or form, or by way of trade, stored in a retrieval system or transmitted in any form or by any means, electronic, mechanical, photocopying, recording, be lent, re-sold, hired out or otherwise circulated in any form of binding or cover other than that in which it is published and without a similar condition, including this condition, being imposed on the subsequent purchaser, without prior permission of the copyright holder.

Cover design Hilary Pitt
Cover images from iStockphoto.com attributed to RixPix©

Publisher Disclaimer:
The events in this memoir are described according to the authors' recollection; recognition and understanding of the events and individuals mentioned are in no way intended to mislead or offend. As such the Publisher does not hold any responsibility for any inaccuracies or opinions expressed by the author. Every effort has been made to acknowledge and gain any permission from organisations and persons mentioned in this book. Any enquiries should be directed to the author.

Printed by IngramSparks (Australia)

ISBN 978-0-646-72891-9

To Family

Contents

PART ONE

PROLOGUE ~ Vienna, 9th May 2006	3
ONE ~ Dawa Goes Home	7
TWO ~ Almost Unjust	16
THREE ~ Journey Of Discovery 1951–1969	23
FOUR ~ Return To Vienna	104
FIVE ~ Journey Of Discovery 1989-2000	107
SIX ~ Dawa's Vienna 2000	116

PART TWO

ONE ~ Arriving In Vienna And Looking Back	144
TWO ~ Vienna, Settling In	190
Vienna, September 2006	201
Vienna, October 2006	202
Vienna, November 2006	213
Vienna, December 2006	214
Vienna, January 2007	221
Vienna, March 2007	238
Vienna, April 2007	253
Bushey, England, 2000	260
Vienna, May 2007	273
Vienna, July 2007	278
Vienna, August 2007	279

Vienna, November 2007	279
January 2008	281
February 2008	287
March 2008	293
EPILOGUE	300
APPENDIX 1 ~ Doris	303
APPENDIX 2 ~ The Vondras	305
APPENDIX 3 ~ The Relocation Of Vienna's Jews From The Walled City To Unterer Werd 1624	308
APPENDIX 4 ~ The Expulsion Of The Jews From Vienna 1669–70 By Holy Roman Emperor Leopold I	310
APPENDIX 5 ~ An Overview Of The History Of The Lowenthal Family And Their Name	313
APPENDIX 6 ~ Generalplan Ost And Lebensraum/Living Space	315
APPENDIX 7 ~ A Brief Historical Outline Of Christian Church Induced Jew Hatred	318
APPENDIX 8 ~ An Outline Of The Growth Of Anti-Semitism In Vienna And Hitler's Rise To Power	321
APPENDIX 9 ~ Revelation, The Teachings Begin	326
APPENDIX 10 ~ Baruch Spinoza's Concept Of God As Presented in Ethics	328
ACKNOWLEDGEMENTS	330

PART ONE

'My Days'
Isaac Rosenberg

My days are but the tombs of buried hours;
Which tombs are hidden in the pilèd years;
But from the mounds there springeth up such flowers
Whose beauty well repays its cost in tears.
Time, like a sexton, pileth mould on mould,
Minutes on minutes till the tombs are high;
But from the dust there falleth grains of gold,
And the dead corpse leaves what will never die.
It may be but a thought, the nursing seed
Of many thoughts, of many a high desire;
Some little act that stirs a noble deed,
Like breath rekindling a smouldering fire.
They only live who have not lived in vain,
For in their works their life returns again.

(1911)

Clara's Whisper

PROLOGUE

VIENNA, 9ᵀᴴ MAY 2006

'This is it!'
'Where?'
'Right here.'

My friendly airport pick-up has come to a halt in front of a set of impressive, glass-panelled double doors, almost as wide as they are tall. With nowhere else to park for more than a brief moment or two, I quickly retrieve my suitcase while rushing my thank-yous and see-you-soons to Kristina's son, Alex, before he must move on. Serendipitously for me, Alex relocated from Berlin to Vienna just a couple of years ago, when I had met him for the first time since he was a little boy of eight in Munich, way back in 1969.

As his car pulls away, I stare at the panel of a dozen or so bell buttons on the wall beside the door. My eyes are too tired to read the names; dammit, I'll have to rummage around in my overloaded shoulder bag to find my glasses. Then, as if on cue, a woman exits one half of the double doors.

On a reflex, and breaking all the rules of protocol, I slip into the entrance hall of the building that will be my home for the next six months.

This is no conventional entrance hall; rather, I have come into an internal driveway that leads to a parking area located within the guts of the building. The driveway is wide enough for a large vehicle to pass through without flattening some hapless pedestrian against its walls.

I notice that the ground is laid with cobblestones and immediately my heart starts to hum. Even the cool, slightly musty air seems delightful, and I inhale the pleasure as I pull my suitcase towards a doorway a few metres to my left.

As the rattle of its wheels echoes across the cobbles, my senses become fully engaged. Laughing deep within, I want to yell at the top of my voice, *'Yes! I'm home!'* I don't, of course, but my smile is so broad that I know it will be a while before it dissipates. For no other reason than this, I know that I have definitely done the right thing.

The lift, almost certainly an afterthought, is squeezed into the narrow well of a winding stone staircase that is trimmed with an art-nouveau wrought-iron balustrade. It is the tiniest lift I have ever encountered and, as if acknowledging that its occupants might experience claustrophobia, its interior is lined with mirrors.

As I ascend to the second floor, I try to avoid catching sight of myself. I don't look my best; in the three years since my mother's death I have experienced many life changes and challenges and when I am tired, like today, it shows – and not only in how my eyes cooperate. Anyway, who enjoys being reminded by such unflattering lighting that one's youthful looks are beginning to recede into the past. There is an added reason for my aversion: the mirrors are replicating me backwards and forwards into infinity, like a hallucinogenic vision scrambling my brain.

Fortunately, I am saved from further depressing thoughts and mind-altering visions by the lift stopping abruptly at the second floor. As I wrestle my case onto the landing, I realise the flipside of entering the building surreptitiously and not checking the nameplates first: I have completely forgotten what number apartment I am looking for. There's nothing for it but to knock on doors until I strike lucky.

One half of a double door adjacent to the lift is slightly ajar, so at least somebody is around who should be able to point me in the right direction. Not wishing to startle the occupant, I give the bell button the lightest of taps. Within a matter of seconds I hear footsteps, and the door is pulled open.

The petite, very elegant woman seems slightly taken aback – hardly surprising as I did enter the building unannounced. Immediately I am certain I have knocked on the right door. '*Frau*[1] Amasi?'

As we confirm our identities, I notice a man standing by another set of tall double doors at the far end of the hallway. Behind him, the room is awash with bright sunlight.

'*Herr*[2] Amasi?'

Walking towards him into what will soon be *my* apartment, I note the polished parquet flooring gently creaking underfoot. I am filled with an intense glow of wellbeing. Heavens, this place sounds so good, smells so good, feels so good; in this apartment there is space and there is light.

As if to confirm that I am in safe hands, my landlord's parents who

---

1   Mrs
2   Mr

are here to hand over the keys project an aura of quiet integrity. Without question, I have landed on my feet; if my heart had already begun to hum, now it is singing at the top of its voice.

It's funny how things turn out. Last year I spent several days in Vienna investigating the rental market in a vain attempt to find a reasonably pleasant, affordable, furnished apartment on a six-month contract. I flew back to London in despair; it seemed that my dream of delving more deeply into my Austrian past would never come to fruition.

Then, about two weeks ago, I was suddenly compelled to look again at the accommodation website Alex had recommended to me a while back. It is much favoured by students and other itinerants for its short-term rentals and the lack of the agent fees that tenants are normally obliged to pay, but it had not filled me with enthusiasm when I'd first looked at it. I did follow up on one possibility while I was in Vienna, only to discard it very quickly. I have no problem with simple – but a dark hovel? Nope, not when there might be a choice.

Now, scrolling down one page after another of shared student accommodation and bedsits, I started to lose heart again. Then my attention was caught by a price tag that suggested neither a hovel nor a luxurious pad that I could not afford.

Steeling myself to click onto the details, I did a double-take. This apartment had two large furnished rooms, one with a serious piece of modern architecture in the form of an enormous L-shaped glass and chrome desk, a separate WC, a generous modern bathroom with bath, shower and washing machine, modern kitchenette and central heating. It was ten minutes by underground to the city centre and the station was just across the road. Most importantly, the rent was within my budget.

Scarcely believing my luck – and wondering what the catch was – I had emailed Alex, asking him to look at the details and give me his thoughts.

'Not directly in the center of the city,' Alex, who is half-American, wrote back, 'so that makes the price, but it still seems to be close enough. Looks good, sounds good – it's a real buy! Shall I take a look at it?'

'If you can spare the time, yes, please. It may not be in the city centre but it's not that far away either – don't forget, I come from London.' If only he knew the distances Londoners are prepared to travel.

Three days later, he rang back. 'I've just had a look at the apartment – take it!' I did, there and then, by email.

Now I am here to take possession – and not only of the apartment.

I thank the universe for hearing me. All I can do now is to trust that it will help me find what, in all truth, I am not certain I am looking for.

ONE

DAWA GOES HOME

ENGLAND, FRIDAY 30ᵀᴴ MAY 2003

I called my mother several times, but she didn't answer. Another three or four steps up the staircase and I tried again. Silence. As I continued upwards, there was no hint of movement from either of her rooms. Perhaps she had nodded off in her armchair? It used to be quite out of character, but now…

I knocked gently on her sitting-room door and waited a few moments before opening it. Peering around to where I had recently started to find her asleep in her chair with her chin on her chest and a book precariously balanced on her lap, she was not there.

Immediately I sensed danger. I returned along the landing towards her bedroom, calling as I went. Nothing. This time I didn't even think about being considerate or polite; instead, I walked straight in.

I felt instant, suffocating panic. The message in the silence was unmistakable. As my eyes took in the expanse of her room, my awareness was instantly drawn towards a shadow to my left. Before I had time to look at it, I heard the scream inside me. When my eyes caught up, I saw my mother on the floor.

Throwing myself down beside her, I grasped her face with both hands. 'Dawa! Oh my God! Dawa!'

Her complexion, which a short while before was still glowing with her customary radiance, was sallow and the sunspots on her skin had a curiously unusual prominence.

I felt for her carotid artery. Nothing. I reached for the wrist of her right arm that was resting by her side, palm uppermost. Her hand was smooth, soft. Nothing. On the floor beside her hand lay her lipstick, slipped from her grasp, unopened, unused.

Dawa was dead. But I couldn't let it be so. It could not be true. She'd only fainted.

I ran across the hallway to the sash window and heaved it open. As I called my husband's name, my despair bounced off the wall of the neighbouring house; it echoed as if it were coming from a distant universe.

Don, my husband, was in the garden. Immediately he was on his way; he didn't know why, but he had caught something terrible in my voice.

I rushed back to my mother and held her face close to mine in a desperate attempt to capture her essence before it vanished forever. I was howling with anguish, yet my thoughts were racing with a speed and lucidity I will never forget. She's gone, gone forever… But it's too soon. We haven't finished. We haven't even said goodbye…

In the midst of it all, I was raging with anger because she had cheated me by leaving me, just as I was beginning to understand the extraordinary complexity that lay behind her gentle exterior. Her unwavering desire to promote happiness and harmony had sometimes frustrated and angered me. Now she had left me behind to ponder the mystery of the woman who, for most of my life, I never really knew.

My mother had experienced separation from her parents and siblings, and the loss of relatives and friends through genocide. She had suffered the loss of *Heimat*[3], with its almost inevitable disorientation. She had gone through divorce and a nervous breakdown – yet she had survived. She may have felt sad about what could not be undone but, having coped and come through relatively unscathed, she appeared to everyone to be the happy person she claimed to be.

There was only one time after her breakdown in the early 1960s that her natural coping strategy fell apart. In the year 2000, with tears in her eyes, she had said to me, 'I can't stop crying.' There had been an obvious cause to explain her uncharacteristic loss of stoicism, and the public display of grief soon passed. She had returned to her usual vibrant self – until about three months before her death when she suddenly withdrew and became all but lost to me.

The day before she died, she'd had an attack of dizziness and nausea; we'd had to call the doctor, and she'd stayed in bed. Eventually she had slept until early the next morning, when she had appeared reborn. I hadn't seen her like that for many weeks but suddenly she was transformed, looking exceptionally beautiful, youthful and vibrant. Yet, only a few hours later, I

---

3   Heimat is a German word translating to ‹home› or ‹homeland›.

was kneeling next to her, knowing that I would never again hear her voice say, '*Mein zartes, kleines Vogerl,*'[4] as she held my hand and gently stroked it.

My mother had been the most loving person, but I'd had the fleeting sense that that recent display of affection was acknowledging something that now would remain unspoken.

Never again would the sight of her elicit a feeling of warmth and comfort for me and a deep love within me for her. Never again would she return from a shopping trip bearing a bunch of flowers because 'I thought you would like them'. Never again would we smile at the different faces we saw in her treasured sea of flowering plants that surrounded our terrace in spring and summer.

Never again would we visit the Jewish Cultural Centre or the Wiener Library like a pair of symbiotic conspirators. Never again would I hold her hand to guide her across a busy road or stroll arm in arm with her through the streets of her beloved Vienna. Never again would we travel to Bohemia, she seeking to replace grief with the warm glow of a distant past, me a pillion passenger on her journey.

Never again could I ask *Who was that? What happened? When did it happen? What's the significance?* Never again would we laugh like children together; never again would we just *be* together. Everything would be never again.

My thoughts were confused, startling, and yet from somewhere deep within me a calm, almost relieved voice was whispering, 'Dawa, it's over. Your pain is over. No more pain.'

Then, almost imperceptibly, there was a slight tug and a barely audible pop from somewhere within my navel and I was calm. From that moment, my only concern was to do right by my mother and to ensure that all those who came to say goodbye, including my father and his second wife Anna, would have as easy a time as possible.

That sense of calm lasted until two days before my mother's funeral when I picked up the phone and heard Anna's shell-shocked voice. 'Are you sitting down?' Then, after a small silence, she added, 'Your father has suffered a very serious stroke.'

***

Two days before my mother's death, we were in her sun-drenched sitting room chatting over cups of fresh coffee and the obligatory *Leckerbissen*[5]. I

---

4   My dainty little bird.
5   Treat.

had felt such relief at having tempted her for the first time in many weeks to take part in something that, during the months before the shadows had overwhelmed her once again, had begun to develop into a ritual for us.

Our conversations were always wide ranging: some aspect of history; the books we were reading; the people we had met; the garden; our two psychologically disturbed and feuding rescue cats; the family; the weak milky brew that has come to pass for coffee in England; politics, Israel (her most passionate soft spot); medical innovations; the latest scientific research … anything and everything.

We had also started to talk more about religion, perhaps because we'd finally recognised that each of us had, seemingly independently of the other, come to tread similar paths.

My mother had felt no need for a dogmatic religious framework to help her exist with her fellow humans and the world in which she lived; to avoid lengthy intellectual explanations of her concept of pantheism that did not come easily to her, she generally preferred to describe herself as an agnostic, a humanist and *Freidenker*[6] – and, if the occasion felt appropriate, a Jew.

Always deeply sensitive to the suffering of others, she instinctively responded to the need for compassion, while adversity and much inner reflection in her adult years had allowed her heart to fully blossom, leaving others feeling safe and accepted.

Dawa loved to reminisce about what she recalled as her mostly carefree and happy childhood in Vienna before it was blown apart by Hitler's march into Austria the day before her twelfth birthday in March 1938, after which her country was almost immediately incorporated into *Grossdeutschland*[7]. Her nineteen-year-old brother Toni had to flee to England six months later; she and her fifteen-year-old sister Elsa had followed on a *Kindertransport*[8] on 27th March 1939.

They left behind their home, parents, grandmother, aunts, uncles and cousins, and their large extended family on her father's side. They relinquished everybody and everything that, until then, had provided all the security they had ever known and would never truly know again.

Her eyes lit up as she told stories of her father's fly-fishing outings on the Danube. The women and younger children of the families used to join him, his friends and Toni at a wooden boathouse where they'd dine on

---

6 Freethinker.
7 Greater Germany.
8 Children's Transport.

freshly caught fish cooked over an open fire. She loved to tell me about her annual summer holidays with her Czech aunts and cousins on her mother's side at her grandfather's house in the small Bohemian village of Popovice, and her more sedate sojourns in fashionable Bad Ischl with two of her father's unmarried sisters, her beloved aunts Clara and Camilla.

I had started to ask my mother questions when I sensed she was receptive, although there were days when I knew not to. I was genuinely interested but I also wanted to get under her skin, to understand what had made her the way she was, and, by implication, what had influenced so much of who I had become.

We talked about almost everything, but anything that touched on her more painful, deeper feelings was strictly out of bounds. She would light-heartedly deflect any movement I made towards her inner world; more direct questions merely elicited a blank expression and a non-committal shrug. I was left frustrated; it was like looking through a shattered windscreen knowing there was something beyond it yet being unable to see clearly.

On that particular afternoon two days before she died, we were talking about my recent trip to Berlin where I had been researching my mother's late uncle Arthur's work as a sculptor, medallist and gemstone intaglio engraver before the Second World War.

She recounted with real regret, even a hint of resentment, the distant relationship she'd had with him and his wife, Aunt Ida, both of whom had fled to England from their home in Berlin in 1935. She reflected upon how much she had been deprived of after she'd arrived in England because she was too young to be of ongoing interest to the childless couple. Nobody had seemed to care about her losses and needs. The same had happened in the 1960s when her older siblings had claimed some small reparation from a Holocaust compensation fund while she had fallen below the qualifying age.

From these tiny pieces of a fragmented mosaic that my mother was unconsciously handing me, I had already sensed that something was catching up with her. Now her unusual tone of voice set alarm bells ringing.

That brief touching on unexplored troubles gave way to deeper reflections as we talked about other kinds of relationships. We discussed their longevity or their transience, the human needs that lay behind them and how disappointing it could be when at least some degree of spontaneous care was not forthcoming. My mother didn't seem bitter, merely slightly frustrated at how it can be.

As the anecdotes continued, I remember urging her to write them down. How often I had said that, and she had promised to do so. However, I'd learned that a happy, interesting recollection as we talked was one thing; risking exposing herself to unwelcome and often supressed memories was completely different. My mother's pen only fleetingly made contact with paper.

We spoke about my sister-in-law, Mary, who was dying of cancer and who now seemed resigned to its terrible conclusion. We both felt useless in the face of her suffering and the effect her premature death would have on my brother Martin and their two children. I told my mother about a phone call I'd received during which, in her own way, Mary had asked for forgiveness for past transgressions. Knowing she had so little time left, she wanted to make her peace.

My mother and I sat in silence for a while as we searched for a subject to distract us, but we were stuck in a groove because next we talked about Don's father, Frank, who had died only two weeks earlier.

On several occasions during the last nine months of Frank's life, my mother had travelled to Cornwall to care for him with her unique gentleness and compassion. Then, after her last stay with him, she stated simply, 'I'm not going back.'

It was at that point I noticed a pronounced change in her sunny disposition. I was aware that she might be looking ahead and wanted to be free to support my brother and his family when she was needed, but there was more to her vehemence than that.

Frank, a distinguished artist, had an adoring circle of elderly female pupils and friends, some of whom had a rather cavalier attitude towards my mother. 'They seem to think I'm only here to make them tea...' This, coupled with remarks from Frank himself, who was now very sick and sometimes not his usual charming self, had struck at the epicentre of her inner world, where a deep-seated sense of rejection and a lack of recognition of her own suffering and needs had finally been disturbed, shattering the construct that had, until then, been her life-sustaining sense of reality.

Worse still, she had recognised the painful truth that her natural *joie de vivre* and willingness to accept others had attracted those who had precious little to give in return. Her tolerance had run its course.

'I like my own company,' she volunteered, sitting surrounded by her books.

My mother's coping strategies had finally been stretched beyond their limits, and from then on she gradually withdrew to a place where I could not reach her. The vibrant, deeply affectionate woman that so many had taken for granted was consumed by a grey fatigue that anti-depressant medication had yet to break through.

She had always enjoyed helping to plan and prepare our meals but now, more often than not, I found myself alone in the kitchen. Her healthy appetite waned as the pain in her stomach grew and her choice of food gradually narrowed to the odd bowl of comforting porridge.

'Mummy, you must eat more. You aren't eating enough…'

No amount of coaxing made the slightest difference. Her response was a blank expression while I longed for the defiant smile that had once greeted me when I'd surprised her with a surreptitious chocolate in her mouth, or when she'd hidden a packet of sweets behind her chair in the hope of avoiding my disapproving eye. 'If you are serious about wanting to keep the weight off, you have to cut that kind of thing out!'

She spent hours in her bedroom with the door firmly closed and only ventured out of it, or her sitting room, for the occasional spot of gardening or to go through the motions for our family's communal evening meals. Most revealingly, she almost lost interest in feeding our two cats that she had always called 'Clio-baby' and 'my little Sukilé'. It was something she'd loved to do, and they had unfailingly taken precedence over humans; her father had taught her never to sit down to eat before the animals were fed, an instruction she had obeyed for most of her life.[9]

She could no longer sleep, even when she had wanted to. Instead, as a former nurse in a cancer hospital who knew more than most, she gave her energy away worrying about Mary. During the rare moments that she drifted off, nightmares often woke her.

A few years earlier she had developed an interest in the symbolism of dreams, often writing them down to see whether she could decipher them. Now there was little need for analysis; her dreams were about loss and fear, of losing her children, of searching for them or fighting for them, of knowing where they were but not being able to reach them. She dreamed about Jews being insulted and humiliated, of prejudice and hatred and the terrible pain of grief and loss.

---

9 Her father had wanted to become a veterinary surgeon; Dawa wasn't certain whether his failure to do so was due to lack of funds or whether he had fallen foul of the unofficial antisemitic policy that was rigorously applied by Vienna's Medveduni/ University of Veterinary Science.

One day she handed me a slip of paper on which she had jotted down her latest dream and waited as I read it. When I finished and looked up, her eyes were glistening. 'Oh, Dawa...' I said, and reached for her, but she turned away and left the room. She never asked for the paper back and I still have it.

It was heartbreaking to watch my mother's torment play out before me and to feel utterly helpless. My feelings were compounded by an inability to step towards her because that would have engaged my own emotions in a way that I was afraid of.

So much unspoken, traumatic history bound us together that even if my mother *had* wanted to talk – which I doubt she could have done – I could not have responded in a way that she needed. I was still haunted by the memory of her descent into suicidal depression when I was ten years old. It threatened my sense of emotional autonomy. Instead, like my mother, I had developed an efficient self-protection mechanism and remained inscrutable. I did not – could not – respond adequately to her despair.

On this, our first *Kaffeetscherl*[10] in a long time and also our last, we talked about death but also the lives that had preceded it.

Frank had been fortunate to have some of his immediate family and final companion with him when he died, and he took his last breath to the words of the latest of many loving poems she had written to him, 'Requiem'. He had remained in his home until almost the end and received so much care from his many friends in his small rural community. He had reached the age of ninety-two with his intellect razor sharp as ever and had followed his artistic passions almost until his death.

Of course it was deeply sad to lose him, but he had led a relatively charmed life with no life-changing trauma. How different his passing had been from that of Dawa's father. He had died alone in a freezing room while my grandmother was running around the Russian-administered sector of post-war Vienna desperately seeking a doctor or some medication to help him. By the time she returned, her husband had slipped away, depriving her of her life's companion and leaving her with an abiding sense of failure.

How different Frank's death was to my grandmother's. She had died alone after days of inadequate care, with nobody close to hold her hand and say goodbye.

My mother and I talked about grief and why we felt it, about grief

---

10   Viennese vernacular for cup of coffee.

tempered by the knowledge someone had lived a relatively unscathed life, and grief rendered unbearable by knowing someone had suffered during their life.

My mother started to cry. 'Poor Maminko, I can't bear to think of her dying alone. Do you know what she once said to me? "What on earth did I do to deserve such an unfortunate life?"'

I sat, paralysed by the fear of our shared emotions, and watched my mother cry. Her tears did not last for long before she forced them back again. Then I heard myself reply angrily to my grandmother's question: 'Because of bloody religion!'.

TWO

ALMOST UNJUST

VIENNA, JUNE 2006

It seems unjust that I am now doing what my mother wanted to do so much. She loved coming to Vienna, and during our brief visits during the last twenty years of her life I always sensed something different about her when we were here. The change wouldn't have been noticeable to those whose inner worlds were less entwined than ours, but to me it was unmistakable.

But even if Dawa were still alive and able to accompany me, what could she possibly do except walk down memory lane once too often and probably trip herself up somewhere along the way? I have plenty of research and other work to keep me busy, but for my mother the lack of safe and reliable social support would cast her adrift.

Could she have established meaningful contact with the Jewish community? Doubtful: superficially they would have done as they were supposed to and welcomed the stranger, but experience had taught her that, despite the community's birth records, if she ever mentioned that her mother had *not* been a Jew, she was never fully accepted as 'one of us'.

The wound that led to this particular psychological scar was inflicted shortly after Dawa fled to England. The mother of her new Czechoslovak school friend and fellow Jewish refugee had commandeered her to switch on the lights during the Sabbath.

'You hypocrite!' her friend had reprimanded her mother, though Dawa was not affronted by the deed itself. It was not so much the hypocrisy of being asked to do something that the woman would not do herself, but what lay behind it: the failure to really accept my mother as a Jew. That scar continued to be opened every so often, even by non-practising secular Jews whose millennia-old conditioning still lurked beneath their thin veneer of more evolved understanding.

It was, however, the orthodox community leadership of Vienna's Jewry that struck the final and sharpest blow. In 2002, my mother received a certificate from Vienna's IKG[11] granting her honorary membership. She was quite touched by this unexpected gesture – until she read the accompanying letter. It was written in German, and she re-read it a number of times to be certain that she had understood its contents correctly.

After first addressing those IKG members whose membership had lapsed as a result of being scattered across the globe during the persecution by Adolf Hitler's version of National Socialism, the letter continued:

> *On the other hand, events have drawn our attention to a group of people whose tragic destiny is of no less import than that of the Community's exiled members: those who according to the principles of Halacha are not Jewish but due to the invocation of the Nuremberg Race Laws were forced to share in the fate of ostracism and persecution.*
>
> *Those who have witnessed the painful consequences of this inner tension, the doubts surrounding one's identity and the unfulfilled longing for a spiritual home, will appreciate how great the moral duty of the Jewish community is towards this group of people…*

If the civic representatives of Vienna's registered Jewish community had intended to do my mother a kindness, their intentions misfired. Even though her own mother was not known to have converted to Judaism, as with her sister Elisabeth (usually known as Elsa or Elsinko) three years earlier, my mother's birth on 13th March 1926 was recorded in the IKG's Register of Births.

There had never been any doubt in the Löwenthal family that the children were wholly Jewish, yet now the IKG that had once accepted my mother as 'one of us' seemed to be informing her that, according to Jewish law, she was not one of them after all.

I don't know whether my mother was aware of a revival of orthodoxy within the civic leadership of Vienna's Jews, or whether she believed the words in the letter had not been considered carefully enough. Whatever, it touched a raw nerve. Perhaps even ignorant of their own local history, the community's current civic representatives appeared to be denying her knowledge not only of herself but of her ethical and spiritual home.

It took her a while to reply, but when she did she made her point simply

---

11   Israelite/Jewish Cultural Community.

but clearly:

Of course I accept the honorary membership with much pleasure, although I have always described myself as a Jew.

I was only just thirteen when I left Vienna and had no knowledge of Halachic principles. Since then I have given the matter much thought and feel as Jewish as I ever have. Unfortunately, I never discussed this with my mother, but I do know that she remained loyally at my father's side and that she also looked after his mother, sisters and other family members. It is she who deserves an honorary membership.

She did not receive a reply. Also, she had not been specific enough; in fact, her mother was an unsung hero who deserved far greater honour.

On the other side of the divide, some people could be disappointing when they inadvertently let deep-seated and often unacknowledged anti-Jewish sentiments slip into routine conversation. Gradually, my mother became increasingly wary of what others might be hiding behind their public self-censorship. It led her to become, with a few rare exceptions, subtly aloof to the end of her days.

Her reticence about sharing herself went deeper than a fear of prejudice. In 1947, after an enforced absence of eight years, my mother was finally granted permission to travel back home to Vienna. When she was there, she rushed up to an old friend in the street and embraced her, saying, 'My God, I'm so happy you're still alive!'

The young woman snapped resentfully, 'Yes, it was all right for you!' then turned and walked away.

A year or so later, my mother was asked by someone in Vienna to befriend an Auschwitz survivor who was now living alone in London. When this young woman discovered that Dawa had spent the war years in England instead of being dehumanised in a concentration camp, she also invoked the 'hierarchy of suffering'. My mother simply could not win; a sense of being stranded in no-man's land left her with no choice but to make it her own.

***

For decades my mother was known in the family as 'Dawa' thanks to my toddler son. We all pronounced the 'aw' in true English fashion (as in 'ouch'), though she, giving a very credible imitation of Zsa-Zsa Gabor, insisted it should be *Daahva*. It wasn't uncommon for my husband Don, who adored her, to add a *daahlink* or *daahlinka* in affectionate acknowledgement of the

Continental connection. Her English was excellent, though; few people ever recognised that she'd been born somewhere other than in England – Wales, perhaps?

Her given name was Camilla but throughout her life, with the exception of friendships made in adulthood, she was called by diminutives. First there was her own invention of My (pronounced *Mee*) when she had barely started to speak; when she was a little older, the family referred to her as Miki, although her closest relatives also referred to her affectionately as Goldi, Milenka, Milenko or Mikilé.

My grandparents, Marie and Oskar Alexander Löwenthal, may well have thought their third child had been born at an auspicious time. How different things were compared to the appalling post-WWI conditions that had led Marie to return to her parental home in Popovice for the birth of her first child, Anton (mostly known as Toni or Tonichku), in September 1919. Their home was now an enormous improvement on the rented rooms in a tenement building in the Viennese suburb of Floridsdorf, where Elsa was born almost four years later.

So much had changed since the end of the First World War. What little was left of the 500-year-old Habsburg Empire had gone on to form Austria's First Republic. The new national government had also agreed to an autonomous municipal government in its former imperial capital, a city that had been devastated by inflation, trade embargoes and the war-time militarisation of many of its factories.

By the end of the war, Vienna had an empty purse and an empty stomach. The country had been brought to its knees economically, and at the same time the city had experienced an additional, unforeseen burden: almost as soon as the war began, more than 130,000 refugees had started to stream in from the empire's eastern dominions.

The majority were destitute Jews fleeing the pogroms perpetrated by advancing Russian troops in the provinces of Galicia and the Bukovina[12], seeking sanctuary at the heart of the empire where many (but certainly not all) already had family connections they hoped would take them in. Their numbers, their dishevelled poverty and, in many cases, their obvious ultra-orthodoxy, left them vulnerable to just about every fear known to mankind.

There were so many that it was not long before the authorities tried to relieve the pressure by dispersing several thousand of them to Salzburg,

---

12   Post-1918 territories of Poland, Ukraine and Rumania.

locations in Upper Austria, and the Austrian province of Moravia. Nonetheless, after the war's end and after many tens of thousands had been repatriated, some 26,000 Jewish refugees still remained in Vienna. Rival political parties had a field day scapegoating them for just about every ill in the city.

As if to add to Vienna's post-war problems, her numbers were newly swollen by thousands of the former Imperial Army's soldiers and large numbers of White-Russian émigrés escaping the revolutionary turmoil back home. The city was bursting at the seams and the housing shortage was chronic.

The appalling squalor of the poor was never a secret to the Viennese. While the urban homes of the better heeled were often spacious, the rented accommodation of the average worker generally consisted of a single room with make-shift cooking facilities. Water – cold – had to be fetched from a shared sink and tap on the communal landing or in the hall. Waterless wooden toilets were usually situated in the central courtyard or cellar; in the worst cases, tenants had to make do with buckets in the cellars.

Before 1914, 3,000 of the city's 100,000 dwellings were recorded as being unoccupied; by the end of the Great War four years later, only a few rooms were standing empty. Most of those were the remnants of the cellar lavatories and unfit for human habitation.

Overcrowding was common. In some of the worst instances, records show that as many as 14,000 of the *Bettgänger*[13] were sleeping in shifts, sharing cramped and primitive conditions without running water or adequate sanitary facilities. There were not only plenty of unscrupulous landlords but also equally unscrupulous tenants who jumped at the opportunity to profit at another's expense.

Poverty was not confined to those on the lowest rung of the socio-economic ladder. Surreal inflation, crashed banks and the evaporation of investments in war bonds meant that many of Vienna's more fortunate inhabitants also suffered a severe blow to their accustomed way of life. Those events were also disastrous for my grandmother Marie, who had always saved. Her dream of buying an allotment on the outskirts of Vienna on which to build a small week-end hut for her future family received its first blow of several and remained unfulfilled.

Overcrowding and unemployment generated a swathe of abject poverty and homelessness, made all the worse by unhygienic conditions, infectious

---

13 Those with no fixed abode who slept on boards in hostels designated for the homeless.

diseases and mental despair. Even those like my grandparents, who were living on a modest, single income, must have found life challenging.

The city needed a radical solution to combat its problems, so it is hardly surprising that its citizens took full advantage of their newly legalised universal suffrage: in May 1919, Viennese men and women voted for the city's first socialist municipal government with a resounding majority.

Less than two years later, the city went further and attained sovereignty over its internal taxation system. With it, its leaders won the freedom to drive through radical social reforms and a strategy was put in place to start the construction of a new Vienna. Through a series of creative tax initiatives, the municipal government set about funding a social welfare system 'from cradle to grave', as well as initiating a cultural programme to accommodate a wide variety of tastes. To many citizens, this was the dawn of a new age that would nourish the mind, body and spirit and create flourishing, healthy communities.

At the time of my mother's birth, Marie and Oskar had just started to benefit from this innovative socialist experiment, and they acquired the lease on a brand-new home in a municipally funded apartment complex.

Homes were allocated according to a points system that considered both the size of a family and the urgency of its circumstances. Despite considerable competition, Marie fought for her new home. No doubt being a paid-up member of the Social Democratic Party helped, but even so she must have felt as if she'd finally won the lottery!

Compared with their accommodation in Floridsdorf, their new home was luxurious. The solid complex was built to a high standard, letting in air and light with respect for the tenants' wellbeing, while the ground floor facing the main road was given over to shops and services for everyday life. Their apartment had four rooms of varying sizes and all the modern conveniences of the day: running water, their own lavatory and a kitchen with gas! Every household was assigned a laundry area in the cellar and space for storage and drying the washing on the top floor. Shielded from the noise and pollution of the outside world, the children could play safely in three attractively landscaped communal courtyards within the complex which also housed a municipally funded library and kindergarten, while the primary school was just a stone's throw away.

After several years as a poorly paid public-defence lawyer, Oskar's private practice was developing into a respectable business that provided a regular income. What more could anybody want? And if one chose to filter out the ever-present anti-Semitic background noise, life could only get better.

THREE

JOURNEY OF DISCOVERY 1951–1969

THE FOREIGN CONNECTION

Over the years, when somebody asked me, 'When did you find out your mother was a Jewish refugee?' I struggled to give a satisfactory answer. Memories of my childhood only produced a hazy awareness that something might be different; there were some events from which I learned more but there was no single revelatory moment. Instead, the unravelling of my foreign background, and the tragedy concealed within it, was an evolutionary process.

One of my earliest memories was of the run-up to Christmas when I was three or four years old. There were often occasions when I didn't understand what my mother and her sister, my Aunt Elsa, were saying to one another but I was a child, preoccupied with my own activities, and they simply passed me by.

It was only when my mother spoke to me directly and deliberately using meaningless vocabulary that I felt threatened by her sudden strangeness. I had been doing my best to give a rendition of 'Jingle Bells' when she started trying to teach me another song with words that meant nothing to me. The unfamiliarity of hearing her 'speaking in tongues' frightened me and I retreated behind the settee, from where I reluctantly attempted to reproduce her alien sounds: *O Tannenbaum, o Tannenbaum, wie treu sind deine Blätter*.

To soothe my anxiety, she explained that it was a Christmas song she used to sing 'at home' when she was a little girl. That was the moment when I started to grasp that she did not come from the place where we lived.

In later years I discovered that I had already been to Vienna at least twice by then, though I only have isolated memories of those visits that seemed to have had no journey attached to them.

I am perhaps between two or three years old, kneeling on the bench seat at my grandmother's kitchen table. She is coaxing some floppy dough into a wafer-thin sheet that gradually covers the entire table and drapes over the sides like a translucent piece of cloth. I keep grabbing hold of it, pulling it even further and further – until a hole appears.

My grandmother says something, half laughing, half irritated. It is fun, and I repeat this game a few more times until my mother picks me up and moves me away from mischief.

I am playing in a park.[14] The sun is very warm. There are enormous wooden barrels turned on their sides in the children's play area, each with a small picnic table fitted to its inside. It's cosy sitting in there with my older brother, Martin. We eat rye-bread sandwiches while our mother watches from a short distance away. I don't consciously notice the enormous flak towers looming over the park. Nor do I know yet who built them or what they signify.

Another time I am about five years old and playing with Martin and our little brother Robert in a sandpit in what I will one day learn is the famous Stadtpark. My mother is watching from one of the benches lining the paths that snake around the gardens. I love it here.

Years later, I learnt that Aunt Elsa had sat on one of those benches with her own young daughter. 'It's so lovely here, isn't it?' she remarked to the elderly woman sharing her bench.

'Yes, so much nicer now that those Jewish women and their brats are no longer around.'

I am sitting in an ice-cream parlour, eating a dessert decorated with a pretty paper umbrella and served in a shallow stainless-steel dish, so much nicer than the soapy-tasting bars in cardboard-like cones from Woolworth's or the Wall's ice-cream van back at home.

My grandmother and I are shopping in the open-air market. Aromas are bursting from mountains of colourful fresh fruit and vegetables. To avoid the heat of the day, we have come early in the morning, but it is already very hot. Thankfully it is much cooler inside the market's butcher shop.

The shopkeeper gives me a thick slice of salami; wherever we go someone usually gives me something to nibble. That never happens in England. The cheeses are delicious, too. I love visiting this place and I even have my own

---

14 I learnt later it was the once beautiful baroque Augarten public park.

little plastic shopping basket. My grandmother seems to know everybody and often stops to chat. It is not just the weather that feels warm.

I recall my grandmother visiting us soon after the *O Tannenbaum* incident. She is called Granny Vienna, to distinguish her from my paternal grandmother, Granny Pinner, whom I see quite often. There has been much excitement leading up to her arrival, and now we are unpacking exotic delights from her seemingly bottomless suitcase. She has brought me a clockwork dancing bear bashing away on cymbals that will amuse me for many days to come.

Granny Vienna is dressed in a beige wrap-over skirt and a cream wool cardigan, with a large cameo brooch pinned below her left shoulder. At first, I am perplexed by the pink wound that almost covers the back of her right hand, but I soon forget it as I experience her warmth and loving cuddles!

Her bedroom smells of Nivea cream and apples, as it always will during her future visits; she uses the Nivea on her face at night and to help soothe the itchy rawness on her hand. The apples? I learned much later that my grandmother firmly believed 'an apple a day keeps the doctor away' and ate one every night. Judging by her beautiful complexion, of which I was very envious when I was a teenager, the combination of cream and fruit worked wonders.

I understood nothing of what she and my mother said to each other, but I no longer felt threatened by the unintelligible sounds. I had simply grown to accept them as part of my life.

GERMANY BECKONS

During the early summer of 1958, our lives took an unexpected turn. My father's new job was about to take us to Winchester, where my mother hoped to replace the post-war drabness of suburban London with the atmosphere of an historic cathedral city. Better still, she would also be within easier reach of her sister Elsa. Then, out of the blue, my entrepreneurial and ambitious father was presented with an opportunity to climb several rungs up the career ladder. We were moving to Germany instead.

I recall the removal van, my mother packing and giving away some of our possessions, then waving good-bye to our neighbours and my playmates as we drove off, but nothing more. What of my best friend Yvonne, who lived a couple of doors away? She was two years my senior and was teaching me to ride her bike. What about Granny Pinner? What about Auntie Elsa and Uncle Michael and their two young children, Lis and baby Sarah with whom Martin and I had just spent a few days being kept out of our busy mother's way? What of my mother's brother Uncle Toni and his wife Auntie Doris, and my cousins Susan and Leah?

I was too young to understand the importance of connections and attachments, let alone the consequences of separation and loss. All I felt was excitement: it was an adventure! Besides, I would finally see my daddy again; he had gone ahead several weeks earlier to start his new job in Germany.

When we arrived in Munich, we stayed in an inn on the city's outskirts where we spent the summer sweltering in the kind of heat I'd only ever experienced in Vienna. The inn was called Die Wachau (which my father jokingly mispronounced as 'Wackow') after the Austrian wine-growing region a short distance from Vienna.

Back then, that was a commonly used juvenile term along the lines of 'Check this out … sexeeee!'. We kids had heard the expression before, and Martin and I thought our father using it was extremely amusing, though not as funny as learning that he was a 'farter' in German![15] We repeated the word ad nauseam until, much to our parents' relief, there was nothing left to laugh about.

It must have been a difficult time for my mother, although I don't remember her being short-tempered; she was not inclined to be impatient or irritable. During the week when my father was at work, she was alone in a hotel in a strange city in a country that must have made her rather uneasy. She had no friends or family, just three lively children aged from three to nine years of age, each with their needs and wants and now without a familiar space or belongings to occupy them.

She did her best to distract us with walks in the woods or tram rides into Munich's centre. On one occasion, a young man on my father's staff took us swimming in an open-air pool; however, we spent most of our time playing in the grounds of the inn's outside dining area and gardens. That was a place where all adults, except my parents, seemed to smoke Ernte 23 and Camel cigarettes and cigars.

Boredom and curiosity got the better of Martin. Obediently, Robert and I helped him amass discarded cigarette butts from beneath the dining tables and chairs. We ripped them apart and collected any remaining tobacco to roll another brand-new – if not quite so smart looking –

---

15   The German word for father is Vater.

cigarette. No doubt feeling very adult, Martin lit up, took a drag and promptly felt horribly sick. He has never been tempted to smoke again.

I might have been bored at times, but I recall being excited by my new environment; paradoxically, it felt familiar even though it was completely different from our home in England. I'd always been a relatively independent child, so I soon became a regular visitor at the wooden newspaper kiosk nearby. In no time at all I had mastered the request, '*Zehn Gummibärle, bitte.*'[16]

I can still recall the scent of the pine-wood kiosk mixed with the sickly smell of wine gums, cheap chocolate and sherbet sticks as I handed over my coins in exchange for a small cone-shaped paper bag containing my day's ration of gummy-bears.

I don't recall wondering why my mother could speak the language; that was just the way it was. Did I know that this language was the same as the one she used to converse with Granny Vienna? I have no idea; I just knew it was different from English.

Weekends provided my mother with a little relief from single parenting. We children were often wedged in the back seat of our English Ford Consul, a vehicle that caused a stir wherever we went because it was still rare to see a GB numberplate, as our parents explored Munich's suburbs and investigated one potential new home after another. Most of them were exactly that: new. Often, they were on building sites, so we had to wait in the car while the adults clambered around trying to envisage their potential.

We hadn't been in Munich for long before I developed an odd sensation of continuous, gnawing hunger that left me craving the inn's dish of tasty, sautéed kidneys. I also discovered Coca Cola and the herbal lemonade Almdudler, yet no matter how much I ate or drank, the hunger would not go away. Some evenings I found it impossible to settle and nagged for *Palatschinken* (pancakes) filled with strawberry or apricot jam. At the age of seven, I was introduced to the pleasures of room service.

On a couple of occasions I even got out of bed and, still dressed in my pyjamas, found my parents in the restaurant so I could scavenge something to eat. I must have been desperate because I had to navigate the crowded tables while the guests watched me with kindly amusement through billowing clouds of smoke. I liked neither the smoke nor the very real physical discomfort of being stared at.

---

16 'Ten gummy bears, please.'

VIENNA

After we had spent several hot weeks living out of suitcases awaiting the completion of the house that would be our home for the next five years, we children and our mother boarded a train for Vienna.

This time I understood that this 'somewhere else' was not just a place called Vienna but also in a country called Austria. In contrast to the long car journey from London with one of our father's colleagues at the wheel, Vienna was only a few hours away. Even so, I still had no idea how it was that Granny Vienna lived in one place and spoke a foreign language, while my mother and her siblings lived in another place and spoke English, even if that English was sometimes interspersed with words that meant nothing to me.

We were greeted at Vienna's Westbahnhof (West train station) with huge hugs, kisses and exclamations of '*Yeshu-Maria!*', which, I gathered, had something to do with us children having grown so much taller since our last meeting.

Once calm was restored, a porter led us to the station forecourt where we piled into a taxi. Fully accustomed to the tricks of the trade, Granny Vienna took charge. Leaning forward from the back seat, she prodded the driver on the shoulder. '*Fahren Sie mich nicht spazieren. Ich kenne mich schon sehr gut aus!*'[17] That, I discovered for the first time, was my grandmother: DO NOT mess with me! Although I hadn't the faintest idea what she was saying, the words rang in my ears until several months later when I finally began to get the hang of the German language.

During that visit I spent many happy times gazing from the open bedroom window of Granny Vienna's second-floor apartment on the Obere Donaustrasse (Upper Danube Street). The street runs along the eastern bank of the busy Danube Canal and has a view across the waterway to the Franz-Josefs-Kai on the west bank where, I later learned, Granny Vienna had worked when she first arrived in town in 1905.

As I stood at the window and she sat next to me, both of us with our elbows on the windowsill, we watched the world go by or fed the birds with finely chopped pork fat mixed with breadcrumbs as they swooped around us.

Vienna felt magical and it excited my senses in a way I hadn't been aware of before. I was mesmerised by the lights flashing on top of the

---

17 'Don't take me for a drive. I'm already very familiar with the place!'

recently erected Ringturm high-rise office building. The screeching of tram wheels from across the water and the sound of cars bumping past on the cobbled street below felt comfortingly familiar. I loved the smells of apples and Nivea, Frankfurters and salami, baking and cooking – and what Martin has identified as the smell of gas from the cooker.

I was enchanted by the creak of the parquet flooring, the large double doors that linked one room to another, and the echo in the huge, slightly musty, ground-floor entrance hall that led through even larger double doors to the pavement outside.

Then there were the sounds and smells of the Karmeliter Markt[18], and the pungent smell of beer and cigarettes mingled with roast pork with caraway seeds, Sauerkraut, Schnitzels, and cucumber salad with chives that escaped from the restaurant below; the mouth-watering aroma of fresh coffee and the sweet fragrance of cakes; the chatter in the cafés; the expanse of the beautiful fin de siècle boulevards, the parks, the mysterious narrow medieval streets in the old city…

Vienna was – home. It is a feeling that remains with me to this day in spite of intermittent bouts of deep anger and even deeper sorrow.

Curiously, within a few days of our arrival my continuous gnawing hunger for salty or sweet food simply disappeared.

Vienna also brought awareness of another aspect of life: there was an abundance of beggars. Many were blind or missing a limb, and most carried cardboard signs with words I would one day understand stated *Kriegsopfer* (war casualty).

There were adults crippled with polio or kyphoscoliosis, and children deformed with hydrocephalus. Some adults honked and spat in the streets, even on the trams, in spite of the prominently displayed signs that warned that spitting was *polizeilich verboten*[19]. I was shocked and disgusted in turn; it seemed that life could be very sad and ugly.

As I stood at the window, Granny Vienna's chubby arm that was wrapped around my waist would disengage sometimes and she would stroke my head with what, even then, I recognised as infinite tenderness, sighing, '*Ach, meine liebe, herzige Salinka.*'[20]

I have never forgotten the sadness that emanated from deep within my grandmother although, thankfully, at that time I had no idea what it was or why it was there.

---

18 Karmelite Market.
19 Against the law.
20 'Ah, my dear, sweet Salinka.'

During my last year in England I had already shown myself responsible enough to walk home from school with a classmate who lived next door. Consequently, nobody raised any objection during this visit when I volunteered to go to the small shop a few minutes around the corner on my own.

Since the language barrier might have led to confusion, Granny Vienna always armed me with a note for the shopkeeper; asking for ten gummy bears was one thing but requesting a litre of fresh milk for my churn, a bottle of buttermilk or some *Kaisersemmel* (crusty bread rolls) was another matter.

I enjoyed being independent but there was another, more mercenary reason for me to help. If there wasn't enough small change in the till, the missing coins below ten Groschen would invariably be replaced by a chewy sweet. I could be a very quick learner!

I remember an occasion when my grandmother and I were walking along the Schottenring boulevard in town. At some point we entered a majestic building where we ended up in a large office with very high ceilings and a huge wooden desk. It was disconcertingly quiet. A conversation took place between the official sitting behind the desk and my grandmother, who declined the offer of a chair and remained standing. I had no idea what they were talking about, and at the time I was not concerned; I just loved being with my granny. Many years later, I learned that she'd been discussing a compensation claim on behalf of her children.

During that visit in the late summer of 1958, we spent a few days in the suburb of Aspern. The still little backwater had given its name to a bloody, two-day Napoleonic battle that had taken place nearby and, until recently, had been home to Vienna's major airport.

This airport was once the base for I/JG135 Squadron of the German Luftwaffe after it had first performed a fly-over at Linz in honour of Hitler's triumphant invasion of Austria earlier in the day of 12th March 1938. On the same day Heinrich Himmler, Reichsführer of the SS and Chief of German Police, arrived to inaugurate a well-prepared campaign of terror against Jews and political opponents. Over a few short days, that campaign resulted in the arrest and detention of some 76,000 Viennese citizens, many of whom were subjected to vicious brutality followed by deportation to even more vicious concentration camps. Many of them never returned.

Back in 1958, to me Aspern was merely the place where Granny

Vienna's sister Auntie Hedwa[21] and her husband Vinzenz – better known to us as Uncle Maly – lived with their daughter Hilda, her husband and their little boy.

On this visit, my second cousin Auntie Hilda[22] was dressed from head to toe in black. She was morose and sometimes decidedly irritable with us children. Her husband, Uncle Willi, had recently been killed when his light aircraft, having taken off from Aspern airfield, crashed into the banks of the river Danube just beyond the city. It was said that he had been flying very low, had entered an air pocket and was killed on impact. We were even taken on a boat trip so that Hilda could show us the spot where her own life had taken an unexpected and tragic turn. Several years later, by way of venting her anger at his recklessness, Aunt Hedwa told Dawa that Uncle Willi had been flying over a nudist camp.

It seems he had also had a penchant for powerful motorbikes; he had almost succeeded in frightening my father to death during a show-off spin on a previous visit.

It was extremely hot, and the dusty semi-rural roads were spattered with potholes and loose stones. I liked it; there was a soporific silence – except when my relatives disturbed it because they were speaking very loudly. I was not used to this almost deafening talking *at*, as opposed to conversing *with*, and it hurt my ears and grated on my nerves.

I remember playing in the sandpit with my third cousin, Willi, who was about three years old. I knew his daddy was dead and felt very sad for him, even though he was terribly annoying. He kept grabbing the spade and the bucket, and just about everything else my brothers or I took hold of, all the while shouting '*Bistubatt! Bistubatt!*'. None of us had the faintest idea what he was saying, but clearly he was frustrated because we were a nuisance to this only child who had not yet learned to share.

I discovered eventually that what he meant was *Bist duppert?*[23],

Out of the mouths of babes!

A NEW HOME, A NEW LIFE

After we returned to Munich in early autumn 1958, we finally moved into our new home. It was a new build on the periphery of a small but expanding village fifteen minutes' walk from the main road of a semi-rural

---

21 Hedwika.
22 It was customary to call adults 'auntie' or 'uncle' whatever their position as a relative. Neighbours were also often addressed in the same way.
23 Viennese slang for 'Bist du deppert?': 'Are you stupid?'

outpost that nestled in a forest to the southeast of the city.

It was such a long time since I'd held my much-missed baby doll that I could barely contain myself as I waited for her and her pram to come off the removal van. I waited in vain.

'They must have got lost on the way...' my mother said. Somehow I didn't believe her, but why would my mother lie to me? Promises of a replacement doll and pram for Christmas did little to ease my sense of loss – until Christmas, of course.

No matter how much I loved my new doll, though, she could never compensate for her predecessor. The doubt about my mother telling the truth continued to rankle, popping into my thoughts for several more years to come. 'Lost' too was my precious dolls' house with its pretty bone-china tableware and delicate furniture that had been given to me by the craftsman who had made it.

Many years later, my mother confessed that she'd given them away because she had run out of space in the removal van. 'It never occurred to me that it would upset you.' In that respect not an awful lot ever really changed throughout our lives together.

Our new home seemed enormous, not only because I was very small but also because what had been intended as a two-apartment house had been converted into a single dwelling for us. Outside there was a spacious garden. Inside there were two sitting rooms (one for the adults and one for us children), a playroom/junk room, four bedrooms, two modern bathrooms (downstairs with pink tiles, upstairs with blue ones), a large attic and an even larger cellar with separate rooms. It had double-glazed windows with built-in roller blinds and exterior shutters – and it had central heating!

Compared with the tiny semi-detached house with its single-pane windows and small electric fires on the spartan post-war council estate we'd left behind in England, our new home seemed worlds away in every respect.

I soon discovered that our village was flanked on all sides by fields. Some small plots had been designated for new homes, but the established houses were set in tree- and shrub-filled gardens that gave an air of permanence and solidity to the place. I was much taken by my new world and soon became more conscious of my surroundings, appreciating nature in a way that I had not been capable of before.

It was not long before some of the locals started knocking at our door

– all men and none of them from our street. My mother later said she suspected that they had been calling with crude attempts to cultivate a relationship with the (presumably rich) English people, though I suspect they were more curious than anything else. Whatever the case, she had not forgotten a certain style of ingratiation she had noticed during her childhood in Vienna where those with wealth or professional status frequently brought out the obsequious worst in people.

For my part, in Munich in 1958 I distinctly remember that being English in Germany seemed to bring with it a certain inexplicable cachet – in those days, at least!

My mother said she had wanted to live closer to a Rudolf Steiner Waldorf school, but our father rejected that consideration out of hand. Logistics, cost, coupled with a disregard for his wife's concern about standard schooling might have influenced him, but he also firmly believed in the maxim, 'When in Rome, do as the Romans'. Although not a socialist, there was also his deep-seated dislike of British 'upper-class' snobbery and the way the desperately aspirational aped it.

As if metaphors had been invented for the occasion, my father grew up in Harrow-on-the-Hill where his parents owned a hardware shop; unfortunately for him, the daily walk to and from his county grammar school in Harrow town at the bottom of the hill also meant running the gauntlet of some obnoxious pupils of the elite Harrow School who lorded it over the pavements at the top of the hill. Bolstered by an inbred sense of superiority, their immaturity sometimes overflowed into infantile mockery when a wearer of a plebs' school uniform had the nerve to claim a share of the same pavement. The experience left an indelible mark on my father; for us, it would be the local state school.

Many years later, Dawa confided that while she had felt a great affinity with Rudolf Steiner's educational ethos, her greatest fear was that we might be exposed to antisemitism in one of Catholic Bavaria's state schools. Living smack-bang in the cradle of Jew-hating National Socialism was challenging enough without the potential for her children to fall foul of a mindset that had not been magically erased.

To the best of my recollection, though, her anxieties turned out to be groundless. I cannot recall any mention of Jews in any context at either of my two schools, at least not in my presence. In those days, the words *Jude* (Jew) and *jüdisch* (Jewish) had become pretty much unutterable in public.

I am grateful that my father's wishes prevailed because my brothers and I enjoyed the freedom and friendships we found in the local school; if we lost something by not going to a Steiner school, we certainly gained a great deal in other respects.

For our mother, to all appearances an Englishwoman who by some quirk of fate happened to speak German, life was not so clean cut. '*Ihre Kinder sind ganz apart.*'[24] Dawa never knew whether the woman had been fishing.

Much to my surprise, on the first day at my new school I sat next to another English girl, Susan. She didn't seem to mind interpreting for me and ensuring that I felt included during break times. Like mine, her mother was also of Viennese origin although, unlike Dawa, she spoke English with a pronounced foreign accent. To the best of my knowledge, though, there was no Jewish connection.

Susan's English father was an ex-RAF pilot employed as a flying instructor at nearby Riem International Airport. I thought he was very dashing when I occasionally saw him arrive home still wearing his flying suit. Maybe that was the influence of my brother Martin's English comics that were full of stories of handsome heroes returning from victorious dogfights against the wicked Hun!

One day when Susan was absent, I was placed under the wing of another classmate. We had rarely spoken before, although I had noted that this girl seemed very reserved and always blushed when she had to speak up during class. My German was still wobbly but, despite our very different personalities, we hit it off immediately. From then on, apart from the occasional and quite vicious spat (my shy but rather territorial friend was no shrinking violet when she was inside the safety of her own four walls) Angelika and I became the closest of friends.[25]

Our mothers became friendly too, and during the summer of my ninth birthday they and we children spent a couple of weeks on a traditional family farmstead in lush, pre-Alpine southern Bavaria. When we weren't all hiking the hilly meadows and forests, picking mushrooms and berries along the way, we children were free to roam the farm where we were introduced to the chickens, the cows, a horse and probably more than I can recall. To add to our sense of freedom, a sparkling, icy cold brook flowed alongside the farm before disappearing into the distance. Little did

---
24   'Your children are quite different.'
25   On the occasions when she witnessed it, Angelika's mother never gave her daughter's nasty behaviour a pass: she very calmly and quietly explained that it was unkind.

I appreciate back then how history was repeating itself.

Gela's[26] mother, Frau Anger, was a born teacher with many talents. She played the accordion and the zither and, as a gift to Martin, during our holiday together she expertly carved a symmetrical pattern at one end of a sturdy stick we had found in the woods. Beneath she added the date: 1960. That walking stick remained in Dawa's possession for many years; now it is in mine.

Angelika's parents, her mother in particular, were devout Catholics. Although *der liebe Gott*[27] as depicted in RE lessons and their textbooks never found any resonance with me, I did relish the preparations for my best friend's confirmation when she was nine years old. Apart from the ritual paraphernalia of fabulously decorated candles, the white satin, silk and lace frocks and even prettier headdresses, there was also plenty of ice-cream and delicious cake, not only on the big day but during the run-up, too. I enjoyed it all and was even a little envious of the frilly clothes – but not once did I feel any inclination to join the club.

Whether or not Frau Anger was aware of the Jewish connection I don't know; curiously, one day and out of the blue, she spread the fingers of both hands to form V shapes and asked me a question I never forgot: 'Sahlee, can you do this?'

By June 1959 I was able to understand and speak German; I even wrote my first letter to Vienna in that language, after a fashion. Reading it now, it has a marked Bavarian dialect. Granny Vienna had been re-named *Oma* (Granny). How must she have felt to finally communicate adequately with at least some of her grandchildren? From then until her death a decade later, we corresponded regularly so that our meetings, while infrequent, were never marred by feelings of unfamiliarity.

Even so, I wish we had seen more of her. From 1952 onwards, as soon as Uncle Toni and my mother had finally set up their own homes with just enough room to put her up, she made what was then a slow and arduous train journey to England every other year. Here she eventually divided her time equally between all three of her children: two weeks with us on the northern outskirts of London; two weeks with Elsa, first on her side of London and later in Sussex, and two weeks in Leeds with Toni. We were never all together.

Before that, my mother and her expanding brood had made that same train journey from England back to Vienna. Although my father (or Elsa,

---
26 Angelika's nickname.
27 Our dear God.

before she married) usually accompanied her in at least one direction, looking back I find it almost impossible to imagine how Dawa coped with three small children in such cramped and restricted conditions, not least when one of them was still in old-fashioned, terry-towelling nappies!

Now we were in Munich, a place where my mother had no particular inclination to be. Despite that, the adventurer in her set aside her fears in order to support her husband in his burgeoning career - and said nothing. My father never knew of her concerns while she consoled herself by imagining that at least we would visit Oma more often.

RELIGION MAKES ITSELF KNOWN

Following my father's birth in 1924, he was baptised into the Church of England. As was – and still is – so often the case, his parents had followed convention for the sake of a quiet life; he, however, kicked against convention. As I learned when I was older, he regarded everything he was taught in school RE lessons, and almost everything he observed about the institutionalised Christian Church, as an affront to his intelligence.

Neither my brothers nor I have any memories of him trying to influence our beliefs with his contempt, beyond a few jocular remarks about 'dog-collars'. When, as a nine-year-old, I asked my mother whether she believed in God, she simply said that we should all be kind and considerate towards one another.

Religion was never discussed. My parents had agreed that we children should be given the freedom to come to our own conclusions. Yet, in spite of the lack of overt parental influence, when I was five years old I insisted on attending Sunday school. Tipped off by my playmates, I joined so that I could also make pretty things with paper cups and coloured paper for Mother's Day.

My mother was only too delighted to have this live wire off her hands for an hour or so; what woman with a bunch of small children wouldn't be? Of course, there is rarely such a thing as a free lunch; I recall being read to from a Ladybird book about someone called Jesus from ancient days, and enjoying the pictures of men and women dressed in brightly coloured flowing robes. The little lambs were sweet, too. I certainly had no appreciation that this had anything to do with religion.

My enthusiasm was short-lived. If my mother was disappointed that her respite was so brief, she didn't make me aware of it. However, she did end up paying me sixpence to spend alternate Sunday afternoons with

Granny Pinner when, for a time, I became fed up with the predictable infringement upon my liberty.

It was only after a few months at my school in Munich, when I could understand more of what was going on around me, that I gradually realised that religion could actually be somewhat divisive.

My primary school consisted of two different institutions gathered under one roof: a Roman Catholic Church school on the first floor, and my multi-denominational school (Catholic and Protestant) on the ground floor. This separation seemed to preclude almost all interaction. Occasionally we spied unknown faces in the bicycle parking area or in the playground and parkland, but it always felt like an unspoken matter of 'them and us'.

This religious apartheid filtered down to us when we were segregated during RE lessons. While my Catholic schoolmates remained in our form room, my Protestant RE lessons took place in the cellar where there was only minimal natural light and, more often than not, stifling heat from the central-heating boiler.

Since there was no secular option in the shape of the philosophy of ethics – least of all metaphysics – for juniors, this time my parents gave in to convention and registered their children as Protestant, members of the Church of England. After all, who would know?

I discovered I was what in Germany is known as Evangelisch – and continued to believe that I was for several years until I eventually learnt that I had never even been baptised. Such was the level of my ignorance. That particular inscription on my internal ID card took quite a while to wear off.

I have sometimes wondered how my mother might have felt if she had been aware of the vicious anti-Jew diatribes penned by the founder of Germany's Protestant movement, homegrown theologian and excommunicated Catholic priest Martin Luther[28]. Certainly, his was an ego not to be messed with!

In Munich, when the formal class register was taken at the beginning of each new school year, I was able to stand up and say with confidence '*Englisch, Evangelisch*[29]' unlike some girls who blushed and squirmed in embarrassment as they were obliged to confirm their national status as *Flüchtling* (refugee). I was bemused, and remain bemused to this day, at

---

28   Luther had expected Germany's marginalised Jews to convert to his brand of Christianity; when they would not, he turned on them.
29   'English, Protestant.'

the need for this very public singling out that caused obvious discomfort, although I had no understanding why people from Poland and Hungary should have had to flee their homelands in the first place.

THE CONSCIOUS BIRTHING OF EMPATHY

I thoroughly enjoyed my new life in Munich. Before too long, the only thing that really reminded me that I had not lived there all my life was that nobody pronounced my name in English fashion. Not that it bothered me, except during the first year or so when sometimes I failed to recognise my name and got into trouble. I eventually tuned in to the alien pronunciation and all was well.

There was a buzz of excitement in the air as we made new friends and our lives entered a different phase. Almost as soon as we moved into our new home, my mother discovered an English family living a couple of streets away. Mrs E. and her two children, four-year-old Bob and his older sister Helen, had remained in Munich while Mr E. had gone ahead to find his footing in a new job in Caracas – something to do with oil.

When our mothers became friendly, we five children benefitted from boisterous outings crammed into the back seat and tiny rear storage compartment of their Volkswagen Beetle, Adolf Hitler's affordable car for the common people.

We had the most fun with Helen. She was of a similar age to Martin, hyperactive, defiant and uncontrollable, and frequently provoked her mother into a state of apoplexy. Not only was she bored to distraction, but there was no father at home who might have constrained her behaviour.

I shudder to remember how easily she influenced me to do her bidding. We three older children sometimes clambered around building sites that, while not sealed off, were obviously out of bounds, and on one occasion we banged on a cellar window to give the unsuspecting occupants a bit of a fright. In my defence, I was still only seven years old, but when I was eventually caught red-handed (having seen danger coming, the other two had already run away) I was marched home with very wet knickers. My mother refused to believe what a brat I'd been – or perhaps she simply chose not to add to my humiliation!

Yet I learned from the experience. Realising that I had upset an elderly couple who were trying to relax over a meal after a long day working on building their house above their heads upset me terribly. I neither denied nor confirmed my 'crime', but I did become much more selective about my activities – even if I was still a far from perfect child.

THE GOOD LIFE

Seeing someone who needs help tends to bring out the best in most of us, and that is how we met the Lassens. Driving home early one Saturday afternoon from a shopping trip in town, my father noticed that a car involved in an accident had a GB numberplate. 'We'd better stop and see if they need any help with the coppers...'

Gerald was a ruddy-faced, ex-army major whose tweed donkey jacket, corduroy trousers and brown brogues immediately signified a common ground beyond nationality. Once all the police formalities were completed and their damaged car towed away, he and his wife Jane squeezed in between us children for a lift home.

They lived in what (to me) seemed like a very old and dark little house on the edge of local woodlands. Here they were attempting to reinvent themselves in civvy street as agents for high-end British tableware. They, too, clearly believed that Germany was ready for the best of British, and the chance to start a new career had fallen into their laps.

My father could be very playful and sometimes scarily strict, but fundamentally he was a good man. Some time later, when he got out of our car to guide a young schoolboy across a busy main road, my hero worship knew no bounds!

Not long after starting at our new school, Martin made friends with a classmate whose mother and aunt became our mother's lifelong 'third circle' friends who only knew her by her formal name. Regine and Kristina were twenty-something divorcees, each with a child: ten-year-old Max, and six-year-old Larissa. They lived with the matriarch of the family, the formidable and elegant Frau Waller and her quiet second husband who was generally referred to as 'Opa' (Granddad).

Still relatively financially comfortable from the sale of Frau Waller's business in another part of Germany, the family's money-earning schemes revolved largely around Opa diverting his artistic craft into engraving name plates for the living quarters of US military personnel in the post-WWII American zone of occupation. While not earning a fortune, name-plating had become a useful source of extra income.

The Americans were potentially useful for something else, too: Regine and Kristina were on the lookout for husbands in what had become a severely depleted post-war marketplace. The US military had a large presence in Munich. The women hosted glamorous parties; they were great fun and soon friendly if transient relations were forged within a circle of diverse cultural backgrounds.

In common with so many women who'd been seduced by smart uniforms and the cornucopia of American goodies available from the US military's own department stores, the sisters believed that marrying an American officer was the route to a prosperous and secure life – especially if they could move across the Atlantic to the land of plenty.

We children benefitted directly from these new connections. While our parents also hosted parties, we took part in some weekend visits to the US Army barracks. While the grown-ups did their thing, our hosts' children took us off to amuse ourselves elsewhere. I can remember a fun fair and lots of sugary stuff, and the cinema where we watched cartoons and munched American popcorn from what seemed like cardboard buckets. There were also the goodies (including copious ice cream) from the American stores and at least one summer week-end outing that I can recall driving in convoy with conspicuous 1950s'-era American limousines that made Larissa horribly car sick.

Even better, my father's friend Uncle Ray moved to nearby Landsberg with his family, which added a welcome sense of continuity to our lives; especially for our father who had left behind several meaningful and mutually stimulating life-long friendships that he was never able to replicate in Germany.

As an RAF pilot, Ray had been seconded to train German Luftwaffe pilots to prepare them for their role in NATO now that the American instructors were gradually withdrawing. Little did I know then that Landsberg prison had provided a sabbatical for a politically ambitious Adolf Hitler to concoct his manifesto *Mein Kampf*.

As life became busy in this Central European culture that still resonated with my mother, little appeared to disturb her enjoyment of life. After ten years stranded in relatively barren suburban land, she blossomed like a swan returning to its lake. My father's new job had provided him with career status and greater financial freedom; it had also opened doors to higher places than he was professionally accustomed to, and he enjoyed the stimulation of new people and conversation. With an attractive and dignified wife at his side, whose social ease made her the perfect executive's wife, he also seemed to grow in stature.

There weren't as many opportunities to indulge his love of live music as there were in London, but there were some. Nor did he have to give up another pleasure in life; instead of making the regular Saturday morning trip from the northern suburbs of London to Parmigiani's Italian delicatessen in Soho, he discovered Munich's equivalent of Fortnum and Mason a short distance from his office. Shopping there, and in the delicatessen about five minutes' drive from our home, he could still obtain his weekend supply of Gorgonzola, other fine cheeses and wafer-thin slices of Italian and German cold cuts.

On Saturday evenings, he and my mother savoured these delicacies as they drank wine and listened to jazz and blues, Neapolitan songs and other genres, as well as the very English humour of *The Goons*, all played on the hi-fi system that my father had lovingly built.

Like every child with happy parents, I felt very happy too. Contrary to my gloomy expectations, I was even happy at my new school.

I liked the teacher who taught me for the first two years. Frau B. was a kind woman in late middle age who always seemed to be dressed in shades of brown. She 'felt' unwell to me but, as a child, I didn't understand the significance of the halitosis, the intense pigmentation changes on her face, neck and hands, and the dark shadows with fat deposits beneath her eyes so it never consciously occurred to me that she really was not in the best of health.

The discipline in her classroom was superbly judged; all thirty-plus of us knew exactly what the boundaries of behaviour were. She was never aggressive, merely firm with an authoritative voice and a look in the eye that told us she meant what she said. Perhaps being a group of only girls for those first two years might have had something to do with it, although I can't recall any poor behaviour after we merged with a boys' class from the third year onwards. It was just the way it was back then.

The tall windows made for a bright classroom with just enough teaching aids without triggering ADHD strung along the walls, and we sat at double desks with a bench attached to them. Everything was neat and tidy and calm, friendly and safe. We learned the basics of the three Rs by rote, chanting the alphabet, spelling rules and times' tables until the brainwashing clicked into place and became second nature. In the first year we practised writing with a sharp, white chalk pencil on miniature blackboards that fitted into our satchels; on one side the slate was blank for drawing pictures with coloured chalk pencils, while the reverse was printed with a grid of lines intended to help us to become accustomed to forming well-proportioned letters.

Instead of having attended kindergarten like my fellow pupils, I had already completed my first year of infant school in England. That must have freed me to get to grips with learning German. With Frau B's patience, Susan's translation efforts and the encouragement of both Angelika and her mother, my first end-of-year school report was deemed very satisfactory.

While I was never interested in competing for the sake of it, after that it was more or less plain sailing – until towards the end of the third year, when I realised that everything around me was beginning to disintegrate.

ALMOST HEAVEN ON EARTH

As far as I was concerned, winters in my new home were tantamount to living in fairyland. In those days we had yet to hear of climate change, let alone global pollution, and snow lasting for most of the winter was still the norm.

During the weeks when my class was on the school's morning shift, I spent many afternoons in the open air. If I was not at the Prinz Regent's ice rink in Munich with Angelika and her mother, the two of us often messed around on her parents' incredibly long skis.

During the first two winters I also joined my brothers and some of the local children to play in the snow. Typical of a group made up predominantly of boys, much of our time was taken up devising games that required a degree of nerve – or ignorance. Running and launching ourselves into skids down the icy street (sometimes helped along with a little cold water to override the effects of grit and salt), ice-skating on the village pond, building a snow ramp into the bowels of a recently excavated building site down which we hurtled on our sledges, or having snowball fights – I took part enthusiastically even if somewhat more cautiously than the boys.

We often stayed outdoors until after winter's sun had gone down and the streetlamps took over. The atmosphere was magical as the beams of electric light made the snowflakes sparkle and the ice shimmer. One year my brothers and I built an igloo in our garden, crawled inside, sat on the snow bench – and froze. At least, I did. I remember trying to imagine what it must be like to be an Eskimo and concluding with absolute certainty that I was lucky not to have been born one. That igloo stood for ages.

When I was in a quieter mood and not playing board or card games with my brothers, I was content to pull up an armchair in front of the big picture window of the 'grown-up' sitting room, wedge my feet into the radiator and lose myself in reading. Other times, I just sat and watched the falling snow; the undisturbed, gentle white silence was pure bliss.

Christmas Day in England had been exciting, but in Munich the festive season took on a magic of its own. It wasn't just the snow, but the warm atmosphere infused with the evocative scent of fern during the December countdown to the big evening on 24th[30] that was still in a league of its own.

Of course, the wise words behind the windows in the advent calendar and the symbolism of the advent wreath – let alone the symbolism of St. Nikolaus and Krampus roaming the streets on 5th December – meant little to me, although the various traditional bakeries, and sweet and spicy hot drinks provided very enjoyable reasons to rejoice during the unfolding of a meaningful tradition.

A typical winter's day began long before daylight, even before we got up at 6.30am when we heard a snowplough clearing the road. It deposited what seemed like mountains of the stuff on the pavement, which then had to be cleared for pedestrians. That responsibility fell to the occupants of the adjoining houses. When there had been a particularly heavy snowfall, it was not unusual to find high drifts against our glass-panelled front door. Opening it, we would be confronted with a white, soundproof wall of snow that had to be pushed back before it collapsed inwards onto the lobby floor.

If we were to get to school on time – and heaven help us if we didn't – shovelling had to start without delay. It was hard work clearing a path from the front porch to the drive at the side of the house, then clearing the snow so my smartly dressed father could drive his car out of the garage, through the wide gate and on to the street. I may be being unfair, but I have few memories of anyone other than my mother doing most of the shovelling during the week. Not that I gave her selflessness any thought; it was simply how it was.

After breakfast, which my mother prepared and we ate in the warm kitchen while she was hard at work outside, we set off to school. While we still attended the local primary, we walked the twenty or so minutes' distance, though sometimes my father gave us a lift if we were leaving at the same time. In winter our car tyres were fitted with snow chains, but even so it sometimes took several attempts to conquer the icy incline to

---

30 In Germany Christmas is celebrated on the evening of 24th December.

the main road into town.

Other times during our first couple of winters, before we all grew too heavy, my mother pulled Robert and me on our wooden sledge. It was fitted with a backrest against which we took turns to recline, wrapped up in a warm blanket. Sometimes we were even given a hot-water bottle to cuddle. It was magical and cosy, and we loved it. So did our mother because, as she later told me, it revived memories of her own childhood when her mother had done exactly the same thing.

Summers seemed to be equally long and no less fun. The peripheral fence of Munich's international airport at Riem was only about ten minutes' walk away along a country track beside fields of maize and wheat. There was an unlocked gate onto the airfield where a shepherd regularly tended a large flock of sheep. We had arrived in Germany at a time of comparative innocence; until the day a few years later when the gates were locked forever to passers-by, my local friend Helga and I sometimes walked and chatted with the shepherd while he whistled commands to his dog as it controlled any straying sheep.

Other days, my brothers and I climbed a rusty ladder to play on the flat roof of an intriguing relic of the war, what I later learnt was a concrete machine-gun bunker. As for watching the passenger aeroplanes land and take off from such close quarters, it was thrilling though it had a particular edge. A few months before we had arrived, an aeroplane carrying the Manchester football team had crashed with cruel consequences into a farmhouse a mere stone's throw away. Its own 'ground zero' was still plain to see.

There was the excitement of the many rides and booths at the annual Oktoberfest[31], coupled with a large sightseeing Zeppelin slowly criss-crossing the skies above Munich during the festivities. With a huge red Trumpf[32] logo emblazoned on its rump, it flew in each afternoon before darkness fell to moor for the night just inside our gate into the airfield. Because the pilots lodged in Helga's house nearby, I was sometimes allowed to stand close as the floating giant hovered a short distance above me.

Before my ninth birthday I walked everywhere; after that, my treasured emerald-green bicycle made life a lot faster, and I could cram much more into my days and go further afield. I also cycled with Martin to the nearest open-air public swimming pool about five kilometres away. Sometimes we

---

31   An annual festival originating in 1810 to celebrate the marriage of the crown prince and future king of Bavaria to a princess of Sachsen-Hildburghausen.
32   German chocolate manufacturer.

rode through the forest; other times we chose the faster cycle track beside the main road until we had to turn off.

At the swimming pool we spent a few hours in the cold, highly chlorinated water, occasionally emerging to thaw out and eat a snack. Once warmed up, and if I hadn't already spent my weekly pocket money, an ice cream or sweet waffle-like sandwich from the snack kiosk was on the menu. Although various mothers – and even Frau Waller – occasionally joined us with Larissa and the younger children, most of the time I could be the free spirit I liked to be.

Rain never bothered me; I either got wet or not, depending on how I was dressed. If the weather was warm, I even derived pleasure from getting soaked to the skin; to me, it was the equivalent of walking barefoot on the grass. I knew my mother would not object because she understood. And on the few occasions when I ended up cold and miserable, there couldn't have been a better person to dry me off and warm me up again.

Apart from the well-established conifers growing along one boundary of our garden, the trees were still immature and unsuitable for climbing, so when I was at Angelika's we used the mature apple and cherry trees in her garden. We clambered around like monkeys, picking and eating fruit, no matter how unripe, and testing just how high we could climb before the branches showed signs of giving way under our weight.

Angelika and I dared each other quite a lot, and her swing was another source of fun. The idea was to swing forward as high as possible to the point of stalling, when the pull of gravity would cause the tension in the chains to buckle. Then one had to hold on for dear life while recalibrating the direction of the swing – or plummet with a jerk towards the ground. I shudder to think of it now.

At home we had a decent-sized paddling pool and a hosepipe with a sprinkler that kept my brothers and me amused for many afternoons. Energetic badminton matches and fairly aggressive ball games ensured that I became tough, very fit and stayed slender! If there was no school the following morning, we often played in the garden until it was either too dark to see or skidding around in the entrails of squashed slugs and worms became too disgusting for us to want to continue.

My mother encouraged reading without ever making an issue of it. Since she and Martin were avid readers, soon after our arrival in Munich we joined the International Library in the city centre. The afternoon tea parties at the British Consulate, with biscuits and cakes from home for expat kids, were fun too, but once Martin and I found our feet locally these social events gradually became redundant.

With the exception of the weekly editions of *Lion* and *Jack and Jill* (and later *Diana*) comics that Granny Pinner sent over to help her grandchildren maintain their English connection, I soon lost interest in the English-language offerings in town. I preferred German fairy tales and folklore as well as children's adventures and gallows' humour in books at our local library. Although I was mostly unaware of it at the time, the stories all contained the theme 'and the moral of the story is…'

By the age of nine I had started browsing the shelves in the adult section, where I was soon hooked on the likes of Attilio Gatti's Africa explorations, Ancient Egyptian history, biographical works and what I now know to be books on anthropology. History and human life fascinated me; sometimes I was so keen to hang on to the information that I copied whole tracts of the text onto a note pad before reluctantly returning the book to its rightful place.

'You're not really reading that, are you? I bet you're only looking at the pictures!' my father said when I showed him something I was copying about Queen Hatshepsut.

'Of course I'm reading it! It's really interesting, about an ancient Egyptian queen who used to dress in men's clothes and wore a false beard.'

He laughed. 'I don't believe you, you're making it up.'

Incandescent at being treated like a silly little girl, I never tried to discuss a book with my father again unless it was one he had given to me. What was the point of inviting derision from somebody who imagined they knew better but against whom I couldn't defend myself? That is what I believed back then, and it was a psychological scab that took many years to fall away.

Unlike several fellow pupils who had been banned from reading newspapers and current-affairs journals because they were considered too young, my brothers and I were free to read whatever happened to be lying around. I became a remarkably well-informed youngster who could name drop the likes of Mrs Bandaranaike, Fidel Castro and the battle cruiser *Admiral Graf Spee* while still playing with my dolls or chasing around on my bicycle.

There was a cinema in the nearest high street with Saturday morning performances suitable for children and teenagers. Charlie Chaplin (silent), dubbed Laurel and Hardy, and adventure films featuring Hollywood heart throbs such as Errol Flynn and Robert Taylor were just a few of the offerings that kept us children happily occupied while giving our parents, especially our mother, a short breather.

I can't remember ever being really bored, except on Sundays when fathers were at home and playtime at friends' houses or with local children was often not possible. The atmosphere beyond our front gate certainly became quieter and curiously formal.

In any event, I soon discovered that complaining of boredom was pointless. 'Then find something to do. I had to, so you can too,' my only-child father would say.

Playful and kind as my father could be, he was never keen on taking part in something that didn't interest him. The more tired he gradually became, the more he wanted to spend weekends at home (after a Saturday morning foray to the local delicatessen) dressed in casual clothes that, on him, still always looked elegant. Even the food on his plate looked more appealing than anybody else's – and tasted better. It was just the way he was. Saturday afternoons were generally reserved for personal maintenance and reading journals so as to remain up to date with his professional and private passions for electronics and music, before giving way to atmospheric evenings of food, wine and beautiful music once we children were in bed.[33]

On Sundays, his communion with the Almighty took place between a late full English-style breakfast (bacon and crumpets depended upon business trips to England), a late lunch, and a light mid-evening supper once we children were in bed. Consequently, the day of rest often signified hunger and headaches and general disorientation for me – and opera and classical music that reached into every corner of the house.

In contrast, our German neighbours tended to rise early on Sundays and dress in formal clothes, with little boys morphing into miniature gentlemen in neat suits, bow ties and trilbies. They attended morning church, took strolls, went out for lunch or visited friends and other family members for afternoon coffee and cake.

Even when we were invited by friends or work colleagues, my father drew the line at bowing to local convention by wearing a suit and he caused considerable mirth with his eccentric Englishman's attire. I, on the other hand, was only too happy to wear a pretty frock and my best shoes.

---

[33] Nobody minded if any of us came downstairs for a quick peek or small taste of adult food.

TANTE[34] MARIANNE

Some months after moving to Germany, my mother's cousin (a few times removed) Tante Marianne, came into our lives.

Her visits always involved little gifts and plenty of affection for us children, but there was something about her that unnerved me. It was not just the smell of mothballs or that she dressed entirely in black; there seemed to be a melancholy about her no matter how much she smiled.

I can remember recoiling awkwardly when she tried to cuddle me, saying mysteriously, *'Die armen Kinder!'*[35] I had no idea what she meant, while my mother later owned up to feeling deeply indignant. What on earth could she possibly have meant?

One day when we were preparing to pay Tante Marianne a visit at her city-centre apartment, I resisted so strongly that my mother eventually explained to me that Marianne's only son, Peter, who I would later learn had been a Harvard (or was it Princeton?) scholarship student, had been killed in a car crash a few years earlier. Not long afterwards, her husband had died of a broken heart. As she was now completely alone, we must be extra kind to Tante Marianne.

From then on, all I ever felt like doing when I saw her was crying. It was many years before I discovered that there was an even greater poignancy to her melancholy that even my mother was still mostly ignorant of.

During our second winter in Germany, a previously unknown great-aunt also made herself known from a distance. Tante Paula lived in Sweden and was my mother's aunt. I had never heard of her before (or maybe I'd been too young for it to register) but now I was delighted to receive the money she sent us children to buy Christmas presents.

My mysterious great-aunt's generosity allowed me to buy my first watch with a detachable, washable, pale blue, plaited-nylon strap. Not many children of my age had watches in those days and I felt very sophisticated!

My very unsophisticated thank-you letter, however, proved to be the sting in the tail. In spite of all the practice on my personal blackboard, my handwriting was always erratic and this time it failed to pass my father's perfectionist eye until I'd rewritten it numerous times. My choice of words suffered the same fate. It proved to be another of those accidentally formative, if unwelcome experiences, although I have felt considerably better having learned that my English grandfather was also sensitive to

---

34 Aunt.
35 'The poor children!'

the use of the written word. He had passed on his high standards to his son, who was probably trying to instil them in me.

I never forgot my great-aunt Paula, even though we never met. More than forty years later, when I read the letters she'd written to my uncle Toni after he had fled to England from Vienna, as well as those she wrote in the aftermath of WWII and the Holocaust, I couldn't help falling in love with this remarkable woman whose humanity, insight and intelligence radiated from every page.

THE BEGINNING OF THE END OF INNOCENCE

After a short time in Munich, and even though my parents never touched on the subject, it was impossible to ignore that there had been a war between Germany and Britain. Apart from Martin's English comic books portraying the adventures of ace fighter pilot Paddy Payne and his squadron who were fighting the wicked Nazis (whom I never equated with the people around me), there were still bomb sites awaiting reconstruction, especially in the vicinity of Munich's Hauptbahnhof, the central mainline station close to our father's office.

More disturbingly, a new girl who joined my class a year or two after my arrival felt it necessary to reassure me that the war had not been her fault. I found that strange: what did the war have to do with us? Later I learned that hundreds of thousands of German soldiers had died (the reality of the multiple millions of dead remained obscured for many years) because we were asked to bring donations to school to help maintain the vast war cemeteries – at least, that was my understanding at the time. In return for our contributions, we were given small prints depicting seemingly infinite rows of white crosses that made me feel very sad.

During the annual remembrance period in my third year at school, my awareness of the war increased. As she recalled the events, a locum teacher kept looking in my direction while repeatedly mentioning the bombing of the city of Dresden and the suffering inflicted upon the German people by *die Engländer* (who always took the rap for all of Great Britain). Perhaps it was impossible to ignore an *Engländer* being present in her classroom; whatever her reasons, it was obvious that there was definitely some bad blood between the Germans and my home country.

The introduction to this bad blood developed one day at the end of morning break. Stormy weather had kept us in our classroom; had I walked back from the playground, I would have finished my sweet in plenty of time after the bell. Even though several others still had hamster cheeks, my teacher Frau G. glowered at me and instructed the class with disdain to 'look at this English girl'. 'Can't you behave like a civilised Central European?' she demanded.

Frau G. confirmed something I had already discovered at infant school in England when a teacher had given me a bad-tempered shove that sent me crashing into some chairs, bloodying my shin and causing a scar that is still visible today. My crime? I had been walking alongside her asking a question at a time when she was more concerned with rushing off for her coffee break.

My mother had been both a children's nurse and a school nurse, so she knew a thing or two about the difference between a normal accident and something more violent. She challenged the teacher, who indignantly denied any knowledge of the incident. She lied shamelessly.

While my German teacher was prone to moralising 'Wer einmal lügt, dem glaubt man nie',[36] she also confirmed something that every child knows: teachers have likes and dislikes, whether they show it or not.

Frau G. was no exception, though her nastiness *was* exceptional. For reasons I never understood, my classmate Hermine was the focus of her venom to the point that the poor girl could barely draw breath without attracting scornful rebukes and petty punishments.

One particular day Hermine repeatedly complained of severe pain as she clutched her abdomen, her pale and blotchy face twisted in agony.

'Dear me, Hermine's always got something going on with her!' Frau G. replied dismissively, clearly determined to stop any further irritating demands on her attention.

The following day, Hermine was absent. The day after that, her mother came into the classroom to say that her daughter would be away for some time; she had arrived home from school in great pain, was diagnosed with acute appendicitis and immediately operated upon.

To my amazement Frau G. feigned complete ignorance and asked why on earth Hermine had failed to say anything to her. I couldn't contain my outrage. I stood up from my desk, which was absolutely forbidden unless you'd been given permission, walked up to the two women and committed a second crime: I reminded our teacher that Hermine had said she was in pain and had been told to stop making a fuss.

My fate was sealed. Reprimands, criticism, sarcasm and punishment

---

36 If you lie once, nobody will believe you again

became part of my daily routine to the point where another teacher was moved to enquire what one earth I'd done to warrant so many detentions.

They took place on days when our lessons were scheduled for the afternoon shift, but if Frau G. hoped to humiliate me by making me turn up an hour early and sit at the back of the morning class, she failed. And anyway, the strange teacher – although obviously bemused – turned out to be remarkably good-humoured about it all!

However, I was disturbed by Frau G.'s injustice. If I'd been guilty as charged I would have accepted the detentions and writing endless punishment lines of *Ich darf nicht schwätzen*[37] on the chin, but I was *not* guilty. Angelika eventually offered to help write my lines (Frau Anger even colluded by tying two pencils together to try and speed up the process), but the unfairness of Frau G.'s false accusations upset me terribly.

Without my knowledge my mother, confused by my supposed change of character at school (and probably not best pleased at having to make me very early lunches), went to see the headmaster to find out what was going on. Of course, that led to further retribution after the headmaster came into our classroom and summoned Frau G. to his office. When she returned, she stood in front of the class and said sarcastically, 'Selly feels she's not loved – but we do all love Selly, don't we?'

Her malice was unmistakable, and I sensed that this would not be the end of the matter. Had my mother any inkling of what she was provoking, she would probably not have intervened and hoped that any unpleasantness would blow over, but quite rightly she tried to protect me from the harsh behaviour of an adult who was supposed to be taking care of me. Unfortunately, it didn't work, but I was pleased that she went out of her way to protect me at a time when, as I found out later, she was suffering deep emotional turmoil.

A few days after my mother's visit, Frau G. disappeared for several weeks. Perhaps it was the stress of the headmaster's reprimand that caused her to succumb to pneumonia. For a brief period, I enjoyed school again – until the day our re-energised teacher took up where she had left off with increased gusto.

I had a curious knack for grasping concepts by sensing them or through flashes of patterns in my mind's eye, so at times I knew the answers without being able to explain how I had arrived at them. Now, when I raised my hand and gave a correct answer or when I finished an assignment faster

---

37   I must not talk in class.

than anybody else, I was accused of cheating. If I made a mistake, I was ridiculed. No matter what I did, it was wrong.

This bullying, which coincided with the stress I was beginning to suffer because of the unfolding crisis at home, destroyed my confidence. Occasional hesitation became an inability to focus or think clearly. To outsiders, it appeared that I was deliberately refusing to put in any effort at school.

This provided Frau G. with further ammunition, and she added regular snorts of '*Faule Liese*'[38] to her weaponry. Looking at a class photograph taken at the time, I am slumped in misery amidst a sea of smiling faces. The elderly couple around the corner no longer had any reason to greet me with '*Da kommt unser Lächeln!*'[39] as I approached them on my bicycle.

My only satisfaction in the midst of this was to watch Frau G.'s fitted brocade jacket change colour as she sweated with anxiety on school inspection day (though I quickly felt quite sorry for her). But in spite of everything, including a poor reference school report, I still passed two (or was it three?) days of external examinations in order to go to grammar school.

In later years, I sometimes fantasised about asking Frau G. whether she had finally grown up. It seems I was not alone. During a class reunion a quarter of a century later, it turned out that Susan had harboured similar dreams. Her nerve failed her, though, or maybe she simply felt sorry for a woman who may well not have had the faintest idea of her effect on we children.

Frau G. also took the RE lessons, the irony of which would be quite amusing if it were not so sad. But, with hindsight, she was very young – and not only in years. 'She's married to an old Nazi,' someone later offered helpfully to try and explain her xenophobia.

For a short time that xenophobia was also aimed at my little brother. '*Aber ich hab doch nichts getan,*'[40] the nonplussed six-year-old protested. Perhaps Frau G. couldn't resist the sweet little boy's plea of innocence, because after that she left him alone.

MY HORIZONS EXPAND

Unless I decided I wanted a change of scenery, my direct route to school

---

38 'Lazybones'.
39 'Here comes our smiler!'
40 'But I didn't do anything.'

(at first on foot and later often on my beloved bicycle) took me to the end of our dusty, potholed side street before turning into the village's slightly wider, tarmac-covered main road. To the south lay fields of wheat, maize and potatoes, beyond which Germany's highest mountain, the snow-capped Zugspitze, beckoned mysteriously on the horizon.

My journeys would have been idyllic had it not been for the open-topped lorries that thundered by transporting wet gravel from a nearby pit, and a boy Martin and I ended up referring to as Snotty Nose – though we were not the only ones.

The lorry drivers usually drove like lunatics. Before it was extended many years later, the road was only just wide enough for two reasonably sized cars to pass without slowing down and it had no pavement, just ditches at either side. There were several occasions when we were fortunate to stay in one piece. Robert was knocked off his feet by a local tradesman as he raced past in a van but apart from severe shock, and thanks to the substantial leather satchel on his back, he survived intact.

Our cleaning lady's son, a sweet little boy of six, was not so fortunate. His death beneath the wheels of one of those lorries was a terrible tragedy for his family, for whom death became an all-too-regular visitor. I caught myself momentarily wishing that Snotty Nose had been killed instead, though I was annoyed to discover that I didn't really enjoy the thought. I loathed the boy because I was afraid of him, but I wasn't capable of such vicious hatred.

Franz must have been about twelve or thirteen and was quite big compared with his peers. He and his much slighter younger brother lived with their father, a hulk of a man who glided along the road in what seemed like slow motion and who, his sons boasted, was a film actor. For a long time I imagined all sorts of glamorous roles until I eventually caught a brief glimpse of him in a film about Mad King Ludwig of Bavaria.

Franz's home was not much more than a quite substantial brick hut, but I didn't give any thought to his family's living conditions beyond feeling rather sad for the boys. I had heard they had no mother – at least not one who lived with them.

The brothers attended a school for children with learning difficulties. As if to reinforce my dislike of him, Franz seemed to have a permanently infected, runny nose that often made me nauseous. Looking back, I have nothing but compassion for him – but this is now and that was then. And I was considerably younger in age than Frau G.

While I have no recollection of it, perhaps I took my cue from the local boys who derided his 'special needs' status. Maybe I was simply in the wrong place at the wrong time. For whatever reason – perhaps with some justification – Franz did not like us '*scheiß Engländer*'.[41] Worse luck for me, being quite a dainty girl, I was clearly an easy target on which he could vent his resentment.

For a while he seemed satisfied with shouting abuse as he passed me in the street, but then he graduated to cuffing me across the head before running off or speeding away on his bicycle. Once he realised I couldn't defend myself, he became more audacious. He would jump out of his hiding place to dance around me like a prize boxer, blocking my escape before giving me a well-placed slap across the face.

Once the seasons changed and snow fell, he graduated to attacking my head with accurate snowballs that he delivered with great force. I had to pass his hiding place as I emerged from beneath the railway bridge that was the only entrance to our village unless I crossed the railway track into a field on the incline below. There was no escaping him if I wanted to get home, and he knew it.

The anticipation of these ambushes became a regular moment of terror, but finally he went too far and hit me with a carefully crafted cannonball of icy snow. The damage was such that Martin beat him up – at least, that's what I was told at the time, though my brother has no recollection of it. Maybe it was my father who felt moved to utter a few choice words?

Whatever, after that last attack the harassment stopped and I was safe again. That episode gave me an insight into the workings of a wounded bully; although I didn't realise it at the time, my experience was a reflection of sinister events that had played themselves out not so many years earlier.

THE PAST CATCHES UP

Frau B. seemed old to me, although she was probably only in her late fifties or early sixties when I first met her. Back then women did tend to look much older much earlier, even more so if they were hard-working countrywomen. She was always dressed from head to toe in black, her dark hair streaked with wiry strands of silver twisted into a bun at the nape of her neck. Whenever she stepped beyond her garden gate she covered her head with a large black scarf, the final touch to her widow's uniform. She was a depressing sight, although not an unusual one; there were many

---

41 'Shitty English people.'

women like her.

Frau B. lived at the end of our street in a much older house than ours. She had a tortoiseshell cat that was almost permanently pregnant. As I passed her garden fence, we had started to chat over the gate. One afternoon I saw several tiny kittens trying to negotiate the steep flight of steps from the entrance of her home. My delight was obvious, so Frau B. invited me in to play with them.

After a few minutes, and to my complete surprise, she offered me one of the kittens. If homes were not found for them, they would have to be drowned she added matter-of-factly. Soon a beautiful ginger tomcat, called either Mieze or Pussy, became an adored and spoilt member of our family. Sometime later he was joined by a beautiful Angora rabbit called Hasi or Bunny who also enjoyed the free run of our home.

A curious friendship developed between Frau B. and me over the following years. Gradually she gave me glimpses of a time during 'the war' that I could only vaguely understand, and that she obviously wished had never happened.

Like Angelika's mother, Frau B. was a devout Catholic. Apart from being irritated by people who lacked respect for one another or did not do their work carefully, I don't recall hearing anything unkind pass her lips.

Her hands were rough, with deep crevices impregnated with stains of soil that spoke of a life of hard manual work. To augment her widow's pension, she worked as a cleaner for a doctor's family. They must have celebrated their good fortune because she took great pride in everything she did, whether it was her paid job or scrubbing her own floor, doing the laundry, making her family's clothes, tending to her vegetable garden, or pruning the flowers and her numerous fruit trees.

In spite of all her work – and she eventually also became her baby granddaughter's carer during the afternoons – she always found time for afternoon coffee and a pastry, served with delicate crockery on a starched tablecloth. She seemed to have had no pretensions to being anything other than a straightforward, decent and respectful human being.

Once a week during the warmer months, Frau B. went into her garden to cut some flowers before visiting the village cemetery to weed and tidy her late husband's grave. Herr B. had been a very handsome man; I knew that from a photograph prominently displayed in the sitting room. He was killed during the war in the field at the end of our road, just a few meters from their house; the Americans had flown over and shot him.

Frau B. didn't elaborate, but I imagined a squadron of fighters strafing the farm workers as their planes screamed overhead. I must have got that idea from Martin's comic books, but the reality was probably not much different.

Much later I learned that Riem airport had become a Luftwaffe (German Air Force) airfield during the war and was almost totally destroyed by American bombing raids in 1945. Later still, I found myself asking why Herr B. was at home and not away fighting for his country. Maybe he had been overseeing foreign forced agricultural labourers and prisoners of war, something about which he would have had little choice.

When Frau B. spoke, it was always in the same unmodulated peasant voice that had so grated on me at Aunt Hedwa's household in Aspern. I recall no hint of anger though, even when she spoke of *die Amerikaner* (the Americans). She demonstrated the same emotional detachment about them as when she tended her husband's grave.

Once she had completed her task, Frau B. invariably made the sign of the cross, tapping her forehead, chest and shoulders in rapid succession. Then she stood in silence for a moment or two as if her thoughts were wandering elsewhere.

Moments later, we would leave the churchyard. She would chat animatedly, fascinating me with her stories about the people whose houses we passed on our way through the village. She told me about one young woman who had left the village to follow her American soldier lover to the USA, leaving behind a young daughter of about eight who had refused to abandon her grandmother. It was not unpleasant gossip, merely a straightforward account of what had happened. I remember thinking how complicated and sad life could be.

'People can be so terrible! I simply had to go over and remove that placard this morning... They have children, and the boy is so sensitive...'

Frau B. explained that an anti-Nazi placard had suddenly appeared tied to the Deppner family's fence across the street. I knew the Deppners because, soon after they moved in, Frau Deppner had invited my mother to send Robert and me to play with their youngest daughter, Kristine. There were three other siblings that I knew of, but they were in their late teens and early twenties, and usually out when I was around. Robert and I obliged, but it was a relationship that eventually fizzled out.

Kristine was nice enough, but she was too young for me to go out of my way for, and Robert, although Kristine's age, was not enthusiastic.

She lacked a certain light-heartedness, which made play somewhat stiff. Added to that, her mother hovered around us, something I found quite unsettling. She wasn't unfriendly – on the contrary – but there seemed to be an element of control involved.

There was something else, too. Both Robert and I recall feeling strangely uncomfortable in their home without ever being able to pinpoint why. In the light of what later emerged, it was hardly surprising; children can be very intuitive, even if they do not know what it is they are sensing.

During the winter of 1960–61, some months before the placard appeared, Kristine was at our house and chatting with my mother. This particular time Kristine was exceptionally downcast; she said she wanted her father to come home for Christmas because 'my daddy is away in Berlin'.

At the time I gave it little thought, but some months later I became conscious of his presence for the first time. Although I was unaware of it because I was at school, my mother was on speaking terms with some local women who occasionally called in for a chat and a coffee on their way round from the nearby corner shops. So did Frau Deppner.

Now that her husband was at home and their strolls took them past our house, they stopped to chat with my mother, though now over the garden gate. A charming Herr Deppner repeatedly encouraged her to keep sending Robert and me over to play, but my mother sensed something was not quite right. However, wary of false accusations, she did her best to ignore the unpleasant sensation in her gut.

Then the placard appeared, and Kristine's father was exposed as former Nazi SS Sturmbannführer (Major) Erich Deppner. Later I discovered that his absence on business in Berlin had been a smokescreen; he was actually being held in custody in Munich while accusations relating to alleged atrocities during the war were investigated. The local (and false) rumour mill had it that he stood accused of the deaths of some 25,000 Jews.

After several months of detention, he was released due to lack of evidence. Several decades on, I discovered that he was eventually brought to trial four years later and charged with one specific atrocity in Amersfoort concentration camp in the Netherlands in 1942. He had been tasked with organising the execution of 77 out of 101 surviving Soviet Russian prisoners of war (mostly conscripts from Uzbekistan). When the firing squad failed to be efficient, he finished off the job. He was found not guilty on a technicality: he had only been following the orders of his superiors.

While it's true that my immediate reaction to his acquittal was disgust and anger, on reflection his vindication made rational sense. The killings had occurred during wartime and war is brutal on both sides; the whole point of both homeland security and the military in times of war is to provide a patriotic, disciplined, single-minded unit to achieve a government's stated objective – by force. Whether one agrees with the objective is another matter entirely. If the firing squad failed to do an efficient job, perhaps it was merciful to release the wounded from their suffering. In a less than perfect world, no matter how repugnant the action, how could the verdict have been anything other than not guilty in this particular case?

However, SS Sturmbannführer Erich Deppner had been a Nazi party member since the age of twenty-two and a member of the SS at twenty-three, so his oath of allegiance to follow orders seemed to contain a darker hue.

As the first commandant of Westerbork transit camp for deportations to slave labour and killing centres in the East, his 'efficiency' almost led to a riot only a few months after the Amersfoort shootings. In his drive to satisfy the deportation numbers set by his superiors, he added fifty children to a transport to Auschwitz – without their parents. To counter the protests, he is reported to have claimed that the children were being sent to a purpose-built children's home within the 'work' camp. Not only that, to fulfil the demand for one thousand transportees, he is reported to have selected a number of newly arrived female detainees who happened to be at the camp's main gate waiting in line to enter.

Due to the disorder his crude actions provoked, Deppner was soon replaced by another commander. Nevertheless, his diligence is reported to have been rewarded with congratulations from his boss and the main architect of the Holocaust, Reichsführer Heinrich Himmler.[42]

Such was Deppner's thoroughness that during clear-up operations against the Dutch resistance (he was advisor to the head of counter-resistance in the Netherlands) he was again called upon to do his best in 1944.

With the Allies advancing towards the Netherlands following the Normandy landings, 1500 Dutch civilians had been rounded up on suspicion of resistance activities and detained in a political prison at the Hook of Holland. They were hastily transferred inland to a special section within Herzogenbusch concentration camp.

---

42   I would urge readers to research the general in command of the SS Army for themselves to gain greater insight into the dark significance of his congratulations.

Employing his counter-intelligence expertise, Deppner is alleged to have drawn up the death list before giving the order for the execution of 450 of those civilian detainees. Infamous as the 'Deppner executions' there were no trials, just a bullet through the back of the neck. As a qualified lawyer, he would have been fully aware that was illegal.

In his book *Ashes in the Wind: The Persecution and Destruction of Dutch Jewry*, Jacques Presser describes Deppner as a *'typical SS-leader, cold as ice, ruthless, a killer with an officer's personality'*. Elsewhere he is described as a brutal, secretive and untrustworthy individual.

As was all too often the case, after his release in 1949 from Soviet prisoner of war detention, his civilian post as head of operations of the Berlin branch of the USA-funded and CIA-backed Organisation Gehlen[43] provides clues as to why, in spite of efforts in the Netherlands, he was never effectively held to account. His expertise in counterintelligence proved too valuable to the Americans (or so they were led to believe) in their efforts to counter expansionist threats posed by the Soviet Union.

Deppner, alias agent V-616, was not an exception: it has been established that at least one hundred former SS officers were employed by General Reinhard Gehlen who, until his dismissal by Hitler in April 1945 for not telling the Führer what he wanted to hear, was the Nazi Chief of Intelligence on the Eastern Front. Such is the pragmatism of realpolitik.

I was too young to appreciate the irony of being invited to play with a superior Aryan's superior daughter; I was also unaware of the ripples of the storm gathering around me. I had started to understand something about 'the war', but I remained ignorant that the murder of Jews (whatever that meant) had anything to do with my family.

One day, prompted by the stir caused by Deppner's unmasking, Frau B. told me about something that had happened to her. On a visit to Munich city centre 'in those days', she was caught up in a crowd of people feverishly raising their arms in the 'Heil Hitler' salute as the Führer drove by in his open-topped limousine.

'I didn't do it,' she said. 'I just stood there.'

By that time, Adolf Hitler's infamy had started to infiltrate my consciousness, and I remember feeling relieved that my friend had not been 'one of them'.

Was she telling the truth? I hope so, but as an adult I have often wondered whether she reinvented a moment she would rather have

---

43 Organisation Gehlen evolved into the 'Bundesnachrichtendienst' (BND), Germany's foreign intelligence service.

forgotten. After all, in 'those days' the prevailing atmosphere was one of intimidation; there was the constant threat of being picked out by the ever-watchful secret police or of being denounced by fellow civilians for the sake of reward points.

I feel bad about my lack of trust, but I cannot help it. If I am wrong, I offer the now-deceased Frau B. my heartfelt apologies. I hope that she would forgive me.

***

It might have been a sense of fun and their own status as newcomers to Munich that first attracted my mother, Regine and Kristina to each other, but there was something else they had in common.

In 1948, when they were in their teens, Regine, Kristina and their mother Frau Waller (who was believed to be a war widow) had fled their home in post-war Soviet-occupied north-eastern Germany. I remained unaware of this for several years until Regine described the terror they had experienced in 1945 when the garrison town they were living in was overrun by advancing Soviet troops.

The often uneducated and indoctrinated conscripts had a reputation for raping ferociously that had travelled ahead of them and sent waves of panic through the female population. What they also heard, however, was that these often superstitious troops were terrified of insanity. With a scary display of protruding tongue and rolling eyes, Regine showed Dawa and me the precautions they'd been instructed to take to save themselves from what they believed was an almost inevitable fate.

Several decades later, I learnt that Frau Waller's story of war-time enrichment was actually opportunistic and distasteful. I was grateful that my mother died before the truth was finally revealed.

While my mother's friends were post-WWII refugees from the north, my playmate Annemie, who lived two doors away, was the daughter of former Yugoslav nationals of German descent.[44] Without a doubt of

[44] From the early Middle Ages onwards Continental Europe had undergone many population migrations eastward (including to Polish and Czech lands) and south-eastward (to within the Danube basin), especially from German speaking territories. Some migrations were pragmatic, some enforced, others encouraged to boost another's local economy. Following the Habsburg empire's gradual push-back of the Ottoman empire in the Balkans, German agricultural workers and artisans were once again encouraged to migrate to re-cultivate and develop vacated lands. After WW1 and Poland's re-emergence as an independent country for the first time in 123 years many ethnic Germans who had lived there over multiple generations were subjected to revenge measures or forced to flee to Germany as penniless and

poorly educated peasant stock, her parents were unfailingly welcoming and generous towards me, while Herr B. even completed my cycling and swimming lessons.

I don't know which side of the fence they sat on, but they were also in the wrong place at the wrong time and ended up in a displaced person's camp nearby. With the help of a repatriation fund, they eventually purchased a plot of land where they lived in the humblest of circumstances in a wooden hut.

When I became friendly with Annemie the family had just moved out of the cellar into the ground floor of the house they were building for themselves. The hut next to the chicken coop had been rented out to another homeless couple with a new baby. The pretty, skinny young woman with the obligatory beehive hair and tight black skirt was always friendly towards us girls; she seemed only too happy for us to sit and chat with her while she ironed her husband's shirts or prepared the evening meal in their cramped, all-purpose room.

A little later that young family moved to a social housing apartment in a new tower block in a nearby suburb. The young woman couldn't stop smiling as she proudly gave the two of us a tour of her kitchen, bathroom, sitting room and separate bedroom!

Though I hadn't been in the least fazed by that young family's living circumstances, it was only years later that I recognised why: when we had stayed with the Malys in Aspern, we had slept next to the chicken coop in what had once been their allotment's hut, while the family lived in a small house they had built themselves a few years after the war.

Now, a little older and slightly more conscious in Munich, nobody needed to tell me how very fortunate I was.

---

oftentimes unwelcome incomers. The same cycle repeated itself in 1945, though in far greater numbers and with greater force. Towards the end of WW2, when the Soviet Union liberated Romania, Hungary, Czechoslovakia and Poland, and communist Marshall Tito's partisans also liberated Yugoslavia from Nazi rule, citizens of German descent were subjected to often murderous vendettas. Thousands fled to Germany and Austria where they were placed in makeshift refugee camps. Others were rounded up and deported to the Soviet Union where they were put to forced labour under appalling conditions. It is estimated that between 500,000 and 2 million ethnic German detainees died in Soviet detention. The release of survivors took place over time, the last in 1956. With rare exceptions, they were repatriated to West Germany. Countless families were destroyed, while the cross-generational trauma continues its course – mostly unacknowledged and in silence.

BECOMING ACQUAINTED WITH MY MOTHER'S FAMILY

On the rare occasions when Oma was with us, I listened spellbound as she told me of her childhood in Bohemia or reminded my mother of amusing events from the days when she still lived zu Hause (at home) in Vienna.

Yes, Uncle Toni had shot a hole in the sitting-room wall when secretly fiddling with their father's target-shooting rifle. Years later I learnt that their grandfather Samuel had been an enthusiastic and skilful marksman; amongst Dawa's memorabilia I even found a booklet he had written marking the occasion when he had sat on the design and construction committee of the third pan-German rifle-club competition in Vienna in 1868.[45] Perhaps that is why I'm a pretty good shot myself?

Hoping to disguise the damage, Toni, Elsa and my mother had feverishly chewed bread rolls and tried to plug the damaged wall with the dough. What nobody had counted on was the bread drying out!

Wagging her index finger in the air, Oma regaled me with stories of why she had so often admonished Toni with 'just wait till your father comes home!' To this day it makes me laugh because sometimes she did the same with Martin when we lived in Munich.

I can still see her rotund, dirndl-clad body, one plump arm flailing, as she chased my brother around the garden after he'd made yet another attempt at fratricide. She's calling out, 'Du Bengel! Na warte bis der Vater nach Hause kommt!'[46]

While she and my mother prepared meals, baked cakes and talked, Oma sometimes sat on a chair piled high with neatly folded bed linen that, after a day or two, required hardly any ironing – if any. Economy and moderation in all things were Oma's Leitmotifs. She removed every vestige of egg white from its shell, scraped butter from its wrapping and cleaned every last fibre of flesh from a bone with a mother-of-pearl pocket-knife that she carried everywhere. I couldn't help absorbing the way in which she respected our resources; to this day it hurts me to witness careless or needless waste.

She gave her undivided care and attention to everything that she did. Now I understand what I did not back then: there was nothing slapdash about her; instead, she always acted consciously, as if in prayer, and the

---
45 Without being political, Samuel's words also reflect a deep regret that the Austro-Prussian war of 1866 had led to the expulsion of Austria from the German Confederation, causing the artificial cleaving of the inextricably linked German people. His words also leave no doubt that he considered himself one of them.
46 'You lout! Just wait until your father comes home!'

results were always good quality.

As I chatted with Oma or listened in to mother-and-daughter conversations, I gradually realised that there were more relatives with foreign names whom I didn't recall hearing about. They lived in Czechoslovakia, a country I knew from my globe to be bordered by several other countries including Germany and Austria.

There was a different inflection in my mother's voice when she spoke about them. Even though they were obviously alive, I recall a sense of being separated from them by a curiously intangible distance. I was still too young to understand the meaning of the Iron Curtain but I must have been aware of something.

During Oma's last two visits with us after we returned to England in 1965, I paid more attention to her reminiscences about relatives I had never met. I learnt about my grandfather Oskar, her beloved 'Ockele', whom she looked forward to reuniting with in death. I found that idea strange and horribly morbid.

There was also Grandfather Oskar's elderly mother, Antonia (in her last years he had affectionately addressed her as Toninka) and his dead sisters, Camilla and Clara. The names of various other cousins on my grandfather's side also appeared occasionally.

Although these people had died what seemed a very long time ago, the warmth with which Oma spoke of them left a lasting impression on me that was curiously tinged with regret. I was learning that the war had put an end to another life before England that I knew nothing about.

Kitchen talk also introduced me to my mother's Uncle Arthur, Grandfather Oskar's older brother. He was a rather sophisticated, cosmopolitan character who was married to glamorous, expensively perfumed and very highly-strung Tante Ida. A few years ago I discovered that Uncle Arthur's death in Lincoln in 1964 had been the catalyst for a series of events that eventually paved the way for our return to England a year later.

DISINTEGRATION

If the school year of 1961–62 was miserable for me, it was an even worse year for my family.

After the initial euphoria of their new and exciting life, my parents' relationship was becoming strained. My father's need to switch off at the weekends from the pressures of work was completely at odds with my mother's need for release from the never-ending work of unsupported parenting.

The situation worsened after my father's best friend Ray was killed during a training flight. Only a short time before, my father had joked that Ray's new black estate car looked more like a hearse than a family car. Soon afterwards, my mother and I were in the kitchen with the radio on in the background. She suddenly stopped in her tracks and focused on every word of the late-afternoon news. A phone call confirmed it: one of the pilots who had died instantly in a mid-air collision during a training flight was my father's oldest and closest friend since his schooldays in Harrow.

It was a shock to us all, but my mother failed to anticipate what happened next. I remember the blood draining from my exhausted father's face as we children rushed to greet him when he returned from a business trip, shouting, 'Uncle Ray is dead! Uncle Ray is dead!' His red-rimmed eyes and silent grief over the following days was another deeply formative experience.

I don't remember the exact sequence of events, but if Ray's fatal collision had touched a certain deep wound within my mother, it was the echo of former SS Sturmbannführer's jackboots and the recollection of his menacing Hugo Boss manufactured uniform that had left her inner world reeling almost out of control: her coping strategy for repressing past trauma had finally met its nemesis.

Shortly before her death she told me, 'Once the war started and there was no hope of seeing my family again for who knew how long – if ever – I knew that if I wanted to live, I would have to become like an ostrich.'

In many respects remaining steadfastly in the present moment and repressing anything uncomfortable served my mother well for the rest of her life. In this instance, however, too many things happened at almost the same time. Erich Deppner's presence in our midst meant that she could no longer avoid the subject she had diligently sought to escape.

She swung to the other extreme and embarked on a quest to learn everything she could about the Holocaust. Although there was nothing like the amount of written material available today, there was certainly enough to keep her occupied and inflict further damage. 'I became obsessed…' she said. That obsession lasted for years and never entirely dissipated.

Back then in Munich, the more my mother learned, the more she was sucked into the suffering of people who had once been part of her childhood; innocent human beings who had ended their days publicly mocked, hatefully abused and directly or indirectly murdered. How could she not be traumatised?

As the stories of their suffering started to occupy her, my father couldn't understand what had possessed his previously easy-going, affectionate and supportive wife.

The violent migraines that had always been a significant and debilitating (and for me terrifying) part of Dawa's life increased in frequency and severity. The dust built up and the house was uncared for. She only ironed the visible parts of my father's shirts – it never occurred to her that he might want to take off his jacket in the office because in her father's day in Vienna men never did. 'I ended up having to send my work shirts to a professional laundry!' my father told me years later as he described her 'neglect'.

My mother never confided in him in a way that made any sense at all; her inner pain was too intense for her to express it in words. Instead, she suffered in distracted silence and my father took her withdrawal as a sign of the abandonment he so feared.

During our last conversation my mother said, 'I think your father felt intimidated by my background.' She believed he'd had a subtle yet long-standing need to diminish her; ironically, his fear that she would reject him finally led him to turn elsewhere.

A casual acquaintance, a young woman my mother had immediately recognised as deeply miserable, eventually provided him with solace. Later it emerged that she was a struggling single parent with an illegitimate child tucked away in a children's home; the child's father had run for the hills when he was told she was pregnant. As a Catholic in a predominantly Catholic environment, her situation had been catastrophic.

The opportunity to console a handsome, successful English executive, who was apparently a neglected husband, was welcome. He sympathised with her difficult circumstances.

Unfortunately, the woman was not only several years younger but also very petite, something that my father used as ammunition against my mother, whose weight suddenly became a new and soul-destroying bone of contention.

Worse, this single woman was not only highly organised but also an insecure adherent to '*Ordnung und Sauberkeit*'[47] so that my mother's easy-going *chutzpah*[48], that my father had once thought such an exotic prize,

---

47 Order and cleanliness.
48 Dawa was too easy-going to worry about 'what the neighbours might think'. On

became an ever-greater irritant.

Perplexed by his unexpected attacks, my mother became increasingly depressed. As the list of her 'defects' grew longer, she drifted into the recurring pattern of comfort eating that had started the day she first set foot on British soil. Back then, Elsa had warned their parents that her sister would develop arms like a lumberjack if she continued to eat as much as she did. Now Dawa once again sought solace in food and predictably put on ever more weight.

'Your father brought a tin of Quality Streets back from England. Instead of sharing them, I sat in bed one evening when he was away and gorged myself on the lot, one after the other. I just couldn't stop... I felt so ashamed...'

Then, in a desperate attempt to appease my father's endless criticism, she lost an enormous amount of weight. Within a short period of time she changed almost beyond recognition – in every respect.

Dawa became addicted to slimming pills (the stimulant Preludine) that helped her shrink to what she hoped was an acceptable size. To add to the problems, she was drinking generous shots of gin to help reduce her increasing tension in social situations. Within a few months of our last family holiday in Italy in the summer of 1961, her moods began to swing violently back and forth like a demented pendulum.

The abuse of her body with drugs, alcohol and starvation, my father's confusing verbal and psychological attacks, and the explosion of previously unexplored emotions related to loss, abandonment and rejection finally led to a mental and physical breakdown from which it took my mother a number of years to fully recover. Yet, even as her heart wept, her pearl necklace lost its lustre and the food and drink she prepared burned and curdled, she never lost sight of my father's wellbeing. She might not have understood the cause of his disaffection – or her own contribution to it – but she understood that he was also suffering and she cared enough about him for that to matter.

> *Don't worry about me*, she wrote to Elsa. *I shall come through one way or the other... It's Ivor I really feel for most at the moment ... but I don't want to be unhappy for too long and if we can't sort things out then I shall have to think of divorce... I feel wicked even thinking about it, because I do still love him after all of this time...*

---

writing a letter of appreciation for her and her husband's enjoyable stay with us, one visitor marvelled at how relaxed they both still felt several days later.

I was ten years old when what had been three mostly happy years in Germany disintegrated into a nightmare. My stressed father's unpredictable yet easily provoked flare-ups terrified me, and my mother's intense suffering affected me deeply.

If Dawa could have talked about the real source of her pain and fragility, my father would probably have been mortified and supportive; instead, he coldly rejected her vulnerability. Many years later he recognised that her behaviour had pushed certain buttons that related to a disturbing period in his own childhood, but she didn't know that and, at the time, neither did he. They really knew very little about themselves, let alone each other.

I literally felt my mother's misery and her depression become my own. She did her best to conceal it from us children, but on the days when there was nothing to distract her from herself and tears were spilling down her motionless face I wanted to die.

To add to my mother's misfortune, their more mature and non-partisan friends Gerald and Jane had given up trying to conquer Germany with fancy tableware and returned to England. On the other hand, as I witnessed on occasion for myself, Frau Waller's past marital misfortunes and those of her daughters led them to subject my mother to unfettered vitriol against my father without showing a glimmer of objectivity or compassion. Worse still, on the rare occasions when my father still socialised, Frau Waller treated him with deliberate, undisguised disdain.

Kristina's daughter Larissa later described the women in her family as good people individually who morphed into a witch's coven when they gathered for a coffee break 'with not a good word for anybody'. Or, as my father said, they were the proverbial vipers' nest.

Dawa found herself stranded without any local support that might have helped her step out of her wounded self and lift her spirits. To add to her isolation, my father was increasingly absent, often on business but sometimes otherwise, so her evenings and nights were far too long and silent.

We didn't have a television because my father, who could be a decidedly old-school autocrat, refused to have what he described as an idiot's lantern in the house. Nor did my mother dare use his hi-fi system to listen to music because he immediately – and angrily – noted any invasion of his domain. She had failed to grasp the depths of his passion for his personal space and its contents; she had still regarded the equipment as a means to an end rather than important in itself.

International phone calls were not only expensive but had to be pre-booked and connected via the operator. Unable to contact either Elsa or trusted, non-partisan friends in England when she needed to, my mother was left alone with the chatter in her head that she could neither offload nor switch off. On the days when she slipped into a bleak world of suicidal despair, she clung to me to keep her company and, by implication, keep her safe. 'Come on, let's go for a walk.'

As she later said, 'If it hadn't been for you children, I would have stuck my head in the oven.'

My mother's disintegration was devastating, while my bewildered, lonely misery was so intense that even now I cannot put it into words. Yet no matter how intently I watched and listened in the hope of making sense of what was happening around me, I could find no explanation.

There was no respite for my mother as more layers of stress and anxiety were piled on. After the erection of the Berlin Wall, she had naively agreed to allow the British consul to use her maiden name and our home address as a 'letterbox' for covert communications from communist East Germany. As she heard the mounting reports of individuals being apprehended on charges of spying against the communist regime, she became even more concerned about my father's safety when he travelled across the border on business trips to the Leipzig trade fair.

Anxiety eventually gave way to paranoia after a letter addressed to Elisabeth Löwenthal dropped through our letterbox. She angrily withdrew her co-operation with the British consul, but there was nothing she could do to erase a message she later described as having come through the radio telling her that her husband should avoid East Germany at all costs because the Stasi had him in their sights. Perhaps it was true, perhaps not; my poor, isolated mother certainly believed it.

Life at home eventually became so unpleasant that I spent as much time as possible out of the house. When I *was* at home, I took to haranguing my mother to allow me to move into a children's home where one of my schoolmates lived. She seemed to be having more fun than I was.

My nagging must eventually have become too much for my mother to bear because one day she stopped me as I was setting out for afternoon school. 'Why on earth don't you want live at home anymore?'

I burst into tears and screamed, 'IT'S SO MISERABLE AT HOME! YOU'RE ALWAYS CRYING – ALL THE ARGUING AND SHOUTING! I HATE IT!'

She stood there silent and wide-eyed, probably too traumatised to respond. Not receiving the reassurance I so badly needed, I ran to school howling my head off – until an uncomfortable realisation stopped me in my tracks. I had forgotten to stop for Gela as I usually did; worse still, my distress was far too revealing of my innermost world which I didn't want to share with anybody. How could I have explained it anyway?

I took a few deep breaths then continued as if nothing had happened. When I returned home from school I said nothing about the episode, leaving my mother free not to mention it again.

Decades later when I was living in Vienna, I recognised that this was the day that I became aware that on some level I was completely alone. It wasn't that I didn't feel loved, my mother was just totally out of her depth.

In 1963, the lease on our house was due to expire. Our landlord, who was now financially back on his feet, wanted his dream home for himself so we children found ourselves spending weekends in the back of the car as we house-hunted again. Curiously, most of the homes we looked at were small and some didn't even have a garage.

When my mother asked about the lack of garages, my father replied, 'There won't be any need for one.' Who was my mother – who had failed her driving test due to an attack of nerves – to argue?

That summer Robert and I spent the latter part of our school holiday with Granny Pinner who now lived on the south coast of Devon. We had a wonderful time being part of her life and enjoying outings with her and her second husband. That was until my little brother's abdominal pains (that both our doctor in Munich and one more recently in England had diagnosed as wind) suddenly got much worse.

Sensing danger, our grandmother called for an ambulance that whisked him away; her quick, decisive action prevented a ruptured appendix. Dawa immediately wanted to fly to be by Robert's side, but our father couldn't see the point. Although their reactions were different, I later learned that both had suffered traumatising hospital experiences in early childhood, at a time when parental visits were still strictly limited if not entirely forbidden: 'The nurses were utterly evil!'.

Since my brother was in hospital and too ill to travel home as planned, I flew back to Munich by myself, as did Robert a couple of weeks later. For good measure, he stepped on a shard of glass on the beach before his departure and landed back in hospital for several more stitches.

When I arrived home, I heard that a date had been set for us to move to a house neither Robert nor I had seen. It was on the opposite side of town in Pasing, a place I only knew from the destination plate of the number 19 tram.

That autumn, on the increasingly rare occasions my father was at home, he spent much of his time designing bespoke wall units for his vast record collection. We all, seemingly including our mother, believed these were intended for the new house. But what Martin had already noticed, though Robert and I had not, was that our father had already moved out some time earlier even though he hadn't taken all his belongings.

I knew that something was happening. On my way home from grammar school in the city one day, I saw him drive past my tram. 'Oh, good!' I thought. 'Daddy will be home tonight.' In fact, it was several more days before we saw him again. Statements from my mother such as 'he must be extremely busy' failed to soothe my uneasiness.

One early evening in late November 1963, just after my mother had returned from an emergency dash to my seriously ill grandmother in Vienna and only days before the packing was due to start, I overheard an exchange between my parents in the kitchen.

'*You* tell them!' my mother said firmly.

Within minutes, my father was sitting with Robert and me. 'I won't be coming with you,' he said, his voice exceptionally gentle as he assumed 'breaking-bad-news-to-small-children' mode.

In spite of his efforts, my heart felt as if it had shattered. Another part of me was too shocked to say anything, let alone cry. Instead, I stood up and went to my bedroom. I hoped to hear footsteps behind me but there were none. Perhaps my parents were too busy consoling my brother who, months later in Pasing, I found curled up on a bed crying his heart out. 'I miss my daddy…'

My parents, especially my father, never knew the extent of my grief. If they assumed I had accepted the news calmly and gone straight to bed, they were very much mistaken.

After the stupor wore off, I burst into tears and spent most of the night sobbing my heart out. When there were no more tears left, I stared out of my bedroom window until dawn broke. As the hours passed, I kept wondering when I would wake up from my nightmare. Obviously, I never did.

Nothing more was said, and I got on with life in the manner in which I was becoming increasingly proficient. Friendly, but inclined to witness others rather than open up to them, I withdrew deeper within myself. Not even my closest friend Angelika knew what was happening, although several years later another school friend remarked, 'You changed completely. I did wonder what had happened to you…'

I was reminded of that evening when my husband Don told me about a conversation with my father, who had spoken admiringly about my inner strength. As an example, he had recalled the way I reacted calmly to his announcement that he was leaving.

My father was right: I have always had a certain inner strength that has helped me move forward where others might have got stuck or even run away. However, being confronted by that memory of my childhood was strange. I didn't want to upset my father by telling him the truth so I said nothing, but I was irritated that he could have imagined I'd been alright. If he was blind to the impact of his actions, it wasn't because he didn't care about me. I was always aware of his love, insofar as he was capable of loving. It was just another human mess in which he cared more about himself than his children.

'Your father would quite happily have had two wives,' Dawa said many decades later.

Maybe if there is genuine affection, coupled with loyalty and equality, an arrangement like that might have its benefits if all parties agree to it, not least in an historic environment where there were more women than men whose role was to provide for safety and security. But my mother, who was not in the least conventional, wasn't fully aware of the dynamics that came into play almost as soon as she had agreed to a separation because my father's behaviour didn't match her concept of a failed marriage.

Already unhinged by stress and drug-induced turmoil, my mother was made worse by his inconsistency. After staying away for many days, he would return to the usual friendly homecomings and they shared a bed, so it was hardly surprising that she didn't understand that my father, who had married far too young, felt he had regained his freedom. She was totally confused by the way in which the pendulum kept swinging between abandonment and normality.

I am sure my father was equally confused about his feelings. His deep-seated loneliness needed big, reassuring gestures, while my more sensitive mother couldn't indulge in exaggerated displays of affection. He was trying to force her to prove something that, to her, did not need to be proven.

What she didn't understand back then was that my father was insecure and needed extra affection, loving touch and caring words. Her disrupted childhood had not prepared her for that.

Given time and mature support they might have resolved their difficulties, but they were both stubborn and they didn't understand each other or themselves. Neither of them could let down their defences and adequately express their feelings; they were no longer speaking the same language.

But instead of taking time out in a neutral space, my father did what so many people do: he leapt headlong into a pair of eagerly awaiting arms that had no intention of indulging an open relationship.

ANOTHER WAY OF LIVING

One grey, slushy day in early December 1963, we left our home and moved into a tiny, newly built mid-terrace house on the opposite side of Munich, away from all our friends and acquaintances. We were without our father, his music and everything else that his presence signified.

In many ways we were also without our mother. She continued to go through the motions of everyday life and tended to our basic needs as best she could, but she was shell-shocked and running on empty. She had no energy for anything other than staying alive for us children and doing her best to adapt to her new circumstances.

That winter I was twelve years old. The most depressing Christmas of our lives to date came and went with a fleeting visit from our father bearing gifts. He was soon gone again. It was many years before the curtains stopped coming down on Christmas Day.

Nobody had mentioned the word 'divorce', something that was comparatively rare back then, particularly in predominantly Catholic Bavaria.

On one level I knew that I was still grieving, but I was old enough to need some sort of intellectual framework to help me understand what I was grieving for. Nobody had died, had they? And every other week, when I had Saturday morning school, my father collected me and drove me home. Yet I had a painful sense of having been abandoned and an almost permanent, often quite debilitating, sharp pain in my stomach.

About seven months after we moved, the bombshell dropped. My Aunt Elsa, who by now was divorced herself and had lost custody of her two children, had received permission to travel abroad with her oldest daughter, my cousin Lis.

On an apparently ordinary day, Lis, Robert and I spent the morning at our local lido. In between the normal stuff kids talk about, Robert suddenly asked Lis, 'What's it like having divorced parents? It must be horrible. I'm so glad mine aren't.' Little did he know that our naïve incomprehension was about to come to an abrupt end.

'By the way, your father and I got divorced today.' That was all my mother said. Softening the blow when she had something troublesome to say was not one of her strengths. My father told me shortly before his death that it was her impulsiveness that had marred many of his homecomings after an arduous business trip or when he wanted to share news of his successes.

If her abruptness was not enough, she had also chosen to tell us in the presence of my aunt Elsa and cousin Lis. How could we possibly react genuinely to such catastrophic news with an audience? I wanted to burst into tears but instead I choked them back, put on a brave face and got on with life. It was what it was. I have no recollection of any overt reactions by my brothers either.

Years later when my mother was living with my family, we spoke about that day, which had become the second greatest regret of her adult life. 'It was very busy at the court. When we were waiting for our hearing, your father said, "Oh, come on, let's go home." But I said, "No, you've brought it this far, you go through with it!"... I was so stupid – I'm sure we could have worked it out.'

Maybe they could have done, maybe not, but when she told me that I was appalled – and said nothing. Dawa also told me that Martin had been furious with her. I wish had known at the time; it might have explained so much.

I never confronted my mother with the consequences of her actions; she already knew them, so why twist the knife? But my irritation lingered for quite a while until one day I looked at my mother and was overcome by a great wave of love for her. This extraordinary and beautiful human being had been alone since she was just thirteen and she had suffered so much trauma. How on earth could I possibly be angry with her?

THE DOWNS AND UPS OF LIFE

Some months after the decree absolute was granted, my mother conceded that she had short-changed herself in the divorce settlement. At the time, with no immediate support and too disturbed to address the financial realities of life, her fair-mindedness had overtaken her.

Believing that my father 'couldn't possibly have enough to live on', she had asked for the generous monthly alimony payments she had been awarded to be reduced. He, in turn, agreed to waive his legal right to ask for a reduction in alimony payments should he have more children. I don't know if there were any cynical intentions behind this agreement, but Anna eventually discovered to her dismay that my father refused to entertain the idea of having more children.

Soon my mother found it impossible to make ends meet no matter how frugally we lived. She could never keep on top of the expense of clothing and feeding three rapidly growing children, and each month began with as many arrears as the last, if not more. She never burdened us children with her financial difficulties but I, for one, certainly noticed the effects.

Seeing no other way out of her predicament, she eventually placed a 'room for rent' advertisement in a local shop window. There was a teacher-training college nearby that had its own student accommodation, but space was limited and the overflow had to live somewhere.

Anticipating the arrival of a lodger, Robert and I vacated our shared bedroom. His bed was moved into our mother's room and I shared her double bed. I don't remember being bothered by this new arrangement; in fact, it was rather cosy.

We didn't have to wait long before there was a knock at the door. Standing on the doorstep were a rather staid-looking woman and her chic nineteen-year-old daughter. They had spent a long, disappointing day trudging from one prospective lodging to another and had pretty much resigned themselves to not finding anything suitable.

Although they left without giving any sign of interest (which my mother took to be a resounding and disappointing 'no'), it wasn't long before Hanneluise moved in, bringing an unexpected but welcome source of sunshine into my mother's lonely life.

Unfortunately, where there is sunshine, there is always a shadow. If my mother had hoped to visit Oma more often after moving to Munich, she was soon disillusioned. After our late-summer visit in 1958, my father took us to Vienna only once about a year later.

My few memories of that short weekend trip are vague flashes of eating breakfast in our hotel dining room, pouring rain and sitting in a café near a model train shop where my father and Martin spent a lot of time choosing tracks and carriages for a very sophisticated model train set.

After that, the pressures of work started to take their toll. My father needed to expand his schoolboy German into a fluent command of technical, business and conversational language. He was running a branch with local staff who had a deeply embedded way of doing things, and his job also involved a lot of travelling to scientific exhibitions in Germany and other European cities. Unsurprisingly, he eventually lost both the energy and the inclination to spend his little free time taking us anywhere, least of all on a four-hour car journey to Vienna and back again on a nerve-wracking Autobahn.[49]

As for travelling without him by train, my mother no longer dared to risk leaving a man who was not suited to being alone at home. Eventually, she also began to feel that her self-sacrificing presence was obligatory until he was ready to call it a day. Therefore, apart from Dawa's emergency dash to her ailing mother the week before we moved to Pasing, we didn't visit Vienna until Oma's death in 1969.

Now that our tiny house had a lodger there was nowhere for Oma to sleep, and my exhausted mother didn't have the strength to find a solution. To make matters worse, Aunt Elsa's written instructions on how to handle Hanneluise's semester breaks suffered from the same inertia. Apart from putting one foot in front of the other, my mother didn't have the energy to do much beyond what was immediately necessary.

Later I discovered that Dawa's silence when Oma enquired about visiting in her letters left my poor grandmother not only grieving for her daughters and grandchildren, ('How can any man leave his children?') but also feeling unwanted.

Despite these problems, life was not completely dark. Our new neighbourhood was very different to our previous one, but it soon revealed itself as a pleasant and opulent one.

The long road that crossed the end of our initially untarmacked and potholed side street was lined with imposing oak trees so that on our way to the bus stop on winter mornings Martin and I often walked through a silent tunnel of undisturbed, glistening snow. On days when I was by myself, all I could hear was my own breath and the crunch of my footsteps – it was like starting the day in fairyland. In spring the trees were alive with songbirds, and in summer the foliage provided welcome shade from the intense early-afternoon sun.

Returning from school in the warmer months, I often chose not to

---

49   German motorway/freeway drivers were notorious for their aggressive and dangerous speeding. Across Germany often deadly pile ups and long delays were part of everyday life.

wait at the end of the number 19 tramline for the connecting bus home but walked through the city park instead where the river Würm flowed past a working water mill. The narrow river had its source in the glacial Lake Starnberg and watching it meander onwards to join forces with the river Amper before flowing into the mighty Danube and onwards into the Black Sea[50] filled me with a sense of mystery. Little did I appreciate back then how everything, in one way or another, is connected to everything else.

There was another advantage to living in Pasing: a modern sports and leisure centre only a fifteen-minute cycle ride away. Activities were on offer all year round; ice- and roller-skating rinks, an indoor swimming pool and lake-style outdoor pools in landscaped gardens for the summer season.

While Martin was on a visit to England during the first summer in our new home, my mother, Robert and I boarded a train to Salzburg. I had no idea what to expect but my mother later admitted she had been very excited and a little apprehensive. It was twenty-seven years since she'd last met her cousin, Luděk. Would they feel the sense of connection they'd had as children?

She need not have worried. As she stepped onto the platform in Salzburg, the two immediately locked eyes then sprinted towards each other with arms held wide.

After what seemed to me like an eternity, we were introduced to Luďa,[51] his wife, Zdena,[52] and their fifteen-year-old son, Luďan. After almost twenty years of totalitarian Communist post-WWII rule, a fissure had finally appeared in the Iron Curtain.

Luďa, my mother's childhood playmate in Popovice, had been granted permission to cross the border into Austria for a short private visit. Oma, Luďa's aunt, had had to guarantee to meet not only all their expenses[53] but also their return home; if she didn't, Oma would be denied future visas necessary for visiting her siblings in Czechoslovakia.

That summer, there were other unexpected changes in our lives. One day, my brothers and I were waiting with great anticipation for our father's arrival; he was taking us on a day trip to the beach at Lake Starnberg.

---

50   I loved studying my school geography book and was ace at playing the game 'Country, Town, River'.
51   Diminutive of Luděk.
52   Diminutive of Zdenka.
53   I have no doubt he will have reciprocated on her next visit to CZ.

Apart from a visit to Munich Zoo some three years earlier, it was a long time since we'd been taken to the lake or anywhere else just for fun, so we were hugely excited when we, together with our cousin Lis, followed him out to the car.

The car wasn't parked outside our house. Instead, we were led up the road and round the corner where we found a young blonde woman sitting in what had always been our mother's seat. Unaware of her existence, it was an unpleasant surprise, though I remember thinking there was no point in dwelling on it: that is how it was now, and that was that.

Martin, on the other hand, ignored Anna completely. At the beach, he pointedly moved away. Fifteen years old, he was having nothing to do with a woman who should have stayed well away from a married man with children.

Anna turned out to be pleasant enough. We may not have had our father to ourselves as we had imagined we would, but the day passed quite reasonably.

For Anna that first encounter must have been a rude awakening to the consequences of getting involved with a man who not only had three children but also had no intention of dismissing them or his ex-wife. Nor was my mother prepared to let Anna remain free of responsibility.

Dawa's opportunity to enlighten the young woman (who later admitted with disarming candour that she'd never given it much thought) came a short time later when my father called in to deliver something for our home. As usual, we expected him to stay for a while, but he was on his way somewhere and Anna was waiting in the car...

Seizing the moment, my mother decided that Anna would no longer be allowed to continue her easy life that focused on my father and herself. This time she insisted on being introduced properly over a cup of coffee so that Anna was faced with reality: her man had three children who were still entitled to a family relationship. The time had come for everybody to behave in a civilised and open manner.

I admit to watching gleefully as Anna, probably fearing an unpleasant confrontation, refused to get out of the car and come into the house. The to-ing and fro-ing continued for a while until she suddenly became aware that several curious young eyes were witnessing her discomfort.

The decidedly odd *Kaffeeklatsch* that followed was undoubtedly a trial for the adults, but my mother made the encounter run as smoothly as it could have done, and my father looked relieved.

With the first hurdle over, several months later (and presumably with Dawa's agreement) our father turned up one Saturday afternoon with another surprise. Standing beside him when we opened the door was Anna's nine-year-old daughter. My brothers and I had no idea she existed.

Sybille was a pretty little urchin with a shy smile and huge, perplexed eyes. She had been uprooted from a happy life in a children's home in a beautiful small resort in the Bavarian Alps to become a latchkey kid in a city-centre apartment. Why would she not be perplexed?

What did I feel? Very sad. If I was jealous, I wasn't aware of it; I felt no animosity towards the little girl whom my mother treated with great warmth and kindness.

As the need for concealment disappeared, acceptance of another way of living took its place. I saw little point in wasting my energy on kicking against something that I couldn't change. Besides, I loved my father so why should I make life even more complicated for either of us?

Anna also took the line of least resistance since she was regularly obliged to host Robert and me. Instead of my father driving me home after Saturday morning school, he started collecting the two of us on odd Sunday afternoons and taking us back to his new place, which boasted a smart wall unit that looked very familiar.

There we whiled away our time with Sybille before spending a leisurely evening enjoying the kind of food and treats my mother could no longer afford to put on our table and watching opera performances or Commissar Maigret on a newly acceptable 'idiot's' lantern.

Suddenly we were spending almost grown-up Sunday evenings being spoilt by our father where once we would already have been in bed ready for school on Monday. I, for one, loved it.

During one of those weekend visits, I eventually discovered that my brothers and I had acquired an adopted sister. Unexpectedly seeing my surname on the front of Sybille's school exercise book gave me a momentary, but uncomfortable, jolt. Why were we never told anything? Why was nothing ever explained? Why all this secrecy?

I didn't realise it at the time, but we were not the only ones receiving an unsolicited education. If regularly giving up her free time to entertain another woman's children had put an end to Anna's guaranteed cosy weekend evenings of married bliss, there was more to come.

My father's contract stipulated annual paid family visits to England. Divorced or not, my mother, having already missed out on at least two of these trips, wanted to see her siblings and friends again during the 1965 Whitsun break whilst my father took his turn looking after the children. In the event, he and Anna took Sybille, Robert and me on a short holiday to Italy, while Martin went with our mother.

Robert and I were self-sufficient and, apart from a minor spat between the two younger ones, we were well behaved. We had no reason to be anything else. Anna was not an unpleasant fixture in our lives. Best of all, we were on holiday with our adored father who, like most weekend fathers, was unfailingly attentive. I got on well with Sybille, who I knew was a completely innocent bystander. On the surface there didn't appear to be much for us to complain about.

DACHAU

After we moved to Pasing, I still attended my school in town. The journey there seemed much longer than before, probably because I was on my own. Yet being alone gave me plenty of opportunity to observe the world around me, especially if I chose not to walk but waited twenty minutes for my connecting bus home.

It wasn't very long before I became aware of another regular bus that went to a place called Dachau. Through a gradual process of osmosis, during which I had read about former SS Sturmbannführer Adolf Eichmann's arrest and subsequent trial in Jerusalem, I had become aware of the names of some concentration camps and something of the evil that they represented. As Dachau forced itself into my consciousness on an almost daily basis, I felt increasingly uncomfortable whenever I caught sight of the destination plate as the bus swept past on its journey north.

Around the same time, I became aware of men who were not too young to be implicated in what had happened in Dachau. I found myself assessing their age and wondering what they were up to during the war.

Did I equate Dachau specifically with Jews or with my mother's family? I honestly don't recall connecting those dots that nobody spoke about, but looking back, I wonder what my mother must have felt. I can't even begin to imagine how seeing this name added to her many existing injuries.

LIFE GOES ON

Hannelu's arrival was, in many ways, my mother's saving grace. Having to share her tiny new kitchen with a young woman with a penchant for frying onions and covering what little work surface there was with jars of homemade pickles and other preserves may at times have been a challenge; however, any irritation was soon cast aside in favour of the bigger picture, not to mention the energy this young student brought into our home. No doubt my mother could also remember what it was like to have to adapt to a strange new environment.

Over the next few months, with Hannelu's encouragement, my mother finally began to remember the attractive, vibrant woman she had once been. In turn, Hannelu, an only child whose father had died on the Russian front shortly before her birth, enjoyed a lively family environment she had never known before. It gave her a sense of security now that she was learning to live away from home. Plus, I liked Hannelu and we became almost like sisters.

Eighteen months after we moved to Pasing, my mother returned from her trip to England determined to leave years of lonely drudgery behind and start participating in life again. She was aware that Hannelu would not be staying forever and, apart from craving some congenial adult company, she needed a regular income to make our lives more secure. But after a fourteen-year absence from the workplace, what was she to do?

A new hospital nearby that was recruiting part-time nursing staff seemed to offer an ideal opportunity, but my mother discovered that her Great Ormond Street nursing qualifications counted for nothing.

Office work was an enigma to her, as was much else for that matter, but she liked meeting people and being helpful. Reception work, maybe?

'They're looking for bi-lingual hostesses at the International Transport Exhibition. What do you think? Should I try?' she asked me.

The exhibition only lasted for a few days, but it was wonderful to watch my mother blossom as she planned her re-entry into the outside world. She even splashed out on a smart suit. Although it cost half of her anticipated first pay packet, it served her well for several years to come.

My job was to style her hair, which lifted her spirits and vastly improved her self-image. Even better was listening to her tales of the day's events that, no matter how humdrum, must have seemed exciting compared to the tedium of her previous existence.

Once she had entered the outside world without coming to any harm, Dawa built on her new-found courage and applied for another job for a few weeks during the summer holiday season. She was happy doing reception work and seeing new and mostly friendly faces every day, but her greatest pleasure came from the conversations she had with her unconventional employers. A married couple, they were professional explorers who had spent long periods in distant and exotic places around the globe.

While I wasn't unhappy with this new stage of my mother's life, I did experience a sense of disconnection because of her absence, even though my trusty bicycle and I were doing a magazine round during some of the afternoons. Later, after she returned to nursing back in England, I had the same feelings when I arrived home from school while she was still at work. I never said anything; instead, I made a promise that no child of mine would have to return to an empty house, no matter how cash strapped I might be. If I couldn't afford to be at home and make ends meet, I would not have children.

I kept that promise, even though for a time it meant economising and walking around for days with only ten pence left in my purse after my carefully calculated weekly grocery shop.

Although Elsa, this time accompanied by both of my young cousins, paid us a short visit, my school holiday in the summer of 1965 was much less fun than it might have been because I was missing the company of my only local friend, Barbara, who lived next door. Her father had already been in the advanced stages of leukaemia when the family moved in the previous year and eventually their reduced financial circumstances forced Barbara to leave school as soon as possible and take up paid apprenticeship at BMW headquarters in Munich.[54] She was fourteen.

The companionship I had enjoyed outside school was gone, but palpable – and audible – stress pervaded the months leading up to her father's death. Sensing the tension, their beautiful Alsatian dog mimicked her stressed-out mistress by barking, snarling and attacking just about everything that moved that was not an immediate family member – except for me.

At first whenever I visited, the dog had to be held back then shut away in another room. Then one day everything changed. I had been doing my best to soothe the distressed creature from the safety of my bedroom window as she stormed around the garden below. Suddenly she stopped in her tracks and approached, peering up at me with her doleful black eyes.

Not knowing that chocolate can be poisonous to dogs, I bit into a miniature Easter egg and threw her half. Thankfully it did not affect her and we became instant friends. Later, when the rest of the family was out at work, I was given a key to let myself into their home. I would spend a few minutes talking with our ashen-faced neighbour as he lay wrapped in

---

54 In Germany, formal apprenticeships have always been respected as a committed route to learning all aspects of a craft or business from the bottom up.

eiderdowns on the sitting-room couch before taking my new friend for a long, and extremely well-behaved, walk.

Barbara's father died during that summer, so did our beloved Bunny; at the same time, our circumstances changed yet again. In spite of Hannelu's welcome presence during term times and my mother's brief work experience, we were still penny-pinching and isolated. I continued to feel unsettled and adrift no matter how used I'd become to living in Munich and considered it home. In many ways we had assimilated. My brothers' Lederhosen[55] and my Dirndls[56] had become second nature; we even communicated almost exclusively in German amongst ourselves unless we wanted to keep our conversations private when we were in public. Back then English was still very much a foreign language!

My mother had an unshakable belief that life is full of endless possibilities if you have the freedom and the courage to follow your dreams, but her life was restricted to caring for us kids and earning a bit of money when she could. She wanted a more rounded life again and, after her Whitsun trip to England, she began to get itchy feet. Soon she was harbouring thoughts of moving to Vienna – or even Madrid.

Kristina had caught her American in uniform and started a new family, although they had all recently returned to Munich when she discovered that her circumstances in the US nowhere near matched her fantasies. Regine had long given up on the American dream; she was about to marry a Spaniard and planned to move to Madrid. Why didn't we go with her? She was keen to have familiar faces to accompany her and her son to an unknown country and she painted vivid pictures of the wonderful life that was waiting for us in the Spanish capital. She even produced a list of schools.

My mother was certainly intrigued by the prospect, but luckily nothing more than that because in the end Regine's keenly anticipated move came to nothing. Mr Spaniard, a commitment-phobe if ever there was one, reneged on the woman who had jumped through every hoop that he placed in her path. She had even applied for her first marriage to be annulled when he ran out of excuses and hid behind the Catholic church. Poor Regine: although they did remain on friendly terms, she'd pinned her hopes on being rescued and she never really recovered.

After our Whitsun holiday in Italy, my father disappeared from the scene. I don't know if we were told what was going on, if we were told

---

55 Traditional leather breeches worn in Bavaria.
56 Traditional German dress

nothing as usual or if we blanked it out, but neither my brothers nor I recall having said goodbye to him. One day we simply learned that he had moved to Frankfurt. Shortly after a company takeover, he had fallen foul of his new, puritanical American bosses who were not prepared to employ a divorced man. Of course, much has changed and these days they would not be able to get away with it.

My father had to follow the work. As an Englishman in Germany long before the days of the European Union or a common market, that was no mean feat. Frankfurt was only a four-hour motorway drive away and business would still bring him to Munich on a regular basis, so for him things could have been a lot worse. Anna was delighted. 'I'd always wanted to live in Frankfurt,' she told me years later.

To add fuel to my mother's restlessness, within a year of the divorce inflation had started eating into her alimony and child-support payments. With this unanticipated set of circumstances, leaving Germany for a beneficial exchange rate and cheaper cost of living seemed to make perfect sense – and England seemed to fit the bill.

We had sometimes speculated about our future, but that speculation ended towards the end of the holidays when my mother announced we were returning to England – at the end of September. Well, why not? Pasing was a pleasant but distant outpost, and our social life wasn't particularly good. What was the point of staying in Munich if our father wasn't there? No doubt she and Elsa will also have discussed the question of 'what next?'.

I had already left my old school in the city and been enrolled in the local grammar school for the next academic year. My mother thought the long journeys were too exhausting and my health was suffering. She was right about the exhaustion and my health – although I doubt that the journeys were their only cause.

Changing schools meant leaving my friends and school companions, whom I rarely saw outside school hours because of the distance, as well as familiar faces who'd been a part of my life since I was seven and eight years old. Going to the local grammar school might have improved my situation but I wasn't averse to a challenge so why not make a complete break and start again in England?

Almost as soon as our departure date was set for the last week of September, my mother's ability to cope started to disintegrate. The anxiety generated by the formalities involved in changing countries, including disentangling from our current lease, inevitably got the better of her still-fragile mind and body.

To help her out, Martin and I prepared an advertisement to sell all our furniture except for a small folding side table our father had made when he was at school. I still have it.

There was a lot of coming and going as we led prospective buyers around our home, striking agreements and watching the remaining vestiges of our old family life disappear one by one, including my faithful emerald-green bicycle. Other than that, I remember little about that period apart from a continuous sensation of cloying nausea and the horrifying discovery that we couldn't take Pussy with us. Paying for six months' quarantine for him was far beyond Dawa's limited funds.

Beyond having given her free rein to buy us children some new clothes (of which she took full quality advantage!), our father had also agreed to pay for our travel and the many administrative and legal expenses, but his pockets were not bottomless. There was no alternative but to leave our cat behind. It was deeply distressing; not only was he one of us, but we were all he had ever known. But what could we do other than have him put to sleep?

We decided to look for someone who would give him a home. Almost immediately Dawa heard about Baroness von Trotha, a philanthropist and great animal lover who lived a few streets away. The hallway in her Gothic villa was permanently left open for all comers and several windows on the ground floor had no glass panes. Cats could enter and leave as they pleased in the knowledge that there would always be shelter and food.

The villa stank like a lion's den, while the baroness herself was sweet and eccentric. Most importantly, she agreed to take in Pussy. Although her ways were not the same as ours, we knew he would be well cared for and free to roam around a garden, something our new home lacked.

I closed off my emotions and concentrated on happy thoughts of returning to England: there was no alternative if I was not to become a complete blubbing mess.

What the rest of us didn't know was that Martin was harbouring alternative plans. On the day of our departure, our father came to drive us to Munich's Hauptbahnhof. Taking it for granted that Martin would soon return from saying his final goodbye to Pussy, we started loading our luggage into the car. Then we waited – and waited.

As one departure deadline replaced another, my mother's irritation developed into blind panic: what on earth had happened to him? Suddenly, my parents got in the car and drove off. A few minutes later they found our brother who had decided not to leave Munich before completing his grammar school education; he had persuaded the Baroness to give him lodgings.

We were in a hurry to catch our train. Since forcing him bodily into the car and tying him down was not an option, there was little my mother could do other than open a suitcase and hand him his clothes.

My mother was beyond distressed but my own shock was quickly tempered by an undercurrent of relief that my angry brother would no longer be blighting our lives. Even so, the discomfort of the separation remained. No doubt for my little brother too.

Less than two hours later, my mother, Robert and I leaned out of the carriage window and waved goodbye to our father and Hannelu as our train pulled away from the platform. A few minutes later we also said goodbye to Munich.

Relieved to be on our way, I sat back and imagined happier times ahead. Best of all, I would soon be seeing Oma, who was waiting for us in our new home that Uncle Toni and his family had just vacated.

I had no idea how challenging these circumstances were for my grandmother, nor did I understand that a deep sense of loss doesn't go away simply because it is ignored. Instead, it will manifest in ways that are not immediately obvious.

Grief for the breakdown of our family and regret at having returned to a damp, cold and alien way of life in England gradually crept up on me and my body started to protest. The list of niggling physical problems grew longer over time, but in the short term I started craving sweet and salty foods again – cornflakes with golden syrup, and cheese and onion crisps drew me like a magnet!

The swinging sixties might have been underway, but apart from watching *Top of the Pops* on BBC TV they did not affect us. Single-pane windows, old-fashioned electric-bar heaters and coin-hungry pay-as-you-go electricity meters were just some of the many retrograde experiences that, in a still comparatively insular environment, I would never feel comfortable with.

Yet there were compensations: we lived in the centre of a small county town where the repertory theatre and library were just around the corner. The cinema was not only across the road but was owned by a neighbour who gave me free entry. Until the place was pulled down a year or so later to make room for a larger theatre complex, I made the most of it.

There was more: less than five minutes' walk away we could cross a river and take long and relaxing strolls in the countryside. In many ways, we enjoyed the best of both worlds that gradually helped push aside the pain of broken bonds.

TRIPS DOWN MEMORY LANE

We never had photo albums; nothing in our house was ever really organised, apart from my father's electronics' paraphernalia, hi-fi system, recording equipment and vast tape and record library, as well as the cine films and slides that came with their own boxes. My father was a product of a generation that considered it a male prerogative to devote time almost exclusively to their own interests.

Dawa, on the other hand, especially after our weekly cleaning lady retired when her son was killed, never had much time to herself. There wasn't anybody else to tend to the never-ending and unpredictable needs of three young children and to keep the house and garden in some semblance of order. Besides, she seemed inclined to go with the flow rather than structure her life entirely according to a set of pre-ordained activities.

Consequently, the collection of family photographs and papers, which were my mother's 'responsibility', were still jumbled up in plastic bags and the odd shoebox. Occasionally we brought them out of the cupboard and rifled through them for an hour or two. I always loved both learning about family and friends, and the sense of togetherness when I sat with my mother to explore the past.

I was intrigued by the old school photographs, portraits, holiday snaps, family photos, notes and postcards, and I was full of questions. Who's that...? Where was this...? How old were you...?

There was pretty blonde Sonja, Dawa's closest friend, with whom she had lost touch because of 'the war'. Whatever happened to her and her lovely 'Omi' (Granny) who looked after her? There were photographs of Tante Camilla, Tante Clara, and 'Father', but I took little notice of them; those relatives had died before I was born – I didn't even know when. I had never known my English grandfather, so there was no emotional attachment to the concept of dead ancestors.

Back in England, these bags and boxes were occasionally brought out again and gradually more information filtered through about the faces and names. Had Sonja survived the war? She had gone to live in Prague... There was Zygmunt, a young Polish fighter pilot who had died during the war. There was a young woman called Jean in a swimsuit, posing against rocks on a beach somewhere. My mother told me that Granny Pinner had 'earmarked her for your Daddy – but then he met me!'.

It is interesting how lessons that are not learned like to repeat themselves. The young man Granny Pinner had loved and hoped to marry was killed during WWI; afraid of being left on the shelf, she had given in to her mother's matchmaking. That matriarch had thought it would be a wonderful gesture in memory of her deceased best friend if the friend's son married her daughter. Sadly, my grandparents had married for all the wrong reasons and ended up not too happy with each other.

There was Hermann Mader, a young boy with thick black hair and the face of a cherub, who had written a dedication on the back of his photograph. His family had been desperately poor – what had happened to him? Had he survived the war? Many years later I realised from the date of the dedication that he had given his photograph to my mother as a memento only days before she fled Vienna. I eventually discovered his name on a couple of Kindertransport lists in the IKG archives in Vienna. I never found out if he made it to England – but neither did I find evidence to suggest he did not survive.

There was the photograph of another sweet-looking boy called Hansi Kann, whose profile bore an uncanny resemblance to my father's at about the same age, and his beautiful mother, Tante Karoline. Hansi was now a concert pianist. There was Elsa's friend, Trudi A; I eventually read in Elsa's diary that, before escaping to Bolivia, Trudi had been photographed for the anti-Semitic Nazi propaganda rag *Der Stürmer*.

There was my mother's autograph album with dedications from childhood friends and schoolmates: Susi W., Edith S., Hermine T. What happened to them? Through these meanderings down memory lane I also learned about more of Elsa's friends of whom we had no photographs. Nevertheless, my mother remembered them: Toni U., Senta, Hansi M. and Elsa's closest friend, Silvia Rennert. They had been dispersed around the world; where were they now?

There was my Uncle Toni's best friend, Ossi W. I learned much later that he had been arrested and interrogated by the Gestapo. He was released in June 1938 after being stripped of his right to live in Austria. He became an 'illegal' in his own country, liable for re-arrest if he didn't leave before a specified date. With little time before the expulsion deadline, he couldn't find a country that would offer him a visa and sanctuary. In desperation, he crossed the river Rhein to Switzerland. Months later, he succeeded in gaining entry to Palestine. Much later still, I read some of the letters he sent from Zürich and Jerusalem to Toni in England; it was humbling to learn how this young man, still only eighteen or nineteen years old, was determined to overcome his sudden dispossession while still deeply concerned about his parents back in Austria. I don't know whether they survived the Holocaust.

During one of these explorations of the past, my mother casually mentioned that she and Elsa had come to England on a train 'during the war'. Somehow, I sensed I should not ask more. Dawa showed no emotion, so I simply accepted that this was what had happened during that still-abstract period called 'the war'. For several more years I remained unaware of the trauma she had suffered.

Somehow, I *had* become aware that she was Jewish, but nobody ever explained what that actually meant beyond vaguely indicating that it was a religion that had not gone down very well. Our family did not do religion, and everybody in my life in Germany had been either Catholic or Protestant. Frankly, I didn't care less who was what religion so long as they didn't try to ram it down my throat or regard me with pity for not believing in '*Der liebe Gott*'.[57]

My only encounter with anybody who was called a Jew during my seven years in Germany had been when I was about ten or eleven years old after my brother Martin made friends with a classmate at grammar school who was Jewish.

My mother may have been pleased that her son had finally encountered somebody from a similar background because she made an effort to befriend the boy's parents. I can't remember who visited whom, though I suspect we went to their home because I do recall an unfamiliar atmosphere. I also remember talk of concentration camps and tattooed ID numbers, which at least one of the couple had on their forearm.

It was the first time I'd come across such things being spoken about openly. My mother and my father were exceptionally serious during these conversations, so they obviously were about something sinister. Too busy playing with the couple's daughter, I didn't pay much attention – but the Holocaust had definitely crept closer.

---

57   Dear God.

The friendship between the two sets of parents was fleeting. Many years later I learnt our mother had been indignant that Martin had been included in a religious ritual without her permission. He can't recall what it was and neither of us knows why it agitated Dawa so much.

For reasons that I didn't appreciate at the time, however, initially there was an attempt to encourage a friendship between the boy's sister and me. I had no strong feelings one way or the other; but always willing to give things a try, I felt quite sanguine when my father delivered me early one Sunday afternoon to their apartment in town.

Once I had been handed over, the girl's parents made themselves scarce leaving the two of us with the au pair. She suggested we might like to take ourselves off to the zoo, so we went on a twenty-minute tram ride to wander around the animal enclosures, lick ice creams and chat. I sensed that my companion was very lonely, which made me uncomfortable. When we got back to her home, that feeling intensified; the silence was only interrupted by the au pair who gave me a hot chocolate and a slice of cake before I went home.

Unfortunately, this brief interlude turned into a real problem. The girl would not let me go! Every time I tried to slip past her to open the front door, she pulled me back under one pretext or another; she was obviously desperate for me not to leave. My desperation to escape this rather creepy neediness was made worse because I didn't want to keep my father waiting at the bus stop where he was going to meet me.

After much to-ing and fro-ing I eventually escaped, but I had already missed two bus connections and was almost an hour late arriving at my destination. I was very upset by what had happed, as well as being anxious about keeping my father waiting.

When I arrived at the bus stop and saw him standing there smiling, I burst into tears with relief – on both counts. He laughed, hugged me and asked, 'What on earth's the matter?'

What nobody had explained to me was that the adults had agreed that if I was running late, a phone call would put my parents in the picture. Had they thought to tell *me*, I could have saved myself a lot of unnecessary anxiety.

That was the last time I was aware of meeting any Jews until we returned to England, when I was introduced to some of Uncle Toni's and Auntie Elsa's friends whom, I discovered, my mother had known for a long time. Kurt had left Austria before the war and never returned; Robert, from

Germany, had also left before the outbreak of war and remained in Britain.

Nobody explained why they were in England, and I did not ask. These adult matters didn't concern me; besides, I didn't know that there was anything else *to* ask. It was just life.

During my stay when I was researching in Vienna, Kurt told me that he and Toni had met in the Pioneer Corps[58] in 1941 after they had both been released from internment on the Isle of Man. Robert met Elsa while serving in the American Army's Civilian Service censorship division in Germany after the war ended in 1945.

Robert was the local optician; he prescribed my first pair of reading glasses about a year after we returned to England because I was afflicted by astigmatism. Thankfully, my eyesight improved as I settled into my new life and I gradually regained perfect vision – until the shock of my mother's sudden death.

My understanding of 'the war' and 'the Jews' gained momentum in 1966. One day my mother and I were having dinner in Robert's home when, to my surprise, we were joined by Mr M., the German teacher at my new school.

I knew he was from Berlin because at times we spoke German when we were alone in the classroom. In the best tradition of his hometown, he used the *Berliner Schnauze* (the Berlin gob), while I – thanks to Frau Angers' lessons – replied in the broadest Bavarian dialect.

I eventually learned that Mr M. was a Jewish refugee whose studies in medicine had been cut short. That certainly benefited me because he was an excellent teacher. His enthusiasm inspired me to move beyond the words on paper and start connecting with what lay beneath them. A rarity in my new school, he wasn't merely 'doing his job'. His wife, who was from the Isle of Man, also taught at my school.

I didn't know about any possible connections between us back then, and I certainly had no idea what being Jewish signified, but I noticed that my mother seemed to feel at home in this group of people with their stimulating conversation and warm, mischievous sense of humour.

***

'You should be ashamed of yourselves. She's a foreigner and she's only been here a few weeks, but she has better spelling and grammar than any of you lot!'

---

58 The Pioneer Corps was a British Army corps founded in 1939 and tasked with carrying out light engineering and construction work.

My teacher meant well but his comments only reinforced my 'otherness'. My slight German accent and basic English vocabulary didn't help much, either. Although my new classmates had been friendly enough, my English teacher's comments placed a wedge between us that never really disappeared. To make matters worse there was one girl who, having initially been quite friendly, seized her moment of power.

Janet was tall, skinny and plain, although she occasionally gave a sweet smile; not that I'd given her appearance a moment's thought until she gave me cause to take a closer look. What I didn't yet understand, though, was that my whole package had proved to be nothing short of a red rag to a bull. She became extremely nasty and did her level best to drag others along with her. Thankfully – and to their credit – she failed, although nobody intervened on my behalf.

It was deeply challenging having to deal with such unnecessary and unpleasant behaviour without any support, especially on top of everything else that I was straining to get to grips with.

I had no choice but to hang in there without responding. No matter what poison poured from her mouth, her eyes or her body language, I didn't react. To her fury, I'd even say a pleasant hello and smile at her. It was tough, but I did not hate back. Why would I want to waste my energy?

I learned another trick that stood me in good stead in years to come: I would take my consciousness into outer space where there was nothing but neutral silence; from that vast distance I looked down upon planet Earth before taking my awareness back down to another country where I knew there was conflict and suffering. It gave me perspective.

Eventually Jane grew tired of provoking me and became more friendly. 'You weren't shy enough… I wanted to teach you a lesson,' she admitted much later. She was fortunate; I could have annihilated her with a few laser-sharp words, but I chose not to because it would have been unkind. Perhaps that is why she picked on me in the first place.

I was delighted when somebody (perhaps my mother?) decided that I should repeat the school year. The new class dynamic was very different; I was no longer considered to be a pesky foreigner who was given one-on-one lunchtime tuition by a couple of conscientious teachers to help me catch up with alien subjects.

Eventually I discovered that one of my fellow pupils was also a Jew; however, it was not being a Jew or even an American that marked Jack out but his habit of sparring with teachers during lessons. He liked to probe and ask questions but unfortunately his tone of voice often oozed boredom and condescension. His father was a satirical cartoonist from New York, which might have contributed to his attitude.

Some teachers made no secret of their antipathy, though I sensed that at least one of them rather admired this sharp-witted, charmless young upstart.

I didn't particularly like Jack, but some of the teachers' attitudes towards him bothered me. However, I had no desire to defend him after my first year at school as a friendless 'German foreigner' who was sometimes greeted with Heil Hitler salutes, clicking heels and cries of 'We're British, we won the war!'.

Some four decades later, after connecting on Facebook, Jack and I met for lunch in the West Country. I recognised him, though he had no recollection of me because we had never interacted. Apart from a couple of teachers whose lessons had inspired him, he'd been bored stiff like me. His previous school experience in America had been with true educators who were doing more than just a job.

He also confessed to lobbing a spit ball or two at our young but hapless (although very pleasant), dog-collar-wearing RE teacher who couldn't rise to the occasion when either of us probed beyond the superficial.[59] He was much like our joyless history teacher who read in a monotone voice from a book during lessons; he seemed not to understand that we pupils were perfectly capable of reading the words for ourselves.

My new English school made me aware of narrow-mindedness, jingoism and inadequacy, but at the same time I encountered selfless generosity. And I discovered that prejudice was not restricted to race, nationality and religion or even social class, a concept that was entirely new to me.

At first, I was perplexed. My parents were divorced but it had never occurred to me that there was anything shameful about that. For my friend Jane, it was different. She was two years ahead of me but she had befriended me on my walk home from school. Eventually we developed a close connection because apart from enjoying long walks in the nearby countryside we shared a love for the theatre, literature and the arts in general. I found that she had a wicked sense of humour and a keen interest in using her intellect and creativity; she was stimulating company.

Jane was sensitive, kind and deeply troubled. She had lived through the acrimonious breakdown of her parents' marriage made worse by her father

---

[59] I had no recollection of the spit balls; maybe they were before my time – or perhaps after I asked to be excused from RE lessons.

having left her mother for a local woman. Some fellow pupils bullied and mocked her, taking swipes at her status as the child of divorced parents.

Jane had absorbed her mother's sense of humiliation and injury, and that made her vulnerable to being singled out by individuals who sensed they could flex their muscles at her expense and get away with it.

DRESDEN HOUSE

In June 1967, almost two years after we'd returned to England, there was great excitement in our home. We hadn't seen Uncle Ted since before we'd moved to Germany and now he was coming to stay for a few days.

During our absence abroad, at a time when small-time farming in England was already becoming redundant (especially for an unmarried man without any reliable support), his mother, the farm's matriarch 'Auntie' Ella, had died. With nothing to lose and everything to gain – or so he thought – Ted had moved to Australia as part of the '£10 Pom' emigration scheme.

I only had vague memories of him from occasional visits to the farm before we went to Munich and I had no idea how he and Ella fitted into our lives, but before Ted arrived my mother started to reminisce. In doing so, another facet of her past was revealed.

When they first arrived in England, Elsa and my mother were taken to live at Dresden House, a large and opulent retirement home for 'ladies in reduced circumstances' near the seafront at Hove. When the manager of the establishment and the person responsible for the girls' day-to-day welfare discovered that her charges had always spent their summer holidays in a tiny village in the Bohemian countryside, she arranged for them to stay on a farm near Aylesbury.

The girls' visit was such a success that it became a regular event. Later, when my mother was a student nurse on secondment to Great Ormond Street Hospital's campus in nearby Hemel Hempstead, she spent some of her limited free time at the farm.

Much later in life Dawa took up the reminiscences where she had left off and, gradually, I learnt more.

The farm environment was not exactly Popovice, but the neighbouring youngsters befriended them. After the war began my mother[60] joined

---

60   I am not certain whether Elsa was able to join her after the first visit because her age within her eventual categorisation as an Enemy Alien Class C placed her under a different set of geographical restrictions from those of her younger sister.

in as a land girl during her school summer holidays. She helped with everything: domestic chores, milking the cows, collecting eggs, gathering hay with old-fashioned hayforks and horse-drawn carts, driving tractors across the fields, and mucking out the barns and stables. Dawa enjoyed every minute of it.

Eventually Italian prisoners of war arrived to supplement the depleted local labour force and working alongside them was enormous fun too. 'They were only too grateful to be out of a war they hadn't wanted and at long last to be given some decent food!' my mother told me.

To make her happy days on the farm complete, my mother had turned her back on silver-screen heart throbs Clark Gable and Tyrone Power in favour of a huge crush on Auntie Ella's son, Ted, a swarthy lad of about eighteen. That is until 1942, when she met the man who was the deepest love of her life.

Blond, blue-eyed and Catholic, Zygmunt Bockowski was one of a remarkable group of young Polish fighter pilots whose courage has earned them a well-deserved place in the history of Britain's airborne defence against Nazi Germany. He and Dawa became engaged and were planning to marry. According to my mother's oldest friend Jean, whose Jewish Polish husband was a fellow airman and Zygmunt's closest friend, he survived numerous dangerous missions over Europe only to be killed on 11th April 1945 – just short of a month before the war in Europe ended. His aircraft collided with that of a kinsman during a routine flight over the fields of England. He was twenty-three. 'His coffin was so small.' Dawa once demonstrated with deep pain in her voice.

'They were all so tired,' Jean told me after Dawa's death.

A few weeks before my mother died, she and Jean paid their last visit to Zygmunt's grave in a cemetery in Essex. My mother, who had been nominated as his next of kin, kept his death certificate to the end of her life. Now it is in my safekeeping.

When Ted arrived at our house some twenty-two years after war's end, he was delighted to see Dawa again – but his pleasure had dissipated by the time he left a week or so later. It seems that he had come back to England to ask my mother to marry him and emigrate to Australia with us children. He was very lonely so far away from home; since he'd always been fond of my mother, who he now thought was 'available', he'd hoped they could help each other out.

My mother had moved on since those days on the farm and now she was also re-discovering her independence. No matter how fond she might have been of Ted, her feelings were not deep enough to even consider such a risky enterprise. Why on earth would she choose to become another man's housekeeper on a sheep farm in the middle of nowhere? Neither was she pleased with her old flame's attempts to interfere in our family dynamics. She had little difficulty in dismissing his offer, though I'm sure she refused in the kindest possible way.

Ted returned to Australia a disappointed man. A few years later, my mother received a letter with no ending; Ted had died penning his last thoughts to her and his nurse had posted them on his behalf.

'He died of loneliness, you know ... poor Ted,' she said to me.

A couple of years later Dawa received another proposal from a man whose company she enjoyed but whose motivation for marriage she didn't fully trust. She was right; after she turned him down, he never invited her out again and within a few months he married one of her colleagues.

OMA IS GONE

On my mother's forty-second birthday we were preparing our evening meal when there was a knock at the door. As she read the telegram, Dawa's smile faded and she turned ashen. 'Mother has died.'

The shock was appalling for all of us. My mother immediately phoned Aspern, only to discover that Oma had already been dead for two days. Our cousin Hilda had sent a telegram to Elsa in London but had made a mistake with the address; not receiving a reply, she'd sent another one to us. My mother couldn't understand why nobody had thought to pick up the phone. It was something that gnawed at her for the rest of her life.

'Why don't you get off the train in Munich on the way back and visit Angelika for a few days?' my mother suggested to me.

'No, she won't be there anymore.' I had no idea where those words came from but, disturbing as the feeling was, I pushed it aside.

Two days later Elsa, my mother and I arrived in Vienna where my second cousin Hilda and her second husband (another Willi, whom I hadn't met before) were waiting at the Westbahnhof. After hugs and condolences, they drove us to Oma's apartment.

As we entered the building I immediately felt as if I'd come home – except this time it was agony. The silence caused by Oma's absence in her apartment was hard to bear.

To make matters worse, Hilda failed to understand that there are times when it is kinder to say nothing and launched into an account of what she had encountered 'when I found Auntie lying dead across her bed'. I would have liked to kick her into silence but, of course, I could not. But the damage was done and it haunted my mother and me for years to come, and probably Elsa too.

There was worse. Oma had dreamed for twenty-one years of joining her Ockele in his grave but it was never going to happen. She had left the Catholic Church to marry Grandfather, though as far as anyone could ascertain she had never converted to Judaism. Now the Jewish authorities were refusing to bury her.

According to Hilda, neither was there a non-denominational option. My mother and Elsa knew nothing about how these things worked,[61] and finding a Catholic Church to bury her had been almost impossible because Oma hadn't paid any church taxes.

Finally, after much '*Bitten und Betteln*',[62] Hilda's local priest in Aspern relented. As I listened to one insult after another being heaped upon my grandmother's humanity, never had I felt more certain that I wanted nothing to do with religion.

I burst into tears. 'What are you crying for? She wasn't *your* mother?' Elsa hissed.

My aunt could be very sharp. It was not the first time she'd chastised me, nor would it be the last, until one day when I was an adult I lost patience and challenged her. I hated doing it because I loved her, but it had to be done. Thankfully I was not aggressive, just on point, and our fundamentally good relationship didn't suffer at all.

Back then, stung into silence, I turned and ran down the winding stone staircase that had once represented so much joy. Back in the large entrance hall, I opened Oma's letterbox and retrieved an envelope she had never opened.

I had written to my grandmother a few days before her death. I had hesitated by the post-box but then, brushing aside an uncomfortable sensation, I pushed the envelope through the slot. As usual, I imagined that by rejecting the unthinkable everything would be fine. Now it hurt terribly to know that Oma had not had the comfort of some caring words from her closest family during her last days.

'Not a patch on Mother's!' The next day, and to put off the moment

---

61   These days, close to the Jewish sector within the Central Cemetery, there is an area designated for inter-faith marriage burials.
62   Pleading and begging.

before we started sorting through Oma's personal possessions, the three of us went for an early lunch in the restaurant downstairs. To our surprise, the proprietor was still the same as when I used to go into the kitchen through the back door to collect some food after a day out, or to buy a bottle of *Malzbier* (malted beer) to accompany the adults' evening meal.

Continuity is embedded in Viennese life.[63] In many ways I envy that, though at times I wonder if it doesn't result in a certain lack of creativity. On that occasion, as if to bring the past into the present, we ordered *Germknödel mit Povidl*.[64] Oma's were always feather-light and delicious; these were heavy, chewy and dull. Outside the weather was bitterly cold and grey. Could our situation possibly have been more depressing?

Back in the apartment, my mother and I finally steeled ourselves to open Oma's wardrobe. Once upon a time there was a tall glass jar filled with *Kräuterzuckerln* (boiled herb sweets) from the Karmelite market, one of which my brothers and I were given as a daily treat. The jar was still there but now it was empty. In a way I was grateful; the taste would have been too evocative, and I was already finding the situation difficult enough.

I loved Oma so much, right from the heart, and knowing how she had spent the last days of her life was deeply painful. My mother was suffering too, walking around in a quiet daze, furtively opening up drawers and peering in as if she were afraid of intruding on Oma's privacy. Elsa, her face impassive, was busy instructing us to do this, do that. It was irritating but I could also sense something else, although I was not certain what. The feeling of aloneness in this place was stifling.

The wardrobe contained few clothes, and it was obvious that not all of them belonged to Oma. She'd never had much because she couldn't see the point of having more than necessary. '*Wozu*?'[65] Besides, she'd had little money and what she had not spent visiting her family in England and Czechoslovakia had sometimes been stolen by lodgers. And her trust in banks was zero.

Hilda couldn't find the bank notes that Oma had saved for her funeral and hidden between the pages of a pile of old newspapers. She and Willi had searched everywhere but they were nowhere to be found.

'Those were Father's!' my mother said, as I held up a pair of leather riding boots, then his overcoat with a black Persian-lamb collar and lined

---

63 The time of writing was 2010. Much has changed since then.
64 Large yeast pastry dumplings filled with concentrated plum purée, served with melted butter, crushed poppy seeds and cinnamon sugar.
65 'What for?'

with moleskin.

Vienna could be very cold in winter. It was mid-March now, but it was freezing. An icy east wind cut like a razor, just as I remembered from those winters in Munich. Back then it had often been too cold to inhale through my mouth, so the fine hairs in my nostrils had frozen and prickled as I'd run to catch my early morning train to school.

There were my grandfather's gloves, a tired-looking three-piece suit, some shirts with detachable collars, a pair of well-made leather shoes and several unused leather elbow patches. This was the closest I had come to the grandparent I had never known, and it was an intense experience.

My mother gently stroked his coat. 'We'll take it back for Martin. I'm sure he would like it, if it fits him.'

I picked up a black, beaded, chiffon wrap-over top. 'Good heavens! That was Tante Clara's!' Dawa exclaimed.

We also found Tante Camilla's embroidered cotton parasol, pairs of fine kid gloves, several ornate and very long hatpins and a couple of old-fashioned hats for which they were probably intended.

'Tante Clara always loved hats and beautiful clothes… You take after her!'

There was a petit-point evening bag with a silver chain and two cabochon amethysts set in the silver clasp. I noticed that my mother's eyes were glistening and becoming slightly pink around the edges. 'Tante Clara made it herself. She used to do the most delicate embroidery… She was a wonderful needlewoman.'

As I pulled out other items of clothing that my mother recalled had belonged to the aunts, I was bemused. Why on earth had Oma kept them all these years after their deaths? It seemed as if she'd been looking after them, as if the aunts were about to return from the dead any day soon.

In the drawers and cupboards there was more: Great-Grandmother Antonia's monogrammed nightdress; a silk-and-lace night bonnet; a treasure trove of hand-embroidered tablecloths, doilies, napkins and pillowcases variously monogrammed with AL, CL and ML – Antonia Löwenthal, Clara Löwenthal, Camilla Löwenthal, Marie Löwenthal.

My mother remembered all of these items and when they were used. She set them aside carefully as if afraid they might disintegrate. 'We'll keep those.'

Following her cue, I set aside Oma's cream cardigan that I remembered from her visit to England. For some reason, I did the same with the parasol, hatpins, kid gloves and the beaded chiffon top.

Over the next two days, my mother and I sorted through Oma's possessions as we packed up and cleared out her flat. Elsa, meanwhile, spent most of her time criss-crossing Vienna tending to the tedious but essential administrative affairs that accompany death.

She had also been exploring the legal procedures involved in taking over the lease of the apartment. As heirs to Oma's 'estate', her children were entitled to inherit the lease, something they desperately wanted to do to avoid losing what was left of 'their' Vienna now that it had started slipping through their fingers forever.

Oma had occupied only a portion of a larger apartment where, ever since I could recall, the rest had been sublet to a giant of a man, the lawyer Dr. Balaban. If he stayed and continued paying rent, perhaps it might be possible to raise the funds to make up the difference. But this dream remained a fantasy; no matter how they juggled ideas and numbers, it was not going to work. Uncle Toni was far away in Canada and had no spare money, while Elsa and my mother in particular were already struggling to make ends meet. The legal fees alone, although quite small, were out of everybody's reach.

To compound matters further, time was short before Dawa and Elsa had to return to England and to work. Depleted after years of stress from breakdowns, divorces and the struggle to come to terms with painful life changes, eventually it all became too overwhelming. Regretfully, they conceded that this was the end of the physical connection with Vienna. All that was left for us to do before we handed back the keys to the landlord was to dispose of everything that couldn't be taken back to England in our suitcases or sent cheaply by freight in a couple of boxes.

We needed to cull the non-essentials while not missing anything important. That meant sorting through a large cardboard box stuffed with photographs, postcards and letters, some of which were tied into neat bundles with ribbons. Others were loose, like so many tickets in a tombola. This was so unlike Oma – had somebody been searching for her money?

Kneeling on the floor, I lifted out the neat bundles. As I untied one of the ribbons, I noticed that the letters still in envelopes were marked with pencilled numbers. I untied another ribbon around more numbered envelopes.

'Oh my goodness, Mummy, these are from Uncle Toni! And these are from you and Elsa!'

After a brief look, my mother set them aside without a word. I continued sorting, calling out the names of the senders and reading aloud the contents of the more obscure mail so she could decide what should go on the 'keep' or the 'throw' pile. She remained detached and efficient; we had little time to linger in the past.

That was until I came across one letter that rattled her deeply. It was quite short, but she snatched it out of my hand before I could finish reading it. 'Throw it away, throw it away!' she shouted as she furiously ripped it to shreds.

She had snapped. Shocked at her sudden metamorphosis, I dared not ask any questions. Instead, I tried to commit its contents to memory for an explanation another day.

Years later, when I finally broached the subject, my mother didn't want to discuss it. The general gist of the letter was: *If the two girls* (or was it women or daughters?) *are still resident in Vienna* (or was it 'at x address?') *on xxxx date, they will be relocated to...* I can distinctly remember thinking Poland but can't recall why.

This was my first tangible encounter with a dark reality that was still being kept from me. I wondered at first whether the document referred to my mother and Elsa, but I suspect it might have been a warning sent to Grandfather by somebody at the IKG about the aunts.

In November 1939, SS Obersturmbannführer Adolf Eichmann had declared that any Jews who had not emigrated from Austria within one year would be deported to Poland. I will never know for certain but, whatever the case might have been, the Holocaust had moved another step closer.

Editing this manuscript in 2013, I re-read one of the letters addressed to my grandfather at war's end and finally began to ponder a possible connection: *...I believe the Head of the IKG was a friend of yours.*

But at the point when I read that letter in Vienna, I was seventeen years old and knew nothing. History lessons at school had yet to catch up, there were no documentaries on television, and this was long before the internet. And my mother remained silent.

Two days after we arrived in Vienna there was a blinding snowstorm. My mother, Elsa and I stood frozen as we said our last farewells to Oma. Her coffin was lowered into a snow-filled grave in a Catholic cemetery far away from her beloved Ockele.

A few minutes earlier, Dawa had asked for the coffin to be opened so she might take one last look at her mother. Completely appalled, she had cried out in English, 'What have they done to her? Mother never wore make-up. Now they've made her look like a tart!' I can only hope that Oma was having a good laugh on the other side of the veil.

'What am I to do without her? She was everything to me...' a grief-stricken elderly woman wailed as we left through the cemetery gates. My mother and Elsa offered some words of comfort before she mounted her bicycle and rode off.

'Who was that?' I asked.

Frau Selka had been Oma's domestic help before the war and before Jews were forbidden to employ 'Aryans' or invite them into their home. I so wanted to put my arms around her, but it didn't seem appropriate. Besides, living in England had made me timid. Where once my friends and I in Munich had linked arms quite unselfconsciously, beyond the family the English still tended see things differently: are you queer or something? No, apart from formal handshakes (also rare), touching another was not a good idea. It took a few years for me to overcome that inhibition.

Three days later we closed the door to Oma's apartment for the last time, descended the stone staircase and walked silently past her letterbox, the name on which would soon be changed.

As our train pulled out of the Westbahnhof and we left behind the comforting mixture of Vienna's sights, sounds and smells, the dignity of my mother and Elsa was heart breaking.

A few hours later our train reached the outskirts of Munich. As we thundered over the bridge past our old local railway station, from where Angelika and I used to travel to school in town, I remembered my words from a few days ago. Our correspondence had petered out quite a while back; perhaps Angelika had moved on, formed new friendships? Like so much else at that time, that thought hurt.

On the other hand, I had something to look forward to: I was stopping off in Frankfurt to spend a few days with my father.

'Your grandma was a remarkable woman!' he told me. I knew that, but unfortunately, I was too young to think about asking my father precisely what he meant.

Forty years on, my mother's old friend Kristina and I reminisced about Oma's visits to Munich. *'Was für eine prächtige Frau!'*[66] she exclaimed. Thankfully, I was aware of so much more by then.

---

66 'What a magnificent woman!'

ANGELIKA

During my college break four months later, I spent a few more days visiting my father again before being delivered to spend a week with Hanneluise and her mother in Swabia. After that I returned to Munich to stay with Kristina and her daughter, Larissa.

I intended looking up Angelika's telephone number to see if she would like me to visit. There was the possibility she would rebuff me, but I was willing to take the risk.

'Did you know one of your old school friends died a little while ago?' Larissa asked me.

I'd heard nothing from the two school friends I was still in touch with, so I wasn't sure to whom she was referring. Suddenly I was on high alert because, although Larissa couldn't remember the girl's name, she said it was the one who lived near me with whom I'd been most friendly.

'You don't mean Angelika, do you?' I asked.

'Yes, that's her. She died – cancer, I think. I'm so sorry...'

I was too shocked to be anything but numb. The next day, having first gathered my courage over coffee and cake with my old friend Frau B., I stood at the familiar garden gate and rang the bell. When the buzzer sounded, I pushed open the gate.

Frau Anger was peering out from the front door. 'Oh! My goodness, Sahlee, where have you come from?' She put her arms around my shoulders and led me into the house that had been my welcoming second home for nearly five years. Now it was in semi-darkness, silent but for the loud ticking of the familiar clock on the sitting-room wall.

I sat down on the seat that was always mine and tears poured down my face as Angelika's mother told me about her only child's struggle during the last year of her short life.

I was close to howling but I knew I must not. If anybody should have been howling, it was Gela's mother. She looked, sounded and felt completely different from the old days; she was only just coping.

Mrs Anger made us both a cup of camomile tea and showed me photographs of a familiar, healthy-looking Gela on her sixteenth birthday, then pictures of Gela with no hair, Gela with a wig, Gela on her seventeenth and last birthday in February. She and her parents had been on a hiking trip to the mountains after they thought she had beaten the disease, cancer on the pleura, only for her to die shortly afterwards on 17th March – the day before Oma's funeral.

'We tried absolutely everything. She was even treated at Dr. Issel's clinic.[67] She was so brave to the very end...'

The first thing I blurted out to my mother when I returned to England was that Angelika was dead. Then I added, 'Oh, Larissa and I went to visit Pussy. When we got there, Baroness von Trotha said he'd been poisoned, she suspects by a neighbour. He died about ten days before I went to visit him.'

'Why didn't she write and tell us?'

I had no answer, as I had no answer as to why nobody had told me of Angelika's death. Perhaps nobody thought it was possible to care from such a distance.

Very soon I developed a sharp pain underneath my right ribcage. It only disappeared four months later after I had one of those lucid dreams, the details of which never disappear.

'What on earth are you doing here?' I asked my friend. 'You're supposed to be dead!'

'Yes, I know!'

I was back in Angelika's garden where the two of us were chatting in a place of indescribable lightness and peace. She looked radiant and said she was fine – would I please tell her mother so that she could stop tormenting herself?

I did sit down to write to the woman who had once treated me like a daughter, but halfway through the letter I stopped and threw it away. How could I possibly tell Frau Anger that I had spoken with Gela? She would think I was mad. I wrote nothing and told nobody about my dream.

Some years later Frau Anger confided in my mother that Gela had appeared to her as well. When she told her priest, he had threatened her with excommunication if she ever dared to repeat such a thing.

He pulled rank as he had been taught: access to a higher level of consciousness was only permitted through the ordained clergy. Ordinary mortals must know their place. It was the Christian Church's spiritual feudalism. It was evil – and, for a while, my friend's mother was admitted to a mental institution. Yet she was fortunate: in centuries gone by she might well have been burned at the stake.

For many years I couldn't bear to hear a ticking clock; and not writing that letter for fear of being ridiculed is one of the greatest regrets of my life.

---

67 Dr. Josef Issels specialised in comprehensive non-pharmacological immunotherapy. His success rate was high.

FOUR

RETURN TO VIENNA

ENGLAND, SPRING 1979

'Darling, I've just seen an ad for what looks like a really reasonably priced three-day holiday to Vienna – flights, hotel, breakfasts and evening meals all included. Wouldn't it be lovely to go back again? What do you think? Shall we…?'

It was ten years since Oma's death but neither of us had had the spare money to visit Vienna again. Apart from the expense, made worse by an unfavourable exchange rate, what would have been the point?

Visiting without anywhere familiar to stay would have been too painful. Our relatives in Aspern were still there, but their family had grown and they didn't have the space to put us up. But now my mother was clearly ready to go back, and, with serendipitous timing, an affordable package had caught her eye. Whatever my own feelings, there was no question that I would not go with her.

During the coach transfer from Schwechat airport to our hotel opposite the Hietzing entrance to Schönbrunn Palace, we overheard a rather tense exchange between the couple sitting behind us. They were speaking heavily accented English.

After a while, my mother and I looked at one another knowingly. 'Excuse me,' my mother said, 'but I couldn't help overhearing. Is this really your first trip back to Vienna since the war?'

The elderly lady looked quite startled. 'Yes, it's my first time back since I had to leave before the war. I didn't really want to come but I must.'

She and her husband – who was also Jewish but not from Vienna – had come back to her birthplace in an attempt to achieve some closure to the memories that she had pushed aside in order to live. 'Retirement and time have a way with them,' she said.

They were on the same package deal as us and over the next few days we gradually heard more of the woman's story across the breakfast and dinner tables. Much of the narrative was wrapped up in codes of 'you know how it was', and 'you know what I mean', while my mother confirmed that, yes, she did know how it was and what she meant. I had the odd sense that this chance meeting was helping to distract Dawa from her own fears.

For me, this was the first real-life encounter with another aspect of my mother's past that she continued to keep at arm's length. We spent the next days touring Vienna. I noticed admiringly that, unlike a tourist, my mother had an easy familiarity with the transport system; she navigated our way around town with the absolute confidence of a local. There seemed to be something different about her, but I couldn't pinpoint exactly what it was.

'The aunts often took me out with them, and I used to love it!' she told me after we left the Hofburg Palace in the old city and walked past Café Demel.

'It used to be one of the finer cafés ... always only the best. The aunts weren't rich but they preferred quality over quantity. I used to have the most wonderful hot chocolate *mit Schlag*[68] and a delicate pastry, of course...'

We didn't go into Demel's on this visit, nor did we visit Oma's grave in Aspern, or anybody else's. We didn't even cross the Danube Canal into our home turf of Leopoldstadt. My mother couldn't bear to do it and I was more than grateful not to have my emotions put to the test.

On our last afternoon, we took a bus to Aspern to pay the Malys and Hilda a lunchtime visit. Aunt Hedwa and Hilda started preparing food; as expected, we were served chicken soup made from a home-reared and home-killed chicken, followed by Schnitzels so large that we could fit nothing else on our plates. By the time we'd ploughed through this enormous feast, Dawa and I were both ready to burst. Even so, despite our protests we were presented with huge helpings of Palatschinken filled with chopped fruit and whipped cream, plus more whipped cream on the top.

We groaned, but what could we do but eat it all? I also felt irritated because, apart from Hedwa, our relatives remained standing throughout the meal watching us eat as we almost made ourselves sick for fear of offending. There and then I vowed I would never again eat too much simply to be polite. There had to be another way of giving and accepting

---

68   With whipped cream.

hospitality.

'Anybody would think we were strangers visiting from another planet,' my mother said after we left. It was nobody's fault, of course, simply the distance created by spending time in two very different worlds.

Nevertheless, by the time we boarded our plane back to England, I knew that my childhood crush on Vienna had developed into a full-blown love affair. I'd been hooked all over again by a place that I was starting to realise was indelibly printed on my psyche. My mother told me one day that she'd chosen my middle name because of its similarity to *'la vie Vienne'*, so maybe that connection was inevitable.

The following year I went back to show Don *my* Vienna. This time we did cross the Marienbrücke (bridge) to Leopoldstadt and walked along the Obere Donaustrasse towards number 57. I'd been feeling so excited about sharing a place that held such intimate memories with my husband that I'd persuaded myself that this time all would be well. It was – until we were within about fifty meters of 'our' building. Suddenly, without warning, I started to tremble, my legs locked and I burst into uncontrollable tears. My poor husband was taken aback as much as I was; he'd certainly never seen me cry like that before.

Once I had pulled myself together enough to place one quivering leg in front of the other, we continued slowly towards our destination. The main entrance door was firmly closed. Because I didn't want to keep walking, we stood around for a while in the hope that somebody might leave or enter the building. We loitered for several long minutes, but when there was no opportunity for us to slip inside or catch a glimpse of the entrance hall, we had to make do with stepping back and gazing up at Oma's window.

As I scanned the building, I noticed for the first time the bullet holes in the plaster facade. It was also the first time that I noticed how tired and neglected it all looked, although the block was not really much different from the rest of Vienna. While many buildings without historical value had been hastily rebuilt after the war with a utilitarian blandness, ageing, pollution and lack of care and attention had taken their toll. The European Union, let alone its restoration funds, had yet to be heard of. But no matter: my love for Vienna was now firmly fixed in my adult psyche.

FIVE

JOURNEY OF DISCOVERY 1989-2000

LONDON 1989

'Oh, by the way, darling, there's going to be a Kindertransport reunion at the Festival Hall. Elsa and I are planning to go.' *Oh, by the way?* That was so typical of my mother.

I had never heard of the Kindertransport. 'What's that about?'

'It's the organisation that brought Elsa and me to England on a train. It's a reunion to commemorate the rescue of thousands of us Jewish children before the war started.'

This was also the first time that I'd heard the word 'rescue', let alone 'of thousands of us Jewish children' in relation to my mother's arrival in England. But I dared not ask more. I don't know why. Perhaps when you want to live you subconsciously know what to do so as not to die? What did I imagine? Perhaps nothing. After all, if you don't know the moon exists, how can you wonder about it?

'Can I come too?'

'Would you like to? Are you sure?' My mother seemed surprised. 'In that case, I'll order you a ticket.'

'Get one for Don, he'll want to come too.'

'Really? Are you sure?'

'Yes, of course!'

In the event, our fourteen-year-old son also accompanied us to London's Festival Hall where we joined a packed audience of 'Kinder' and many of their descendants to remember the rescue of some ten thousand Jewish children from Nazi Germany and Nazi annexed territories.[69]

I had no idea what to expect, but it soon became obvious that many of the people there knew each other, though my mother and aunt didn't

---

69   Austria and Czech lands.

know anybody.

As the scene was set, I was already incredulous; when we were shown film footage of Jewish child refugees arriving on British soil with labels tied around their necks, I was shocked. Was this my mother? I'd had no idea!

For the first time I was confronted with the magnitude of what had happened to her when she was even younger than my son, who was still and will always be my baby.

I thought of Oma and Grandfather, who were forced to give up their children in the hope that they might be safe. I contemplated what my mother and Elsa must have felt, as well as the thousands of sorrows concealed behind the mostly expressionless faces in the auditorium around me. I tried to imagine the unimaginable: the sacrifice, the loss to parents and children alike.

By the time we left the Festival Hall later that afternoon, I was lost for words. The painful circumstances wrapped in the innocuous sentence 'I came to England on a train' had finally hit home and were deeply disturbing. My mother and Elsa, however, were discussing their journeys home. It was a signal, and I did what was required of me: I kept my thoughts and feelings to myself.

I didn't engage with my own emotional response until some seven years later when it came back to punch me in the solar plexus.

***

'There's an organisation for people like you.' Elsa's face was mask-like, her tone devoid of emotion, although there was that hint of irritation. Typical: as wonderful as Elsa was in so many ways, she had little patience with those who displayed painful emotion. I didn't understand that it was because she was so desperately afraid of her own. My mother, looking slightly withdrawn but composed, said nothing.

My cousin Sarah had wanted to see Diane Samuels' play *Kindertransport* at our local repertory theatre and our mothers had agreed to go with her. Certainly, where Dawa was concerned, what better way to share something that needed to be acknowledged without actually talking about it? I had declined; the short excerpt shown recently on television had been enough for me to know it would be too painful. I would cry. A lot. And I must not do that.

I picked the three of them up after the performance and, when I asked about the play, Sarah immediately began to sob. So did I. I couldn't help it;

it was an uncontrollable reflex made worse by seeing our mothers standing paralysed in their wasteland of unexpressed grief. They needed somebody to put their arms around them and hug them, but they did what I had also learnt to do: drew a wall around themselves that nobody must infiltrate.

At the time I still didn't know how Sarah functioned because we'd never really talked. One thing was certain, though: we all needed comfort, and nobody could give or receive it. However, at that point I learned for the first time that there was an organisation for people like us who were suffering our parents' sorrows.

By then I'd seen Claude Lanzmann's *Shoah* and several other documentaries about the Holocaust that portrayed the atrocities perpetrated upon the Jews and other 'undesirables'. I knew the names of the major players in the Nazi regime and was familiar with the existence of many of the concentration and labour camps, and the barbarity that took place inside their high walls and barbed-wire fences. I had watched the gratuitous violence and humiliation Jews were subjected to after the Anschluss[70] as well as the Germany- and Austria-wide pogrom of Kristallnacht[71] and its catastrophic aftermath.

I had seen footage of Hitler's jubilant entry into Vienna the day after my mother's twelfth birthday, the crowds falling over themselves with deafening enthusiasm, even though I wasn't aware that much of it was a well-orchestrated piece of theatre.[72] Many in that crowd were probably ignorant of what was really happening in their country.

Yet I knew nothing of my mother's and her family's experiences in Vienna, only that the aunts Camilla and Clara were deported to Terezin and never returned home. I'd only discovered that accidentally when I'd found my mother reading a book about the artists of Terezin. Since then, she had briefly hinted that other relatives had suffered the same fate. But I knew so little that I could keep my history at an emotional distance.

Then I learned that, despite being christened into the Catholic Church at birth, neither Tante Marianne, whom I had met as a child in Munich, nor her young son Peter, had escaped the poisonous tentacles of the invented Nuremberg Race Laws.[73]

---

70 The Nazi regimes annexation of Austria and incorporation into Greater Germany.
71 Also known as the Night of Broken Glass; a pogrom against Jews across Germany and Austria during the night November 9-10, 1938
72 The Nazi authorities had ordered businesses to close early, instructing their employees to line the streets.
73 Nazi race laws introduced in Germany on 15th September 1935 that included

Marianne's husband had not been a Jew, so no matter what her own Jewish parental background, she and Peter had qualified for 'protected' status and were not automatically condemned to deportation to a concentration camp. However, in the end her and Peter's 'protected' status had counted for nothing. During the winter of 1944/5 all three of them were eventually rounded up in their hometown of Prague and packed off to Terezin concentration camp. Learning that the woman who'd been so keen to hug me when I was a child had suffered so much came as a painful shock. With it, the holocaust moved another step closer.

Marianne, Peter[74] and her husband had survived, but liberation did not signal the end to their troubles. When they returned to Prague after liberation, they found that their home had been confiscated. A neighbour gave them sanctuary but soon they were caught up in a tidal wave of violent post-war expulsions of ethnic Germans from Czech soil. Revenge for recent transgressions and historical unfinished business was finding expression; as a family with a foot on either side of the divide, they could not win.

Fortunately, once they had settled in Munich, Marianne's husband's professional reputation led to his appointment as a senior state prosecutor sitting on a special commission for war-crime tribunals. There was at least some justice, although undoubtedly not as much as he wished for.

ELSA GOES HOME

On October 27th, 1996, my mother wrote in her diary: *Elsa died today, what am I to do? I'm glad it's over for her but for us it is so terribly sad. What will I do?*

For weeks my aunt had suffered the Irish patient across from her hospital bed lambasting 'the Jews', but finally she had succumbed to the after-effects of a massive stroke. Once again, I found myself listening to my mother's hollow voice, one that I remembered so well from another phone call twenty-two years earlier: 'Darling, Toni has died.'

Eighteen months after Elsa's death, my mother came to live with my family. I had always known that this would happen sooner or later. Don and I had bought a large house some years earlier with enough space to accommodate visitors from home and abroad and also my mother when

---

a methodology to establish degrees of Jewishness. 'Full' Jews were stripped of their civic rights.
74 Of the 15,000 children held in Terezin between 1942-44 less than 150 survived.

the time came.

After she moved in, our conversations about her childhood, family and friends back in Vienna started to change. Losing her sister and fellow traveller had left her bereft, and I soon found myself taking on the role of Elsa's proxy as Dawa tried to find some measure of resolution to at least one aspect of unfinished business.

After the two girls arrived in England in March 1939, they continued to correspond with friends who had successfully fled Austria, as well as with those who were still trying to escape. Some eventually got away, others did not. Five months later war was declared. The flow of letters gradually reduced to a trickle before eventually drying up completely.

By the end of the war six years later reconnecting with friends was a lost hope, apart from a couple of exceptions. Many had moved to other countries and continents, while the less fortunate had simply disappeared.

Hoping that she might have survived in Czechoslovakia, my grandparents had made every effort to track down Sonja, Dawa's best friend, through the Red Cross but the trail went cold. However, the question in the back of Dawa's mind: 'I wonder what happened to...' never really went away.

My mother and Elsa had often reflected on the past and wondered. Now that Elsa was gone, my mother's questions and tension did what they had always done: transferred to me. I had grown up with an awareness of all these people, even when there were no photographs to put faces to. After Elsa's death, there were faces in photographs where once there had only been names, and I, too, began to wonder.

Neither my mother nor I knew that years earlier Elsa had placed search notices for her friend Silvia in both the AJR[75] Journal and the *Jerusalem Post* but received no replies. She never did find out what had happened to Silvia and her younger brother.

'Well, Dawa, if you really want to trace these people you have to *do* something about it!' I had said and Don, who had heard our exchange, was immediately on hand with advice. 'I've just been reading that you can do people searches on the internet!'

Don was not only a computer genius but he also read everything, hoovering up the written word. He had seen an article in one of his computer journals that listed some relevant websites.

That news came at just the right time. My mother's need for certainty

---

75 Association for Jewish Refugees.

about the past had reached its crescendo a while ago, but I hadn't had the spare time to carry out more conventional, labour-intensive and emotionally draining searches that I knew she would not be able to cope with.

It was Boxing Day and I had what seemed like flu. I was feeling thoroughly lousy and exhausted and – for once – had decided to give in to what my body was attempting to tell me. However, although I was feverish, I wasn't knocked out enough to go back to bed without fretting about all the things I had to keep on top of: the household chores and the mountain of my university work.

'Do go and lie down and take a rest, just for once. You'll feel so much better for it!' As usual, Dawa's plea fell on deaf ears. Then I thought of something I could do that wasn't strenuous and might divert me. And on that day, it felt right.

'Okay, Dawa, give me a list of names and I'll do an internet search for them. You never know!'

I entered one name after another into a couple of people-search websites but in the end all I had to show was a single possible match with Herman Mader, that beautiful, black-haired cherub who had dedicated his photograph to my mother more than sixty years ago. Most of the people on my list were girls and I was fairly certain that the chances of finding them under their maiden names were remote. But at least I could send an email enquiring if this was *the* Herman Mader, last heard of in Vienna in 1939.

I sat back, wondering what to do next. My mother had made every effort not to build up her hopes, but she couldn't help it and now she was deeply disappointed.

'Dawa, can you remember any names of brothers?' I asked.

The only one she could come up with was Silvia Rennert's brother, Martin. Saying nothing I returned to my computer, silently imploring the universe to let this be our lucky day. Nothing.

There was only one site left for me to explore, and I typed in Martin Rennert. Almost immediately a list of about a dozen M. and Martin Rennerts appeared, together with places of residence and email addresses. Most were in America, others scattered across the world; there were a couple in Germany.

I knew that Silvia and her brother were two of only about a thousand unaccompanied Jewish children who were granted American visas and had escaped to New York in the autumn of 1939. My grandparents had somehow discovered that their parents had been murdered after being deported to a concentration camp. Perhaps Aunt Elsa's friend and her brother had remained in America?

Are you by any chance Martin Rennert from Vienna but last heard of in 1939 in New York? If so, please contact.

As I prepared to email all the names on the list, I was a little hesitant about the two German ones. Would Martin really have gone to Germany instead of back to Austria? But anything was possible, so I sent the message off to the first of the two remaining Martin Rennerts.

Just as I was about to click on the 'send' icon for the second Martin Rennert in Berlin, my mother put her head around my office door. 'How's it going? Any luck?'

Her face lit up when she heard what I had found. Then, inexplicably, when I told her I was about to message another possibility in Berlin, she reacted with uncharacteristic irritation. 'Don't bother, it can't possibly be him. He would never have gone to Berlin!'

Thirty-six hours later, with the exception of one from the man in Berlin, I had received disappointing replies to all my emails. Even Herman Mader was not the one we were looking for, although he wished me the best of luck.

Part of me was relieved. The fear of bringing more pain than pleasure to the people my mother wanted to find had made me anxious. Knowing what had happened to Silvia and Martin's parents, how could I be certain that they could cope with having the past recalled so abruptly? I had no idea where life had led them; perhaps they would simply like to forget and not be reminded ever again?

Certainly, my mother would have been delighted if somebody from her past reappeared, but she had not lost her parents under terrible circumstances. Yes, she was very close to the aunts and had even been distraught in 1939 when she'd read that Tante Camilla hadn't been well– but that was still not quite the same. There was nothing I could do other than give up my worries to the universe and hope that nobody came to any harm when absolutely none was intended.

I rarely used email in those days, so I stopped logging on to check for a reply from Berlin; it was the Christmas break and most people had better things to do than sit at their computers. However, for some reason I was convinced all was not lost even though my mother's hopes had been so high that now she felt deflated and wanted to let go.

I waited a couple of days before logging on again.

I lived in Vienna for almost 24 years (till '85) and actually was born in NY City, but considerably after 1939. Why do you want to know? Please reply.

On the face of it, our last hope had been blown away because this man was clearly not 'our' Martin; even so, I was certain that we had finally made some progress. Could this possibly be a son?

Without saying anything to my mother, I replied with a brief outline of Elsa's friendship with Silvia. Then it was back to waiting – again.

***

The cloudless night sky around us was erupting with fireworks as we stood in a friend's garden seeing in the new millennium. It had been a lovely evening, although another part of me couldn't help thinking what a let-down many would experience in the coming weeks after the hype surrounding the build-up to the year 2000 and the New Year resolutions that went with it had exhausted themselves. Then, as I stared at the stars, I suddenly thought, *I must check my emails first thing in the morning.*

I had a reply.

I believe you have found the right person, although I also think your mother must have made a mistake about the first name. My father left Vienna the same way as his sister Silvia, also in 1939.

This man Martin seemed very cautious and did not divulge his father's name, nor did he tell me where he lived now or whether Silvia was still alive. He wanted to correspond some more before passing on any details. I, on the other hand, knew with certainty that we had found who were looking for and replied with more information that would surely convince him of my integrity.

This time I didn't have to wait long for the response from Berlin:

I am very happy indeed. I also am sure that you have found the right person. My father's name is Erwin ... anyway, the –in is the same.

'Dawa, just imagine where we would be if you hadn't remembered the wrong name! How weird is that!'

As Martin told me later, we met in cyberspace at a time when the Holocaust had caught up with him too. He was experiencing a deep need to connect with a part of the past that his father, who had returned to

Vienna with his young family in the early 1960s, had only recently started to talk about more openly.

A few days later when I tried some more searches, the website on which I'd found the Rennerts had disappeared... Synchronicity had certainly helped me out in the nick of time!

SIX

DAWA'S VIENNA 2000

THE SILENCE IS BROKEN

'Darling, look what I've found! I thought you might be interested in reading them.' My mother handed me several letters, some with worn envelopes, others with none. There were also four tired-looking buff postcards. So, this was what all that rummaging around in the loft and the long silence that followed had been about!

The top envelope had a number three pencilled on the front and was addressed to Dr. Oskar Alex. Löwenthal, Schweidlgasse 13/6, Wien, Österreich. The post-office stamp stated: Brighton & Hove, Sussex, 8.30pm, 29th March 1939. The sender was Elisab. Löwenthal, Brighton, Dresden House, Albany Villas, Hove.

I had completely forgotten about them but now I recalled the bundles of letters in Oma's apartment more than thirty years earlier. Inside the envelope, the sender's address was embossed in elegant, upper-case letters on high-quality writing paper. In stark contrast, the handwriting was erratic and sloped progressively downwards from left to right.

> *Dearest Parents!*
> *We are very glad that the whole journey is now behind us. The border control was considerate towards us. Out of the whole transport only 10 suitcases were searched. In London the Committee took us over. We waited for an hour and then Mr Beddington, his wife, Uncle and Toni arrived. Mr B. is a friendly old gentleman and Mrs B. a beautiful old lady. I didn't speak much with Uncle or Toni. The poor boy looks awful. First of all, we drove through town to Victoria Station, where we went to the restaurant. Each of us was served half a chicken, ham and tea. My immediately pounced on her chicken. I couldn't eat mine. I felt very embarrassed but I didn't touch it. Mrs B. was also accompanied by a young lady. Her name*

is Miss Hawkins. We were put in her care and travelled to Brighton. The weather is marvellous. The sea is beautiful. We are staying in a large and fabulously elegant house. Carpets everywhere. Miky and I have two bedrooms next to each other. They are simply furnished but nice. A lot of other people live in the house as well (I think). I don't know who they are. It is so elegant here that I feel quite nervous. Miky, on the other hand, feels completely at ease. She didn't get sea-sick. The second night we slept in a first-class cabin. I shall write in more detail tomorrow. Please forgive my atrocious scrawl **but I am very agitated!**[76] *It's afternoon now and I'm writing in Miss Hawkins' room. I shall write in more detail tomorrow. At the moment I'm still very tense. Miss Hawkins thinks that my English is very good (probably in comparison with My). I made a real effort to use all of my vocabulary in conversation. My likes it here. Farewell. E.*

Lots of love and kisses to all. Tomorrow I shall write in greater detail.

Upside down, in the top-left corner and carefully avoiding the embossing, there was a short additional message in a contrastingly firm hand:

Many millions of kisses to you all. I will write to you in detail tomorrow. Your My

The second envelope was very fragile and barely intact. The postage stamp bore the words *Deutsches Reich* and on the reverse was a strip of four, black-framed, rectangular rubber stamps, each containing an announcement in German that neatly established the atmosphere of the time: '*for reasons of currency control opened by customs*'. It was addressed to Misses Elisabeth and My Löwenthal, c/o Miss Hawkins, Dresden House, 18 Albany Villas, Brighton-Hove, Sussex, England. There was no indication of the sender, although the word *Wien*[77] was just about legible on the ink stamps thumped across the customs' marks.

Inside the torn envelope were three folded sheets dated 4th April 1939 and filled with neat script. At first I was reminded of Oma's handwriting but when I looked at the signature there was just a strange squiggle.

Dearest darlings,

How anxious we are for you! How we miss you in every nook and cranny, how it hurts us to see your empty chairs at the dinner table. We think of you all day long and in the sleepless hours of the night. But we

---

76 Written in English.
77 Vienna

can at least be reassured that you are in the best of care and that kind, understanding people have taken you in and will look after you in the best possible way. We are infinitely grateful to them, and you too must be grateful – <u>and show it</u>! On no account must you cause Miss Hawkins any trouble or unhappiness and ask her to please put into writing your gratitude to Mr and Mrs B. Sweethearts, do not neglect to speak to Miss H. about this, it is very important. We are of course confident that you will be polite and well-behaved as always and will earn the good-will and liking that you enjoyed here. All your relatives and friends are full of praise for you. Uncle Josef has already been here to ask after you (do send him and Uncle Karl and his sisters a card straight away). Mrs Selka and Irma, Auntie Tildy, everybody, want to know how you are. Do write to Pest[78] as soon as possible and say thank you for the chocolate. Uncle Willi in M. Ostrau is thinking of you too and is happy that you have arrived safely. Have you sent Aunt Paula your address clearly and precisely? She would like to send you some pocket-money so that you can buy stamps. Who has given you stamps so far? Did Uncle Arthur think of it? You must thank him sincerely for his efforts, don't forget! He has earned it of you. In your next letter send greetings to Auntie Roserl, Mrs Selka and Irma and mention how much you enjoyed their gifts of confectionary. They will be so pleased! You were very good to write straight away. You can imagine how heavy hearted we were and how we tremble to hear detailed news from you. You must always write in precise detail about the smallest little thing so that we know everything about your daily lives and we do not lose touch, God forbid! How we live, well, that you know, just that it becomes more difficult all the time. It is a good thing that you have gone away, we would not be able to give you any fresh food or vegetables. Well, as I have already said, just keep writing in detail. I am going to attach a long questionnaire to this letter and beg of you, my sweethearts, answer it. Do I need to tell you how anxious your mother is for you? But she makes every effort to appear brave, at least on the outside. Father learns your letters off by heart (I think he reads them at least three times an hour). Tell our dear Toni that Father carries his photo around with him and shows it off with pride. The dear, good boy. Give him much love from all of us, as we send you, much loved, sweet children, all our love and a thousand kisses!

Granny, Auntie Milla and your loving Auntie Clara

---

78   Budapest

Part One ~ Chapter Six

My heart was already breaking, but the words on the third and last page sent a shockwave through me with a force I could never have anticipated:

My dear, dear Elserl and you, dear little Myki, do say your prayers at mealtimes and at least recite the Shema morning and evenings. Were you able to celebrate Pessach and were you given Mazzoth? Dear treasured children, you are so far away and all that is left for us to do for you now is to pray that God will protect you and ask you to remain well-behaved and keep in mind your duty to Judaism.

Again and yet again, countless kisses from all of us.

I'd had no idea. What duty? To what Judaism?

I turned to the postcards. Two of them were numbered 1 and 2 and, like letter number 3, were addressed to Dr. Oskar Löwenthal at Schweidlgasse – although this time not at number 13/6, but 13/4. Assuming this must be one of those errors that creep in unnoticed, I didn't give it another thought.

Postcard number 1 was dated 28th March 1939 and postmarked REGENSBURG. The disturbed handwriting was immediately recognisable.

Dear Grandmother, Parents and Aunts!
We had a fairly good first night. My slept mostly on the floor. I didn't sleep at all, but I'm not tired. The last station was Passau. It is half past four now. The postcard was given to us. Lots of kisses,
Elsa and My

The familiar, characteristically strong, open and evenly flowing handwriting on postcard number 2, also dated 28th March 1939, was equally recognisable.

Dear Grandmother Parents and Aunts
We passed safely through Cologne and have just passed Düsseldorf.
Lots of love
My and Elsa
Letter to follow

I turned to the remaining two cards, also addressed to Dr. Löwenthal at Schweidlgasse 13/4. The sender was Clara Ottilie Löwenthal, Theresienstadt,[79] Postgasse 8, Bohemia, Protectorate. Thumped across the front of both cards were the heavily underlined words:

Reply only *with postcards in the German language.*

16/10/43

---

79 Terezin ghetto and concentration camp, Czech Republic.

My most beloved brother and sisters!

I thank you so much for the little parcel and the news, especially from Grossbyrn and Broed. They are elixirs of life, do kiss the children a 1000 times for me. Unfortunately I have to send you bad news: in spite of every medical skill and care our dear good Willy died on 7.10 – he was a 'special' case. With little Willy dead and big Willy not here, I am alone in my helplessness. Brother and sister, please write more often and in more detail of your lives. From Dmastekovo there is no sign?

I kiss you a 1000 times, your Clara

Greetings to everybody else.

Do pass the above news on!

Oh my God.

'Dawa, I didn't know people were allowed to send post and receive parcels from concentration camps.'

'Writing from Theresienstadt was strictly limited and everything was censored – the same went for receiving parcels. But don't imagine large packages. They had next to nothing in Vienna either, and everything was rationed. For the remaining Jews there was next to nothing. If it hadn't been for Mother... Oh, and don't be fooled by Clara's address, it was a charade to fool the Red Cross inspection. The conditions were absolutely appalling – they were dying in their thousands, they were starving and there were epidemics... The way they were treated was absolutely foul. They suffered so terribly...'

'The bastards! Who are these "Willys" Clara's wrote about? And what did she mean by "special case"?'

'They were Father's Löwenthal cousins. One of them lived in Märisch Ostrau...'

'Where's that?'

'It's Ostrava, in Moravia. "Special case" was code for murdered, I suppose. I think he might have been beaten. Big Willy – he must have been transported onwards, probably to Auschwitz or somewhere like that.'

'And what does she mean by Grossbyrn and Broed?'

'Great Britain, and probably Ungarisch Brod[80] ... lots of relatives used to live there, and in Budapest.'

'And Dmastekovo?'

'I don't really know but I have wondered whether perhaps she was referring to the Allies.'

---

80 Uhersky Brod, Czech Republic.

Dreading what I would find, I turned to the last postcard. It, too, was from Terezin.

17th February, 1944

Dear brother, sister and sister-in-law.

Your cards of 8.11 and 17.12.43 have assured me, unexpectedly and thank God, of your good health. Deepest thanks for the much valued news. Lalage has unfortunately suffered several heart attacks, as well as double pleurisy and lumbago, hence great pain. As to your question about Dr. Weinberger I must tell you that his behaviour was so mean from the beginning and that he deserted us. Write often and in detail and kiss the beloved children, may God protect them, and may they not forget Grandmama and the aunts too soon! On 12.3 is the first anniversary of our dear sister's death. I return all greetings, and greet and kiss you, Your Clara

The muscles in my throat were so tight that I could barely speak but I had to know. 'Dawa, who was Lalage?'

'That was Tante Clara. When Father was little he used to call her Lala. It's code, because Theresienstadt was supposed to be like a spa town for "privileged" Jews but it was a sham. They didn't want anybody to know what was really going on.'

'And what's this about Dr. Weinberger? Who was he?'

'One of Father's many Weinberger cousins. When he was thrown out of his home, he went to live with them in Schweidlgasse. He was deported with the aunts. I'm not sure what she meant … perhaps that was code, too. Who knows what they did to them? He didn't come back.'

Listening to my mother and trying to digest what I'd just learned, I could hardly contain my distress. Its intensity took us both by surprise. My mother was looking at me with troubled eyes but neither of us spoke; there was no need for inadequate words.

Whether Dawa was aware of it or not, a veil of forgetfulness had been ripped apart and I knew that my life would never be the same again. That had not been her intention, and I knew she was already sorry, but we were preparing for a trip to Vienna in a few days' time and she wanted me to be aware of something she had not known how to articulate.

We had already planned to pass briefly through Austria on our drive back from Bohemia later in the summer, when Dawa intended to say a last farewell while finally initiating me into *her* Vienna. I understood why, although the implications felt deeply uncomfortable. However, we had brought forward that leg of the trip because our reasons for making the journey had taken on a new dynamic. Silvia Rennert was still living in America, but we were going to visit her brother, who was not called Martin but Erwin.

The last time Dawa and I had been to Vienna together was some sixteen years earlier. Sadly, what had begun as a happy family occasion with Don and our son had become a rather depressing affair.

Towards the end of a brief afternoon visit with our relatives Hedwa and Hilda in Aspern, my mother had asked where she could buy flowers to place on Oma's grave before leaving town. The visit to Oma's grave would be our first together since we'd buried her.

'She's not there anymore. Didn't you know?' Hedwa said.

Hedwa and Hilda were dismayed; my mother and I were horrified.

For the first time that morning we had driven past where Dawa used to live in Lassallestrasse, as well as the building in Schweidlgasse where her grandmother and the aunts had lived before the war. The drive past had been brief, commentary free, and had not left much of an impression. Now we were too shocked to do anything but listen incredulously to the explanation.

The renewal of the lease on the burial plot had become due some time earlier and Hedwa had proposed to Elsa that, if there were no funds or a desire to keep it going, the Maly family could take over the plot; Oma's remains would be removed and placed in the ossuary. My mother had not been consulted or informed, and now there was nothing she could do about it: no Oma, no grave. Nothing.[81]

We maintained a strained politeness for the rest of the visit, but once back in the car my mother fell silent as she tried to come to grips with what she had just heard. Apart from the loss of her mother's grave, her opinions and feelings had not counted – yet again.

I, on the other hand, suddenly snapped out of my shock and started to cry before choking back my tears so that I didn't upset my young son. He understood neither German nor the enormity of what had just happened – and how on earth could I have explained it to him?

Two days later, my healthy and fit mother became breathless. Within a short period of time her heart began to fail, leaving her reliant on medication for the rest of her life. Her wounded heart had finally, quite literally, broken.

---

81 Elsa took early retirement due to intermittent memory loss; perhaps this explains why my mother was unaware.

***

Despite history and the emotions associated with the place my love of Vienna was still pretty much intact, but after that last visit there had been no reason to return. We could not visit Oma's grave, and I had also become aware of an undercurrent of irritation within me towards a sense of entitlement that neither my mother nor I could claim.

Dawa had visited with friends and family members a couple of times but, financially strapped as ever, those visits had been in passing. When her one-time travel companions and chauffeurs had either died or could no longer accompany her, it had seemed a long and expensive trip to make merely to spend a few hours reminiscing over coffee and cake.

Suddenly, with the contact established with Erwin Rennert, we had a purpose. However, as our travel date drew closer my mother found herself increasingly wrestling with her fears as the prospect of coming face to face with another aspect of the past filled her with terror.

Two days before our planned departure, she asked me to cancel our flights. Sensing that it would be a mistake to backtrack when we had come so far, it took all my powers of persuasion to help her follow through with what she had started. Besides, the plane tickets were non-refundable; could she really justify throwing our precious money away?

BACK IN VIENNA

Arriving in Vienna, we were greeted by one of those balmy evenings I remembered so well. We both laughed as we caught each other taking deep breaths of *our* air; it was still the same and didn't fail to hit the sweet spot.

By the time we'd checked in to our hotel room it was almost ten o'clock in the evening; even so, we couldn't resist taking a walk. The Italian ice-cream parlour that used to serve me ice creams with miniature paper umbrellas in its original location had since moved just down the road on the Schwedenplatz. It was heaving so we didn't stop – though we were determined to return at some point – but continued northwards along the less frenetic Frans-Josefs-Kai.

We were deep in conversation and failed to notice that we'd already reached the Augartenbrücke (bridge). What else to do but look across to 57 Obere Donaustrasse? I'd not been anywhere near the building since I'd shown it to Don more than twenty years earlier. Now it was so near yet so far away. Then there was that sharp sting in the tail.

Suddenly feeling wretched, we turned around and strode in the direction of something sweet. A couple were just leaving the ice-cream parlour and we were able take over their seats. The choice of traditional and new ice-cream flavours and the array of concoctions with fruit or liqueurs or sweet toppings (and of course, with or without *Schlagobers* [82]) was quite overwhelming.

So was the impatience of the waitress, who was not only very busy but also had a vested interest in serving her customers as quickly as possible. She immediately pounced on us, order pad at the ready, pencil poised. If we'd lived in Vienna, maybe we'd have been familiar with the grand selection on offer, but we didn't live there and we weren't. Intimidated into making an almost instant choice, my mother stuck an imaginary pin into the name of a dish with an enticingly long list of ingredients *mit Schlag*. My hunger had waned considerably, so I ordered the smallest dish of mixed ice cream.

I settled our bill as soon as the waitress brought our order, then sat back and took a closer look at my mother's towering creation of multi-coloured ice creams and sorbets. I looked at my prissy little dish of chocolate, hazelnut and coffee ice cream. 'Dick und Doof!'[83]

My mother was only a split second behind me in recognising a running private joke and we doubled up with laughter.

After a few minutes of burrowing through an Everest of whipped cream, my mother's mood changed noticeably. I braced myself as I recognised her preoccupied expression. 'I simply can't stop crying,' she said.

As always, her tears, whether visible or not, became my tears. We left hastily and went back to our hotel room. That night my mother's misery was so tangible that I found it impossible to sleep. Tomorrow couldn't come soon enough.

THE RENNERTS

If I'd needed proof that my mother was feeling deeply stressed, I'd have had it at breakfast. Uncharacteristically, she complained from beginning to end. Even I, who have been known to pull something carelessly substandard to shreds in seconds, found the almost endless stream of complaints (no matter how justified) exasperating.

After we'd eaten, we returned to our room to arrange a meeting with

---

82 Whipped cream.
83 Laurel and Hardy known in Germany as Dick und Doof: Fat and Stupid.

Erwin before drawing up an itinerary for our tour of my mother's Vienna. The phone rang: it was Konrad, another of Erwin's sons, and he wanted to meet us.

We met in Café Bräunerhof a couple of hours later. Some three hours later, we arranged to see him again the next day because he wanted to take us to the DOEW[84] where they held records of Holocaust victims who'd been deported and murdered.

We didn't know about the DOEW, but being so far removed from anything other than superficial contact with the Jewish community, let alone those who actually spoke about such things in detail, why would we? Perhaps this would be an opportunity for my mother to find out exactly what had happened to the aunts and so many of her other relatives, but for now we were going to have afternoon tea with Erwin and his wife, Ruth, on *our* side of the Danube Canal in Leopoldstadt.

Erwin recognised my mother instantly, not necessarily because he remembered her but because he definitely remembered Elsa. Only a few days earlier Don and I had watched my mother watering the plants in the garden wearing one of Elsa's dresses; her hair had even been cut and styled very much like her late sister's. Usually strong and erect, she had recently started to stoop like Elsa, and she'd even begun to brood like Elsa. Now it crossed my mind that perhaps it had been Elsa who was so afraid of the past.

I had yet to read Elsa's diary from the nine months before their flight from Vienna. When I did, I learned of her fear of eventually meeting her friends again one day and discovering that they no longer had anything in common.

My mother and I had already spoken to Erwin a couple of times over the phone from England, but apart from being told that he was delighted that we had found him, we didn't know him at all. Despite that, I had an intense urge to hug him, if only for Elsa's sake. I didn't; he seemed rather fragile and a strange woman's embrace might have been overwhelming. Instead, we shook hands warmly, though I did kiss his cheek lightly before we took the lift to his apartment where Ruth was waiting at the open door.

She was smiling widely, saying, 'I'm so happy to have you here!', something she repeated several times during our visit.

Two hours later, when the entrance door to the apartment building closed behind us, I was clutching a volume of Erwin's limericks as well as

---

84   Documentation Centre of Austrian Resistance.

a copy of his recently published autobiography, *Der Welt in die Quere*.

'It depends on how much you allow yourself to feel,' he had replied when I'd asked if writing it had not been too painful. Maybe this was the reason Erwin had, at times, used the apparently flippant writing style that had so irritated Martin? Knowing that Erwin had recently made his story public, I was relieved not to have to keep wondering if we'd been the catalyst for unwanted memories.

Back on the pavement, neither of us spoke. For my mother the encounter with Erwin after many years of wondering had been quite overwhelming, but in terms of communication so pleasantly easy. We'd covered so much ground that I couldn't recall all that had been said, but I retained a strong impression of the humanity that underpinned his philosophy of life: live as positively and as fully as possible for the sake of those who went before and whose spirit is still around us.

I appreciated his survival strategy, though I wondered if his optimism and faith comforted him in his darker moments.

In late 1939, when he was just thirteen years old, he and his sixteen-year-old sister had said goodbye to their mother and father before making the train journey to the Italian port of Genoa. There, they boarded a ship carrying Jewish refugees aiming for New York and where they were taken in by dutiful – but childless and clueless – distant relatives who were good people yet complete strangers.

After six complicated years, during which he hitch-hiked and 'tramped' his way alone to California and back, eighteen-year-old Erwin returned to Continental Europe as an enlisted soldier. Much like Elsa, he eventually made it to Vienna, only to learn that his parents had fallen victim to the 1942 frenzy of roundups and deportations of the 'final solution to the Jewish question' and had never returned. He and Elsa also probably only missed one another by a small margin.

Later Erwin also learned that his parents had suffered the tortuous journey in overcrowded cattle wagons to the extermination camp at Maly Trostenets in Belorussia. Shortly after their arrival, as per usual, they and their fellow travellers were tricked into undressing and handing over their few belongings before being forced to run into the forest. There they were shot as they stood by the edge of their already dug mass grave. Why on earth would Erwin not have his darker moments?

Part One ~ Chapter Six

MY MOTHER'S VIENNA

It was now just after 6pm, towards the end of a long and intense day. I was sure my mother would be ready to return to the safety of the old city and our hotel, but she was not. 'Let's go this way,' she said.

As we walked through side streets, she remembered their names and found something to say about almost all of them. So-and-so lived here … her grandparents lived a little further down the road … Mother lived there with her friend when she was a freelance cook … Dawa focused doggedly only on the pleasant aspects of 'before the war'.

After a while, as if taken by surprise, she announced, 'It's beginning to feel less threatening.'

I was grateful to Erwin and Ruth who had been so kind and welcoming, and had allayed her fears: for once, there had not been even the slightest hint of a hierarchy of suffering.

Eventually we reached Pfeffergasse and Dawa said, 'Father's cousins, Onkel Karl Löwenthal and his sisters Cäzilia and Rosalie used to live here.'

This was the first I'd heard of them and an emotional pain shot through my heart. The sisters were not married, and my mother couldn't recall whether Karl ever had been. He'd run a coffee and tea import business. Apparently, the family were the embodiment of 'goodness, Judaism as it should be', although I didn't have a clue what exactly she meant by that.

'Zilly' and 'Salie' were sweet women who looked like a couple of dainty little birds. Dawa also recalled their other brother Onkel Willi from before he moved to Ostrava, though she didn't remember when. They were all deported to concentration camps; she knew that they were in their mid to late sixties at the time of their deaths, but not where they were murdered.

'While we're here, I'll show you where I used to go to school.'

A little further was Patzmanitengasse. My mother had enjoyed her secondary school; some of her friends were Jewish, some not, but it had never mattered.

A few weeks after the Anschluss, the headmaster had urged the Jewish children to go home as quickly as possible because he'd received a warning of what was about to happen. By the time my mother reached the exit, many anxious parents were already there to grab their children. They were surrounded by a mob of uniformed Hitler Youth brandishing sticks, yelling threats and shrieking '*Jude verrecke!*' [85] Seeing no familiar faces amongst

---

85 'A miserable death to Jews!'

the waiting parents, my mother had panicked and fled.

Somewhere along the way, she ran through an open door and up several flights of stairs until there was nowhere else to go. There she cowered for what seemed like hours; even after everything fell silent, she didn't dare move.

In the meantime, Oma had arrived at the school and panicked when there was no sign of her daughter.

It was Onkel Karl who eventually found my mother. 'Don't be afraid,' he'd reassured her, brandishing his silver-topped cane. 'Come with me. I'll show them what for!'

'It was ridiculous,' my mother told me. 'He was such a slight little man and couldn't have stopped any of them. But he had such authority that I had complete confidence about going back onto the street with him.' Then she added impatiently, 'I was such a coward! If it had been Elsa, she would have bared her teeth and gone for them!'

'Oh, Dawa! You were only a little girl!'

My mother never did go back to school and she had no formal education until a year later in England.

We continued walking in the same direction, then my mother pointed. 'Schweidlgasse is just up there.'

She changed course and we returned to Heinestrasse, from where we headed for the nearby Praterstern roundabout. I was quite relieved; Clara's words from Terezin were still painfully fresh in my mind, so for my mother this must surely have been too close for comfort.

As we walked the length of the Praterstrasse, my mother continued recounting stories of her childhood and pointing out who lived where and what shop belonged to whom.

Eventually we turned into Tempelgasse. Dawa reflected that her parents must have agreed to bring their children up in the Jewish faith because on high days and holidays the family occasionally attended the Great Temple that had stood there. Mostly, though not often, they'd used the Stadttempel[86] in Seitenstettengasse.

The Great Temple had been truly magnificent but was torched to the ground during Kristallnacht.

'You can have no idea of the primitive, brutish violence. The next day the destruction was ghastly. Grandmother's and the aunts' domestic help was so traumatised she went insane – she killed herself. She wasn't the

---

86   City Temple.

only one. They came for Father. There were about eight members of the SA,[87] really *gscherrt*.[88] I was with him in his office when they stormed in and he told me to leave, but I refused. It was the only act of real bravery I ever committed in my entire life. I stayed right there between them – why I thought I could protect him I can't imagine.'

Her father had been quite extraordinary. He remained so calm and spoke to them in a normal tone of voice, connecting one human being to another. He told them he was as loyal to Austria as they were, and that he had fought in the war. He took a book down from the shelf and read something to them, reasoned with them quite calmly. Then they left.[89]

The aunts had been listening behind the door, and after the SA had gone the three of them fell into each other's arms. 'Father must have been terrified, but I would never have known it.'

'How come you were in his office that night?'

'Because we were all living there!' My mother seemed irritated, as if I should have known that. 'They threw us out of Lassalle Hof. Grandmother lived upstairs and Father's consulting room was in the aunts' flat downstairs. When we moved in, they slept upstairs. Father had put the lease in Mother's name so they couldn't throw us out all over again. We all came and went really… In the long run they all had to live downstairs.'

We crossed to the other side of the narrow street and looked back at a memorial in the shape of four tall, stark columns. The silence lasted for what seemed like several minutes; no doubt my mother was superimposing the image of a lost magnificence upon them that I couldn't begin to imagine.

My mind wasn't on temples; I was still struggling to make sense of what she had told me. Just as we were about to return to Praterstrasse, she pointed towards the street to the other end of Tempelgasse only a few meters away. 'That's Ferdinandstrasse. Mother lived and worked there before she got married.'

A few minutes later we had more or less closed the circle and crossed the Aspern Bridge to the Urania by the Franz-Josefs-Kai. As well as being a public observatory and cultural centre, the Urania had once been *the* place to enjoy good cinema. My mother's friend Gerda, whom she had met two years earlier through the AJR, had stood somewhere near there

---

87 Paramilitary wing of the Nazi party.
88 Coarse.
89 After Dawa's death I found Grandfather's WWI bravery medal. Had he been fast on his feet? Or had the SA followed instructions not to harass war veterans? Perhaps both.

in March 1938 and watched Hitler's motorcade drive past on its way to his headquarters at the Hotel Imperial. My mother also remembered seeing Hitler's motorcade by the Praterstern as it travelled towards the town centre.

'What on earth were you doing there on a day like that?'

'I was probably either going to or coming from Grandmother's because of my birthday. The crowds were hysterical, *rabiat*,[90] absolutely ghastly. I can remember wishing that somebody would drop a heavy plant pot on Hitler's head.'

That moment had marked the beginning of the end of my mother's childhood and of the way of life she had known.

Later in the evening, over a meal in the back streets of the old town, we talked about the people we had met. We didn't know them well, but there had been an unmistakable thread of humanity running through our conversation with Erwin and Ruth. We agreed that Elsa would have appreciated that, too.

'I'm so pleased we came,' my mother said.

So was I as I scribbled notes first on a crumpled old envelope I found in the bottom of my bag and then on a paper napkin, praying I'd be able to decipher them later

DOEW

In the DOEW, the large map of Europe on the wall pinpointed the locations of the Nazi regime's extermination camps, labour camps and ghettos. There were so many that printing the full numbers of those murdered in each one would have caused a problem of overlap. Instead, there was an instruction: 'Multiply the figures shown by 1000'.

Konrad evidently knew his way around and soon a number of files were placed before us. My mother was hoping to find information about her father's period of forced labour, something else that, 'by the way', I had only recently heard about for the first time.

Unfortunately, these particular files contained only housing register data. We were shown into an office where a woman was working at a computer. She told us that the DOEW Holocaust victims' database was being continuously updated with as much information as they could gather.

My mother sat by the desk while Konrad and I remained standing.

---

90   Savage.

One by one, Dawa provided a name for which to search. The woman at the computer read out her findings then handed over a printout of each person's data:

Klara Ottilie Löwenthal. Date of Birth 30.04.1875. Last Address: Wien 2, Schweidlgasse 13/4. Date of Deportation: 14.07.1942. Place of Deportation: Theresienstadt. Date of Death: 18.04.1944. Place of Death: Theresienstadt.

Camilla Löwenthal. Date of Birth 21.09.1876. Last Address: Wien 2, Schweidlgasse 13/4. Date of Deportation: 14.07.1942. Place of Deportation: Theresienstadt. Fate: Death without Confirmation.

This was confusing. I had gained the impression that Camilla was most likely transported onwards to Auschwitz, while Clara's postcard gave a precise date of death even if the records held no information. Perhaps I had misunderstood, or something had got lost in translation. Whatever: she had been murdered.

The cramp in my throat was clawing into my jaws and my ears. The realisation that only a few days ago I was holding what might have been Clara's last communication with the outside world before she died was deeply disturbing. She had been in a desperately bad way; had she had a premonition? Was that why she'd said she hoped the children would not forget their aunts and grandmother too soon?

Now, though, my mother's expression gave nothing away. At least she knew for certain when Clara had died.

Karl Löwenthal: Born Vienna. Date of Birth: 18.02.1879. Last Address: Wien 2, Pfeffergasse 3/20. Profession: Merchant. Date of Deportation: 02.06.1942. Place of Deportation: Maly Trostenets. Fate: Death with Confirmation.

Rosalie Löwenthal: Born Vienna. Date of Birth: 28.05.1872. Last Address: Wien 2, Pfeffergasse 3/20. Deported 20.06.1942. Place of Deportation: Theresienstadt. Transported to Treblinka 19.09.1942. Fate: Death with Confirmation.

As she listened to the findings being read aloud, Dawa remained expressionless and silent but, when she heard the horror laden word TREBLINKA, she could no longer contain herself. Her voice full of pain, she exclaimed, 'Poor Tante Salie,' before retreating again behind inscrutability.

My eyes filled with tears but what could I do other than turn away and mop them up? My emotions would not help my mother, whose ability to shut down was nowhere near as limitless as she would have had us all believe.

The woman behind the computer was also expressionless; she hadn't even smiled when we'd entered her office. Part of me appreciated that it must be a challenge to maintain her equilibrium, but her professional distance was beginning to grate. She continued matter-of-factly:

> Cäzilia Löwenthal: Born Petersdorf, Hungary. Date of Birth: 28.04.1870. Last Address: Wien 2 Pfeffergasse 3/20. Place of Deportation: Theresienstadt. Fate: Death with Confirmation.
>
> Wilhelm Löwenthal: Born Wolkersdorf, NÖ. Date of Birth: 11.07.1876. Deported from Mährisch Ostrau (Ostrava) 22.09.1942. Place of Deportation: Theresienstadt. Date of Death: 07.09.1943.

My mother had come armed with a long mental list of other relatives whose names I hadn't heard of before breakfast that morning: Fürst, Sternfeld, Lustig, Braun, Körner. The litany of murder might have continued for some time, but she'd had enough for one day.

Turning away from her personal pain, she decided to use this unexpected source of information on behalf of her friend Gerda. There was some data about Gerda's family, but nothing specific about her parents' fate. They had come from the small town of Oswiecin (Auschwitz) in Poland but because they had lived out of the country for more than five years, their Polish citizenship, in tandem with their rights to residency in Austria, had been revoked following the Anschluss.

Without any legal means of escaping the hell that Jewish Vienna had become, Gerda and her family travelled by train to the German border at Aachen, praying they would find sanctuary on the other side. Their prayers had gone unheeded; they were forced to turn around.

There was worse to come. The theft of Jewish businesses and property had already become a legalised feeding frenzy, but Gerda's parents could never have imagined the reaction of their once-friendly neighbours who had seen the family leaving their home carrying suitcases. Squatters had moved into their home and refused point blank to let the family back in. Now they were not only pariah Jews but dispossessed and homeless.

With not much more to lose, it was decided that Gerda (although until her disenfranchisement an Austrian citizen due her birth but just over the qualifying age for the Kindertransport) should try to escape again, alone.

This time, as she stood in the queue for border control beside the train at

Aachen, the whistle for the departure to safety on the other side sounded just as it was her turn to show her papers. 'Go!' the passport control officer shouted, waving the remaining unchecked passengers back onto the train and to freedom. Gerda had made it.

'I must have had a guardian angel,' she had told my mother.

Her parents were eventually rounded up and deported from Vienna. By some miracle, her father escaped a 'rabbit run' shooting at Maly Trostenets. He had even written a few times to his daughter in England from somewhere in the Soviet Union before falling silent.

What was worse: knowing the whole truth or not knowing anything?

MEETING THE LÖWENTHALS

When we met Erwin and Ruth in town the following afternoon for coffee and cake, the heat was so debilitating that even 32°C later in the evening was a welcome relief. By 9am the following morning, though, the temperature forecast for midday had already been ahead of itself. We had earmarked the day for visiting the Zentralfriedhof;[91] it was out of town and my mother assured me its many tree-lined avenues would make it a little cooler.

It was the Feast of Corpus Christi, one of the many Christian public holidays that the British tend to know little about but I remembered fondly from my schooldays in Catholic Bavaria. Perhaps that explained why our train to the cemetery in the suburb of Simmering was full of women carrying flowers, plants and garden tools in their bulging carrier bags.

To be truthful, I had come to dislike cemeteries intensely. Some of the history that can be found in them is fascinating, but the grief of loss stored in them still tended to get the better of me if I stayed in them too long. No doubt Oma's funeral had lot to do with that, but I suspect the real reason was the funeral of one of Robert's six-year-old classmates in Munich.

The boy's mother had just returned home from hospital after giving birth and was on her way to meet him from school with his new sibling. Seeing her coming, the excited little boy had rushed across the main road and straight into an oncoming car. The depth of his grief-stricken mother's suffering at his graveside had traumatised me, so cemeteries and I still did not mix well.

We'd been on the train for several minutes when my mother said,

---

91   Central Cemetery.

'When Grandmother died in 1942, Father had to walk all the way from Schweidlgasse. Jews weren't allowed to drive or use public transport without special permission related to forced labour. There was no other way of getting there, and he was the only family member anywhere near fit enough. I so hope he had a friend to accompany him…'

It was a few years since my mother had last been there with Elsa. When we went through the huge wrought-iron gate near the train stop, she realised that we had approached the cemetery from the wrong direction; we should have taken a tram instead of the railway. 'Damn, it's going to be a long walk!' she said.

Nothing could have prepared me for the scale of the place. In spite of hugging the shade, both of us were dripping with perspiration by the time we'd navigated our way to the Jewish sector. Unfortunately, my mother discovered that she'd also forgotten to bring Grandfather's 'address' with her. Even if she had, the area was so overgrown that it was almost impossible to identify the rows and where one grave ended and the next one began. As for identifying individual headstones, there was little chance except for some seriously ostentatious edifices!

The graves in the Christian sector were well maintained but this section was an unruly jungle. I was shocked, though my mother had seen this before. 'There's nobody left to come and look after them,' she said.

That made morbid sense – but what had happened to the voluntary initiative to tidy up the place that we'd heard about a while back? Maybe it had just been one of those feel-good-factor one offs to alleviate guilt? Or had we got the wrong end of the stick?

On her previous visit, my mother and Elsa had searched without finding their father's grave until, in desperation, Elsa had stood on a small mound and shouted: 'Father, where are you?'. Her eyes had immediately homed in on a grey headstone with the two hands, the symbol of the Kohanim[92].

Kohanim? I still had only a vague notion what that might signify but at least it gave me a better idea of what to look for – and if that failed, I could always try Elsa's trick again!

We were knee-deep in grass, weeds and ivy, trampling across other people's graves as we searched for my grandfather. It seemed disrespectful, and we both apologised repeatedly to those lying underfoot as we continued to feel our way along.

'Dawa, this really isn't doing you any good at all. You need to cool down.

---

92 Traditionally members of the Jewish priesthood prior to the destruction of the Second Temple in 70AD.

Don't you think we should just stand still under—'

'I've found him! There he is!'

'Where?'

'Over there, slightly to the right. It's not as overgrown as last time. Maybe it was Hilda – she did send me a photograph of herself tidying up.'

I wondered if Hilda had also been caught up in the wave of guilt-expunging enthusiasm. I didn't like my thoughts, but I was angry on so many counts. Then I checked myself as I remembered Hilda telling me how much she had loved Onkel, and how painful it had been during the war when she'd had to pretend not to know him as she passed him in the street.

It was 1941 when she was still only a schoolgirl of about eleven and had run up to Onkel, who was wearing the now-obligatory yellow *Judenstern*[93] on the left breast of his clothes. She'd expected to chat with him as she'd always done, but he had pleaded with her, 'Hildushka, please! You mustn't talk to me in public, you could all get into terrible trouble!'

'My God,' Hilda had said to us, 'those were such terrible times!'

The hands of the Kohanim were clearly visible at the top of the headstone, although thick ivy obscured most of the other inscriptions. Ripping it away took a while before I could stand back and take a good look – only to be taken by surprise all over again.

In between the Hebrew inscriptions that neither Dawa nor I could understand, I saw from the words in the Latin alphabet that not only my grandfather but also his father Samuel were buried there. I hadn't expected that, nor that Samuel's older twin brothers, Ignaz and Gideon, would be there too. Gideon was the father of the Pfeffergasse Löwenthals. The three brothers had been born in Kojetin, near Olomouc in Moravia.

'I have a photograph Elsa had of the three of them. I'll show it to you when we get home,' Dawa said.

I knew nothing about them, but neither had my mother known much until after Elsa's death. What she *did* know was that the original gravestone had been damaged during the Nazi era and Oma had paid for a new one when Grandfather died in 1947; after Dawa's death I even found the invoice for it.

A couple of months earlier, a client had offered us a cruise on one of their ships. One of the disembarkations was in Israel. I knew that Dawa had felt unusually at ease in Israel while I knew I had been there before,

---

93 Star of David, rather than the round yellow patch of the Middle Ages.

but I didn't realise that something had moved her to take a stone from the Dead Sea. Now she was rummaging through her shoulder bag before emptying its contents onto the grass. Finally, she admitted defeat and accepted that she had left the stone in England.[94]

We looked around for another stone before giving up when we couldn't find anything suitable. Wandering over to a less neglected area by the main path, we found a group of newer graves surrounded by short grass and gravelly soil. Stones! We pointed and laughed. Unfortunately, they had been placed on graves and were not just lying around. It was tempting, but we weren't about to raid another person's last resting place.

We embarked on what turned out to be quite a lengthy hunt, bending down, picking up and discarding stones for what seemed like an eternity, until eventually we found what we wanted.

My mother wrote her name on her stone and I followed her example. I wasn't certain whether this was a modern convention, but it was symbolic of the personal nature of what remained unspoken: 'Father, Grandfather, family, we are here *and* we remember you.'

Placing our stones carefully on the plinth we said in unison, 'Shalom.'

'Next time, I must bring the Dead Sea stone,' my mother said.

Ah, *next time*!

MORE OF MY MOTHER'S VIENNA

After an early morning start on our third day in town, we returned to the café near our hotel for coffee and a late-morning snack before braving the heat once more and setting out for the Prater – not the fairground but its extensive parklands.

This was the café where we had occasionally stopped on our way back to Oma's after an afternoon playing in the Stadtpark. I could clearly recall the sweet hot chocolate with a thick blob of freshly whipped cream. When we'd first gone in the previous day, we'd still been a little disorientated and it had taken us both a few minutes to recognise where we actually were. In our excitement we'd phoned Martin in England: 'Guess where we are!'

When we'd mentioned to the waitress that we used to come here some forty-five years ago, she'd told us that until recently the café had been owned by the same family for more than 120 years. My mother had already pointed out a lot of continuity to me that morning: the baker, the tailor, the ladies' clothes shop, the book shop, the shoe shop, the jewellery shop, this

---

94 Placing a stone on a Jewish grave is a custom with several supposed explanations.

café and that café, all of which were familiar. The successful confrontation with her past and that comforting continuity had persuaded her to take another step in revising her plans concerning Vienna, and she was now discussing the idea of renting an apartment for a few weeks – next time!

We tossed around the pros and cons of the idea, rather excited by the thought while fairly sure that Dawa would not be able to afford it. Then we went by underground to the Praterstern station that marked the main entrance to the Prater Park.

It was considerably cooler in the park, and we set out along the Hauptallee. The allée stretched into what seemed like infinity but my mother was on a mission, aiming for a lake called the Heustadlwasser. The breeze whispering through the leaves of the chestnut trees was magical, but I was not certain how she would cope after walking so much during the last two days. She, on the other hand, seemed unperturbed as she recounted memories of happy days and family outings. I wished that I'd had a tape recorder. Maybe she should write them down when we got home?

I heard about their domestic helper, who used to visit her boyfriend in a smoky pub when she was supposed to be taking my very young mother for a walk in the fresh air. Dawa was instructed in no uncertain terms not to *tell*, so my mother learned how to use blackmail to get her way.

'Dawa,' I protested. 'I had no idea you were so wicked!'

'Never underestimate children!' my mother laughed.

I heard of her visits to the Prater fairground with Toni as they detoured on the way to Schweidlgasse before my mother was old enough to walk there by herself. Her brother sometimes pretended to be a foppish gentleman so that she had had to rest her hand on his as he held it aloft and swaggered through the crowds. In fact, he'd been under strict instructions not to get separated from her, but holding her hand properly would have been far too embarrassing. He had loved to impress his kid sister with his prowess when he walloped the *Watschenmann* in the face, always trying to beat his previous best score on the slapometer!

'I thought Toni was wonderful, but with hindsight he was probably just letting off steam. He was never too keen on being my chaperone, let alone visiting Grandmother or the aunts. He was a young teenager and they were far too old and sedate for him. Poor Toni, he felt terribly guilty later on. He used to blush with embarrassment when he was asked to lead the prayer at table. Grandmother's household was a lot more *frumm*[95] than ours.'

Unlike Toni, who spent much of the weekends by his father's side developing insights as they explored the nature of man and the world around them, Dawa had loved taking turns with Elsa to spend alternate Saturdays with the aunts. She was about six years old when she'd been left to stay over for the first time after the family's Friday sabbath meal, but she had screamed and howled and created such a scene that they'd ended up taking her back home in a taxi.

After that, because she knew she had a choice, Dawa had come to look forward to staying with them. When she was ill at the age of seven and needed peace and quiet, she had spent even more time in their doting care. She'd had trouble sleeping but Tante Camilla had stroked her hand and calmed her down, then my mother had often dropped off to the sound of beautiful piano playing somewhere in the distance. She had felt as if she were in heaven.

The aunts had taken her to interesting places around town. When they walked through parks, Dawa was encouraged to take a closer look at the plants and flowers as the aunts expressed their own delight with '*schau, wie schön!*'.[96] Other times they took her to good restaurants and cafés. It seems Oma had wanted her children to learn to be comfortable with the more sophisticated and refined aspects of life – and who better to initiate them than the aunts who'd had the best academic education available to girls and even moved in aristocratic circles? There was another reason, too: teaching about life and appreciating nature's beauty had been the overarching motivation.

'Let's sit down for a while.' My mother motioned to the closest of the many benches lining the allée.

'Not long before the Anschluss, Tante Clara and Elsa were sitting on a bench here when one of those aristocrats and another woman came riding by on their horses. They were speaking in English and complaining about "those awful Jews". Poor Aunt, she understood every word and was *ganz niedergeschmettert*.[97]

'Later, after Hitler came, we Jews were forbidden to sit on most park benches. By the time I went to England, all public recreational areas were out of bounds. We children could get away with ignoring a lot of the

---

95 Righteous, observant.
96 'Look, how beautiful!'
97 Devastated.

Verboten[98] signs – we did it *justament*[99] – but for the adults it was another matter.'

Some Nazi apparatchiks had even marched a large group of Jews down to the Prater Park, forced them to their hands and knees before ordering them to eat the grass like a herd of animals. Others were made to do gymnastics for hours on end until they dropped with exhaustion.

'I thought we were lucky in Munich but, goodness, you were *so* lucky!' It just tumbled out and I could have kicked myself because my family had everything taken away in such a demeaning and tragic manner.

We had just reached the shore of the Heustadlwasser where the Löwenthal and Maly children used to mess about in the water while their parents sat at a table by the wooden kiosk and had their own version of fun.

'I could be such a little brat,' Dawa told me. 'Elsa and Toni always wanted to go off as a twosome, it was always a case of them and me, but I didn't want to stay with Hilda and Hubert because they were so young. I wanted to be with the older ones. Whenever I started howling, the owner of this kiosk used to give me a pastry or something to shut me up. Father once won a legal case for him and he was so grateful that we children were invited to clear the biscuits and sweets from their Christmas trees. There were always little presents hidden amongst them…'

She paused and slipped off somewhere else for a few moments before adding, 'I'm fairly certain that a number of grateful non-Jewish clients and friends must have helped out Mother and Father during the war.'

How I had needed to hear that!

'I think this is far enough for one day,' Dawa said. 'Let's go back and cut across to Lasallehof.'

How she could remember all the side streets was beyond me. By the time we reached our destination, I'd been shown at least half a dozen homes of former school friends, 'It was such a lovely group', as well as those from the 'Jewish club' she had joined after the Hitler Youth incident. Most of the boys and girls had vanished, never to return, and she didn't know what had happened to them. She knew that a couple had certainly got away to Peru or somewhere in South America.

Susi's parents were *Freidenker*.[100] 'That really appealed to me. They were such lovely people…'

---

98   Forbidden.
99   Out of defiance.
100 Freethinkers.

Dawa and Susi used to sit and chat in a large bay window that she pointed out to me, or they came down to play with the other children in the playground next to where we were standing. She had no idea what had happened to Susi and her parents; freethinkers or not, they were still Jewish.

Lasallehof resembled a huge rectangular fortress surrounded on all four sides by streets. The main entrance to its inner courtyards was on Lasallestrasse, a major road that led to the bridge over the Danube a couple of minutes' walk away. That entrance was much more imposing.

We passed through a quite humble archway in Vorgartenstrasse only a short distance across the road from what had been my mother's primary school. She was happy there, even though she hadn't been able to write properly until the age of nine and had been quite slow to learn. First, she had almost died of whooping cough; Oma had only kept her going by placing small drops of diluted honey under her tongue with a pipette. Then she'd become ill with rheumatic fever; not long after recovering from that, she had come down with Sydenham Chorea. One day she had kept pulling faces; nobody knew what was wrong with her until her arms and legs started to jerk uncontrollably as well. Her teacher had immediately sent for Oma.

Frau Rothansl, Stefanie Rothansl, was such a lovely woman and always so kind. I couldn't concentrate, nothing went in, I couldn't hold a pencil properly. The slightest stress was intolerable, I'd start howling or screaming about the silliest things and I developed a fearful temper. Just somebody moving past me in a hurry used to set me off. That's when the migraines started. Everyone had to be really careful around me. I know it affected poor Elsinko because she always thought Mother loved me more than her.

'Mother was wonderful, although I didn't really appreciate it at the time. I always nagged for something sweet, but all she gave me was a piece of fresh liquorice root to chew. I thought she was being really mean – but, oh, the Chaudeau[101] without the wine, I loved that. Oh, and lots of fish and fresh fruit and vegetables!'

Oma may not have known the biochemistry of it all, but she was definitely ahead of the game. As my mother spoke, I found myself mentally scanning the inside of her young body and observing the destructive inflammation that invaded her cells. Then I thought of my son, whose bout of meningitis at the age of eight changed his cognitive faculties and

---

101 Eggnog.

stress-coping mechanisms for years to come. I wished I had known then what I knew now.

'Where is everybody?' Dawa asked. 'It's so deathly quiet! It used to be so full of life...'

'Perhaps most women are out at work these days?' I offered.

My mother motioned to our left. 'The kindergarten was over there.'

When the weather was good, the children had played outside; that's where the photograph of her class was taken, in which she was pinching the boy next to her because he had dumped the skin from his hot chocolate into hers.

'I never tolerated any nonsense from anybody in those days. I had so much spirit back then. I think a lot of it drowned in the Channel in 1939.'

The library was housed in the same part of the building as the kindergarten. 'Elsa and Toni were always in there, but I couldn't have cared less – that came much later. This was our entrance. Just round here was our balcony... Mother made sure it was always full of beautiful plants. She grew some herbs, too.'

Looking up, I could envisage a young Oma tending her plants to the vibrant sounds of another era, before I returned to the silence around us.

'Is that where the photograph of Elsa was taken, the one with the spotted dress and headscarf?' Indeed it was, during the summer after they had moved in when Elsa was about three years old.

My mother had been born there almost as soon as their part of the complex was completed. Their neighbours were from all walks of life, yet my mother couldn't recall anybody caring who was what. Still, her father was always shown a great deal of deference which he had disliked intensely; it had made him feel uncomfortable.

'Imagine the dismay when Frau Dr. Löwenthal' – my mother emphasised the 'doctor' with a wicked little smile – 'was arrested during the uprising. *Die Schande!*'[102]

During the socialist uprising in 1934, fierce gun battles had raged all around them. Eventually the right-wing militia stormed the building in search of weapons. My mother had been absolutely petrified but Oma had chased after them, shouting, 'You thugs! She's an old woman, leave her alone. You'll frighten her to death!'

She'd tried to pull them away and prevent them from breaking down the door to the old lady's apartment just above them. Oma was charged

---

102 'The disgrace!'

with obstruction; my grandfather was appalled that his wife had put herself in such danger.

'But I think secretly he was very proud of her. She spent a week in prison. I found the whole affair very upsetting – I wasn't quite eight at the time. Mother always said it was one of the best times of her life, like being at university. She peeled potatoes with professors, a bit like Toni did when he was interned in the Isle of Man.'

Now my mother was really laughing: could they also have been peeling potatoes metaphorically, just as Toni had written of how much Aunt Ida had loved Father because the two had 'plucked chickens' together?

My grandfather had to sign for Oma's belongings when she was imprisoned, and he was shocked by the amount of money in her handbag. She was very careful with her housekeeping, always saving because she disliked being dependent. Maybe she was still holding on to her dream of a small allotment with a weekend hut? Later, when Jews were no longer permitted to continue in their professions, everybody had been very grateful for her secret stash!

So this was my Oma: not merely that warm, funny and kindly old lady I had loved so much but a fearless woman who had thumped her fist on the desk at the Gestapo headquarters.

Somebody had denounced Hedwa for permitting Hubert and Hilda to spend weekends with the lonely and deeply depressed aunts after my mother and Elsa had left. Hedwa had been too afraid to face the authorities herself, so Oma went in her stead. 'How dare you tell me who I can and cannot invite into my home!' she had thundered.

The young officer behind the desk had once been a school pal of Toni's. Recognising Frau Dr. Löwenthal, he eventually motioned to the door and said quietly, 'You may go.'

Later I learned of another young man, an unhappy enlisted soldier who had been a philosophy student. Oma had been kind towards him during a raid on their home. They had talked, and he had helped her by passing on warnings of upcoming raids.

In the afternoon, we joined Erwin and Ruth in their home for tea and a pastry treat for my mother: *Buchteln*. The buns were delicately sweet and as light as air. It was a perfect ending to an extraordinary few days.

When we returned to England my mother was exhausted but much relieved. For my part, there was a curious little voice whispering in my ear: 'There is more… There is more…'

Part 2

ONE

ARRIVING IN VIENNA AND LOOKING BACK

VIENNA, JUNE 2006

At last I can simply sit and breathe as I contemplate with some disbelief that finally I really *have* made it! The logistical gymnastics since taking possession of the keys to the apartment are over. Don has returned to England with my car and now, for the first time in my life, I will be living on my own. So will he.

But I am not afraid and I hope that neither is he. I am not a pathological loner even if independence and self-sufficiency have generally come fairly easily to me. To be honest, I am rather looking forward to having most of my time and energy to myself, unencumbered by the daily needs of others. Life is life, of course, and while no reasonably well-adjusted individual would seek to disconnect totally from social interactions, a little open-ended 'me' time will be beneficial – perhaps for both of us.

Not that either one of us will be able to empty our brains and float on a cloud of ether! Don has complicated house renovations to complete, but it's a creative project he's been anticipating with excitement. What's more, he has an element of obstinacy; as always, he will make something work that others have declared impossible. He is at his most vital when the creation also includes others he can enthuse to move beyond their perceived limits.

Before beginning the work *I* am about to embark on, I have to get to grips with the inner workings of a city that, apart from a deep psychological attachment and a limited geographic familiarity, is alien to me.

There is much I will have to learn just to keep my daily life afloat. There is a lot of research to complete, follow up on and expand. It is rather daunting when I stop to think about it, but I must keep faith that once the ball starts rolling everything will create its own momentum and somehow fall into place.

Last month, when I first took over the apartment, the weather was already warm; now it is early June and very hot. Ha! This is the Vienna I remember and love, so I have no complaints on that score! If this summer remains true to form, the few clothes I have brought with me will see me through to the end of the season.

It had been quite a challenge to fit everything into the car. Apart from my bedlinen, laptop, printer and several books, my most precious cargo was a dozen or so ring binders containing letters, box files filled with disconnected clues, and a selection of photographs.

The colour photograph of our son and daughter-in-law, taken at their wedding earlier this year, now has pride of place on a bookshelf in the sitting room and is mentally labelled 'the present'. The shelf below, 'the past', is dedicated to my mother and members of her family. The sepia photographs are from before the war. When I sit back in my armchair, which exudes a faint aura of the Orient, I can look at them as their faces peer at me from across the room.

I don't doubt that connecting daily with them, whether consciously or not, will lead me to wherever it is I need to go. If that sounds crazy – well, that's how the process works for me when the time is right. And the time has definitely come.

The ring binders and box files now live on a smart glass shelving unit beside a beautiful glass and chrome desk at the far end of my spacious bedroom, which will be my workstation for the next six months. My landlord is a young architect who lived here before relocating to New York and I suspect his profession goes a long way towards explaining the desk's minimalist extravagance.

On the other hand, several undeniably kitschy items hanging on some of the walls look out of place. Perhaps they are simply convenient space fillers to provide some colour on the wide expanse of white-painted plaster?

So much water has passed under the bridge since I toured my mother's Vienna back in the year 2000 that it is almost impossible to quantify the changes that have taken place not only within me, but also in my circumstances.

That trip revealed so many hidden aspects of my mother's life and my own background. After we returned home, Dawa continued to hand me more letters to read and by the end of my university break that summer I had read, transcribed and translated some sixty or so of them – and I seemed to have cried more than I had done in my entire life.

'Darling, if it's too painful, don't do it!' My mother's concern fell on deaf ears and I know that another part of her was very pleased that I *was* doing it. She wanted me to know; she wanted her story and the stories of those who could no longer speak for themselves to be heard. She wanted their benign influence to be recognised and their lives honoured so that they would not be consigned to oblivion as if they had never existed. Until recently, that had seemed to be their fate.

My mother could easily have decided that I already knew enough and pretended that there were no more letters, but she understood only too well the pernicious nature of unfinished business. Consequently there had been regular knocks on my office door: 'Sallienchen, here, I've found some more!'

The steady trickle of letters landing on my desk continued unabated until, by the time of her death three years later, the collection had already grown to well over two hundred documents. Then, when I eventually found the courage to sort through her possessions, I was astonished to discover even more. Much of the correspondence was dated between October 1938 and October 1942, but other letters had been written between 1945 and 1952, and some well into the 1960s.

Apart from the letters from my mother, her sister Elsa and her brother Toni that we had found here in Vienna more than three decades earlier, there were many that they had managed to preserve despite numerous relocations during the intervening years. The letters Elsa had received were found amongst her possessions after she died; Toni's were packed away in one of several boxes of personal correspondence, books, pre-WWII German art journals, as well as other documentation and press cuttings relating to Uncle Arthur. These had been left behind in 1965 when Toni and his family embarked on yet another new life in Canada.

The weeks before their departure had been fraught, not least because Toni was laid low with repeated infections in the stump of his amputated leg. Perhaps he had simply not found the time or energy to decide what to do with those unwelcome reminders of painful events.

When Toni returned for a brief visit to England a few years later, he did not retrieve them. Curiously, however, several times after his death - and independently of each other - both my mother and I heard the distinctive thud of his walking stick moving around the attic above our bedrooms. What, each of us had speculated, might he have been looking for?

When I finally assembled the many finds, I had letters from my mother's parents, the aunts Camilla, Clara and Paula, and even Uncle Arthur; there were also letters from Toni's, Elsa's and Grandfather's friends and extended family who had succeeded in fleeing to the USA, South America, Italy, China, Switzerland and Palestine.

There were school reports,[103] death notices, personal letters and postcards from the mid-nineteenth and early twentieth centuries, those comparatively halcyon years afforded by the constitutional freedoms that had begun with the Austro-Hungarian Empire's full emancipation of the Jews in 1867 before the black clouds of a new threat started to gather on the horizon in the early 1930s.

As a whole – and beyond persecution – they provided witness of decent and considerate human beings going about their lives with care and kindness and reflective intelligence.

Another unexpected find was an exercise book labelled '*Geschichte der Literatur*',[104] Elisabeth Löwenthal, Wien 6, Rahlgasse 4, 5a'. Inside, the schoolyear date was September 1937. The first half of the book contained some impressive work that I fancy would cause most of today's fourteen-year-old school pupils (at least, British ones) to blanche; the second half had been filled in reverse from the back cover, beginning on 13th May 1938.

It was the diary Elsa had kept secretly until shortly before her flight to England, and it revealed a young teenager's experience of fundamental loss. She was only one of so very many.

Deciphering the different handwriting had been challenging at times, as had been following some of the Austrian vernacular and colloquialisms. While my mother was still alive, I had often asked her to explain certain expressions and events to me. She always obliged and seemed pleased with my interest, but it was obvious that there were numerous letters she had

---

103   Great-grandfather Samuel and his twin brothers Ignaz and Gideon enjoyed a secular education at the Piarist grammar school in Olomouc/Moravia/CZ, where they were top-grade students. A few years after their father Wolf Löwenthal died on 9th September 1849 his teenage sons left home. Where Gideon went I do not know, but according to Elsa's diary Tante Camilla told her that Ignaz (16) and Samuel (14) arrived in Vienna with only their books and the clothes on their backs and had slept on 'boards'. How they survived is a mystery, but a college report attests to Samuel's Sunday attendance at public polytechnic lectures.
104   History of Literature.

not read since the time when they had been written. There were even some that Elsa, who was always concerned for the welfare of others, had not shown her so as to not cause her little sister even more heartache.[105]

As lost memories were dredged up for Dawa, they mingled with repressed emotions associated with more conscious memories. To make the experience even more overwhelming, as my mother re-read earlier letters from Vienna she was forced to re-evaluate some of her beliefs. 'I always thought Mother had given me away far too easily.'[106] she said.

I was faced with a dilemma that was compounded by an uncomfortable sense that time was short, so I continued working on the letters whenever I could while not involving my mother unless I found transcription or translation impossible.

Sometimes I only showed Dawa a word or sentence I was struggling with while covering up the rest. If she was curious and tried to read any further, I took the letter away and changed the subject.

I returned repeatedly to the translations, wanting to do full justice to the people who had written the documents, but that had consequences. I became absorbed in the letter-writers' inner worlds and I identified ever more closely with each of them in turn. What had begun as uncomfortable speculation eventually gave way to experiencing their deep loss.

Mass ignorance had colluded with the deluded egomania of a fanatical few to violate the soul of my mother, her entire family and the many millions of innocent human beings like them. Now that the veil of forgetfulness had been lifted, my soul, too, began to weep openly.

If that were not challenging enough, I was angry about the insidious way in which the past had affected *my* childhood and the childhoods of my brothers and cousins.

I determined that even though nothing could be done to change what had happened to those who had gone before me, I would do everything to soothe our family's collective subconscious. Our ancestors would be remembered as the warm flesh-and-blood human beings they had been, not just the jumble of meaningless names they were in danger of becoming. So began the first stage of my mission of rectification.

∗∗∗

---

105 Elsa even wrote to her ex-father in law asking him to be kinder to his ex-wife (her own ex-mother in law).
106 When they said goodbye Oma had put on a brave face to avoid causing her daughters even more lasting pain.

I was also determined to learn about that lost part of me called 'Judaism'. What did it signify?

I had been rather perplexed when my aunt Elsa had announced, 'There's an organisation for people like you.' but I was too busy to give the matter much thought. That was until about a year after my mother had moved in with my family and I joined her in her sitting room.

'What are you reading?' I asked.

'The *AJR Journal*'

'What's that?' I had never heard of it, let alone of the formal Association of Jewish Refugees. That was hardly surprising; not only had the pile of journals beside her armchair belonged to Elsa, but in spite of the Kindertransport reunion years earlier my mother had always kept both the 'Jewish' and the refugee part of her life very much to herself. At least, in front of me.

That day, when I read through the journal myself, I was impressed by the breadth and depth of some of the articles. However it was only later, when I read other editions, that I came across the organisation Elsa had referred to as being for 'people like me': The Association for Children of Jewish Refugees.

Curious, but in the dark as to what I might encounter, I made contact and soon found myself boarding a coach for a visit to the Beth Shalom Holocaust Centre near Nottingham. Most of my fellow travellers were members of the surrounding North London Jewish communities so many of them knew each other or had contacts in common. They exchanged family and school gossip, discussed community events and upcoming holy days, often spattering the conversations with an 'in-speak' that was alien to me.

Curious to learn what being Jewish was really about, I persevered and accepted an offer to attend a Passover seder. My mother merely watched me and said nothing.

My seder hosts were members of the ACJR who had volunteered to help those 'like me' to start reconnecting to Jewish life. They were very welcoming, even if their other guests seemed rather unsure of this visitor from another realm. To be honest, no matter how welcoming they might have been, I would still have felt like an intruder at a private party. How could it have been otherwise? I was a stranger in a well-established group, knowing almost nothing of the historical event that was being remembered and not understanding the symbolic acts and tentative Hebrew readings,

More importantly, the outer rituals of the Seder itself failed to touch me.

My curiosity took a beating and I put it on the back burner - until I stumbled into territory that resonated with me.

The members of the Second Generation Network were immediate descendants of Jewish refugees from Nazi persecution or of concentration camp survivors. It was a much more diverse group compared with the one I had encountered through my exposure to the ACJR. There were those who had been brought up by two Jewish parents in varying degrees of religious conservatism or liberalism, but there were also those who were secular, or with mixed backgrounds like mine and far removed from any overt Jewish influences. There were even those who hadn't known about their Jewish or refugee backgrounds until well into middle age, when their lives and everything they had previously held to be true had been replaced with new knowledge that had brought considerable inner turmoil.

What we had in common, though, was a deep desire to connect with others who might understand that frustrating sense of a void demanding to be filled.

I didn't gain much from the substance of the gatherings, but I did make some new acquaintances who have accompanied me as I began exploring the past. We are not bosom pals but we understand one another where others could not, and for that I am grateful. I am also grateful that our meetings took place at the Wiener Library where there is a wealth of learning about all aspects of the Holocaust.

With it, my fascination with the multi-dimensional web of cause-and-effect found yet another stimulus and I grabbed it as if my life depended upon it. Even though I was working hard for my university degree, I somehow found the time to attend lectures, seminars and conferences at the Wiener Library, the Leo Baeck Institute, and other venues in central and north London.

I also discovered a diverse range of stimulating literary and artistic events at the Jewish Cultural Centre in Hampstead to which my mother (and often Don) happily accompanied me. Through these, I sensed that my mother was finally rediscovering an environment that resonated deeply with her inner world.

One day, following a talk about the Romanian artist and former Jewish slave labourer Arnold Daghani, I contacted the art historian presenter. Dr. Deborah Schultz invited the three of us to take a closer look at the large body of Daghani's work held at the Centre for German Jewish Studies at

Sussex University. A little later I was invited to join her and the Centre's director, Professor Edward Timms, on a field trip to the Felix Nussbaum Haus[107] in Osnabrück. It was a haunting experience.

Together with German and Austrian Jewish refugees, I was soon regularly attending events related to Jewish experiences during the Nazi era hosted by the professor. My mother was curious enough to join me a couple of times, but she soon became bored with the emphasis on academic research that she thought contributed nothing to changing the average human psyche.

While a stimulating new dimension to my own education was opening up for me, for Dawa skirting around the edges of a community of 'people like her' gradually brought home what she had lost: the support of a community connected by a common background of ethics and learning, and also by a trauma that those who had not experienced it could never understand.

She wanted to reconnect. She began to notice announcements about regular and more local get-togethers organised under the auspices of the AJR. There she met Gerda who, it turned out, lived only a short bus ride away. The once-a-month afternoon teas included interesting talks and musical performances, but for my mother they also provided a deeply comforting dimension: a physical reunion in the shared Jewish essence.

It also gave Dawa a chance to do what came naturally to her and help those who could not help themselves. After she'd retired from nursing, and before she came to live with my family, she had sometimes stepped in to support people who were struggling on their own; now she became an AJR volunteer.

With a new sense of purpose, her sparkle returned as she took a bus once or twice a week to spend a few hours with an elderly Austrian refugee who lived alone and was mostly housebound. I gave her lifts whenever I could, so I was introduced to her new acquaintances, and little by little my mother opened up - about other people's experiences. For me, it marked the beginning of a steep and deeply moving learning curve.

There was something else too. 'Why is it,' Dawa once asked with a mischievous twinkle in her eyes, 'that relatives who rarely – if ever – lift a finger suddenly start worrying about their inheritances?'.

---

107 Felix Nussbaum, German Jewish surrealist painter born 11th December 1904 in Osnabrück, Germany. Nussbaum was murdered in Auschwitz sometime between 20th September 1944 and 27th January 1945. His paintings are housed in the Nussbaum Haus, a purpose-built museum designed by architect Daniel Libeskind.

Part Two ~ Chapter One

***

2002: ANOTHER DOOR OPENS

My mother had spent the morning getting very hot and dusty in my overcrowded loft as she emptied yet another one of those many cardboard boxes in which she'd been finding so much she had forgotten. Now she was really excited. 'Look what I've come across!'

This time it was a collection of old English newspaper cuttings together with a whole page from a 1932 edition of a Berlin daily newspaper. The cuttings were records of various exhibitions of her Uncle Arthur's work as a sculptor and medallist, while the whole page contained a lengthy article about a sumptuous two-handled crystal cup called the *Dionysos Kristall* that had been sculpted by the artist Artur Löwental.[108]

The occasion had made the headlines when the patron who had commissioned the work presented it to the City of Berlin; now, seventy years later, I was reading about it.

Ironically, had Arthur completed the piece just one year later I might never have learned about it. The City of Berlin would never have accepted the gift and there would have been no reports about its existence because the Nazi regime and its followers didn't like to recognise the achievements of Jews, no matter how assimilated or secular they were.

Two years after being fêted in the press, Arthur and his wife, Ida, left Berlin and arrived in Britain on 20th November 1935.

'Don't worry, leave most things here. It will all blow over in a few months!' his friendly admirer Herr Krupp[109] had advised. The same Herr Krupp who, as a participant in the symbiotic dark arts of self-interest and hunger for power (or, as US President Eisenhower later expressed in his retirement speech, *'the dangerous influence of the military-industrial complex within the halls of political power'*) had been bankrolling Adolf Hitler's NSDAP.[110]

What I didn't know when we found the newspaper cuttings was that, according to John Turner's research, Arthur returned to Berlin on more than one occasion after leaving Germany and was able to retrieve a number of his smaller works and valuables. He even paid a short visit to Vienna after the Anschluss.[111] Presumably these trips were facilitated

---

108 Arthur preferred to omit the *h* following the t in his first and surname.
109 Industrial magnate and arms manufacturer.
110 National Socialist Democratic Workers Party/Nazi.
111 Germany's Annexation of Austria.

by his connections in high places and his Czech passport; following the dissolution of the Austria-Hungarian Empire in 1918, he and Aunt Ida had declined Austrian citizenship in favour of that of his parents' birthplace, newly independent Czechoslovakia.

After the end of WWII, Arthur made renewed attempts through official channels to retrieve his many personal artworks, valuable books and collectors' items that he hoped were still in occupied Berlin, though I don't know whether he succeeded.

The newspaper cuttings opened an unexpected door. Over the following months, I tracked down a large body of Arthur's work in European museums, including many in Berlin and Vienna. Serendipity and goodwill became my companions as the curators gave generously of their time; Wolfgang Steguweit, the Chief Curator of the Numismatic Collection of the National Museums of Berlin, who knew nothing of Arthur's life and career in England, deserves my special thanks for his empathy and continuing personal engagement.

After my mother's death, I found a copy of an article published in the March 1932 edition of the German art magazine *Der Kunstwanderer* dedicated to the Dionysos Cup and its creator. It gave a detailed description in Arthur's own words of the complex technical process involved in engineering the tools for shaping the cup out of one piece of rock crystal and engraving the classical Greek bacchanalian scene in relief upon it. There were photographs of the remarkable end result – and yet, despite my lengthy investigations, the cup itself remained elusive. Eventually I conceded that either this masterpiece had been destroyed during the wartime bombing of Berlin or, like countless other works of art, had disappeared as part of war booty.

If it is still safe, perhaps it will come to light again one day. I hope that will be sooner rather than later so that I can enjoy it – and perhaps even see it returned to Berlin.

I started to focus my attention on learning more about the efforts to rescue Jewish children from Nazi-controlled Germany and Austria. Soon I became dissatisfied with pared down second-hand accounts and decided to go straight to source - primary research.

At the London Metropolitan Museum, the archivist specialising in Nazi-era Jewish affairs (whose name I have regrettably forgotten) was very generous with his time. Apart from numerous other documents, I also read through eighteen months of minutes of meetings of the executive of the Council for German Jewry from 15th March 1938 onwards. I was shocked by the horrific hardships that Jews born (or long-term residents) in Austria had been exposed to so suddenly after the Anschluss three days earlier. I was equally in awe of the ongoing efforts of the Jewish elite of different religious and secular hues in Britain and America to assist and try to rescue all Jews and non-Aryans of mixed Jewish and gentile backgrounds. Their engagement on behalf of the long-resident but now disenfranchised Polish Jews in Germany and Austria, who had been forced in their thousands across the border into Poland with nowhere to go, was deeply moving.

It was a lesson in united purpose. For the first time I came across Lord Bearsted, occasional chair of the executive, and Lord Reading, chair of the executive of the Movement for the Care of Children from Germany.

MRS EMANUEL

Four months before she died and only weeks before her last dark night of the soul overwhelmed her, my mother wanted to accompany me to Sussex University for their Holocaust Memorial Day presentation: 'You never know, perhaps I might just bump into Ralph Emanuel!'

That's when I learned that Mrs Emanuel had immediately been very welcoming when she and Elsa arrived in Hove, and had invited the two girls to attend a Seder in her home a few days later. The Emanuel family as a whole had been very kind and now, if possible, Dawa hoped to tell their son Ralph, who had been about the same age as her, how deeply grateful she had always felt.

It was not to be. For the first (and only) time my car's engine overheated just half an hour into our journey to Sussex and we had to be towed to our local garage before being taken home in the pick-up truck. The Emanuels, who had neither faces nor stories attached to them, faded into the background of the whirlwind of my life.

Several months after my mother's death I came across two letters Dawa and Elsa had written to Vienna on 3rd April 1939. They describe a lively and enjoyable Seder at the Emanuels' home, and also the most beautiful Friday and Saturday liberal synagogue services they had ever attended. Mrs Emanuel, an orthodox Jew, had organised these at the request of another person whose name Elsa did not recognise. The letters showed the extent of the welcome the girls received into their new world and hinted at a wider network in action in which Mrs Emanuel had taken centre stage in Hove.[112]

A few months later I received an e-mail from the Centre for German Jewish Studies. It had inadvertently included their entire mailing list, and within a second my eyes homed in on the name Emanuel.

Following another one of those 'are you by any chance' e-mails, I had lunch with Ralph and his wife, Muriel, at their home in north London's Hampstead. Each was a true Mensch; it is difficult to imagine two more delightful, kind, generous and intelligent human beings. Sadly Muriel died soon afterwards, but Ralph and I have remained in touch and I have begun to appreciate even more what has been lost.

***

Two years after Dawa's death and only a few weeks before what would have been Elsa's eighty-second birthday on July 21st, I had felt moved to ask my second cousin, Luda's granddaughter Katja, to translate a letter Elsa had written in Czech to her mother in Vienna on 22nd July 1939.

> *Dearest Maminko!*
> *Thank you so much for your dear letter and good wishes. I also got your lovely chocolates which made me very happy. Miss Hawkins gave me a powder compact and took me to the cinema and afterwards we dined in a restaurant.*
>
> *Miss Beard knitted a grey-blue pullover for me. Mrs B. sent me a little handbag made of silk and with beads.*
>
> *One of the ladies who likes me very much gave me a leather writing case with a zip. Another one a box of chocolates, and so on.*

---

[112] After my stay in Vienna, I re-read a letter Toni had sent from London to his father on 10th January 1939. He reported that Uncle Arthur had not only been making enquiries with many prominent people about how he could best help his brother and family get out of Austria, but that he had also visited a well-known rabbi who had promised to do what he could for Elsa and my mother. Two weeks later Toni wrote that Arthur had received a telephone call from a Mrs Mattuck to inform him of two placements if Grandfather agreed that the girls would be accommodated separately – and if they agreed not to reclaim them if they came to Britain later. Only then, with my wider knowledge, was I able to put two and two together. Mrs Mattuck was the wife of Britain's first Liberal Rabbi, Israel Isidor Mattuck. He had helped form the union of Liberal and Progressive Synagogues and the World Union of Progressive Judaism; he was also the Chairman of the Society of Jews and Christians and the author of several books on aspects of Judaism. Evidently Mrs Mattuck was helping coordinate the various local rescue committees that had sprung up in Britain. Neither their name nor the 'well-known' rabbi could have meant anything to my mother when she read the letters some six decades later. What Elsa knew, I cannot say.

> *Mr Beddington wanted to take us out in London, but Mrs B. is so ill that he can't leave her. She has cancer and the doctors say there is no hope. But Mr B., and we too, hope she will get better.*
>
> *This Saturday we will be going to London with Miss Hawkins, we are invited to Aunt and Uncle for Tea. Toni has not been to visit because the weather has been awful.*
>
> *Yesterday, we had a garden party. It was the first time that Mr B. didn't come. He wrote a letter which was pinned on a board in the hallway in which he said how sorry he was not to be able to come and see his 'two little daughters'. On this day they bring out a very large silver bowl into which each lady puts a rose. At the end, one of the trustees called out 'and now our children' and everyone started to clap. The party itself I found very boring, but the food was delicious.*
>
> *I had a pair of new court shoes on which were uncomfortable because I am only used to wearing sandals. I was very tired, everyone came to look at us, so we had to smile at everyone. The Mayor of Brighton was also there, a funny little chap with tiny eyes and an enormous mayoral chain around his neck with lots of medals on it.*
>
> *I sent a card to Luda for his birthday. In one of the theatres, they performed a play by Karel Capek. It had very good reviews.*
>
> *With all my love and greetings, your Elsa*
> *I include a photo of Miss B. and me.*

'How remarkable that you should call us just as we are going through our archives and files to put together a history of Dresden House!' the current manager of the establishment marvelled. On researching, they had found an entry in the minutes of meetings of the board of governors of Dresden House in which was noted a request by the lady residents to offer sanctuary to one or two Jewish girls from Nazi Germany. Apart from a request made considerably later to the board of governors for financial assistance for Elsa's education, they had not been able to put the wider story together.

'Perhaps you would like to join us for our very special "Day of the Rose" in a couple of weeks' time?' the manager asked.

Everything about the day was as Elsa had described it, including the food. As I was shown around the extraordinary place, I recognised the rooms, facilities and layout just as Dawa had described them – even though they were a little tired.

When I was taken through the glass-panelled hallway that joined the two rows of houses on either side of the croquet lawn and gardens, I glanced at a notice board; pinned to it was a photograph of Dawa and Elsa sitting on the grass in the countryside. The girls had sent a copy home to Vienna (which was now in my possession) to show what a good time they were having. The photograph had been found in an office drawer in Dresden House; nobody knew who the girls were, but they had put the photograph on display anyway.

Seven months later, the non-denominational Dresden House retirement home for ladies in reduced circumstances, founded in 1911 by a female cousin of Reginald Beddington, closed down forever. The Georgian villas that made up the complex have since been restored to the individual sophisticated residences they had formerly been.

IAN, FORMERLY KNOWN AS HANS

Ian, formerly known as Hans, was another refugee who was forced out of a world that had exercised a lifelong influence upon him.

Witty, articulate, erudite, this incorrigible lover of women, poet and political animal became not only my good friend but in some respects my mentor. Despite him being thirty years my senior, we seemed to understand each other without the need for words.

We met at Sussex University some years ago. Three months before I left for Vienna, we arranged to meet there for our usual coffee and an overdue catch-up before attending a seminar. On the day, out of character and disturbingly unavailable on his mobile phone, Ian failed to turn up.

Like my mother, Hans had fled Vienna in 1939 but, unlike her, he had never been a registered member of the Jewish community; on the contrary, he had once been a devout Catholic. His mother came from a secular Jewish family, while his father's lineage was 'Aryan' Catholic; it was only shortly before Hans was due to start primary school that his Freethinker parents began to consider what religion he and his younger brother should be affiliated to. In those days, that could still mean the difference between acceptance through conformity versus outsider status.

Hans' parents were not only Freethinkers, they were also activists in the post-WWI Social Democratic Party before it ripped itself into factions of doves and hawks and every hue in between. Adolf Hitler's Jew-blaming and Jew-hating National Socialism infiltrating from across the border may have been the reason why, at the age of six, Hans and his younger brother were christened into the Catholic Church.

Later, at his Piarist grammar school where pupils of all denominations enjoyed a famously rigorous academic education, Hans fell under the influence of some proselytising Jesuit teachers. The once enthusiastic 'Red Falcon'[113] voluntarily turned his back on Karl Marx and became a passionate apostle in a Jesuit youth movement whose aim was to promote moral conduct through the veneration of the Virgin Mary.

His devotion to the Jesuit cause was rewarded when he was chosen to participate in a group confirmation led by Vienna's Archbishop Cardinal Theodor Innitzer. He also enjoyed another distinction: Austrian federal chancellor Dr. Dollfuss became the confirmed group's godfather.

Hans was not alone in this metamorphosis: his Jewish mother and her parents also converted to Catholicism. According to him, this had been another act of well-considered pragmatism.

Over the next few years the adults wore their new pious coats very publicly. No doubt they felt certain that they, much like the Marranos[114] in the Iberian Peninsula, had done the right thing to maintain their material security and physical safety. Little did they suspect they were about to be outmanoeuvred by the Nazi regime.

As the Austrian Social Democratic party tore itself into shreds of extreme and often violent disagreement, Hans' parents left the party and in 1933 joined devout-Catholic Dollfuss's newly created non-partisan Fatherland Front movement instead. But that dream also remained just that: a dream.[115]

Hans' Catholicism only helped him in one small way after the Anschluss when the Nazi Nuremberg Race Laws of 1935 rendered him a first-degree half-caste[116]; technically he was tolerated and not subject to the many restrictions applied to a 'full-blooded' Jew.[117]

The reality turned out to be not so straightforward. In common with all 'full-blooded' Jewish children who had not already dropped out or

---

113   Member of the Social Democrats' children's movement that was dissolved by decree by the Dollfuss government.
114   The name given to those Jews of Spain and Portugal who converted to Christianity either voluntarily or by Catholic Royal coercion during the fifteenth and sixteenth centuries, but who continued - as best they could - to practise their religion in secret.
115   Dollfuss was assassinated on 25th July 1934 during a failed putsch attempt by Austrian Nazis.
116   An individual with two Jewish grandparents but not a registered member of the Jewish community.
117   An individual with two Jewish parents, or with two Jewish grandparents and a registered member of the Jewish community.

been expelled from their primary and secondary schools, academically precocious Hans soon found his high marks falling no matter how well he performed or how hard he studied.

These children were never going to be academically good enough to remain in mainstream Aryan schools - although, as first-degree half-castes, boys like Hans *were* eligible for conscription into the Nazi military machine.

When we first met, he had described his and his brother's flight from Vienna as a 'do-it-yourself-Kindertransport'. I didn't ask for details at the time; for some reason I sensed his discomfort and knew not to. Later, I understood why.

I discovered during my research in the IKG archives that Hans, together with many others with half-caste status, had fallen foul of the Jewish Community rescue committee's rules which stated that they could only directly assist registered community members who had been declared non-citizens in their own country. Instead, the Quakers had stepped in to help many children in his unenviable position.

Hans' mother obtained a visa for England by securing employment as a domestic worker; his father remained in Vienna, believing optimistically (much like the once-deluded Herr Krupp) that common sense would soon prevail. He was proved very wrong.

Exactly five years to the day after sixteen-year-old Hans fled Vienna from the Westbahnhof, he finally returned to Continental Europe, this time as a tank crew member called Ian. He took part in the 7th Armoured Division's invasion of Nazi occupied France, (the Normandy Landings) on 6th June 1944.

By the time the war in Europe ended in May 1945, his beloved grandmother, who had played an important hands-on role in his happy childhood, had been deported and murdered in Terezin concentration camp.

As with many people of mixed parentage where others sought to decide who was what, Ian's sense of identity and belonging took a battering from which he never fully recovered. In many respects it is hardly surprising; as a child he had known nothing of the politics of power and survival and, as he put it, he had been a very late starter in finding his own mind and passions.

No doubt his Freethinker parents would have been happy to know that he finally found his more authentic self in a safer world; sadly, however, his many sorrows and their almost frantic displacements caught up with him three months ago when he suffered a catastrophic stroke.

Now my friend is lying in a hospital bed back in England. He can think but cannot move, can communicate only with great difficulty, and has little prospect of ever recovering his physical faculties. For him it is an emotionally painful end to a troubled life; he has no means of feeding his ever-curious mind or dissipating his inner tensions with the many activities with which he has always filled his days.

'The only place I ever felt at home was during my war service with the Hussars,' Hans confided in his daughter. All for one and one for all.

THE NOOSE TIGHTENS

In May 1938 the marks for Elsa's schoolwork had begun to be downgraded. Dismissed Jewish school teachers continued to do their best in hastily organised makeshift classrooms in a Jewish orphanage. It was then that my aunt recorded in her diary: *My[118] is already going to a special school.*

A few days later on 1st June, as the noose continued to tighten, she wrote:

> On Sunday I was at Granny's. Suddenly the phone rang and I ran into the kitchen to call Aunt. She came and as soon as she picked up the receiver I could hear (I was standing in the doorway) continuous talking. Poor Aunt Camilla tried in vain to push her bonnet away from her ear. She whispered her cautious 'Pardon?' a couple of times and then it suddenly went quiet. All she could make out was 'Staffel R40, Herr Dr. should stay at home today'. I had to put my coat on and rush home. My poor mother got a terrible fright, as did Father* but he hadn't wanted to show it, so he said in the jolliest of voices 'Let them come and get me, but first I have to eat my fill.' In the afternoon he quickly went and put his things in order. But nothing happened, nor the next day.

Then Elsa added: *Because they arrested about 90 lawyers on Saturday

Somebody somewhere must have been on his side because Grandfather had certainly had a very narrow escape. A short while later another several hundred 'undesirables' were herded onto trains and delivered to hard-labour prison camps in Germany, which were soon to morph into the mass death camps we now know so much about. The Nazi regime had started establishing these extensions to the penal system immediately

---

118 Nickname for Dawa.

upon coming to power in Germany in 1933 – including at Dachau.

Any optimism Grandfather harboured that civilised behaviour would prevail soon disappeared. He recognised that he would have to go with the flow, though he clung to the hope that the situation would improve. Meanwhile he had to face reality. Upon Hitler's accession to power in Germany, antisemitic Austrian Nazi sympathisers had already begun flexing their aggressive muscles on Vienna's Jews, laying the groundwork for what was to come.

Now that Austria had been incorporated into Gross Deutschland (Greater Germany) the full force of the Nazi regime's propaganda machine, the disenfranchisement and the violence that came with it was unleashed upon the Jews with the destructive speed of molten lava. Grandfather had to consider following in the footsteps of not only his brother Arthur but of tens of thousands of German Jews who had already been forced to look around for sanctuary abroad – and he needed to do it quickly.

Unfortunately, even if he'd had the private means to assure his family's independent livelihood in a foreign country, the Nazi regime forbade the transfer abroad of any Jewish-held financial assets.

There was also the issue of another country's self-preserving domestic economic policies to consider, policies that had to recognise the fear of stolen jobs and any number of antisemitic biases prodded to the fore by right-wing organisations and their counterparts in the media. Grandfather's expertise in Austrian law would have been useless in another country's legal system, so what work could he do – or would he be allowed to do – and who would offer him a job if he didn't speak the language well enough?

But those were not the only aspects of Grandfather's dilemma. Many Jews did leave their elderly relatives behind with the pragmatic, if distressing, rationalisation that the younger generation must be given the opportunity to continue to live a meaningful and safer life[119] – and perhaps find the means to bring out their older relatives later on. But since he had not been entirely erased from everyday life by incarceration or forced expulsion, how could he voluntarily choose to leave his ninety-year old mother and his two unmarried and ageing sisters to fend for themselves now that every other relative was scrambling to get away?

---

119   I have wondered whether the decision to send their children abroad might in part have been a throwback to the once not unusual Ashkenazi Jewish practice of sending children to other Jewish communities to further their education or vocational skills.

Grandfather found himself in an impossible position but at least he could use every ounce of his energy to ensure his children's safety by whatever means possible until the current political circumstances turned around.

Elsa's diary 7th September 1938

My is causing us great heartache. She's now attending the emigration school. Aunt Clara is crying her eyes out. To send such a child away, when she's so sensitive and so very attached to her mother.

According to my mother, Grandfather was never a political or religious nationalist. As far as he was concerned 'Tomorrow Israel' was a metaphor. But now, despite his family's diligent commitment over the generations to being fully assimilated, loyal and responsible Austrian citizens, he had little choice but to enrol my twelve-year old mother in the Zionist Youth Aliyah movement.[120]

Unaware of any undercurrents, my mother enjoyed her days spent at her 'club' so much that she happily participated in Hachshara (preparation/training) for eventual physical Aliyah (emigration) to Palestine.

Dawa never forgot the young men and women who cared so enthusiastically for her and other sometimes exceptionally traumatised children. In the 'club' they rediscovered, even if only temporarily, some light-heartedness and optimism.

'We regained our self-confidence after having suddenly become such a filthy word,' she said. Besides, compared to what was happening in Austria, the bright picture of the new communal life awaiting them on a kibbutz in Erez Israel (Land of Israel) was quite irresistible – for a while.

During the summer of 1938, for reasons nobody could have anticipated, life also became complicated for Toni. His birth in Popovice had only been registered with the secular authorities, and there was no documentary evidence that he had been circumcised as a Jew – because he hadn't been.

I don't know why, though an incident shortly after his birth might have something to do with it. During an 'open day' to celebrate the birth of her first child and to introduce him to the villagers of Popovice, Oma had caught a local peasant woman trying to unfasten her baby's clothing. Supposedly the woman had said, 'They say that Jewish men have devil's tails and I've never seen one before.' Or, perhaps, had Grandfather been a

---

120 A metaphor for building upon experience in order to do things better tomorrow, Aliya (spiritual ascent), had become a necessary physical construct at a time when few were prepared to help the Jews of Europe.

quiet freethinker?

Unfortunately for Toni, who had never been in any doubt that he was one of 'we Jews', his new status as a first-degree half-caste had rendered him liable for the unthinkable: the military came knocking at his door.

They don't want to accept him as a Jew, Elsa wrote in her diary, though I don't know whether she was referring to the IKG or to the German authorities. The need to leave Austria had suddenly become urgent and Toni had to leave without delay – but how and where to?

With no prospect of obtaining a visa, let alone a resident's permit in another country without evidence that he had the means to support himself, appeals were made to Uncle Arthur to help.

Three years earlier, the written support of influential benefactors in England, together with his prominence as a respected artist with connections in the highest places in Germany, had eased Arthur's way into Britain. In 1938, when visas had become mandatory, he extended a formal invitation for Toni to live with him and Aunt Ida; he also guaranteed his nephew's expenses until Toni was granted a work permit or found sanctuary in America – if he succeeded in joining the list of restrictive Jewish refugee quotas in the first place.

In the meantime, Toni started taking English lessons from one of his tutors, Eduard Wimmer-Wisgrill, at Vienna's School of Applied Arts, though by his own admission he didn't do very well. The celebrated designer Wimmer-Wisgrill had previously lived and worked in New York; aware that his Jewish students would have to leave sooner or later, he hoped to leverage his influence to their benefit as best he could.

After navigating seemingly endless bureaucratic hurdles deliberately put in the path of the Jewish émigrés, Toni finally departed for London with a personal reference and a letter of introduction from his tutor to possible employers.

Elsa's diary, Vienna Sunday 11th September 1938

Anton left an hour ago. He received his visa the day before yesterday, after he and Father had already queued up from the evening before. He was given a suit with long trousers and a new hat. The fuss the aunts made of him was deeply touching. Yesterday we paid a good-bye visit to the Löwenthals.[121] They gave Tony 5RM. He immediately said to me 'you can have them, after all, I have no use for them now'. Poor father looks terrible. Now that he has succeeded in getting his only son out, he has no

---

121 Karl, Rosalie and Cäzilie in Pfeffergasse.

purpose left. I acted all bright and cheery and was determined not to cry. Father went to fetch a taxi and then came the most unpleasant moment. I had wanted to say good-bye to him laughing so as not to cause him even more heartache. But he had already been over to My and I could hear her throwing up behind the curtain. Every bit of resolve just disappeared. Then he approached me with tears in his eyes and, although trying desperately hard, only managed an awkward smile. As fast as I could I told myself 'but he will be better off in London', yet as he stood there before me with that hat that was far too new, only one thought took over: now you won't see him for a very, very long time. He kissed me in silence. We didn't say a single word. I quickly turned away and disappeared into the bedroom. Then I turned to Miky[122] who was still howling and we felt so embarrassed that we started to laugh. Miky immediately went into Toni's deserted room to see what he had left behind.

While Elsa was determined to be stoic in the face of her brother's departure, my mother had discovered a survival mechanism that would see her through almost to the end of her days: transformation by returning to the present moment through humour and light-hearted displacement. 'I couldn't stop vomiting... What else was I supposed to do?'

On his stopover at the German border at Aachen on 12th September 1938 Toni posted a card to his family back home.

Dear Father,
Please give my love to everybody, especially to little Kamilla.
I have arrived safely here in Aachen. We have just had the customs check and shall be leaving again at 9am for Ostend, where I should be arriving at 10.20am. That's why I must now send a telegram to Uncle. Love and kisses to you and everybody else, Your Toni.

THE SCRAMBLE TO GET AWAY

Toni was gone. Elsa was still clinging to hope of going to live with Aunt Blazena's family in Czechoslovakia but plans for my mother's escape abroad had just been dashed: she was not included on the first Youth Aliyah transport to Palestine as had been expected.

Nobody had really wanted her to go but it seemed the only option to get her to safety and some semblance of a meaningful life within a community environment based upon the Jewish ethos of mutual care.

---

122   Another nickname for Dawa.

Now, as the departure date came closer, my mother was told she would not be going after all.

Perhaps to soften the blow, she was told that Aunt Clara had intervened, saying that my mother's migraines and the Mediterranean heat would be detrimental to her health. In fact, while the Youth Aliyah movement was originally founded in Berlin immediately after Hitler's rise to power, its intention was to provide a means of emigration to Palestine for teenagers between the ages of fifteen to seventeen. Since Palestine was a British protectorate and did not make it easy for Jews to immigrate, the British government had refused to extend visas to unaccompanied children below the age of fifteen.

Dawa was relieved to know that she would be staying home in Vienna. However, towards the end of her life she reflected, 'I should have gone to a kibbutz, it would have been so much better for me.' Perhaps.

Meanwhile, after several months of worsening school grades, unpleasantness and even outright intimidation by some classmates, Elsa and her fellow Jewish pupils were officially excluded from mainstream education.[123]

The scramble to escape was gathering momentum, so much so that when an offer was made by friends of friends in France to take Elsa in as an 'au pair', there was an interview between Grandfather, Elsa and a go-between at the Jewish community's emigration headquarters.

Elsa confided in her diary that she probably hadn't given a particularly self-assured account of herself; whatever the reason, something hadn't gelled because the idea was soon shelved. Instead, all hopes came to rest on her going to live with Aunt Blazena's family in Czechoslovakia. If official permission could be obtained, she would be able to continue her grammar school education to the end within a family environment. It seemed a good solution: after all, Elsa was bilingual, knew her relatives well and loved her mother's homeland that was only a stone's throw away.

Aunt Blazena's husband, Uncle Josef, was not only steeped in politics but also had connections in the local government of their home town of Hradec Kralove. Surely he could navigate a way around the complex bureaucracy on Elsa's behalf? Yet when he'd done everything he could, the bureaucratic wheels still continued to turn at a frustratingly slow pace prompting Elsa to shout despairingly in her diary: *'I don't know what's*

---

123 One of Elsa's teachers tried to be helpful by suggesting she might consider converting to Christianity; she appeared to have had no understanding of the current racial context.

going to happen to me ... I can't get away from here ...'.

Their hopes were dashed soon after Toni's departure when the British government, unprepared for another military conflict and perhaps even refusing to stare reality in the face, co-signed the Munich Agreement[124] that effectively handed Hitler manna from heaven: the unopposed annexation of Czechoslovakia's German-speaking Sudetenland. The agreement was signed just after midnight on 30th September 1938. The German military began their invasion the next day.

The fleeing Jewish population sought sanctuary in other Czechoslovak towns, including Hradec Kralove. The reaction of the local population was less than sympathetic and Elsa would probably have been neither welcome nor safe there. She had little choice but to join her friend Silvia and other contemporaries in the youth Aliyah's Hachshara.

Just ten days after the agreed annexation of the Sudetenland, the pogroms of Kristallnacht changed everything. The situation of the Jews in general, but particularly those in Vienna, was now suddenly and obviously untenable. If no government would make it easier for adults and families to find sanctuary then at least the children must be rescued.

The official rescue effort moved into overdrive, instigated by the German Jewish leadership in Berlin and the Quakers, in collaboration with the Central British Fund for German Jewry.[125] After much negotiation with the British government and a debate in Parliament, the 'Kindertransport' rescue operation was inaugurated – on condition that all travel costs and living expenses would be met by voluntary groups and private individuals.

Kristallnacht also changed everything for my mother. She was already suffering from anxiety; now she couldn't sleep and refused to move from her parents' side. She found it almost impossible to eat and she lost weight. The frequency of her migraines increased and she came down with one cold after another. If a place on a Kindertransport came up when she was unwell, she would not be allowed to travel. More stress.

THE END OF HOME

On 27th March 1939, two weeks after Dawa's thirteenth birthday and twelve days after Nazi Germany reneged on its assurances and occupied

---

124 Signatories to the Munich Agreement were German Chancellor Adolf Hitler, UK Prime Minister Neville Chamberlain, fascist Italy's prime minister Benito Mussolini, and Prime Minister of France Edouard Daladier. Czechoslovakia's President Edvard Beneš had not been invited to the conference.

125 These days known as World Jewish Relief.

the remainder of sovereign Czechoslovakia, and after months of hopes being raised and dashed, my mother and Elsa took their seats on a Kindertransport train destined for London. It was 23.45pm.[126]

Soon after their departure, one of the accompanying chaperones[127] arrived with large sheets of corrugated cardboard and suggested the children take it in turns to lie down and sleep. None of the other children in her carriage moved, but my mother – never one for inhibitions and suddenly exhausted by the release of tension – took up the offer and promptly fell asleep for what seemed 'like hours'.

On a small buff postcard marked 28.03.1939 Elsa wrote:

> *Dear Grandmother, Parents and Aunts!*
> *We had a fairly good first night. My slept mostly on the floor. I didn't sleep at all, but I'm not tired. The last station was Passau. Now it is half past four. The postcard was given to us.*
> *Lots of kisses, Elsa and My*

When their train pulled in at Nuremberg, Dawa recalled they were given mugs of hot drink poured out of 'watering cans' and some bread and butter. Neither she nor Elsa ate the offerings;[128] she couldn't recall whether the other children in the compartment did, but nobody seemed to want to touch anything from German hands. In fact, according to the archives the IKG had negotiated the warm drinks and snacks with the station catering services and had paid good money for them.

My mother said, 'There was such a sweet little girl of about nine or ten sitting in the corner of the compartment and looking very lonely. We offered her some food and tried to talk to her but she was too traumatised... She spent the entire journey just staring straight ahead... I've never forgotten her and often wonder what happened to her.'

On a second postcard, also date stamped 18.03.1939, my mother wrote:

> *Dear Grandmother, Parents and Aunts!*
> *We passed safely through Cologne and have just passed Düsseldorf.*
> *Many greetings*
> *My and Elsa*
> *Letter to follow*

---

126 According to the archives, the Nazi authorities feared that daytime departures might provoke a public backlash.
127 According to the archives, the chaperones were only approved by the Nazi authorities under threat of collateral damage in Vienna if they failed to return upon delivery of their charges.
128 Oma had provided them with plenty of home-made food.

When their train stopped at Aachen, the German border control officers examined only a few of the many suitcases, although my mother remembered that they 'seemed menacing and fear was in the air'.

After crossing the border, they stopped once again in Holland where noticeably more cheerful Dutch people distributed warm orangeade and cheese rolls. As they travelled towards the coast, my mother kept herself occupied by watching the houses as their train passed by. 'I can clearly remember all the mother-in-law's tongues in the windows. I suppose it might have helped prevent passengers from seeing in because many houses didn't have their curtains drawn even though it was already dark.'

'I can't remember how we got on board the ship, whether we were given a meal … but I remember in the morning looking at myself in the washroom mirror and feeling awful.

'We all had labels around our necks and somehow we got on a train. We were given an egg sandwich and some fruit for the journey to London that seemed unending. The countryside was bare, it was raining and windy and very cold. We all seemed depressed.

'As we got nearer to Liverpool Street Station, all we saw were miles of railway cottages with washing blowing in the wind looking grey and grubby rather than clean, and all the chimneys had dark-grey smoke coming out. My heart sank. We arrived at Liverpool Street, which was such a dark and dirty looking station, and were herded into a large hall full of people.'

An hour later, after the rescue committee had processed their paperwork, the girls were surprised to hear a familiar voice calling out from the crowd of adults milling around waiting to pick up their charges. It was Toni!

My mother was shocked. The robust, healthy-looking brother she hadn't seen for six months had lost weight, his trousers were too long, his shoes (that had been bought to last) were curling up at the toes, and as he held his hat that was no longer 'too new' in his hand he 'looked so awkward, the poor chap'.

Toni had been considerably more fortunate than most who had no relatives to support them financially or psychologically, but he had still suffered and he looked bedraggled. How easy it is to look like an alien.

Toni and Uncle Arthur had come to greet the girls and to meet their new legal guardians, Mr and Mrs Beddington. They were also introduced to a younger woman called Miss Hawkins who would be accompanying the girls to their new home in Hove. My mother was confused: weren't they supposed to be going to a children's home run by her new guardians?

If my mother was shocked by her brother's appearance, he, in turn, noticed something about his little sister.

*London,
30th March*

Dearest Parents!

Yesterday the two girls arrived safe and well in London. There was no sign of any possible strain such a long journey could have caused. At first we thought they were two Eskimos, they were so wrapped up and rosy cheeked.[129] *With Camilla I saw something entirely new: terribly slitty eyes, which she can only have acquired recently, or perhaps it was the stress after all which reflected itself another way in her face. As Mr Beddington was introducing Mrs Beddington and Miss Hawkins (the manager*[130] *in Hove, near Brighton) before handing over the children, she grabbed me by the arm and asked 'Toni, what's going to happen to us now? Where are we going?' But that seems to have been only a momentary worry because she immediately turned to checking whether her new watch was still working... Mr and Mrs Beddington are very nice and kindly people. Mrs B. looks like dear God Himself. She is an older lady but of strong character and has blue eyes with a really joyous sparkle. She told me that they had all been so afraid that the girls would not be able to come and had already given up all hope...*[131] *Uncle had the best of impressions of Mr and Mrs B. and Miss H. and is of the opinion that they couldn't have hit upon better luck.*

Enclosed: also two forms for Father and Mother, about England, which give more detailed information.

Yesterday I received a very nice letter from Courtaulds (a sort of reference) to help me with my application for a work permit. No doubt the girls will send a much more detailed report than me and I remain with a thousand greetings and kisses for you and Grandmother and Aunts Clara

---

129 What Toni did not know was that the girls had worn as many layers of clothing as possible because their luggage allowance was only one small suitcase. The family had also been concerned about the damp winter weather that had prompted Toni to write home for some warmer underwear (which he could not afford to buy).
130 Theo Hawkins' official title was Lady Superintendent.
131 The Refugee Committee's move to larger premises at Woburn House in order to accommodate the volume of administrative work and practical services, as well as intermittent delays in communication between London and Vienna, caused several weeks of uncertainty and anxiety to the refugees, their families and their new British hosts.

and Camilla and Aunt Hedwa and Uncle Maly, Hubert and Hilda
Your son Toni

Formalities and introductions completed, Uncle Arthur and Toni said goodbye and left the girls to climb into the Beddingtons' chauffeur-driven car for the journey across town to Victoria Station where they were taken to lunch at the Grosvenor Hotel.

Hove, 29th March 1939

Dearest Parents!
...Mr B. is a friendly old gentleman and Mrs B. a beautiful old lady. I didn't speak much with Uncle or Toni. The poor boy looks awful... Each of us was served half a chicken, ham and tea. My immediately pounced on her chicken. I couldn't eat mine.[132] *I felt very embarrassed but I didn't touch it. Mrs B. was also accompanied by a young lady. Her name is Miss Hawkins. We were put in her care and travelled to Brighton. The weather is marvellous. The sea is beautiful. We are staying in a large and fabulously elegant house. Carpets everywhere. Miky and I have two bedrooms next to each other. They are simply furnished but nice. A lot of other people live in the house as well (I think). I don't know who they are. It is so elegant here that I feel quite anxious. Miky, on the other hand, feels completely at ease. She didn't get sea-sick. The second night we slept in a first class cabin.*[133] *I shall write in more detail tomorrow. Please forgive my atrocious scrawl but I am very agitated! It's afternoon now and I am writing in Miss Hawkins' room. I shall write in more detail tomorrow. At the moment I am still feeling very nervous. Miss Hawkins thinks that my English is very good (probably in comparison with Miky). I made a real effort to use all of my vocabulary in conversation. My likes it here. Farewell. E.*
Lots of love and kisses to all. Tomorrow I shall write in greater detail.

Arthur had been quite right in his assessment of his nieces' good fortune. Although the girls were unaware of it, Reginald and Sybil Beddington were independently wealthy and well-connected scions of the Anglo-Jewish community; with their place near the top of the pyramid, their commitment to the Jewish command for philanthropy had become a way

---

132 Elsa had already eaten her fill of the food Oma had made for their long journey; they even had plenty left over.
133 Toni wrote to Vienna that because of the administrative delays to the Kindertransport the girls' new guardian was even considering paying for them to fly to England; could it be that he also paid for their first class cabin?

of life.

Sybil Beddington regularly sent little notes and thoughtful gifts to the girls, doing her best to help them feel less adrift and build a connection even though she could not be with them.

43 Lowndes Square, London S.W.1.
23rd June 1939

Dear Mrs Löwenthal,

The delay in responding to your kind letter can be put down to two reasons. Firstly, I am ashamed to admit that I am not too familiar with the German language and had to have your letter translated for me by a friend. Now I am having this letter translated by the same friend since I can imagine that you would prefer to receive a letter in German rather than in English.

The second reason is that I have been ill and am still in hospital and did not want to have a letter written to you until I was well enough to dictate it myself.

My husband and I thank you for your kind words and can promise you that not only we, but also Miss Hawkins will do only our very best for your sweet daughters. I shall also write to Miss Hawkins to inform her of the contents of your letter and to impress upon her your concern that small aberrations of behaviour should not be ignored. I do know that she herself feels and is of the same opinion as we are, that it is not true love to be too indulgent, and I am sure that Miss Hawkins will correct any small trifles (as you put it) with discipline as well as with love.

Because of my illness I have so far only been able to meet Elsa and Mikie once, which was on the day of their arrival; but I immediately felt drawn to them and had hoped to spend many lovely days with them. My illness has so far prevented me from doing so.

My husband went to Brighton to visit your children and returned home with the same warm feeling towards them that we had felt on the very first day. A lady in Brighton with whom I am very good friends (Mrs Livesay) has a little daughter who is my godchild. Jean Livesay is the same age as your Elsa and I hope that the two girls will become close friends as I am sure Jean is the kind of girl you would like your daughters to make friends with.

I know that Miss Hawkins is already very attached to your daughters and will do everything in her power to take your place while they are entrusted to her care. By that I mean that she will not only love and care for your daughters, but she will endeavour to prepare them to cope with the trials of life which may come their way when they are adults.

The ladies who are employed in the home are all competing with one another to make your daughters happy and I can only hope that my health will improve enough to gain the strength to visit them from time to time and to try and ensure a happy future for them.

I would also like to thank your mother-in-law and your sisters-in-law for their kind words and to reiterate how pleased my husband and I were to receive your so very kind letter.

Yours sincerely
Sybil E. Beddington

Sadly, one month after Britain and France declared war on Germany on 3rd September 1939, Sybil Beddington, the woman whose inner light had shone so bright, died of cancer.

'It was a tragedy for me,' my mother said as she reflected on her life at Dresden House. She had lived in grand luxury and been met with great benevolence and generosity; she and Elsa had been exceptionally fortunate.

In the first few months they were kept busy with enjoyable activities, which they described in detailed letters to their family back home. They had complete freedom to use all the recreational facilities at Dresden House including a billiard room and croquet lawn.

Theo Hawkins allowed them to use her private sitting room as their own, to play records on the gramophone and entertain their friends. There was also a table with chairs where they could have afternoon tea or do their homework. To Elsa's delight, Dresden House also had a library with comfortable armchairs and tall glass cabinets filled with books.

The girls did their best to appear as if everything was 'normal' and 'at home', just as everyone around them was trying to make it, but that was on the surface; the truth of their grief-stricken inner worlds when they retreated to their bedrooms was another matter entirely.

Almost immediately after they arrived in Hove, the girls were introduced to religious services and to schul (Torah school) at the local liberal synagogue. Rabbi Dr. Heinrich Lemle, who spoke English, was from Germany; he had been a rabbi in Frankfurt and was briefly interned in Buchenwald concentration camp until the efforts of the American Joint Distribution Committee resulted in his release and flight to Britain. 'He and his wife were very kind. I spent quite a lot of time in their home. They had a little boy of about eighteen months, blue-eyed and blond curly hair,'

Dawa recalled.

Elsa initially reported that she was reluctant to follow the rabbi's prompting and study for her belated bat mitzvah (confirmation), but she soon changed her mind. She found herself enjoying the three-way sparring with her fellow student, an intense and sharp-witted seventeen-year-old boy, and the rabbi who, Elsa suggested to her father, must have been driven almost to despair by the boy's fixation with questioning the minutest of details. I am inclined to suspect the rabbi would have been delighted.

Hove 22nd July 1939

My dear Granny!

Thank you very much for your dear letter. I showed it to the ladies and they all greatly admired the beautiful handwriting. I was very happy to get your birthday wishes and tried to be very merry. I thought of you all day long because I knew you would be thinking of me. I was very pleased with the sweets, as was Micky, who immediately took her share. I was given many small presents. Mrs Beddington sent me a very delightful handbag made of beige silk, with a pretty clasp made of little stones.

I may be confirmed in the autumn. At any rate I'm busily attending the confirmation lessons. The Rabbi is very modern. He recently arrived from Frankfurt. We usually argue a lot in the lessons (that's to say the Rabbi, me and a 17 year-old student). I don't know enough good English to express myself as I would like but if I think of something good, I just say it in German, whereupon the Rabbi then translates it into English.

Friday evenings I always go to synagogue and during the 'silent prayer' I always think of you all.

On the evening of the 9th there's going to be a service in German, just for refugees, in commemoration of all the destroyed temples in our history.

I hope you are well, dear Granny and close with a thousand kisses, your loyal granddaughter
Elsa

Less than two months later, just after war broke out, thirty-year old Rabbi Lemle and his young family migrated to Brazil.[134] His departure marked the beginning of the end of the girls' regular attendance at synagogue services. His departure also marked the gradual end to a structured contact

---

134 Dr. Henrique (formerly Heinrich) Lemle served as rabbi to the liberal Jewish community in Rio de Janeiro and founded the German-Brazilian Jewish Congregation. He also co-founded the Christian-Jewish Fraternal Council in Brazil. He died in Brazil in 1978.

with the wider (if very anglicised) liberal Jewish community that might have provided my mother and Elsa with some sense of continuity and belonging.

By the second week of May 1940, German troops had invaded and overrun Western Europe and were fighting their way ever closer towards its coastlines, including those facing southern England. The British government decided to tighten restrictions on adult refugees and others of German and Austrian descent.

No matter what their circumstances, they were all now considered potential enemies to Britain and potential friends to the Nazi regime – from which most had fled. Under the Aliens Restrictions Act, Toni was categorised an 'Enemy Alien Class C' and forbidden to go near the coast. His enjoyable visits to see his sisters in Hove that Elsa had so enthusiastically written home about were suddenly over.

Shortly afterwards, the National Security Aliens Tribunal applied the same categorisation to Elsa and Dawa. Since she was still considered too young to constitute a threat, my mother was allowed to remain at Dresden House but Elsa, who was almost seventeen, had to leave Hove and relocate further inland.

The Dunkirk evacuation of Allied troops had just taken place, Calais had fallen and the Nazis were firmly entrenched less than twenty-one miles off the south coast of England. With a German sea and airborne invasion looming, Elsa had become a potential foe.

London
16th June 1940

Dear Elsa,

Thank you very much for your letter but was actually expecting it from London,[135] so it quite took my breath away when I saw the Oxford post mark. And I had so been looking forward to another visit from you. Thank you so much for your kind offer to help me out but this past week I earned 30 shillings and am now hoping I will slowly be able to pull myself out of the dumps. Uncle Arthur sends his warmest greetings – I spoke with him on the phone this morning – and when I told him of your changed circumstances, he said "Better that than the other."

Now, before I write more about myself and my new-found wisdoms I want to ask you to describe everything in the minutest detail in your next

---

135 Toni had erroneously assumed that Elsa would move to the London home of her legal guardian, Reginald Beddington.

letter; what were your last days in Hove like, what Kamilla did, what it's like at your new school, whether you are having a somewhat better relationship with your room mates, describe them to me a little, although after reading your first few lines I have an idea what sad types they are (further below I'll give you a description of their counterparts amongst the blokes), how the boarding house is run, whether the food is any good etc.

I would love to provide you with some solace but I'm certain that everything I say will sound just like the usual platitudes – garnered from the narrower moralists and then rather badly regurgitated – so I prefer to just follow my train of thoughts in the hope of cheering you up. I just wish you a really thick elephant skin so that you can survive safe and sound all the stupid things that will get your gall during the initial period of adjustment. Remember: 'We never swallow anything as hot as it has been dished up'.

Now to the aforementioned counterparts. The behaviour of young people on their own who join a larger group always manifests in such ways as you have just described, screeching and giggling at bedtime, pillow fights and so forth. These are germ cells of the mass or herding instinct, so to speak. An individual on their own would never behave in such a way; the courage to forget oneself and participate in the transgression of others only occurs with the comforting certainty that the others have suddenly forgotten themselves too, and the desire of the individual to become one with the mass – if not to surpass it with greater gimmicks – becomes ever more powerful. That kind of thing provides a momentary sensation of self-worth. Unfortunately, people only realise much later what this worth really signifies. But actually, it is a fact that the majority never awakes from this delusion, merely remain the yeast in the dough, which continues to rise and bring forth all the phenomena that we, especially, have experienced during the last few years. It is all too easy to join in the baying rather than follow one's own good sense. And I have to confess that I too have all-too-often forgotten myself in this way. But thankfully I always woke up just in time.

For example, I once went on a skiing course in Filzmoos and shared the room with 6 other boys. The performance they put on before bedtime! First, they chose a victim (don't worry, wasn't me) whom they robbed of his pyjamas and on whom they attempted various forms of castration. After a while these particular fun and games were given up as impractical and we restricted ourselves to pillow fights and the singing of rude ditties. Of course, this eventually led to exhaustion and so the heroes turned to a more manly farting competition. Every effort was rated and if somebody could only manage to squeeze a little squeak from his cheeks, he was instantly judged an example of unmanliness. Well, finally it all came to an end and the aspiring men went to sleep. Thank goodness, because one evening was enough. A chap sprained an ankle – he was staying a little further away on a farm – changed accommodation and I swapped with him, so that I managed to enjoy the skiing course without farting competitions. Later on, I learnt through the indiscreet remarks of my fellow female pupils who had been on their own skiing course in St.Veit that they had had similar adventures – and then even surpassed us with their inventiveness. One of them dressed up like a young peasant and went calling on some crazy creature (who was always babbling on about one adventure or another). To everyone's greatest amusement she fell completely into the trap and started necking with the so-called peasant boy. He played his part so well that the fool only realised her mistake towards the end and went hysterical.

With all of that I just wanted to show you that it's always the same and that you actually haven't stumbled across particularly silly creatures. I am quite sure your friends will soon tire of it and behave more normally. You can be sure that their behaviour will be completely different when they are on their own and aren't falling on primitive mass instincts. Surely you will have observed how, after a performance with which the audience is not familiar, nobody dares to clap and the wild applause only begins when the hired claque gets going. Once the allure of the new has faded, the applause becomes weaker, as does the performance. I'm certain I am not mistaken in thinking that your companions are only subconsciously giving you the run around to impress you.

When I have finished this letter I will write to Kamilla as well, I suspect that she will be missing you as much as you do her ... I hope with all my heart that you will find a decent friend who will meet your needs. There is also a well-known library in Oxford, if you are interested make some enquiries. At first one is always a bit self-conscious and feels awkward but believe me, I can tell you from my own experience, that disappears after five visits. Once you acquire a familiarity with the searching of catalogues (they are always a problem for a newcomer because you can never find what you want) it will become a joy. You will be able to learn about *everything you are interested in and would never learn at school because, of course, every teacher is restricted to their subject and then only imparts to the pupil what he deems important and what time will permit...*

...I send you lots of love and kisses, your loyal brother Toni. Write back soon!

PS. Take my fertile letter writing as an example and write a lot to me too. If I appear to be amusing myself too much, don't think that I am not thinking about your miserable situation, I just want to provide a little light relief and to distract you. I can understand only too well that you would like to smash everything up – after all, it is only laziness that prevents us from giving in to fits of anger!

Five days later, Toni wrote again to Elsa.

London
23rd June 1940

Dearest Elsa!
Many thanks for your nice letter. If I had realised that you have got used to things so well, I really would not have wasted so much good brain lard. It should be used sparingly so as not to suddenly end up without any. But I am really very pleased that you have calmed down somewhat. Your suggestion that I should write short stories is a little ahead of time; it's not just a question of the exercise itself but one should really have lived a lot in order to be able to exploit little episodes from one's experience through literature. And you will probably be aware that I haven't experienced anything yet.

Unfortunately, business is useless. I do still have enough to live on this week and am hoping that it will pick up again, but I am trying to get into agriculture. Uncle has promised to talk to a few people in the various committees.

Otherwise, I am 'very well'.[136] *But do write me a letter with lots of detail. Please. Mine is not so long today because I feel devoid of ideas but am hoping that it will improve soon and then you can expect another 8-10 pages of schmooze.*

At the moment I am reading 'Radetzkymarsch' by Joseph Roth. Quite good. If you've already been to any of the libraries, do try to find the following work: 'The Savage Hits Back' written by a German

---

136 'very well' was written in English.

anthropologist who had to get away from the Nazis. It deals with the subject of how the coloured races see us, the whites. It will amuse you deliciously to see with what accuracy and fabulous observation quite ordinary negroes whom many regard as 'wild' portray the characteristics and defects of the whites in their sculptures and paintings. <u>Do not miss it</u>. It is very, very educational! I will tell you the exact name of the author next time.

That's the limit of my lard for today.
Lots of love and kisses from your brother Toni

A few days later Toni was ordered to report for his internment on the Isle of Man. This marked, with only a couple of exceptions, the beginning of his correspondence with Elsa in English.

House 9
Hutchinson Internment Camp
Douglas
Isle of Man
Tuesday 13th August 1940

Dear Elsa!
I am afraid you did not get my letter, which I wrote to you just after my arrival here, on or around 15th July. I knew that our letters are not the quickest, as now everyone in this house has got his, you may easily imagine how happy I feel. If I have to write that I am living better here than before internment (the pure truth) it is then to judge by the fact that the last weeks of liberty and misery I got a small help of 17/6s from the Komittee. I don't feel the depression of the internment as much as I work all day in the kitchen. But last week I had a small mishap. I cut off a bit of my thumb with the bread slicing machine. It was rather painful because one third of the nail went with it. But the Doc says I can take off the bandages in a week. But to get a normal thumb again will last perhaps a year. Here are many nice people, but a lot of blinking fools too. The only possibility to get out of here will be my affidavit to U.S. which I hope to get in about one to two years. If the U.S.A. will keep out of the bloody trouble. The 25 lines to write are nearly spent so I close with best regards to Miki, Miss Hawkins and Beard. With love, your sincere brother
Toni.

One year earlier, just after her sixteenth birthday in July 1939, which had coincided with the annual Dresden House garden party, Elsa had written to her parents in Vienna:

...Mr Beddington didn't come because Mrs B. is very ill, and he won't leave her. It is very sad, but she has cancer. People here are very strange and speak about things which we would avoid even trying to mention. For example, Miss H. recently said 'If anything happens to poor Mrs B., you mustn't be surprised if Mr B. comes here more often and invites you more often too. It's just that he is going to be very lonely.'

Until he became more deeply involved in contributing to the war effort, Reginald Beddington did indeed visit Dresden House more frequently. My mother soon found herself enrolled as their alibi as he and Theo Hawkins canoodled on the back seat of his chauffeur-driven Bentley ('Miki dear, do lean forward a little') or almost devoured one another at the cinema as if she were not sitting next to them.

'It was revolting and, looking back, they should have been ashamed of themselves, it was the stuff of the farmyard!'

To make matters even more uncomfortable, one day she even interrupted the two adults in Theo's sitting room – in flagrante! 'It was excruciatingly embarrassing!'

At other times, she and Theo visited her guardian at his London home or his country estate but, 'At least they behaved themselves when the butler was around!' my mother laughed.

Two months after the war ended, Theo returned to Hove where she initially moved into a smart apartment building. Four months later she relocated to less salubrious accommodation further along the coast. From there Toni, who had joined her after initially recuperating from his war wounds at Dresden House, wrote to Elsa on 5th December 1945:

Yesterday I was at Roehampton and had that limb delivered. Can walk around quite successfully, but it is very tiring. Am going next Monday to the hospital for further instruction in the walking school... The birdie hasn't changed except for some signs of an approaching climacterium of which she told me some time ago, in guarded language... Her old sugar-daddy still keeps coming along. For the last four weeks she has been telling everyone that she intends to invest some of her savings in an expensive fur coat. Still, my old suspicious brain sees in all this talk an attempt at camouflaging the fact that her sugar-daddy might give her some fur coat as consolation prize for a disappointment on the marriage market.

When Theo Hawkins left Dresden House, her young stand-in, Kathleen Beard, took over responsibility for my mother. The two of them had always enjoyed an easy-going relationship; within weeks of their arrival, Elsa had noted that it would be easy to wrap the young woman around a finger because, though very 'posh' and adept at picking holes in all and sundry when out in public,[137] she was not only devoid of feelings but had no mind of her own.

Consequently, after Theo's departure mature adult mentorship for Dawa was nowhere to be found. She was left to her own devices and became her own boss. All credit to the early influence of her family in Vienna that she neither went off the rails nor behaved disrespectfully! Perhaps her father's and Aunt Clara's words were still ringing distantly in her ears.

Several decades later I drove my mother to visit Theo at her home and we spent a pleasant afternoon together. Subsequently my mother received a letter that ended with the words '...*for I do love you so much*'. For a long time I wondered whether Theo, an habitually impulsive adventurer, had been reflecting upon her choices; later I found letters she had written to Elsa after she moved to Oxford in which she signed herself off in the same affectionate way. She was undeniably a genuinely good woman.

There can be little doubt that this well-intentioned and caring middle-class spinster was not immune to the flattering attentions of the chairman of the Board of Dresden House, Reginald Beddington CBE. Neither did he seem to have been immune to her attention when his wife died. Gratitude in the face of kindness can easily be confused with romantic love.

Perhaps Theo was not fully aware of the deeply entrenched British class system. Whilst it was acceptable to move outside one's social circle to sow wild oats or find comfort, ultimately the tribal lineage had to be kept pure. With rare exceptions, that was the way it had always been – and still is.

IN SEARCH OF JUDAISM

After my initial efforts to learn more about Judaism – as distinct from 'being Jewish' – I remained deeply dissatisfied. Perhaps attending some Friday-night shabbat services might give me greater insight? But there was a snag: although not ultra-orthodox, my local synagogue was nevertheless an orthodox one.

Over the years I had driven past it on countless occasions and seen community members arriving for services and other events. I had even been on friendly terms with a couple of women within the community

---

[137] Elsa wrote that she feigned to play along with her silliness.

until our lives took us in different directions. I instinctively knew that 'doing as we are supposed to' (whilst also keeping a close eye on who was wearing what) had nothing to do with what I was searching for. Besides, if I had ever revealed that my maternal grandmother was a gentile, that would probably have been the end of my association with the synagogue.

'If your grandmother wasn't Jewish then your mother isn't either,' another very nice Jewish acquaintance once said, albeit disappointed that I was not 'one of us'. 'That's the rule, because at least you know who the mother is.' Oh.

So I gave up, until by chance I noticed a small newspaper advertisement placed by an independent synagogue in north London founded by liberal German-Jewish refugees in the 1930s. Perhaps that might be a better fit?

I attended some Friday shabbat services where the congregants were not only friendly but also felt curiously familiar. What's more, there was no obvious security at the entrance, let alone a high metal gate and an armed guard. The Rabbi's intellectual approach, combined with a deep humanitarian warmth and thought-provoking sermons, found an easy home within me. To make my Friday evenings complete, the cantor's singing almost sent me to heaven – which, of course, was probably its underlying purpose!

One Friday evening a young child was introduced to the congregation. It was a moving event, but one that highlighted the sense of being an outsider that had been with me for so much of my life. This was the glue, the sense of belonging that held members together within the security of a trusted community. Even if one no longer had immediate family, the community was available and you were not on your own.

In an increasingly mobile world, the importance of such a security net cannot be overestimated, particularly for Jews who know more than most about being both physically rootless and social outcasts.

Although my mother made a number of new friends during her life, after fleeing her home in Austria she experienced a deep-seated sense of insecurity. She did her best to live in the moment, but she assumed a mask to disguise a sense of not belonging. When I experienced what being a part of a community can be like, I felt both saddened and angry about what had been lost to her, to me and my brothers and to those like us.

As I was leaving the synagogue that same Friday, I felt a hand on my shoulder. Behind me was the Rabbi. Looking into my eyes, he said nothing. On the spur of the moment I said, 'I would like to come and speak with you.'

He proved to be not only very kind but also understanding where the touchy subject of my mother's predicament within Halacha was concerned. 'But she suffered along with all of them for it!' he said.

I was still ignorant of the diversity of denominations within Judaism. Neither was I aware that a part of Vienna's Jewry had once been ahead of the game in loosening the knot around matrilineal descent.

The freedom of movement granted to the Jews of the Austrian Empire following their emancipation in the second half of the nineteenth century contributed to a further broadening of Jewish thought and a marked increase in Jewish men 'marrying out'. Beyond the dilution of long-standing traditions, the absence of these men posed a threat to the cultural, financial, and social viability of formal, organised Jewish communities. In response, Vienna's emerging liberal and progressive groups loosened the traditionally strict Orthodox interpretation of Jewish descent as passing only through the mother. Children of Jewish fathers were also accepted as Jews, provided there was a commitment to raise them with a Jewish identity shaped by Jewish ethical and spiritual values.

However, sitting in the Rabbi's office, when he asked what I knew about Judaism, the only answer I could give was the truth: 'I've been doing my level best to find out, but not a lot.'

He gave me a list of books to read and promised to put my application forward to their committee if I wished to formally join his synagogue's community. Irrespective of my decision, he also said he would do right by my mother and give her a Jewish burial when the time came.

Arriving home that day, I studied the list of books and realised that I had already read most of them plus others in the same vein or by the same authors. Did that mean I knew more than I realised even though felt I understood very little?

When I informed my mother of the Rabbi's offer, she smiled but seemed unconcerned. After her death, in quiet defiance of rules and regulations, we buried some of her ashes with those of her sister in the forest by their beloved Popovice. In symbolic re-unification of her splintered family, we deposited more ashes in other meaningful locations in Bohemia, Austria and Canada. To acknowledge my mother's belief in the unity of all things, some ashes have been sprinkled in other far-flung locations across the globe; she even attended our son's wedding in Australia! Ashes to ashes, dust to dust.

My attendance at Friday evening synagogue services in north London lasted only a couple of months. The congregants were welcoming, the services were interesting and curiously resonant, but in essence there was nothing I didn't already know. Yes, I became familiar with some biblical events and their associated high days and holy days, but I was looking for more. If I was going to find the golden nugget, I had to look elsewhere. In the meantime, I determined to find out whether or not Oma had converted to Judaism.

On a visit to Vienna, and by one of those synchronistic quirks of fate, I was unexpectedly taken to meet the Chief Rabbi of Austria in his office. He requested documentation from the community records located within the same building and was able to confirm that there was no evidence of conversion. He copied details from the birth records and gave me a handwritten note in both German and Hebrew: *Your mother was born Jewish. Take this to the Beth Din*[138] – *just don't say too much.*

I never did. Years later I stumbled across a newspaper interview with the Chief Rabbi in which he said, 'You can interpret *halacha* to include or exclude. We include.'

UNCLE ARTHUR

I never did meet Uncle Arthur. By the time I was born, he and Aunt Ida had already been living far away in Lincoln for almost ten years, and direct contact with my mother was limited to the exchange of annual Christmas cards.

No matter how guilty he came to feel for ignoring her and Elsa during the war years – *I feel very ashamed as their uncle having them so neglected (sic). Please tell them that I think always about it with bitter regret* [139] - he continued only to make enquiries and send good wishes to Dawa via Toni. Despite that, he still complained about my mother's tardy letter-writing habits!

As for Ida, she never communicated with my mother or Elsa during the war. The girls' two visits to their uncle and aunt's home in London after

---

138 Jewish court/committee of experts.
139 Grandfather and Oma spent the war years believing that Arthur and Ida were keeping a careful eye on their daughters; when he heard that was not the case, Grandfather wrote to his brother expressing his bitter disappointment. Grandfather was also unaware of his brother's very real mental and physical health challenges that arose from his intense wartime work for the Ministry of Defence, which will be covered later.

their arrival in England had been kindly but somewhat odd affairs, not least because Ida had neglected to speak English in the presence of Theo Hawkins, who had accompanied them. When she spoke to Arthur, she also spattered her speech with Italian and French, none of which Arthur thought to translate.[140] In fact, Ida's language of choice when conversing with Arthur was Italian.

Another planned lunchtime visit even had to be re-arranged because Ida had refused to extend the invitation to Theo.

Ida was a multilingual, well-travelled Jewish woman of sparkling intellect and heightened intuition, but now she was a refugee in advanced middle age who had seen too much to be polite and superficial. She had no opportunities to socialise with equals and to learn English in the process, and her life in England became painfully insular. 'I can see past what is presented, and what I see I often don't like,' she told Toni.

To make matters worse, she bristled like a porcupine if she thought she was not being taken seriously. The reserved manner of women in English polite society might also have contributed to her isolation because she never felt true empathy. In her unhappiness she became her own worst enemy as her charm and charisma gave way to withdrawal and volcanic explosions of temper.

Toni soon learnt to tiptoe around Ida, but his sisters failed the test: they did not adore her sufficiently and she took it personally. For the duration of the war, and while Arthur was fully occupied with his own war work, the girls were ignored when they needed family support.

Toni's gender, age and shared passions meant that he could forge a more intimate relationship with his father's brother. Arthur took him under his wing in 1938, and during the war and immediately afterwards he continued to keep a fatherly eye on him through their correspondence. Later, as life settled down and Toni matured, their relationship evolved into one of equals; they enjoyed common interests and showed a genuine fraternal concern for each other.

Things changed in 1964. For many years Toni had been assured by Arthur[141] that he would one day become the guardian of a large body of his work as well as rare books, personal papers, archaeological artefacts and

---

140 Aunt Camilla wrote to Toni soon after his arrival in England and commented that, in Arthur's home, he had more chance of learning Italian than English; she asked whether he was making the most of the opportunity.

141 I have discovered through my research that Arthur was described as a latter-day Benvenuto Cellini and 'the greatest engraver of precious stones since the Renaissance'.

other antiquities that had not already been sold in order to survive. There was also a small house in Lincoln that would help Toni take the financial step up that had continued to elude him.

It was not to be.

After Ida's death on 30th January 1958, Arthur was left lonely and bereft. He suffered repeated chest infections, his eyesight deteriorated and his hands became weaker, making the exacting work that in later life had distracted him from maudlin thoughts increasingly difficult.

He slipped into a depression. Toni and Doris offered him a home with their young family in Leeds but, not wishing to give up his privacy nor the creative sanctuary of his studio and workshop, Arthur declined.

One of his friends came up with a possible solution: he introduced Arthur to a younger couple who lived near Lincoln and needed extra income. Having soon established a very friendly relationship with Dr. and Mrs Bauer[142] who were also aware that their potential lodger was hoping to receive a large sum from his claim for Jewish reparations,[143] a possible solution became material reality. Arthur agreed to rent out his house and pay for two rooms in their sprawling but dilapidated home to be upgraded into his living quarters. The cellar was converted at his expense into his studio and workshop.

A year after Ida's death Arthur moved into his new apartment and, in his own words, felt cosier than ever before. With all sustenance now provided in return for a contribution, unbeknownst to Toni his once lonely and anxious but now grateful 79-year-old uncle changed his will. Mrs Bauer became the sole beneficiary 'because of her unfailing kindness and care for my welfare since the death of my wife and in recognition of the great happiness which she and her husband have given me.'.

The discovery of the betrayal of their close relationship, trust and family upon Arthur's death on 16th November 1964 was devastating for Toni. After a vigorous but failed attempt to challenge the will, he threw in the towel and took his wife Doris's advice to leave the past behind and emigrate to Canada.[144]

---

142 Dr. Bauer was a Polish medical doctor who served in the military on behalf of the Allies during the war. He returned to England in 1947 to settle with his second wife and son from his first marriage. Forging a new professional life was a struggle until he found a permanent position in Lincoln and was eventually able to purchase a dilapidated vicarage on the outskirts of the city. Toni visited with the couple and is not known to have voiced any misgivings.
143 I do not know if Arthur was successful in his application.
144 For a precis of Doris' deeply moving wartime experience please see Appendix 1

Part Two ~ Chapter One

A couple of years after Arthur had moved into his new home, Toni, Doris and their two young daughters moved from Leeds to a small town in Surrey so that Toni might be closer to London whilst also reviving his craft as an antique book restorer. This also meant that he was closer to Elsa, who was recently divorced and once again living in the capital. Now that he was emigrating to Canada, Toni became deeply concerned as to how his sister would cope without his support. To complicate matters further, her children's weekend access visits often took place at a halfway house: Toni's home.

From the time of Elsa's arrival in England, and throughout the war and its challenging aftermath, she and Toni had always looked to each other for support. No matter how much she might have wished him well and hoped that Canada would open up greater opportunities for him, his absence was bound to be a terrible blow. For my mother in Munich, it also meant that moving to Vienna – or anywhere else – was no longer an option because Elsa needed her.

Two days after Toni, Doris and my cousins left England at the end of September 1965, my mother, Robert and I moved into their maisonette. In part, we filled a void Elsa would have found too difficult to cope with.

I learned some thirty-five years later that Toni had left behind all the legal correspondence relating to the contested will and well over one hundred letters he had received from Arthur between August 1940 and his death in 1964.

When my mother moved in with my family, she was accompanied by a small mountain of boxes. Not all of them were her own and the contents of some had not seen the light of day since Toni had stored them in what became our loft in 1965. Now, at the age of forty-seven, I became more closely acquainted with my great-uncle Arthur of whom I knew next to nothing beyond my mother's report of his sensitive hands and urbane demeanour. The only piece of his work that I had seen was the bronze medallion portrait of his mother, my great grandmother Antonia Löwenthal, on Dawa's bookshelf.

During the months after my mother's death, I opened the folder of Arthur's letters to Toni on a number of occasions then set it aside. I knew that once I started exploring them there would be no going back; reading them would involve a great deal of time and focus and quite possibly painful emotions.

After a few months, however, I found myself listlessly flicking through

Arthur's letters when my eyes homed in on one particular word. I had been told that Arthur had once enjoyed a friendly relationship with Albert Einstein, but since my mother knew nothing concrete it might not have been true. There it was, in a letter to Toni dated 19th June 1948:

> *... By the way, I had after a silence of nearly 30 years a long and touching letter by the American friend of my youth 'Jimmy' and another fine letter by Einstein. I just got an invitation by the Royal Academy for the big Soirée on June the 30th...*

A few days later I received four scanned documents from the Albert Einstein Archives in Jerusalem. The shortest one was the last page of a letter of uncertain date written by Arthur from Lugano in Switzerland requesting Einstein's intervention on behalf of someone named Carlo Klein, who was now in a desperate position because his application for residency in Switzerland had been refused.

I had no idea who this man was, but there were Kleins in my Jewish Moravian ancestry. A distant cousin perhaps? Who knows. At the bottom of the page was a draft reply believed to have been penned by Einstein's wife, Elsa.

The second letter, dated 24th March 1930, was written by Einstein to the director of the Metropolitan Museum in New York. It was a hymn in praise of Arthur's work, specifically mentioning two bronze portrait medallions and a bust of Einstein himself acquired by the Prussian State Mint and the Kaiser Friedrich Museum respectively. It concluded with a request for recommendations as to who might help Arthur create further wonderful carvings and engravings in precious stones now that impoverished Europe was no longer a place for working artists.

Perhaps Einstein had been hoping to facilitate Arthur's exit to America; certainly he wanted to promote his value as an artist. Only a week later, he sent a handwritten letter to Max Liebermann, the president of the Academy of Arts in Berlin. He praised the portrait medallions and the bust, which he in *'my amateur opinion'* believed to be the best of the many he had sat for. If the Academy agreed with his verdict, would it consider displaying for the benefit of the artist?

Six months later, Einstein was at it again. This time he passed Arthur's address in Berlin, Fasanenstrasse 55, to a Mr Boyce Thompson in New York who was the foremost expert in, and collector of, gemstone carving. Einstein suggested Thompson might find it of mutual interest to make contact.

But that was not all. The archivist in Jerusalem informed me: *For many years nobody ever mentioned Arthur Löwenthal's name here, and now, interestingly enough, within a few weeks' time, two requests pertain to this sculptor.*

I was not alone in wanting to learn more about my great uncle!

A few days later, after serendipity had introduced me to my fellow researcher, John Turner, via the Jewish National & University Library in Jerusalem, we were exchanging excited e-mails.

John, a numismatics' enthusiast, lived near Lincoln and was writing a book about Arthur! He sent me copy of a letter he had recently received in response to an advertisement he'd placed in the *Jewish Chronicle* requesting information on the sculptor Arthur Immanuel Löwenthal.

The only person to respond was none other than Curt Carter, Toni's old friend whom I had met a couple of times when we returned to England in 1965 and had since lost touch with. Disappointingly for John, Curt's letter contained precious little of any relevance to his research, but I struck gold because Curt had included a brief outline of Toni's account of the day on which his leg was injured during the last weeks of war!

In fact, I had struck a large seam of gold. A few weeks later John and I met at the Usher Gallery in Lincoln. From snippets gleaned from my mother I was already aware that Arthur had a connection with the museum, though my enquiry at the very beginning of my search for the Dionysos Cup had remained unanswered.

Following a number of other silences elsewhere in England, I turned my attention to Germany and Austria where I experienced a heartwarming willingness by various institutions to help mend some of the Holocaust's broken ties. John's research for his book was entirely focused upon Arthur's medallion work; since he hadn't mentioned anything else to me beyond numismatics, I had no idea what was lying in wait at the Usher Gallery.

I recognised some medallions from the large body of his work held at the Bode Museum in Berlin, but I'd never seen many of the other pieces. These included his casts of a 1944 medallion of Winston Churchill and a silver 1945 Churchill Victory medal; a bronze medallion of Sir George Francis Hill, the numismatics' expert and former Director of the British Museum, whom I learned much later had championed Arthur's entry into Britain in 1935, and two plaster busts of unnamed women who show an uncanny resemblance to the young aunts Paula and Clara. There was a rock crystal intaglio of the violinist Fritz Kreisler, Arthur's childhood friend with whom he is said to have also shared digs in his youth, and a carnelian intaglio of an unknown man I am certain was my grandfather Oskar in his younger years. Could it be the one that I read Arthur had asked Oma to send him after his brother's death in 1947?

There was the 'Panther Vase', a small chalice with two handles in the shape of panthers carved out of one piece of rock crystal. It was very plain and unpolished, and the base was damaged, but still…

As I had already read Arthur's detailed description of how he went about the Dionysos in the German arts journal *Der Kunstwanderer*, I could appreciate what may not immediately be apparent to the uninitiated eye.

Arthur was an obsessive artist who set out to become expert in all forms and techniques of sculping, including the precision engineering of the tools used. I discovered in another German art journal that his obsession had taken the rebellious sixteen-year-old schoolboy to Italy, where he had learned the craft of wood carving, before returning to Vienna to complete his grammar school education about three years later. He went on to study sculpting at the Academy of Arts under the tutelage of Edmund Heller, a founding member of the Vienna Secession,[145] and the renowned medallist and sculptor Josef Tautenhayn.

That day in Lincoln, the curator of the Usher Gallery had something else to show me. After a walk along several corridors we reached a nondescript door, on the other side of which was a small, windowless storeroom. Inside it was pitch dark but as the light was switched on I was startled by what I saw.

'Oh my goodness, there's Einstein … and there's Beethoven. I've been searching for *him* for the past two years!'

---

145 An art movement closely related to Art Nouveau.

TWO

VIENNA

SETTLING IN

Since I had to wait a few weeks before being given access to the IKG archive, I made the most of my time. After registering with the local authority and opening a bank account, I took long walks through my new neighbourhood and gradually discovered shops, services, cafés and restaurants.

I had to get reader's cards for the National Library and the Municipal and National Archives; I also needed to find out which archive held which material before I could start to drill through the layers to find the hoped-for golden nuggets.

My infatuation with the apartment developed into a full-blown love affair. It was not just the light, space, tall double doors and the faintly creaking parquet flooring that felt so good, but also the atmosphere. However, it was very hot. The weather had been sweltering since I'd arrived and despite closing the windows and blinds the temperature on the apartment's sunny side rarely fell below 30°C.

To my surprise, despite the heat and the early morning traffic beneath my bedroom window, I slept well and felt more relaxed than I had for some time. I was in Vienna – and I had no responsibilities other than to follow my passion.

There was a lot of desk work to be done but when it became unbearably hot I often filled my knapsack with books, notepad and pens, plus a large bottle of water and some snacks, and took the Number 10 tram the few stops to Schönbrunn Palace with its shaded parklands and quiet gardens. I spent many hours there reading, reflecting and clarifying my thoughts as I strolled beneath a mostly clear blue sky. If it hadn't been for an ancient theme of 'them and us' emerging between the lines, I would have felt as if in heaven.

Other times I crossed the Danube Canal to wander aimlessly through the cooler back streets of my past, smelling, feeling, listening, observing and remembering with fondness and affection. Curiously – and unconsciously – I found myself repeatedly returning to the Karmelite Market of my childhood. Browsing through a book one day, I discovered that Nazi thugs had decimated the place during a 1938 rampage to evict the many Jewish stall holders.

It caused me to reflect more deeply upon Oma living alone for some thirty years surrounded by the ghosts that others had chosen to keep at a safe distance. I also found myself contemplating how migrating to Vienna on a quest for an independent and more fulfilling life had catapulted her into a trajectory of potential she could never have imagined, let alone anticipated.

OMA

Oma lived in the Austrian capital for some sixty-four of her eighty-four years, but she was born in Zábĕhlice[146]/[147] on 19th December 1885 when she was christened into the Catholic Church and named after her father's sister, Marie.[148]

In common with many hopeful economic migrants during the early years of urban industrialisation, Marie's parents Vojtek and Josefa Vondra had left their rural home in search of a brighter future closer to the capital some 60kms to the north.

Cousin Luda told me that his grandfather Vojtek found employment in a warehouse, loading heavy barrels of pickles. Legend has it that he was extremely strong and impressed his workmates by lifting weights far beyond their capabilities. Unfortunately, he eventually found himself in financial difficulty; in truth, he was probably too poorly equipped to compete in a free market that thrived on separating the educated from the ignorant, the men from the boys, the sharp operators from the more ethical or naïve.

Hard labour requires regular and nourishing food, but it is doubtful that Vojtek's income could have adequately fed and supported himself and his growing family in the manner he had envisaged. Faced with long hours of intense physical labour while living in an increasingly polluted and

---
146 A former suburb, now part of Prague.
147 For an outline of the Vondras and the feudal system in which they existed before their move to Prague, see Appendix 2.
148 Czech variant of Maria.

crowded environment, his disillusionment finally got the better of him.

Vojtek loaded a cart and retreated on foot with his young family to Popovice, 50kms to the south of the capital. This small village was the ancestral home of Josefa's mother, Anna.

The family home in Popovice was a typical one-storey dwelling with just enough land and livestock to provide for the most immediate necessities of life. At certain times of the year Vojtek worked as a woodcutter in the abundant surrounding forests belonging to the estate of an aristocrat with close connections to the Austrian ruling elite.

Vojtek bitterly resented the overbearing Austro-German influence in his homeland, where for more than two centuries the German-speaking overlords had treated the peasants with contempt. He became a vocal supporter of the growing nationalist movement,

Having to take on an official German first name and to be bilingual to accommodate a streamlining of the empire's bureaucratic machine were just two of the many insults he experienced.[149] As time passed, his anger and sense of being oppressed turned him into a moody individual with a quick temper.

Vojtek (who was also known on paper as Adalbert) made no secret of his political leanings. He is said to have embarked on regular anti-imperial tirades in the small neighbouring market town of Postupice until he offended local officialdom once too often and found himself banned from the place. So the story goes, he simply grew a beard and continued venturing into town unrecognised – but no longer ranting.

My mother loved to mimic how, in later mellower years, he gave an exaggerated and amusing performance of his morning *toilette,* brushing and caressing his beard as if his life depended upon it, while his impressive moustache received added finger-tip preening.

The only surviving photograph of great-grandmother Josefa as a young woman shows a sturdy, attractive woman, but by the time she died her spirit and looks had been broken by life's capriciousness. Beside coping with her intelligent but frustrated and moody husband, she gave birth to five more children that we know of after Marie: Josef in 1888; Blazena in 1892; Emila in 1894; Antonin in 1899 and Hedwika in 1901.

The family ate fresh, wholesome food or homemade pickles and preserves according to the seasons and the children were fit and robust, but even so theirs was not an easy existence. Without transport (except

---

149 The streamlining of an empire's bureaucratic machine and the language used within it was a practice predating the Greek empire.

for a horse-drawn cart), running water (let alone hot water) or any of the timesaving devices that we take for granted, life was hard and relentless for everyone and particularly for the women whose work never ended.

In 1905, aged just seventeen and distressed by the end of his first love affair, their son Josef picked up a hunting rifle, walked into the barn and shot himself dead. As if losing a child under such tragic circumstances was not painful enough, he had to be buried in un-consecrated ground by the boundary wall of the village cemetery. In the eyes of the Catholic Church his suicide had condemned him to eternal hellfire, something that marked the beginning of a long shadow over my grandmother's soul.

A year later, much of Popovice was submerged when the banks of its large fish pond overflowed, spilling its contents onto the houses on the incline below. Most of the Vondra possessions were either lost or ruined, including a treasured family heirloom, a large tome of *de Materia Medica*. Its pages were said to have been filled with dried pressed plants accompanied by explanations of their therapeutic applications.

I can remember Oma speaking of it as she described with a wistful smile and a distant look in her eyes the walks deep into the woods and across the meadows with her mother Josefa, seeking out plants and receiving instruction as generations of daughters before her must have done.

Marie didn't know then that her knowledge of natural remedies would rescue many people in distress during the privations of World War II. Neither did she know that I would one day pick up a book on the science of therapeutic nutrition and, at the age of forty-eight, become absorbed into a long family tradition of naturopathic medicine.

The family's house was so badly damaged by the flood that it was abandoned in favour of building a brand new one. To help finance its construction, twenty-year old Marie put her ambition of travelling to the New World on hold and contributed 6000Kr of her hard-earned savings towards a compensation pay-out so that her father could fulfil his dream of better things.

Nestling at the foot of one of the many undulating and lush hills that make this part of Bohemia so achingly beautiful, the handsome new house was reportedly the first two-storey domestic dwelling in the village. It was painted in traditional Habsburg yellow and was large enough for the right flank of the ground floor to be rented out to the local gendarmerie, providing Vojtek with a welcome boost to his income.

In later years his four married daughters returned every summer to escape the heat of their urban apartments and to reconnect with one another, and eventually eight grandchildren kicked off their shoes and ran free with the village youngsters. Sadly, the summer of 1937 was the final Löwenthal visit from Vienna and the beginning of the end of their idyll.

I have been told that great-grandmother Josefa was a warm-hearted, if at times reactive, mother whose children loved her deeply. Losing Josef must have been a terrible blow for her, but it was not the last. In 1917 Antonin, affectionately known as Tondo and an unwilling conscript fighting with the Austro-Hungarian Imperial Army in the Dolomites, sustained a severe spinal injury. Evidently he had volunteered to cross enemy lines to help his unit infiltrate Italian-held territory when he was shot. Ironically, the Czech nationalist in him had intended to defect to the Italian side where his older brother-in-law and budding politician, Josef, was already doing his own bit against the Austrians.

Antonin was brought back from the front and hospitalised in Klosterneuburg, on the outskirts of Vienna, where Grandfather went to visit him in on 19th September 1917. He had just returned from a visit to Popovice where Oma was staying with her family.[150] According to Dawa, Tondo is said to have eventually been repatriated to Bohemia. His mother, helped later by Oma, tended his gangrenous torso, although nobody has been able to verify this version of events. Wherever reality might lie, Tondo, a self-assured and sturdy young man whose youthful bravado had ended in his own tragedy, finally succumbed to his wounds in 1920 at the age of twenty-one.

One day, that same year, Josefa headed for the barn where she picked up a wood-cleaving axe; instead of splitting a piece of wood, she chopped off her hand and bled to death.

Vojtek had lost his two sons and now his wife. Marie had lost her adored little brother Antonin, after whom she had named her own first child, my Uncle Toni, and now she had lost her mother. Whether it was suicide or not, Josefa was buried alongside her eldest son in un-consecrated ground.[151] What conflicting emotions Marie must have suffered as she stood by the graves of these two beloved would-be exiles from God's grace.

---

150 Grandfather had already served on the WWI battle front, but as a reservist officer in the Imperial Army he had been sent on a machine gun instructor's course in Bohemia. He was given official permission to detour via Popovice on his way back to Vienna.

151 On a visit to Popovice with Dawa some eighty years later, a cousin told us that Josefa and Josef were reburied in the family grave during the communist era.

MARIE

Marie Vondra was an intelligent and curious young woman frustrated by the restrictions of her immediate surroundings; above all, she objected to the power the Catholic clergy held over village life.

Many decades later I laughed out loud as she recalled (in Austrian German with a Viennese inflection heavily laden with a Czech peasant's accent) the convoluted detours she'd had to take on her short walk to school to avoid the priest who insisted that all the girls kiss his outstretched hand. Although heavily censored for my young ears, there was no mistaking my grandmother's view of how this jobbing man of the cloth received his daily pleasure when he was not – as I learned many years later – engaged in claiming it behind closed doors.

Marie's formal education, which she received thanks to the social reforms instituted by Empress Maria Theresa, ended at the age of fourteen. She was then expected to care for her siblings and the homestead until a suitable candidate for marriage showed up or leave home and go further afield to earn a living.

The arrival of her sister Hedwika in 1901 is said to have galvanised her into action. A month after her sixteenth birthday Marie packed her bags, said farewell to her family and the restrictions of village life, and headed for the Czech Moravian region's capital of Brno. There, she followed in her godmother's footsteps and started work on the lowest rung of the domestic-service ladder.

But Marie had a plan. By the time she arrived in Vienna three years later, she'd had three jobs and risen to the elevated status of 'cook'. From then until her marriage in 1917, she was almost continuously employed and gathered glowing references for her ability, reliability and honesty.

In those days female domestic servants were commonplace and cheap to employ. Most had live-in accommodation: at worst, a straw mattress on the kitchen or scullery floor, at best a small, box- or attic room. Poor country girls did not expect anything more, but a skilled cook in a well-heeled household generally fared better.

Marie was determined to have her independence in Vienna instead of being obliged to respond around the clock to her employer's every whim. She and a fellow cook joined forces to rent their own accommodation, a shared, sub-tenanted room. Despite its limitations, it also gave her a much-needed retreat from the crowded city's assaults on her senses.

VIENNA AND THE JEWS

Marie's work was either in the I. District (which until the 1850s had spanned the entirety of the old walled city) or in the II. District of Leopoldstadt (Leopold Town), where Jewish migrants tended to settle due to the pull of historical ties and the proximity of the Nordbahnhof (North Station).

The vast, splendid railway station and administrative complex was the impressive entry point to the capital when they arrived from the empire's central-eastern crownlands of Bohemia, Moravia, Galicia and Bukovina. It was also the area where those few Jews permitted to live in Vienna were confined in 1624[152] until their eviction from Vienna and the whole of Lower Austria in 1670 by decree of Holy Roman Emperor Leopold I.[153]

By the time Marie arrived in Vienna, Leopoldstadt was once again home to a growing Jewish community that was legally free to come and go as it pleased in most aspects of life,[154] even if the law and everyday reality could at times remain somewhat at odds with one another. That history might repeat itself under these new constitutional protections within a more civilised and enlightened society would probably not have occurred to many Jews; sadly, their newly won freedom from restrictions and persecution turned out to be a mere blip in time.

Constitutions may be written, borders may seem to be secure, but devious power-hungry man's determined inventiveness should never be underestimated!

NOW IT'S THE TURN OF THE SLAVS

I don't know if Marie knew that she was walking straight into a snake's pit of anti-Slav xenophobia when she decided to migrate to Vienna. While overt anti-Jewism (in the meantime reinvented as a supposedly more rational but unashamedly xenophobic anti-Semitism) still continued in some quarters, Vienna in 1905 was witnessing the decline of imperialism and the birth pangs of democracy and human rights. That resulted in disruptions to the status quo that many native Viennese did not like at all.

The Vienna-based empire had sought to suppress Czech national and

---

152 For a fuller description of the relocation of Vienna's Jews to Unterer Werd see Appendix 3.
153 For a fuller description of the expulsion of Vienna's Jews in 1669/70 see Appendix 4.
154 There were exclusionary quotas within the bureaucratic system and university courses.

individual freedoms but the about-face of its 1867 constitution enshrined the right for all nationalities within its dominion to raise their children in their mother tongue, and the equality of all traditional languages in their own schools, public offices and public life. The rise in Czech economic growth and self-assertion set in motion the erosion of Austrian domination in its internal affairs.

If that had been a bitter pill for the habituated *Herrenvolk* (supremacist) mentality to swallow, there was more to come. Czech migration to Vienna where, if their minority status exceeded twenty-five per cent of the city's population they would be entitled to enjoy the same constitutional rights as a native, also continued to gather momentum.

When Czech politicians insisted that Vienna should also have to function on a bilingual basis if Prague was not given over to the exclusive use of the Czech language, the political posturing took on a belligerent nationalistic slant that continued for several turbulent years.

The introduction of democratic universal male suffrage in 1906 didn't help matters either, fanning the embers of nationalist panic as the centuries' old unchallenged Austrian monopoly over the local economy was perceived to be coming under ever greater threat from hordes of Slavic 'Wenzels' who, it was considered, should have stayed at home where they belonged.

Hysterical polemics and 'damned lies and statistics' flowed forth as various ambitious native Austrian candidates across the political spectrum sought to prove that the Slavic Czechs were intent on taking over all aspects of Austria's political, institutional and economic life.

Nationalist extremists on both sides of the border were involved in terrorist attacks, while peaceable Czechs in Vienna were subjected to business boycotts, riots and mob violence.

No doubt there were some incomers who were either too lacking in self-awareness to notice, or simply had no intention of doing in Rome as the Romans did. Caught in the middle was the average Czech migrant who just wanted to get on with life and assimilate, if not wholly integrate.

Instead, they often found themselves looking over their shoulders while walking on eggshells lest they do or say something that might raise their heads above the parapet. They feared further aggravating the locals' fears of being deliberately usurped, despite these having no solid foundation in reality. Harmless acts, such as gathering in small groups to catch up with one another in their native language or visiting the amusement arcades and parklands of the Prater, could provoke verbal abuse or even physical assault.

For Marie, who was extraordinarily strong in so many ways and very sensitive in others, the pervading undercurrent of antagonism was deeply affecting. For that reason alone, small wonder she'd been saving for her escape to America, the Land of the Free.[155] However, fate intervened before she could return to her ambition after helping finance her father's house in Popovice.

22nd January 1916, from the WWI trenches on the Eastern Front.

> *My most treasured and beloved Marie!*
>
> *...I am in a state of complete peace of mind, but only superficially. I think to myself if all goes well, I shall come home to you. If things go badly and I am unlucky then I simply won't come home, and I will be spared much. For example, I will not have to be afraid of the day when I might say it would have been better if I had been killed back then. That would all be well and good, but what would happen to you? And it is these thoughts, you know, that leave me no peace... You need just as much love as I do, yet the two of us have had too little of it and I know very well that a life in the shadow would be too long for you – just as I know how sensitive your heart and soul are... Furthermore, I cannot bear the thought that strange, stupid and wicked people might come your way, and that cold, harsh words and deeds will hurt you without anybody being there to protect you, to be with you...*
>
> *The post is being collected now, so unfortunately, I must end and can only kiss you as passionately and embrace you as tightly in my thoughts as I once did in reality.*
>
> *Your Oskar*

GRANDFATHER

When she first saw the skinny grammar-school pupil Oskar Alexander Löwenthal in the Moravian capital Brno, Marie Vondra was still a lowly domestic servant employed in the home of relatives he had come to visit. A few years later the resourceful young cook and the newly impoverished law student bumped into one another in the streets of Vienna. Oskar encountered an independent, determined young woman, while Marie

---

155 Cousin Ludan told me that a close relative of Great-grandfather Vojtec had got into a brawl; afraid that he had inflicted serious injuries for which he might be imprisoned, he had fled to America. Had that relative perhaps planted the idea of the American dream in Oma's mind?

found a man of quiet reason, quick wit and easy humour. He alone knew how to blow her clouds away. Each one also found something else: their fellow pariah.

There was attraction, empathy and mutual respect and, within a couple of years, Oskar in particular wanted to plan for their marriage. Unfortunately, neither one of them had much money, so the future bride needed to keep saving.

There were university fees to be paid too. The Löwenthals had not been badly off when Oskar's father, Samuel, was employed as a senior design engineer with the Royal and Imperial Northern Railway. Oskar's mother, Antonia, had continued to enjoy the lifestyle she'd been accustomed to as the pampered only child of prosperous parents, while Oskar and his four older siblings, Paula, Clara, Camilla, and Arthur, had benefitted from the best secular schooling available.

Unfortunately, soon after retiring 68-year-old Samuel died from stomach ulcer complications; this was in 1905, the year before Oskar was due to go to university. Antonia was totally ignorant of financial affairs and money slipped rapidly through her fingers.

For reasons that are not clear, municipal records show that Oskar soon left the parental home and moved to another address. Archive documents relating to his tenure at the University of Vienna also show that he'd acquired another legal guardian after his father's death, Julius Beckmann, but nothing explains the lack of funds to pay his tuition fees in full.

Although private Latin tutoring generated some income, the university records reflect that it was not always enough, which made his attendance at lectures inconsistent. He failed an end-of-year exam, after which he was given dispensation to pay only half of the university fees and was allowed to continue with his studies. What *is* known for certain is that when Marie learnt of his financial challenges, her self-sacrifice enabled her future husband to complete his course.

There was nothing she could do about the aggressive anti-Semitic posturing of the nationalistic student groups within the Burschenschaften,[156]/[157]/[158] however. Perhaps emboldened by Vienna's

---

156   Association of University Students.
157   In 1905 the University of Vienna introduced an unofficial antisemitic policy; it was specifically designed to exclude Jewish students, especially from the faculty of law. The policy was rescinded in 1906 but the historically antisemitic Burschenschaften had a violent field day.
158   Before the coining of the concept 'anti-Semitism', the University of Vienna (historically a Catholic institution) had for centuries been a hotbed of anti-Judaism,

incumbent mayor Karl Lueger's vote-garnering, anti-Jew diatribes, they were once again dredging often violent depths.

In what the chief archivist at the University of Vienna suggested might have been an act of solidarity while under such overt persecution Oskar, who considered himself a fully acculturated Austrian national of Jewish descent, whose Moravian ancestors had communicated amongst themselves exclusively in German,[159] wrote on his university registration form that his mother tongue was '*Deutsch*' (German). With no formal prompt, he added *Jüdische Nationalität* (Jewish nationality).

Whatever the case might have been, writing to Toni in England thirty years later he reminded his somewhat tetchy son of the obligation that, no matter what one's personal differences in behaviour and demeanour, all Jews must support one another when under persecution.

Once Oskar's fees started to be paid in full, his attendance at lectures improved. He passed his final law exams in 1912 and gained his doctorate two years later. Then, just as life seemed to be proceeding in an orderly manner, the outbreak of WWI threw his and Marie's plans into the air.

In the immediate years leading up to their marriage in January 1917, Marie renounced the freelance life and returned to more secure live-in employment. Oskar, having served as an officer on the eastern front, became a public defence lawyer at the High Court and *'Lieutenant in the Reserve of the Imperial Infantry Regiment nr. 82'*.

Although there is no evidence that Marie converted to Judaism, she did leave the Catholic Church to comply with its anti mixed-marriage rules. Even if she had wanted to convert, how would she have found the time and money to study Torah to any meaningful – and acceptable – depth?

In any event, and in contrast with Arthur and Ida's 1910 marriage in Vienna's Seitenstetter synagogue,[160] Oskar and Marie had a non-

---

although Jewish converts to Catholicism were accepted on its faculty. In particular the German journalist and politician Wilhelm Marr popularised the xenophobic, but ostensibly more rational concept of anti-Semitism in the second half of the nineteenth century when he blamed the 'foreign' Semites for all ills. Later in life he is said to have recanted, recognising that the industrial revolution had been the true cause of society's upheavals.

159   When German was imposed as the official language in Bohemia and Moravia by the Habsburg Empire, wealthy as well as secularly educated Jews adopted it as their primary language.

160   Like his siblings, Arthur was not conventionally 'religious' and nor was Ida; perhaps he had been keeping his more 'frumm' mother happy. Grandfather does not seem to have been concerned with keeping up appearances.

denominational civil ceremony witnessed by two members of the Imperial Opera. Oma loved to sing, so perhaps their witnesses were friends from a church choir?

Vienna, September 2006

THE PAST CONTINUES TO CATCH UP

Lothar Hölbling, the head of the IKG archives, not only gave me privileged access to the microfilmed post-Anschluss collection of documents but also helped me a great deal.[161]

What I had already learned in the London Metropolitan Archives was shocking and awe-inspiring in equal measure, but back then I was investigating from a relatively safe distance. In Vienna, it was different. I started with the intention of scanning the microfilmed forms, lists, reports and letters in the hope of finding the Löwenthal name but gradually I became immersed in individual human tragedies, the pain of which started to affect me deeply.

There was nobody in Vienna or at home with whom I could share the experience; although my family shared their problems with me, I didn't feel I could burden them with mine.

Then I learned that my friend, mentor and confidant Ian, formerly known as Hans, had died, which made me feel both sad and curiously lost though I was glad he was free again.

I was due to leave Vienna at the end of the following month, but as soon as that thought crossed my mind I was almost floored by debilitating palpitations. Something was obviously playing itself out beneath the surface, but what? My son reassured me that I wouldn't be leaving forever and could always come back; I knew that, but after talking it over with Don I decided to renew my rental agreement for a further six months. I felt very bad in many ways, but I simply could not leave the city.

Although I felt better for doing that, every fleeting thought about departing still sent the palpitations into overdrive.

---

161 At the time the microfilmed archives had only just been received from Israel. The IKG archive department did not have the facilities to accommodate public access so I was exceptionally privileged.

Part Two ~ Chapter Two

Vienna, October 2006

MANNERS

The number 10 tram stop was only a few meters away from my apartment. It was one of my favourite places because it signalled the beginning of a break when I felt my brain and my heart were about to explode after a day at the laptop or contemplating my research findings.

Walking around the parklands at Schönbrunn Palace, only a few minutes' ride away, gave me the mental freedom I needed to allow the bigger picture of what I had been attempting to grasp fall into place.

One afternoon I was waiting with growing despondency for my tram, almost certain that any sunlight would have disappeared before I reached the park. That was when I became aware that I was contravening a cardinal rule of my upbringing: *don't stare!*

Seven years in Germany had made me aware of manners that were different to those in England, but 'don't stare' had remained firmly imprinted on my mind.

When my mother fled to England, she was a child with little understanding of the boundaries she needed to navigate in order to maintain harmony. During formal occasions she knew she should be more restrained and allow the adults to take precedence, but generally she was a chatterbox who said what she thought, asked questions and gazed intently when she was curious.

Once in England, her learning curve became steeper. Her sister Elsa wrote to Vienna: *As far as My is concerned, she feels very at ease here and is content. She hasn't become in the least a little humbler and always says exactly what she wants.*

Elsa's reprimands were frequent and often ruthless, so much so that my mother was almost relieved when her sister had to move to Oxford in 1940.

But some things had filtered down from Vienna[162] and by the time my mother had children herself a kindly 'don't stare, darling' had become part

---

162 Dawa was brought up in an environment that encouraged speaking with thoughtful authenticity in a kindly manner that would not cause embarrassment or provoke a thoughtless knee-jerk reaction. She became a master of subtlety, leaving it to the recipient to process the meaningful 'Aha!' moment in their own time. In the case of wilful deafness, her more direct words were often spoken more from pain than in anger. Unsurprisingly, there were those who took advantage of her kind and sophisticated nature, not least because she was a woman.

of her child-rearing manual.

So there I was, looking at a young man on crutches who was waiting at the tram stop across the road. I wondered what his story was. What had happened to him? Motorcycle accident? Car crash? Military casualty? Industrial mishap? Fallen under a tram? Disease, cancer, diabetes...? Why no prosthesis? Still too sore? Not bothered, maybe? Attention seeking? Denial?

As I stood there speculating, he took his arm out of the crook of his left crutch, raised his stump – hands free – at a right angle to his body and placed the crutch beneath it to serve as a support for what was left of his leg.

He removed a small tin from a jacket pocket and a lighter and a pack of cigarette papers from another. Placing them on his thigh, which was now serving as a bench-top, he rolled a cigarette then lit it and inhaled deeply and pleasurably.

As the young man stood there smoking, with his thigh still resting on the grip of his crutch, my thoughts turned to Uncle Toni, who had probably been about the same age when his leg was amputated in 1945.

UNCLE TONI

My first conscious memory of Toni is of when he came to stay with us when I was about three years old.

My overriding feeling for him has remained one of deep affection tinged with the sadness of loss. Knowing that my mother was so attached to him might go some way towards explaining that, but also Toni was one of those rare individuals who could provoke intense warmth and respect from others.

Apart from my mother, there have only been two people who have moved me so profoundly: Oma was one of them, Toni was the other. They both had that indefinable 'something' because their own hearts were more open than most.

During that visit when I was little, Toni took me with him to post a letter. When we approached the post box, I reached for the envelope and begged him to pick me up so that I could put it in the slot. He told me to be careful; if I put my hand too far inside, my fingers would be bitten off by a creature whose duty it was to prevent its home from being used as a rubbish bin. His warning made such an impression upon me that, even to this day, I still remember the threat of sharp teeth waiting to snap when I post a letter.

The story scared me but Toni didn't, and I loved being with him. One morning when impatience got the better of me, I ran into his bedroom, only to be stopped in my tracks by the incomprehensible sight of his trousers almost standing next to his bed, albeit it without an upper body attached to them. The body was lying in bed. I can still see the shoe of Toni's left foot with the trouser leg wrinkling around the ankle, while the braces were hitched up over the top of his thigh, in the place above which one would normally expect to see the rest of the body. The other trouser leg was hanging empty and lifeless, like a windsock on a still summer's day.

My terror must have been obvious, but before I could launch into the wailing fit that was building inside me, Toni began to explain to me. My fear evaporated almost immediately. I can't recall what he said, but from then on I accepted his limp and that he leaned on a stick. Much later I understood that his need for a prosthesis was the result of an injury sustained in WWII.

***

My tram was still nowhere to be seen, though the young man's had arrived and he had gone. Now that my thoughts were no longer occupied, I started thinking about how ill at ease I'd been feeling since returning from London a few days earlier. In England I had been fine, very relaxed, all the more so for having followed up some clues from Curt Carter's latest letters.

With Don's encyclopaedic knowledge of military history and methods of documentation, we had isolated war diaries at the National Archives and pinpointed the exact time and place of the skirmish in which Toni was wounded during the Allied advance across the Rhine in April 1945.

Since I have very little tolerance for loose ends, tying up this one had felt pretty good. Having pieced together the strands of my earlier research, I had also completed as best I could Toni's untold story for Helen Fry's book *His Majesty's Most Loyal Enemy Aliens*.[163]

I should have been feeling pretty good but I didn't; instead, my thoughts and emotions were jumping all over the place. Every outing beyond the apartment had become such a trial that I wondered whether my cousin Leah, Toni's psychotherapist daughter, might not have had a point when she had recently voiced concerns about my mental health.

My discomfort had to have something to do with Vienna, but what?

---

163 Sutton Publishing 2007: Hardback ISBN 978-7509-4700-8; Paperback ISBN 978-0-7509-4701-5

I was there voluntarily and the city was familiar. I *liked* being there – but something deep inside me had been disturbed and I had no idea what it was.

One thing that had discomfited me had been an encounter with a man who'd boarded my train a few weeks into my stay. He'd sat opposite me and stared quite shamelessly at my face, the way I remembered people staring in Munich when I was a child.

He had a large crucifix hanging around his neck. After what seemed like an eternity, his gaze moved down and his expression changed as he noticed my necklace. The delicate gold chain had belonged to Tante Camilla and, against all the rules, had been sewn into the lining of my mother's coat when she'd fled Vienna.[164] Now it held a heart-shaped charm (also sewn into her coat by the aunts) and the tiny gold 'Glückstern' (lucky star) Oma had given me when I was ten years old.

There was also a slightly larger Star of David. Our cousin Hubert, my mother's cousin and playmate back in Vienna who had died in London only five months before her, had given it to her. His own childhood had also been lost to the Holocaust, his innocence to predatory Nazi officers. The Star of David had been in remembrance of *Onkel* and *die Tanten* whose gentle patience and loving kindness he had never forgotten.[165]

The man on the train looked repeatedly at my necklace then at my face, and I felt increasingly threatened. Finally he stood up to get off the train, but he subjected me to another long, intense glare. I couldn't recall ever having been at the receiving end of such deep antipathy, and afterwards I stopped wearing my necklace unless the Star of David was hidden beneath my clothes.

That episode had left me wary about what others might be concealing behind their smiles when I mentioned my background, and I had become even more sensitive to undercurrents. I also sensed another kind of discomfort in other people; were they wondering what *I* might be thinking about *them*? Did I blame them in some way for what had happened in the

---

164 Dawa was not alone in this.
165 Hubert had felt safe and loved when he was with the Löwenthals; in contrast, when there were no Löwenthals present to hold him to a higher standard, Uncle Maly often had vicious outbursts of temper and hit Hubert and Hedwa 'for no good reason…he shouldn't have done it anyway…'. Dawa was terrified of him and loathed him: 'I feel that was the only thing I hated in my childhood.' She also acknowledged that Uncle Maly, while poorly educated, had been the most gifted of gardeners who cultivated abundant fruit trees, flowering shrubs and flowers, their perfume often pervading the Löwenthal home in Lasalle Hof.

past?

I MEET HEINRICH

Although they had no obvious relevance to the file that contained them, I found a number of portrait photographs of children. One photograph was markedly different to the others; it was of an older teenage boy dressed in a dark suit and a white, open-necked shirt. Gazing straight into the lens, he cut a dashing figure, relaxed and self-confident as he posed against a backdrop of what seemed to be the Danube Canal.

Looking at the name, I read Heinrich Gertler. My vision blurred and my heart missed a beat before starting to race. I *knew* Heinrich: I had been inside his head because I had read his letters. However, there was no congruence between the desperate tone of those letters and the confident young man in the picture.

I had read countless heartbreaking letters penned by parents, grandparents and children, some of them pleading with the organisers of the Kindertransport and adult-rescue committees in the most emotional of terms, but Heinrich's were different.

Judging by the many errors in his second letter, which demonstrated a poorer knowledge of German, he didn't write his first plea for rescue himself. It had been deeply upsetting to read because I was becoming horribly familiar with the appalling reality behind the objective statements of fact.

<u>Vienna 21st May 1939</u> to Lord Bearsted, Central British Fund for German Jewry, London:[166]

> *Noble patron Lord Stead (sic)!*
> *I permit myself to turn to you, honoured benefactor, with the following:*
> *Please, my parents had a grocery shop in Vienna, the same having been taken away from them on 10th May 1938 and they are not in a position to look after me.*
> *My father was arrested on 10th November 1938 and was in Dachau concentration camp until 8th March 1939.*
> *Due to his war service he was released and must leave German territory on 26th May: so that I shall have to remain here alone without seeing any future ahead of me.*

---

166   Ref: Archive IKG Vienna, Jerusalem Holding, A/W1971 Kinderauswanderung, Q22 Frame 700.

I am a deaf and mute boy of 17 and am good at any task put before me, furthermore I have a good final school report.

I have read that you can bring children to England, for which £50 surety is required. But I know nobody in England and my parents are very poor. I therefore ask you, honoured Lord, to help me come to England, so that I too can become a useful human being. Not only I but also my parents will be most grateful to you. And God will repay you. I ask you once again to help an unfortunate child.

I look forward to receiving your reply soon.
I am also enclosing my photograph.
I and my parents thank you in advance,
Yours most sincerely,
Heinrich Gertler

London 25th May 1939 from Ms Exiner, the Movement for the Care of Children from Germany to Miss Schwarz, Social Welfare Department, IKG Vienna:[167]

We regret that we can do nothing for this boy, as, within the framework of our organisation, we are only able to bring over children who are one hundred per cent mentally and physically healthy.

We request that you get in touch with this boy.

Heinrich's second letter was all the more pathetic because it was raw, in his own words and poorly written.[168]

Vienna 3rd June 1939 to Lord Bearsted, British Central Fund for German Jewry, London:[169]

Dear Lord Stead (sic)
I am very sad that you have not written an answer to me.
Please, you write no answer to me. I must know why you have not answered me. I have written two letters to you but you do not answer me.
My mother is leaving for England tomorrow. My father is leaving for Palestine next week. My parents and siblings are now leaving already, but I do not leave. Please arrange permission for me to come. I was in the Vienna Jewish Community Office. I want to leave and go abroad.

---

167 Ref: Archive IKG Vienna, Jerusalem Holding, A/W1971 Kinderauswanderung, Q22 Frame 0697
168 This is an approximate translation in which grammar has been corrected.
169 Ref: Archive IKG Vienna, A/W1971 Kinderauswanderung, Q22 Frame 0698

Vienna Community Office says 'you must write to Lord Stead and he will sort you out'. Please answer soon. Please do not forget!
  Heinrich Gertler

London 13th June 1939 from Ms Exiner. Movement for the Care of Children from Germany to Miss Schwarz, Welfare Department, Vienna Jewish Community:[170]

We refer to our letter of 25th May.
The boy has written again, saying he has had no reply. We enclose his original letter and would ask you to invite the boy in and explain to him – as we have already informed you in our letter of 25th May – that we can only bring one hundred per cent mentally and physically healthy children to England.
We would like to avoid the boy receiving a rejection from our end.

The last letter was stamped with *KV informiert*': *Kindes Vater informiert* (child's father informed).

I was shocked by how deeply Heinrich's photograph affected me. Returning home, I immediately opened my laptop and checked the DOEW database of Austrian holocaust victims. Desperately hoping for no results when I typed in his name, I found one with a short summary of the bare facts:

Heinrich Gertler, Born 7th July 1922. Deported to Litzmannstadt (Lodz). Date of deportation 15th October 1941.

My eyes went straight to where I knew I would find his fate: *Location of death unknown. Last known address: Schweidlgasse 13.*

I instantly dissolved into tears. Heinrich had left his family home and for some reason ended up living in the same apartment building as my grandparents, my great-grandmother and my two great-aunts. My mother's family would have known him and, if he really was alone, would have treated him as they would their own son. Somewhere deep within I felt a slight relief. Unless he had been picked up in the street without warning, they might have also said goodbye to him on his way out to the collection lorry.

Was it watching Heinrich being taken away that had galvanised my grandmother into risking her own safety by joining the underground, or had she already been helping Heinrich? Certainly, Heinrich's father did

---

170 Ref: Archive IKG Vienna, Jerusalem Holding, A/W1971 Kinderauswanderung, Q22 Frame 0696.

not leave for Palestine according to the schedule described in his son's pitiful letters, although he was eventually deported from the family home in the summer of 1942 and delivered straight to the killing fields of Maly Trostenets. Did the father stay behind to protect his son, only to end up being murdered too? And what had happened to Heinrich's mother and siblings? So many questions, so few answers, so much injustice.

I later learned that Heinrich's occupation in the Lodz ghetto was electrician's apprentice. His address was Siegfried Strasse 70, Flat 1. How many others were crammed into Flat 1, and how long did the boy survive without being able to communicate effectively in the hellish conditions that were an unimaginable challenge to those in possession of all their faculties?

To quote from a report dated 17th July 1942 by the Gestapo in German occupied Lodz (now known as Litzmannstadt) to the incumbent Governor Greiser in Poznan:

> *The deterioration of the Jews' physical condition has had an adverse effect on work and productivity. Consequently, the Jewish Leaders' Committee has decided to draft all children aged 10 and above for labour to keep up with the army's orders.*[171] *Despite the poor nutrition, the Jews are still trying to do their work properly. Roughly 70,000 Jews are employed in the ghetto to fill the army's orders, and we shall be able to use them for work in three shifts until the end of the year... The Jews' medical condition has worsened threefold... For several months, average mortality has exceeded 1,800 a month.*[172]

---

171 The wider reality is more complex and beyond the healthy imagination. The overriding motivation of the ghetto's Jewish leader, Mordechai Chaim Rumbovsky, who found himself confronted with a diabolic challenge, was to ensure that as many Jews as possible could remain 'useful' (for which they received below subsistence rations) and perhaps live to see another dawn. Of the 210,000 Jews and 5000 Roma (who were segregated in separate buildings), thousands simply died of hunger and disease wherever they had stopped because they could no longer move, mostly in the streets of the ghetto that was sealed off from the rest of Lodz with deep layers of high barbed-wire fencing. Thousands of others were sent to be gassed. For more detail go to: https://encyclopedia.ushmm.org/content/en/article/lodz and https://encyclopedia.ushmm.org/contents/en/article/give-me-your-children-voices-from-the-lodz-ghetto

172 Ref: Michal Unger. The Last Ghetto: Life in the Lodz Ghetto, Yad Vashem, 1992. P12.

ALTRUISM?

I decided to check the database for the names of the other innocent children I had met through their photographs. One-third of them were deported and murdered. If any of their parents or siblings survived, how could they ever get over it?

Richard Mandel Born 25th August 1928. Deported to Maly Trostenets on 6th May 1942. Died 11th May 1942.

Richard's sister Irene Mandel Born 10th March 1931. Deported to Maly Trostenets on 6th May 1942. Died 11th May 1942

Anna Süss Born 7th November 1924. Deported to Lodz ghetto on 2nd November 1941. Place and date of death unknown.

Herbert Scherzer Born 16th June 1935. Deported to Riga on 3rd December 1941. Place and date of death unknown.

Lotte Wachs Born 18th February 1926. Deported to Modliboryce ghetto 5th March 1941. Place and date of death unknown.

Gitla Rakowicz Born 12th December 1925. Deported to Lodz ghetto on 2nd November 1941. Place and date of death unknown.

Gitla's two siblings ***Marjem*** born 6th September 1928, and ***Wilhelm***, born 1st March 1931 as well as their mother ***Cywie***, suffered the same fate.

Her father ***Benjamin***, aged 44, was deported to Buchenwald on 15th November 1939. Date of death 28th December 1939.

Karl Rosenbaum Born 1st June 1928. Deported to Modliboryce ghetto on 5th March 1941. Place and date of death unknown.

Selma Streigold Born 3rd September 1932. Deported to Terezin 1st October 1942. Transported to Auschwitz 18th May 1944. Date of death unknown.

Selma's brother ***Herbert***, born 30th June 1929 and her mother ***Chaje*** suffered the same fate.

Selma's father ***Moritz***, *aged 39*, date of death 30th December 1938 after six weeks in Dachau.

Berta Kerzner Born 2nd May 1930. Deported to Modliboryce ghetto on 5th March 1941. Place and date of death unknown. Berta's parents **Friedrich** and **Rosa** suffered the same fate.

Susanne Bauer, Born 1st June 1936. Deported to Terezin 20th August 1942. Transported to Auschwitz 16th October 1944. Dead but no further details.

So Heinrich was also dead. I immediately remembered other children who were refused a place on the Kindertransport because they were not 'one hundred percent mentally and physically healthy'. One little boy was turned away because he was a diabetic, although his condition had been fully controlled with medication. A little girl was turned away due to a 'strawberry' birthmark on her cheek. Another girl was turned away because she was a little behind at school.

There must have been more, because I came across a number of these admonitions:

2nd January 1939 from the Movement for the Care of Children from Germany, in London to the Welfare Department of Vienna Jewish Community Office concerning two sisters:[173]

> *I must inform you of the following so that from now on the medical examinations are carried out with greater rigour. X[174] is, according to medical opinion, mentally retarded[175] is also a bed wetter. X[176] is also mentally retarded and a bed wetter.*
>
> *We have given an undertaking to the Home Office that within the framework of our Movement we shall only accept children who are one hundred percent mentally and physically healthy. The same applies to guaranteed children and I ask you to apply this rule to the letter.*

10th March 1939 Movement for the Care of Children from Germany, London, to the Welfare Department of Vienna Jewish Community Office:[177]

---

173 REF: Archive IKG Vienna, Jerusalem Holding, AW1970 Kinderauswanderung, Q18 Frame 574.
174 Name of an eight year old.
175 Could be translated as intellectually underdeveloped.
176 Name of a fifteen year old.
177 Ref: Archive IKG Vienna, Jerusalem Holding, AW 1971 Kinderauswanderung, Q19 Frame 143.

We would once more like to make it clear that we are unable, under any circumstances, to bring backward children to England, even though they may attend normal schools and have a guarantor.

When I searched through my dossier, I came across some other scanned correspondence clipped together with a photograph of the child in question. I had no idea why I was collecting all this information apart from feeling compelled to do so.[178]

Sabine Horn was fourteen years old when she gazed at the camera through her round spectacles. There was something deeply affecting about her, perhaps an inner quality that might have compensated for her lot in life. She was not conventionally pretty, although the 'fault' in question is not one that is immediately obvious.

<u>18th June 1939</u> Welfare Department of the Vienna Jewish Community Office to Movement for the Care of Children from Germany, London:[179]

Permit us to draw your attention to the above-mentioned girl who is a double orphan. We enclose all relevant documentation. However, we would like to make you aware of the fact that, as you can see from the medical certificate, this girl has very visible surgical scarring to her face.

I looked again at the medical certificate, signed by Dr. Joseph Grünberger, 16th June 1939. Sabine had scarring as a result of an operation to a bilateral cleft lip; additionally, she had undergone an operation to a cleft palate.

<u>Dr. Joseph Grünberger 16th June 1939</u>:[180]

The effect of the operation is a halfway good one.

It seems Dr. Grünberger tried to do his best, and the case worker probably crossed her fingers in the hope she might slip Sabine beneath the radar. Instead, she received another letter from across the Channel with very clear instructions not to submit any similar cases. To put it bluntly – and British government directives aside – Sabine was simply <u>considered too</u> ugly; she would have had difficulty finding anybody to care

---

178   Many years later I was able to assist others who were seeking information about their murdered family members.
179   Ref: Archive IKG Vienna, Jerusalem Holding, AW197 Kinderauswandering, Q21 Frame 795.
180   Ref: Archive IKG Vienna, Jerusalem Holding, AW 1971 Kinderauswanderung, Q21 Frame 0798.

for her or employ her. No doubt she was not regarded as a particularly good representative specimen of the Jewish people. I had read too much to imagine otherwise.

Once again I pulled up the DOEW holocaust victim database:

> **Sabine Horn** Born 9th February 1925. Deported to Maly Trostenets 14th September 1942. Died 18th September 1942.

To be precise, murdered upon arrival.

VIENNA, NOVEMBER 2006

TANTE CAMILLA?

The tension had got me by the jugular again and my muscles felt like sheaths of steel. My jaws were so tightly clenched that I was afraid my teeth would crack. I was hungry all the time but my digestion seemed to have given up so that I had a permanent ball of lead in my stomach. In spite of doing my best to eat little but often, I had lost 5kg; although it was not yet a disaster because I'd put on more than that after Dawa's death and hadn't been able to shed it.

I was starting to dislike going out, especially on public transport, because I had the irrational feeling that people knew I was a foreigner, an outsider and probably a Jew, that I didn't belong here. Had I stepped back in time?

The sad truth was that, much as I loved Vienna, Vienna was now making a mess of me.

About ten days earlier, I'd settled in front of the TV for the evening hoping to find something to make me laugh and relax. I was flicking from one channel to another until I lingered on the impish face of an old lady. I can't recall her words but I soon realised that she was giving an account of her incarceration in Terezin concentration camp. How could I not watch?

The documentary was both fascinating and deeply moving. It drew me in until, without warning, I was gasping for air. In a clip from a Nazi film showing a column of women moving towards and then past the camera, I had caught a fleeting glance of my mother's aunt, Camilla.

I eventually collected my wits enough to find paper and pencil and scribble down *Die Pianistin von Terezin* (*The Pianist of Terezin*). The old lady was the remarkable Alice Herz-Sommer.

Could the woman I'd seen really have been Tante Camilla or was I imagining it? If that were the case, why had I reflexed so violently? I had to find out.

After establishing the name of the documentary production company, I asked them where and when the footage had been taken. If it was from Terezin, and if I had the date it was filmed, I could cross-reference it with the date when the aunts were deported from Vienna. Although the company couldn't give me the precise information, they suggested I might be able to get it from the archives in Berlin. In the meantime, they sent me a video copy of the documentary.

I watched the relevant frames again and again. Like a ghost, Tante Camilla was there and then gone but I eventually succeeded in isolating the relevant frame. It was slightly fuzzy but I could see she was thinner, exhausted, yet her head was held high. She had a particular 'look' that seemed so very familiar.

I had brought a small box of photographs from England to help me explore a world before my time. Tante Camilla's face was fuller – but she still had that look.

Her world fell apart in March 1938. Later, she knew that once her frail mother died, she would find her own name on the next deportation list. I thought of the losses, privations and humiliations she endured for the next four years: the lack of food and basic essentials, the tortuous train journey in the height of summer without adequate food, drink and sanitation. She must have known that she was walking towards one of the many doorways to hell on earth.

If it was not her in the footage it didn't matter; that woman would have been somebody else's Tante Camilla.

***

Something extraordinary happened a few mornings later. I woke up knowing that I had been feeling my mother's dread at having to leave home.

The palpitations stopped.

Vienna, December 2006

OPENING UP TO THE PAST

Two years before she died, my mother finally dared to openly ask what it must have been like for her parents in Vienna during the war and the Holocaust. How had they coped with the loss of so many relatives, friends and neighbours, the humiliations and privations and the constant fear? How had they survived the allied bombings and the final battle for Vienna in April 1945 that had caused so much devastation? How had they survived at all, especially after her father had been put to forced labour and food rationing had been exceptionally meagre for the Jewish population? What had he been forced to do? There was a hazy memory of being told he had unloaded freight boats on the Danube docks, as well as associated hard labour and digging elsewhere.

Dawa also remembered something of Oma's work for the resistance, that she'd had a code name and gathered intelligence as part of a cell within a chain of gentiles who hid and fed Jews and moved them from one 'safe' house to another. They even succeeded in spiriting some of them out of Vienna. Oma had hidden Jews in their apartment building, which had caused my grandfather great anxiety.

The more questions Dawa asked, the more she became angry with herself for not having acknowledged her widowed mother's suffering and endurance when they were finally reunited in 1947. By then, though, suppressing trauma had become the only way for her to continue living without falling apart.

By the time my stateless and passport-less mother obtained permission to travel home to Vienna, her father had already been dead for three months. He had died almost eight years after that cold night of 27th March 1939 when he had sent her away, not knowing when or if they would ever see each other again.

When Dawa returned home, so much terror and suffering had taken place that the few weeks she'd spent with her mother were marked by tears and stress-relieving laughter. 'We cried and laughed hysterically.' She didn't ask many questions and pushed what was said or alluded to into the recesses of her memory. Yet now my mother was finally ready to learn the truth.

HANS KANN

'If you really want to find out, you must do something about it,' I told my mother. 'Do you know anybody who could tell you something?'

'The only person I can think of is Hansi Kann,' Dawa replied.

When my mother returned home in the late spring of 1947, she had belatedly celebrated her twenty-first birthday with Hans and his parents.

That beautiful young boy in my mother's photograph collection had, together with his father, been conscripted into forced labour alongside my grandfather. They had escaped the Holocaust due to the protection afforded by Tante Karoline's Aryan status.

The couple had been sitting, laughing and enveloped in clouds of cigarette smoke, at my grandfather's bedside the night before he suddenly succumbed to pneumonia.

Oma had begged them to put away their cigarettes but her Ockele was having such fun with his friends that they ignored her. Initially, my mother consoled herself with the thought that, thanks to them, her father died laughing. Oma, on the other hand, never entirely forgave her friends for disrespecting her wishes and their culpability in his premature death.

Unfortunately, the last contact between my mother and Hans had been when he was performing at London's Wigmore Hall more than forty years earlier. While she wanted to get in touch with him again, part of her was afraid to do so. He had seemed strangely remote when she and my father had met him after his concert; perhaps he wanted to put the past behind him. The Nazis had imprisoned his mother for two years and he had suffered a breakdown during his time of hard labour; should she remind him of things he might prefer to forget?

Because I knew that she was desperate to find the missing pieces of a puzzle, I decided to contact Hans without her knowledge. I assured him that I would understand if he preferred not to revisit the past but he seemed eager to meet during my forthcoming trip to Vienna. He told me about his father, his mother, his son and his wife, his music and his career, although he seemed determined to evade 'the topic'.

All he revealed was that he'd been only fifteen when he was first 'conscripted' to somewhere around the Praterlände area on the main arm of the Danube. Any further details were firmly concealed behind a façade of banter and affected indifference. Hans mentioned that his mother, to whom he was deeply attached, was imprisoned during the war for listening to the BBC, but then he moved on.

Later, during my research in Vienna, I found Gestapo photographs taken at the time of his mother's arrest. They show the pretty, vivacious Tante Karoline that my mother remembered from 'before the war' with dark rings around her eyes, looking considerably older than her forty-one years.

Hans' own nemesis came one day when he stumbled under the weight of a heavy load of cargo and dropped it as he fell. For a growing teenager suffering from chronic stress and undernourishment, and weakened by hard labour, the fear of punishment proved too much. Auschwitz was only ever a train ride away.

In January 1946, at the age of nineteen and only nine months after his liberation, he performed at the Musikverein, Vienna's famous concert hall. First Oma, then my mother kept the newspaper article that said he had played compositions by Händel, Scarlatti, Mozart, Chopin, Mendelssohn and Liszt.

I wondered what he had felt. How many of his admirers in Vienna then and in the decades that followed knew of his Jewish background or what he had endured because of it?

THE BOOK THING

I have a thing about books: I want to possess them and be surrounded by them but I am frustrated by the thought that I will not live long enough to read everything I want to read. Then there were my mother's books; having to let go of some of them after her death because of lack of space made me extremely anxious.

Books have something to do with continuity; perhaps I have inherited that sense from my mother. For her, books not only expanded her inner world, but they also represented a lifeline to a world of which she had been robbed and to which she could never return. To dispose of them would have been a betrayal of their previous owners.

Consequently her bookshelves were eventually filled with double rows of books, stacked behind her sofa, beside her armchair and stored in boxes and bags in my loft.

Eighteen months after Dawa's death, I finally gathered the courage to sort through them. I spent days leafing through each one, finding a good reason *not* to let go of it and cursing the fact that I would never have the time to discover all their treasures.

I was also haunted by the fear of betraying the dead by disposing of Dawa's library, of breaking a tangible bridge to my family's past without which some of them would be consigned to oblivion.

Then I found an unexpected treasure. As I opened yet another old book, a small, neatly cut square of newspaper fluttered out. I picked it up and read the words: *'Die für heute auf dem Rapid-Platz angesetzten Spiele wurden abgesagt ... Meisterschaft der Liga...'*

It was about football. When I turned it over, there was an announcement printed within a black border:

Unser lieber, unvergeßlicher Arbeitskollege
Rechtsanwalt
Dr. Oskar A. Löwenthal
Ist am 7. März 1947 plötzlich verschieden.
Das Begräbnis findet Sonntag, den 16. März, um 10 Uhr auf dem Zentralfriedhof, I. Tor (Israel. Abt.), statt.
Es wird um zahlreiche Beteiligung gebeten.

Our dear, unforgettable work colleague
Lawyer
Dr. Oskar A. Löwenthal
Passed away suddenly on 7th March 1947.
The funeral will take place on 16th March at 10am at the Zentralfriedhof,
 Gate I (Jewish Sector).
Large attendance is requested.

Then my heart missed several beats:

In Namen der Zwangsarbeiter
Der Leergutsammelstelle Wien:
Leopold Weinberger.

In the Name of the Forced Labourers
Of the Empty Container Depot Vienna:
Leopold Weinberger.

A depot near Hans Kann's Praterlände: this was where the health of my grandfather, who loved life, people, animals, the sun, nature and fresh air, had started to fail.

A few months later, during another trip with Don to Vienna to attach a memorial plaque to the Löwenthal gravestone, we found a document at the DOEW providing the administrative address of his 'employers': Engerthstrasse 230, a vast Red Vienna apartment complex taken over during the war to house the headquarters of the Wehrmacht's XVII Army Corps.

I also found his 'Replacement Employment Record Book' hidden away amongst my mother's possessions.

Commencement of occupation: 26th August 1942. Employer: Wehrmacht. Type of Business: Provisions Depot. Type of work: Depot Worker. 7am – 21pm.

HERR DR. VOGEL BRINGS THE PAST INTO THE PRESENT

I received an e-mail from Erwin Rennert's son, Frederick, about a symposium he thought I might like to attend at ESRA, Vienna's Jewish community's psychosocial centre, where support is offered to anyone who might be suffering as a consequence of the Holocaust.

The topic was Jewish 'returnees' to Vienna after the end of the war. Etti, a lady I'd met at lunch at Frederick's home, was due to speak; she had been a child refugee who had returned to Vienna with her parents after the war.

My immediate impulse was to cry off; I was still tired from my recent train journey from Frankfurt and couldn't muster any enthusiasm. Then a quiet voice changed my mind and I submitted a last-minute registration request.

Among the speakers was a strikingly handsome elderly gentlemen who gave an account of his work with returnees, most of whom were survivors who had endured arduous journeys back to Vienna from concentration camps across Europe. More often than not they returned to nobody and nothing.

The returnees were exhausted and traumatised after years of physical and psychological suffering; most of them would never be completely whole again. At times it was very difficult for this speaker - and it was not easy for those of us who were listening to him.

When he finished recalling those he had done his best to help, a member of the audience asked him about his own experience during the Holocaust.

Late in life my mother fondly recalled her time as a member of a 'Jewish Club' where she not only learnt about 'Eretz Ysrael'[181] but, most importantly, 'we sang and danced and had such fun ... the youngsters who led the various group were just marvellous ... I wonder what happened to them ...'

Our speaker had been one of those group leaders within what I now knew was the Zionist youth movement Hashomer Hatzair and had taken over as the organisation's local leader in the year before its dissolution by the Nazis in 1941. Unlike the majority of the movement's members, like his father he was protected from deportation because of his mother's Aryan status.

Since there was almost no paid civilian employment for Jews, whether 'Mischling' (half-caste) or not, and 'Aryan' spouses were often denied jobs, he and his father reluctantly applied to work at the empty container

---

181 Land of Israel.

section in the Wehrmacht's wider provisions depot.

Their luck ran out in 1942, when months of transports to concentration camps and ghettos (if not straight to the killing fields) practically rendered Vienna *Judenrein* (cleansed of Jews); it also depleted it of the supply of almost-free labour. Now it was the turn of the 'protected' Jews and 'half-castes' to join the remaining contingent of foreign forced labourers brought in from territories conquered by Germany.

Hearing the word *Zwangsarbeit* (forced labour), then *Leergutsammelstelle* (empty container depot), followed by *Wehrmacht* and *Praterlände*, I was certain that this man would have known my grandfather. Rarely had I been so immediately certain of anything in my life.

As soon as his presentation ended, I did something entirely out of character: I rushed forward and blurted out that it was imperative that I speak with him on a private matter and asked him to give me a contact number.

To my surprise he did. In return, I scribbled my name on a scrap of paper so that he might have at least some point of reference when this strange woman eventually called him. His name was Dr. Martin Vogel.

MY FIRST MEETING WITH GRANDFATHER

A few days later I was sitting in Café Schottenring, one of Vienna's traditional coffee houses, waiting for Dr. Vogel to arrive. Diners were relaxing over late lunches or coffee and cake whilst the pianist played pleasant music. I caught myself wishing that I, too, was merely there to while away a relaxing half hour.

Instead, I was anxious. Dr. Vogel had seemed impatient and abrupt on the phone. Was this gruffness because of approaching deafness or because he was reluctant to have memories stirred up by a strange woman who seemed to think he might have known some relative of hers whose name he couldn't catch?[182]

As a tram pulled away on the other side of the Schottenring boulevard, an athletic elderly gentleman with a wonderful head of thick white hair was waiting at the pedestrian crossing. My date had arrived! At the same time, I noticed the model train shop from forty-five years ago.

Dr. Vogel disappeared momentarily before the café door opened. He

---

182   Dr. Vogel hadn't been able to hear me properly during our telephone call and, not understanding what I was talking about, he had asked his wife to just arrange a meeting instead.

spotted me instantly even though I was at the far end of the busy lounge. As he approached my table, I stood up to shake his hand and thank him for coming. He sat down with the body language of somebody about to leave. 'Well, what is it you want to know? What do you want to ask me?' he barked.

I repeated more fully what I had already tried to convey during our unsatisfactory telephone conversation.

'What was his name?'

'Oskar Löwenthal.'

Almost before I finished speaking, he said, 'Dr. Oskar Löwenthal?' The expression on his face changed instantly. His voice rose by several decibels and he exclaimed, '*Ja! Das war ja ein prächtiger Mann!*' ('Oh! What a magnificent man!')

A curious pain shot through my heart and I found myself stifling an urge to cry. Before I had a chance to say more, Dr. Vogel added, 'In fact, I've just come from having lunch with the widow of my closest friend who was also with us during those forced labour days. Hansi…'

'You don't mean Hans Kann, do you?' I asked incredulously. Yes, he did. I didn't know about Hans Kann's recent death and felt sadness mixed with gratitude for having met him before it became impossible.

Two and a half hours later, I knew for certain that my mother's memory of her father had not been viewed through rose-tinted lenses. Elsa's and Oma's affection and admiration for him had already left me regretting that I'd never known him; when I'd read his letters to his children after they left for England, that regret had grown. I felt closer to the father my mother was deprived of and the grandfather I had never known. I was also very angry.

'If you like, we could meet again and perhaps I can tell you more. In the meantime, I know somebody else who might well have known your grandfather during those days, I will give him a ring and let you know.'

VIENNA, JANUARY 2007

HERR DR. KÖNIG

Dr. Vogel was as good as his word, and after returning from a Christmas break in England I had a phone conversation with Dr. Joseph König, a fellow forced labourer and now curator of the Leopoldstadt District Museum.

'Your grandfather was an imposing and highly cultured man who was also able to assert himself,' he said, before inviting me for a meeting at the museum.

The museum was closed to the public for the day but Dr. König unlocked the door and welcomed me with a beaming smile: 'I am so delighted to be able to meet Herr Dr. Löwenthal's granddaughter!'

Dr. König had been a young teenager when he was conscripted into forced labour. His father was a Jew, his mother a Catholic. She did not step out of the Church and he was christened at birth and brought up as a Catholic, but the Nuremberg Race Laws had caught them out. He admitted that he had resented being lumped together with so many Jews with whom he had nothing in common. I dare say he wasn't the only one to feel that way either – and he was only a boy, after all.

His memories of Grandfather during their time of forced labour were fewer, some different, but most resonated with what Dr. Vogel had already told me. But he did remember both of my grandparents more clearly as neighbours because he had lived opposite them on Schweidlgasse. He had also experienced the final Battle for Vienna in April 1945 that had taken place on their doorsteps; I already knew from one of the letters that Oma had suffered a head injury, but now I found out how.[183]

As Dr. König went into graphic detail of the artillery attack they endured for several days, twenty-four hours a day, part of me felt deeply uncomfortable for stirring up such traumatic memories, but I also believed that he really did have a need to talk about it – and I provided him with the opportunity.

'We were hiding in the cellars while they destroyed the buildings above us. We'd run out of water. One young lad couldn't bear it any longer and decided to risk going out in search. They shot him. It could have been me. If it had lasted any longer, we would all have gone insane.'

Before I said good-bye, he gave me a book he had published with photographs of Vienna's destruction. It was still haunting him and he needed people to know. Then he pressed another book into my hands: Toni Morrison's novel *Beloved*. 'I always recommend it to Museum visitors.'

Sadly, Dr. König was not long of this world.

---

183 I have since wondered whether the large burn wound on the back of Oma's hand might also have been sustained during the artillery attack: when as a child I had asked Dawa what the cause was she said that Oma was 'struck by lightning'.

THE JEWISH CONNECTION

'Of course, had I stayed at home we would probably have come to blows sooner or later.' It was only towards the end of her life that my mother admitted Grandfather's highly tuned intellect would have struggled to accommodate his teenage daughters' inclinations towards popular culture.

Elsa was so afraid of him being disappointed by her that she kept her teenage dream of becoming an actress to herself. Instead, she and her best friend Silvia sneaked off to watch Hollywood movies and secretly had their portraits taken to prepare for their film careers. Grandfather never knew.

As for my mother, the idea of spending hours on her schoolwork just to earn high marks never appealed. If she passed the tests to squeeze through from one school year to the next, that was fine by her; she preferred to go with her own impulses and never feigned any interest in academia. That pursuit of instant gratification would eventually have proved a challenge to her father's commitment to diligence.

But who knows? If Elsa's interest in acting had been serious, he might have seen the matter differently. After all, he gave his son permission to leave grammar school at the age of fifteen and paid for him to attend Vienna's School of Applied Arts.

Grandfather was born in Vienna on 21st October 1885, and considered himself an Austrian citizen whose family history also rendered him a Jew. His parents, Samuel and Antonia (née Eisler), came from Czech Moravia, a crown land that in their day was still under the jurisdiction of Bohemian Prague and, therefore, also under imperial rule emanating from Vienna. That is, until Czechoslovakia's declaration of independence on 28th October 1918, which my Bohemian Czech nationalist great-grandfather, Vojtek Vondra, will have celebrated with enthusiasm![184]

According to Dawa (who must have learnt this from Oma), Grandfather Oskar enjoyed a very close relationship with his father Samuel from whom he gained an understanding of the principles of engineering.

According to Dr. Vogel, Grandfather was highly cultured and knowledgeable in many spheres. According to my mother, he also had a vibrant love of life and people. His friendships spanned a wide spectrum of social and professional backgrounds and he had never been concerned with religious affiliation. What counted was that someone was curious to

---

184 For an overview of the history of the Löwenthal family and their name, see Appendix 5.

explore, discuss and to grow, as well as prepared to laugh at life's foibles. Clearly, Grandfather was not afraid of his own shadow.

When Grandfather and Oma entertained friends for Sunday afternoon coffee and cake, men and women discussed all manner of subjects and laughed a great deal. I know from my own experience that Oma had a wonderful sense of humour, although Dawa said she was more inclined towards observation and inner reflection. My extrovert grandfather loved to tell amusing, instructive anecdotes. Dawa recognised that she was brought up in an environment where she had absorbed a great deal without being consciously aware of it.

While listening in, she had learned that during the impoverished post-WWI period (and before Lasalle Hof) Oma had shared what food they had with those less fortunate, while Grandfather dispensed free legal advice in local factories. After they moved to Lasalle Hof, he continued to visit those factories once a week until the Nazi regime took over in 1938 and his licence to practise was soon revoked.

He also undercharged at times so that poorer citizens could benefit from legal representation. A letter from one of his friends after his death refers to his commitment to justice for everyone.

The Löwenthal children became accustomed to sharing the dining table with beggars whom Grandfather had invited in from the street below. Oma was at peace with his philanthropic gestures, even though she disliked the fleas and lice that she had to contend with.

The children grew up aware of their own good fortune and knowing they should never look down upon those who were less privileged. As an adult, although Dawa never brought strangers in from the street, she always had an open door (at times even a bed) to support those in need.

> *'She opens her mouth with Wisdom, and in her tongue is the law of kindness. She opens her hand to the poor; yes, she reaches out her filled hands to the needy.' Proverb 31 vs 20,26.*

> *To dear Mummy T, Happy Birthday and with grateful thanks for your loving welcomes (especially the hugs and the food), from two of your many children, Lindianna and Paul.'*

That was my mother.

What she had also internalised was that no job, however menial, was beneath her dignity – not least in the absence of choice.

GRADUALLY ASSEMBLING THE CLUES

After Grandfather succeeded in sending his children to safety abroad, he did not remain idle. While Uncle Arthur was advocating on his brother's behalf in England, he took one of the vocational training courses organised by the IKG. These were intended to offer a way to gain financial independence in another country while not being perceived as a threat to the local labour force.

Unlike Uncle Arthur's prominence as an artist, Grandfather's Austrian legal qualifications had relegated him to the bottom of the list of 'potentially useful' émigrés to Britain, so he enrolled in a course to train as a butler. Perhaps he and Oma hoped they could find work in a wealthy British household and somehow reunite the family?

In the meantime, while my mother was secretly dreaming of one day living with her parents in a Richmond apartment block she had passed on her bus journeys to London, she and Elsa approached everybody they knew in the hope of striking lucky. At Grandfather's written request, followed by a desperate plea from Silvia, they also advocated on behalf of Elsa's friend and her younger brother, although without success. While one couple seemed very interested, they decided to adopt English children.

With his tongue firmly in his cheek Grandfather wrote to Toni on 29th July 1939:

> *My most beloved Toni!... To your enquiry as to how I got on with my butler course, let me tell you that due to my good prior knowledge I passed with flying colours and received a certificate.*

Oma and Grandfather also took daily English lessons with their new lodger and self-taught linguist, Dr. Johann Weinberger. However, their hearts were torn at the thought of leaving Vienna. A few weeks before war was declared, Grandfather wrote to Elsa: '...*your mother refuses to desert the aunts...*'

Oma stuck to her resolve until there was nothing more she could do for her sisters-in-law beyond sending them small parcels to Terezin concentration camp.

On 15th October 1942 13804250 Pte (private). A. Loewenthal, 229 Coy P(ioneer). C(orps). Marlborough wrote to Elsa, in English:

> *Dear Elsa,*
> *Do you remember the text of the last reply from Vienna? Well I have now got a bit of very bad news from uncle via Sweden, and although I*

hesitated first to let you know of it at all, I believe it is best not to be quiet about it, especially in these times an age of nineteen should have made you grown up and enable you to bear bad news when it comes.

A few weeks after Grandmother's death our two aunts Camilla and Clara were deported from Vienna. All endeavours, even by Aunt Paula's Chef[85] *through the Red Cross and other channels to get their new address were of no success. You and I are aware of the uselessness of commonplace phrases, therefore I cannot write any more comments. Do you think it advisable to write to Camilla about it? Do write me as soon as you can.*

I end now with my best wishes, and all my love
Your sincere brother Toni

Written around the margin of the letter, he added:

According to some news, a camp has been made at Theresienstadt[186] *for Austrian Jews and so some hope may still exist.*

By the time Grandfather was put to forced labour in August 1942, the effort to rid Austria of its own remaining Jews had already reached the frenzied end stage. After the first wave of deportations of 19,024 Jews to ghettos in Nazi-occupied Poland between February and November 1941, things remained relatively quiet up to the end of April 1942, with 'only' 6201 further deportations.

Meanwhile, the methodology to speed up the Final Solution had undergone a change before it was eventually rubber stamped at the Berlin Wannsee Conference in January 1942 with its resolution to put 'Operation Reinhard'[187] (within the context of the wider 'Generalplan Ost'[188]) into action.

The initial plan of the 'Final Solution to the Jewish Question' was to 'emigrate' the Jews of Germany and Austria through extreme intimidation, but it had suffered because of other countries' reluctance to take them in.[189] The emigration that was facilitated by legal means was eventually reduced

---

185   Boss.
186   Terezin, Bohemia.
187   The extermination of all deported European Jews corralled within the German-occupied territories of Poland.
188   For a more detailed account of the genocidal Generalplan Ost within the context of Hitler's long-standing expansionist ambition for Lebensraum/Living Space, see Appendix 6.
189   The abject failure of the 'Evian Conference' of July 1938 in which 32 countries participated to discuss the plight of Germany's and Austria's Jews proved be the death knell for six million Jews from across Europe.

to a relative trickle by Britain's declaration of war in September 1939.

The second stage of the Generalplan Ost, namely to exterminate all deported Jews from Nazi-occupied European countries through hard labour, starvation, general brutality and poor medical care, was now to be speeded up by means of industrial-scale mass murder.

Squads of 'Einsatzgruppen', consisting of Nazi SS units and police, had already carried out mass shootings and gassings in mobile wagons when German troops invaded the western territories of the Soviet Union. This provided the green light for similar actions in the rest of Nazi-occupied Europe.

Ruthlessness was the name of the game; ruthlessness[190] as an unwavering means to an end. Totalitarian. Authoritarian. Because the end justified the means - including lying through your teeth to the rest of the world to obfuscate the truth.

In the three months from the beginning of May to the end of July 1942, 14,916 Jews, including Grandfather's sisters Camilla and Clara, their cousin and lodger Dr. Johann Weinberger, and cousins Rosalie and Cäzilie, were rounded up and deported to concentration camps. A further 7,997, including dainty 'Onkel' Karl, were sent directly to the killing fields of Maly Trostenets, Sobibor and Auschwitz.

The terror of the mass round-ups and deportations to render Vienna (and thus Austria) 'Judenrein' (cleansed of Jews) continued unabated for a further three months until the only ones who remained were temporarily protected management and employees of the IKG, those Jews still protected by an 'Aryan' spouse or parent, and those successfully hidden or assisted by members of the resistance.[191]

In one five-day period in May 1942, 281 apartments were cleared of 1,748 inhabitants; by the end of that month, a total of 6,968 Jews had been deported, 3,000 of whom were sent to their immediate deaths at Maly Trostenets.

The aunts Camilla and Clara had been spared from earlier deportation because of an internal IKG policy that temporarily held back anybody responsible for the care of an immediate relative who was incapable of

---

190   In his manifesto *Mein Kampf* Hitler claims that, in the spirit of 'the end justifies the means', he consciously developed a ruthless mindset during the turbulent and violent times prevailing at the beginning of his political career in Munich. He also claims to have chosen to banish any trace of guilt or compassion from his consciousness.
191   Between 600-1000 Jews are estimated to have survived in Vienna due to the intervention of gentiles.

walking on their own. Great-grandmother Antonia died aged ninety-two on 10th June 1942, and her death was her daughters' death knell.

After the aunts were rounded up they were taken to a local school, one of several collection points dotted around the second district. In spite of the IKG's best efforts to alleviate their suffering, the cramped and entirely unsuitable conditions were deeply challenging and distressing – and even more so in the heat of the summer.

Under the ever-watchful eyes of unpredictable SS officers, they waited until the required number of transportees demanded by the Nazi authorities had been delivered and their paperwork processed. In some instances, from round-up to deportation could take anything up to two weeks.

On the day of their deportation, 14th July 1942, Camilla Angelika Löwenthal aged sixty-five (No o14334), and Clara Ottilie Löwenthal, aged sixty-seven (No o14335), were obliged to sign a document headed *Declaration of Wealth pertaining to Jews evacuated to the Eastern Territories.* Apart from a few Reichsmarks in cash and documents related to their small private pension entitlements, there was nothing to steal.[192]

Grandfather tried to prevent at least one 'stealing spree' through legal means; in the municipal archives I discovered a document in which the aunts gifted their furniture to Oma 'in lieu of board and lodgings' in the event they might eventually have to move into an 'old-people's home'. My mother often wondered what had happened to some expensive pieces of furniture she never saw again; probably they were sold in order to live or eventually destroyed during the final battle for Vienna.

Remarkably, their bone-China tea service survived and I still have it. A number of other things also made it through, including my mother's tiny toddler's chocolate drinking cup, Oma's dinner service, assorted glasses, books, linen, photographs and clothes. I can only imagine that Oma, always foresightful, practical and thorough, packed them away carefully in the cellar for safekeeping during the many months of relentless Allied bombing raids in1944 and '45.

In the months of the deportations, and before Grandfather was put to forced labour at the Wehrmacht, he was under strict instructions not to open the door to anybody or leave their apartment if Oma was not with him. For those obliged to wear the yellow Star of David, life had become too dangerous; without a gentile spouse or parent providing protection

---

192 I have not been able to ascertain how much of their pensions they actually received; levying exorbitant taxes on Jewish assets became standard practice.

anything might happen.

Little did anybody imagine Ausheber returning to break directly into their home once its unprotected inhabitants had been deported.

THE MECHANICS

Ausheber (lifters, extractors) were IKG employees charged with rounding up their fellow Jews whom the local Nazi administration had earmarked for specific deportation transports. Although the Nazis stipulated who was to be deported and which dwellings were to be emptied, it was the leaders of the Ausheber squads who had to ensure that each transport quota was filled. Domestic dwellings, old people's homes, orphanages, hospitals, institutions for the blind and the mentally or physically impaired were all included.

If somebody evaded the net, a substitute might be picked up at random to complete the numbers. It seems reprehensible, and many have debated the morality of the Ausheber, but they were being watched by Nazi soldiers waiting by the transport lorries and they wanted to survive. It was an unenviable position. Having 'faith' is easier said than done – not least when faith is merely a word and not an internalised state of being.

It was made clear to the IKG leadership that if they failed to co-operate with the roundups, Nazi thugs would do the job for them. The Jewish leadership hoped to make the process as orderly and civilised as possible to avoid as much distress as they could, but even so the suffering was immense – and so were the later recriminations against the leading members of the IKG.

The management of the IKG appointed the Ausheber squad leaders and their foot soldiers. To try and delay the fate of remaining Jews where possible, the IKG had 'employed' as many individuals as they could under the pretext that their jobs were essential to running both the Nazi-overseen Jewish administration and its much-needed social services, including soup kitchens and distribution points for rationed necessities. Every single Ausheber would have been aware that refusing to acquiesce to Nazi orders endangered their own physical safety and that of their immediate family.

Some individuals carried out their task with zeal and brutality and undoubtedly relished their power; others used the opportunity to settle old scores. They had found resonance within a system that had been borne out of weakness. Most did not escape it themselves.

On one occasion Oma arrived home to find two Ausheber attempting to break in through a window: one was holding a ladder for the other. She is said to have gone ballistic. On two other occasions they succeeded in taking Grandfather to the deportation assembly point, but fortunately Oma found out in time and was able to show he was under legal protection and that he must be released.

I can't help smiling at the thought of my fearless Oma giving them a piece of her mind! Yet, according to Dr. Vogel, even while labouring for the Wehrmacht the 'Sword of Damocles' continued to be a relentless companion because individuals were still being disappeared from one day to the next under one pretext or another, possibly to make up the numbers.

THE PAST COMES EVER CLOSER

I was sitting in the warm comfort of Café Schottenring again, trying to digest Dr. Vogel's words in order to bring my grandfather back to life.

Dr. Vogel recalled that the Jewish forced labourers came from all walks of life. Because they were always hungry, tired and under extreme duress, friction was inevitable but Grandfather would calm them down by working through their grievances. 'You know, he really was quite magnificent!' Dr. Vogel repeated admiringly.

Although the most gruelling labour was generally reserved for teenage boys and young men, the experience was trial for everyone, not least the work party Dr. Vogel's father and Grandfather had been assigned to. They toiled year round in all weathers with few breaks and insufficient food.

Officially they worked in the empty container and catering supply depots of the Wehrmacht barracks, but some were assigned to other work parties or driven by lorry to locations around Vienna. Grandfather dug and built, loaded and unloaded; following the Allied bombing raids during the final year of the war, he cleared rubble and cinders and removed dead bodies.

Dr. Vogel emphasised that almost all the career military officers of the Wehrmacht behaved decently towards him and his fellow forced labourers. Apart from the viciousness of the unpredictable SS Division members stationed at the barracks, it was the local civilian overseers whose behaviour was most reprehensible. 'They had felt like nobodies and it was their moment of power,' he said.

Beatings and humiliation were common. Because Grandfather was highly respected as a source of wisdom, the overseers kept a particularly close eye on him. One beating resulted in him having a damaged arm that was never properly treated. No doubt Frau Dr. Löwenthal did her best under almost impossible circumstances, but it was a Wehrmacht officer who provided some salves and bandages for what turned into an infected arm and hand. Dr. Vogel had a similar experience of being assisted by a Wehrmacht officer.

Dr. Vogel added, 'Your grandfather also did a lot of latrine cleaning. They were not what you understand by latrines, these were just basic. But let's not go there.'

He explained that Grandfather was a man who believed we should take responsibility for our own emotions, so attempts by others to diminish him was futile. His mantra was 'forgive them for they know not what they do', and this perspective also helped others establish some sense of balance. As for the dirty jobs – well, somebody had to do them.

As if to soften the blow for me, Dr. Vogel added that on several occasions Grandfather was called into an office within the barracks to do personal legal work for Wehrmacht officers, such as writing their wills.

'But please, don't think he was a collaborator – he most certainly was not! He had no choice, but it did help keep the others off his back for a while.'

I recalled Dawa telling me that Grandfather believed that seeing the best in everyone and meeting them with love and respect was the way forward for the common good, but now it seemed that he'd had to learn the painful way that no amount of enlightened wisdom could save him from those who were entrenched in resentment and victimhood. The overseers were so afraid of their own weakness that, as Dr. Vogel recounted, 'They wanted to reduce us to subservient obedience because it made them feel powerful as long as we were at their mercy.' My grandfather had encouraged his fellow labourers not to comply with a sense of shame but with the strength of understanding.

Another assault Grandfather and others endured was having to treat decomposing foodstuffs with the insecticide Zyklon B,[193] a highly toxic hydrogen-cyanide powder. Shaken out of containers with no protection, it caused considerable problems to both eyes and lungs.

After the war Grandfather must have written about it to a friend in America, who advised him to seek out an old medical colleague who would help him with the syndrome he described. Was this why his cold had suddenly turned to pneumonia and been fatal? If a legal quirk had

---

193   Used for mass murders in the Nazi gas chambers.

saved him from being worked, starved or tortured to death, or summarily shot or gassed, had 'they' still won?

Grandfather, together with former military comrades from the First World War, had once been a volunteer fire fighter but, like most white-collar professionals living in city apartment blocks he had never performed any significant manual labour. His hands soon ended up pretty much in shreds.

Strangely, he was the only one left in their group still wearing leather shoes. Everybody else had been reduced to crude wooden clogs. As Dr. Vogel told me this, I couldn't help but smile: was this because of Grandfather's belief in quality and care rather than quantity? Or had one of his non-Jewish friends helped him out yet again, like the old WWI comrade who risked his own safety to have coffee and tea delivered to Grandfather with the written request that he distribute it to family and friends?

I gradually came to recognise that this unsung hero, whose letter I still have, was one of many, although nowhere near enough to tip the scales of probability. The collusion of the power of terror on the one hand and the mentality of victimhood on the other were still too great.

The Wehrmacht's official working hours were one thing; the reality was another. Forced labourers could be kept for however long it took to complete an assignment, after which they had to walk home in a blacked-out Vienna where Jews were under curfew not knowing who they would encounter and how they would be treated.

During the extensive bombing raids of 1944 and 1945, labourers working in the depot were not permitted to use air-raid shelters; instead they dug shallow trenches that proved useless against the pressure of the blasts as bombs struck the Danube industrial docks and freight railway lines nearby. Other times they sought protection under the trees in the Prater. Some died and were buried under the rubble.

Was this what Aunt Paula had referred to in her letter to my mother some months after war's end, when mail had begun to trickle through again? *From 1942 onwards your father was a forced labourer for the Nazis and was buried three times at his place of work...*

Although the bombings were terrifying, they were welcome because they kept the hope of liberation alive.

What Dr. Vogel did not reveal until three years later was that forced labourers eventually also worked on the construction of the capital's anti-aircraft flak towers, including those two concrete thugs I failed to notice during my childhood visits to the Augarten.

On a short return trip to Vienna, a couple of hours before a meeting with Dr. Vogel, the radio in my hotel room was quietly playing in the background. I caught the words 'flak towers' before the newsreader reported on the various disagreements about what to do with those hideous concrete relics from WWII. Suggestions of turning some of them into various forms of recreational venues had been met with resistance by those who deemed it disrespectful to the forced and slave labourers who had built them.

When I broached the subject with Dr. Vogel later that day, he confirmed that forced labourers from the Wehrmacht provisions depot were seconded to construct the Augarten flak towers alongside foreign slave labourers. It was fairly late in the war and they were aware that the Nazi war machine was no longer functioning so well. Some in their group who had knowledge of engineering wanted to try and sabotage the structure but they were found out – or betrayed. Those implicated, including Grandfather, were sent to carry out more gruelling labour further out of town.

Dr. Vogel did not want to go into further detail beyond saying it had not been for long. Much as I wanted to know more, I didn't feel entitled to push and we moved on.

Now though, in Café Schottenring, I heard that when the war was over the Vogel family continued to visit Grandfather and Oma in their newly allocated apartment in Obere Donaustrasse. 'Your grandmother was an amazingly good cook and made the most delicious food.'

I laughed. 'That's certainly something I *do* know about!'

By the end of the war, there was already a desperate shortage of basic foods in Vienna; within months the situation evolved into near famine, made worse by the summer drought and crop failures of 1946. Initial rationing of international food donations was soon reduced to subsistence calorie levels that, for a population living under extreme physical and mental stress, was not easy to bear. It proved so detrimental for growing children that several hundred of the most undernourished were sent to private homes in Belgium to recuperate.

I know from letters that Aunt Paula succeeded in sending a private food parcel with an official Swedish food convoy, and there was also at least one package from a friend in America that eventually made its way to Obere Donaustrasse. Although Oma had a reputation for conjuring up delicious meals with next to nothing, perhaps she and Grandfather had again been sharing their food?

When Dr. Vogel had met Grandfather at the Wehrmacht depot, his first impression was of a rather serious and unapproachable man but that impression soon changed. He said that my grandfather turned out to be the warmest person you could imagine, with a wonderful sense of humour while being highly intelligent and deeply reflective. He lived according to The Book. His natural way of being seemed to be one ongoing 'mitzvah'.

I didn't know what he meant because my mother had told me that theirs had not been a conventionally religious home. When I did eventually delve into the essence of Judaism, I cried with joy and sorrow; such living from a loving heart is rare.

Grandfather's letter to Toni in the summer of 1939 described his attempts to fill his now disenfranchised days and grieving, sleepless nights. It ended with the words:

> *Thus I flee time and, thank the Lord, grow older and older every day usque ad finem... Delighted by my new life-style I certainly am not; however, since this misfortune is not of my own making I know myself to be free of guilt, which is a great comfort to me.*

'Your grandmother was a nice lady. She had an exceptionally highly developed sense of justice,' Dr. Vogel told me.

Although he knew nothing of Oma's secret resistance activities, he lamented the fact that nobody had given these women the credit they deserved for their bravery and sacrifices. Instead of divorcing their Jewish husbands as they were pressured to do, they protected them and their children under the most difficult and dangerous of circumstances. These non-Jewish women suffered a great deal, not only because of their losses and their anxiety about their loved ones but because they were subjected to humiliation, verbal and even physical abuse, and at times were ostracised.

'Just going to the shops could be a terrible experience,' Dr. Vogel said. 'When my mother grew old, she confused the present with the past. She would go searching for food in dustbins and rubbish bins and was always in fear of being bullied.'

I remember that Oma was said to have done the same, even becoming paranoid that once again 'they're all talking about me behind my back'. It breaks my heart.

POST-WAR TRAUMA

The armed conflict might have been over but Grandfather's war never really ended. When information about the pitiless assaults on his two elderly sisters began to filter through via the few returnees, his own suffering paled into insignificance.

When the magnitude of what he was being asked to forgive became ever clearer, the challenge to his sense of humility was too great. His belief in the goodness inherent in every human being and seeing all as worthy of love was rocked to the core and he found it impossible to forgive. Perhaps it had been too soon.

Then Dr. Vogel added, 'My wife was in a concentration camp. She suffered so much more than I did. How can one really ever forgive that?'

And how, in our civilised world, Grandfather had asked, could it ever have come to that in the first place?

'Because the apparent civility is mostly an enforced one.' My cynicism just tumbled out of my mouth.[194] Dr. Vogel nodded in agreement.

How challenging it must have been for my grief-stricken and exhausted Grandfather, who was no longer the life and soul at everybody's party but questioning over and over again, to receive a letter from a friend advising him from the sanitised distance of America to stop ruminating, to put it all behind him and get on with normal life! This friend wanted his Oskar back, the man who had always shone the light for others. He appeared to have no concept of my grandfather's experiences.

Some fifty-six years later, following the 9/11 attack on the Twin Towers, my mother received a letter from New York: *Only now are we able to begin to imagine what it must have been like in Europe during the war.*

Even before the Battle for Vienna had ended, all municipal supply sources of electricity, gas and water had been destroyed. Nothing could be cooked in the usual manner, while even the most basic food was in short supply. Although two bridges across the main Danube river to the east of the city had remained intact, by the end of the last battle every other bridge across the Danube Canal that connected Leopoldstadt to the rest of Vienna had been either blown up or was too dangerous to use.

A quarter of the city's buildings had been reduced to rubble and more than 200,000 inhabitants had no permanent roof over their heads.

---

194 More precisely what I meant is that civilised behaviour is all too often the result of the fear of judicial punishment rather than of an internalised ethical or moral compass.

Looting by locals and liberated foreign slave labourers was rampant. Yet this was only a microcosm within the macrocosm of a pulverised would-be-glorious thousand-year German Empire.

As if matters were not already challenging enough, after the main Soviet liberating forces continued their advance beyond Vienna their holding troops often behaved appallingly. Woman were not safe: many thousands of girls and women are estimated to have been raped, with many mutilated and murdered, despite the soldiers having been informed by their commander that Vienna was not to be considered a *fallen* city, but a *liberated* one.

Perhaps these soldiers did not understand the difference or perhaps they simply did not care. Whatever the case, they merely repeated what the lowest of the low of victors of war have always done and still do: assuming the gang rape of women and girls to be one of the self-entitled spoils of war, a primitive, age-old act of retribution and reward. Fully aware of what was happening, Tante Paula even wrote to Toni suggesting that his mother, being a fluent Czech speaker, would probably be able to look after herself.

As brutal as the rapes in Vienna might have been, they did not match the scale or level of barbarity elsewhere, especially in the eastern territories of Germany. No matter their political leanings, no matter where they were, how young, old, able-bodied or infirm, all females in their path were defenceless against such overpowering and primitive male aggression.

I cannot imagine that the war ever really ended for any of those girls and women who survived – mostly in silence. As for the prolific rape and sexual abuse of Jewish girls and women held captive in Nazi concentration camps, it doesn't bear thinking about.

And pity the innocent men who, whether consciously or not, have been and will be made to suffer for the sins of the fathers.

Some six months after war's end, my grandparents received the painful news of their own son's brush with death.

Vienna
27th November 1945

My dear, poor Toni!
You wrote to us but you never mentioned anything of your misfortune. If you only knew how you have always been and still are forever in my thoughts. What will you do when you are discharged from the army? For God's sake, you haven't even got a home. Who will look after you? If only

you were with me, my poor Toni. You left home in good health and now you are an invalid. It is so terrible for me, I can barely take it in, but I see so much misery around me and so many poor mothers who still don't know where their sons are and are waiting helplessly for them. They say to me if only they would return home, even with a leg missing. Please write and tell me exactly how it all happened. I only hope that I will see you and the girls again. And poor Milenka[195] has suffered such a tragedy with her fiancé too. But what can I do when I can't help anybody? Such a terrible war must never befall humanity again. Everybody has suffered so dreadfully, I have discovered how evil man is and was, and that he has brought this catastrophe upon himself. Whether humanity will become any better, I don't know.

I kiss you both and remain your mother who thinks of you always. May God take care of you and write soon.

Dr. Vogel told me that, to add to his grief, Grandfather was contacted by a number of friends and acquaintances who had emigrated upon the Anschluss asking him to find out what had happened to their possessions that had been packed and delivered to the railway depot ready for shipment abroad. Grandfather discovered that everything had been 'impounded' – in other words, stolen.

Vienna
February 3rd 1946

My most beloved Toni… The greatest joy is learning that your prosthesis is so good that it almost feels like an integral part of your body… here the lack of materials means that most war wounded are still walking around on crutches… We are awaiting your reply with great anticipation… I kiss and embrace you, Your father Oskar Löwenthal… One more thing: the war is over and you no longer have to be concerned for yourself or for us. Can't you now put aside the Protestant name?[196]

In spite of the pervading bleakness, Grandfather channelled his energy into normalising their lives with plans for springtime fly-fishing outings

---

195 Dawa.
196 In German, *Namen der evangelischen* literally means *Protestant name*. But it also carries echoes of the word for *evangelisers*. I can't help wondering whether Grandfather meant it in a different sense - something closer to the sophisticated Jewish idea of working on *being the change* yourself, rather than trying to persuade someone else of a good idea.

at his favourite spots on the Danube.

'We were all going to go to Schönau together in the forthcoming spring, but sadly he died. I will take you there when the weather is warmer,' Dr. Vogel promised.

I wonder whether Grandfather's spirit had perhaps been so saddened that, when he was suffering from pneumonia, chronically malnourished, and drained of energy during another bitterly cold winter without adequate heating, it became easier to let go than to fight to stay alive. Additionally, he knew that the mentoring of his son into maturity and the fathering of his daughters was over, and his wife had proved herself stronger than he could have imagined.

Writing to Toni in early 1939, Elsa had already pronounced her father's faith in the imminent victory of the best of humanity an illusion; now, in his letter to Toni of 3rd February 1946, Grandfather added:

> ...Mother is sitting across from me and is also writing to you and to Milenka. Thank the Lord Mother is now feeling much better; there is not much to report about me; I am growing – or rather am – older every day, and even though I no longer find life beautiful it is still interesting. Can you recall enough Latin to understand 'in veni portum, spes et fortuna valete!'[197]

Back in the warm and bustling café, it was time for Dr. Vogel and me to go our separate ways. 'Let's meet again in a few days' time,' he said. 'There is so much more I would like to tell you.'

I was delighted to agree, but several eventful weeks passed before I could take up his generous offer.

VIENNA, MARCH 2007

REVOLVING DOORS

'Come on Miki dear, we'll go for a brisk walk along the seafront! It'll blow the cobwebs away and do you no end of good!' Theo used to cajole chirpily. Then she would pull back her shoulders and straighten her spine, theatrically demonstrating the daily trick for dissipating the build-up of inner tensions that nobody knew how to give the homesick young refugee an opportunity to talk about.

'They all kept me so busy with this that and the other that I couldn't

---

[197] 'I have arrived at the port, hope and good fortune adieu!'

focus on anything in the end,' Dawa told me.

During the first year in particular, the lady residents of Dresden House had kept Elsa and Dawa busy with outings along the coast, to the shops and for walks in the countryside; others gave them painting lesson, drawing lessons, singing lessons, elocution lessons (how now brown cow....Moses supposes his toesies are roses but Moses supposes erroneously, for nobody's toesies are posies of roses as Moses supposes his toesies to be!) piano lessons, croquet lessons. All were beneficial, but they left my mother little space to breathe.

Hove, 1st June 1939

Dear Aunt Clara!
...Miss H. really makes a great effort to make things as pleasant as possible for us. She is very kind and natural (perhaps even too much so; a real nature's child and outdoor person) and very much in the moment. That is to say she never considers anything she does (by which I mean what she does during her time off work). For example, at tea-time she will suddenly say: 'It's a beautiful day today, we must do something.' And already she's running to get her handbag and hat (us too) and runs to catch a bus going into the countryside or along the coast.

Like most English people, she is emotionally cold and never allows even a little bit of sentimentality to interfere. She is accustomed to happily accepting anything that comes her way, not to give anything much consideration but to make a quick decision, and she asks the same of us.

I think that expectation is a very good thing to help one get over many things. I'm very glad that I'm here because I used to spend too much time living in my thoughts. Miss H. never leaves us alone for long and always pulls me out of my distractions. For that I am very grateful. Furthermore, she has taught me to always appear very self-confident and under no circumstances to show any silly embarrassment.

I have a lot of contact with other people here and have completely lost any lack of self-confidence. I am very pleased about that too, only I'm afraid that it might manifest as indifference.
...I kiss you with all my heart, your Elsa.

Theo once found Dawa exhausted and grieving, curled up on her sofa pretending to be asleep; without saying a word she gently covered her with a blanket. My mother never forgot that loving gesture. She was also certain that her many tears in the secrecy of her own bedroom did not go unrecognised - but how could anyone talk to her about it without making things even worse. And, no matter how kind and friendly and generous everybody at Dresden House was, neither Elsa nor Dawa ever received a hug or a caring touch.

These days we know so much more about letting out grief rather than keeping a stiff upper lip and putting on a brave face, and giving loving hugs and touch even if nothing about the situation can be changed. Yet this is now and that was then.

***

The sweltering heat during the weeks before I accessed the IKG's post-Anschluss archives often left me with no option but to seek refuge in the parklands of Schönbrunn Palace. Winter, however, kept me inside particularly when it was unpleasantly cold and foggy, or snowing heavily.

Sometimes, though, the pervasive tension that was growing inside me forced me to take the short No 10 tram ride to the end of the line at Hietzing to the palace's western gate. Beyond it lies a peaceful network of gardens and gravelled avenues that I claimed as my back garden and exercise yard.

It was during one of those late-afternoon walks that there was a sudden heavy snowfall. As the wind subsided and the snow became increasingly dense, the silence made me nostalgic for the long winters of my childhood in Munich. Unfortunately, I wasn't dressed for the occasion and soon the biting cold turned my thoughts to my mother's thick fur coat. What I would have given for it at that moment!

The coat was far too big and heavy for me, but three years after Dawa's death I still hadn't been able to part with it. She had often opened it to pull me inside to the warmth of her body which, during the bleak years of her disintegration, had given me a much-needed sense of security.

Recalling that coat brought unhappy memories to the fore, and once again I cursed how everything seemed to lead back to the Holocaust.

It reminded me of the pain my mother had alluded to in the year before she died when she had tried to explain the shadow it had cast across her soul, her choices and consequently our entire family life. She described how events had begun merging with the past, triggering the release of memories she had fought hard to leave behind; memories in which the suffering of her relatives and the millions of others who lived deep within her consciousness robbed her of the ability to be in the present without referring to a disturbing and painful past.

'During my last winter in Vienna, Jews were constantly being hauled out of their homes to shovel snow, even with their bare hands … People just loved to stand around jeering, some were so primitive, it was terrible … Tante Camilla had a weak heart... Mother often argued with the Brownshirts, or whoever else was orchestrating things, to let her take Aunt's place … it usually worked … When I think about it … she was so brave … but it was awful seeing people you respected being so humiliated.'

On the winter's day when Dawa had shared her memory of Oma's selflessness, a reflex had led me to remind her of the early winter mornings in Munich when she had often cleared the snow around our house while our father and we children sat eating breakfast in centrally-heated comfort. 'Why on earth did you do it?' I asked.

There was a long pause before she replied, 'Because I was stupid.'

I understood what she meant and felt sad that she was beginning to be angry with herself, so I remained silent.

After a while, she continued. 'Just recently, when it was so bitterly cold, I couldn't help thinking of the aunts and all those poor people in concentration camps … forced to stand on parade for hours on end in the freezing winters, often dressed in next to nothing, ill, starving … the fear of not knowing what was going to happen to them.'

MICHAEL

Michael and I arranged to meet for breakfast at Café Sperl. I had never been there before but had recently read that the establishment was wrecked in 1931 when antisemitic thugs wielding metal bars decided to end a Jewish New Year party. Looking around, that seemed quite unbelievable.

The last time Michael and I had met was more than two years earlier when he was still living and working in England; since then he had relocated to Munich. Now he was paying his home town a short visit and had a few hours downtime.

My mobile phone rang: Michael had been circling the neighbourhood for ten minutes searching for a parking space. He had given up and suggested I get in his car and we drive elsewhere. 'Have you ever been to St. Leopold's Kirche at—?' I didn't catch the rest of the question but I wasn't aware of having visited a church of that name.

'No, I haven't. Where is it?'

'It's just out of town – it's a beautiful place. You'll really like it … we'll go there.'

Michael was a complex and driven man capable of great warmth, humour and wisdom and also of cruel sarcasm, abruptness and nastiness. I had always known that his inner world was deeply troubled: 'Men have to pretend to be something they are not.' A challenging job and a complex domestic life had recently made it increasingly difficult to negotiate his ever-changing moods. I chose to remain the witness, knowing that, like all of us, he was an individual tip of an ancestral iceberg and coping the best way he knew how. If he succeeded in hitting some painful bullseyes now and again, well, it was up to me to take responsibility and ask myself why.

To my relief, when we met he seemed to be in good humour. However, that only lasted for a few minutes before almost everything I said was met with dismissive irritation. When we touched on where Dawa used to live, he even corrected my pronunciation of Lasalle Hof. I chose not to retaliate and to tell him that Ferdinand Lasalle was not a Spaniard!

He had met and spoken with Dawa on occasion, but when I mentioned her death he seemed impatient with my need to explore what had happened to her. The day before she had died she'd said triumphantly, 'It's so good to be alive after all ... I'd been feeling so ill for so long ... perhaps all the toxins have gone.' Afterwards I hadn't been able to find any trace of her medications.

When I made a more general comment about my incomer status in Vienna, he took umbrage. 'As an outsider, I'm finding it really difficult to get passed the portals to Viennese life...' I said, my tongue half in my cheek.

'There's no such thing as Viennese life!'

My flippancy seemed to have got me into trouble! 'You know exactly what I mean.' I defended myself but I didn't bother to elaborate.

'You've got friends here, haven't you?' Michael asked me.

'I suppose so.' In reality, they were friendly acquaintances but I decided not to quibble. 'The trouble is, with one of the couples I have the distinct impression of being used more as a buffer between warring parties, which isn't exactly my idea of fun.'

'Isn't that how it is with all marriages?'

'Really?' I felt like adding, *Well, things haven't necessarily always been roses, but not in my experience.* Instead, I bit my tongue.

'If you really want to experience a genuine Viennese café, that's the place to go,' Michael announced a few minutes later, pointing to one of the grubby concrete blocks we were passing.

'Why's that? Is the coffee especially good?'

'No, not particularly, but it's an authentic Viennese café – really basic and very smoky.' He was obviously making a point about what he imagined was my lack of knowledge of the *real* Vienna.

I started to pay more attention to our surroundings. We were entering an area of tenement buildings that seemed vaguely familiar and I realised we were only a few minutes' walk from my apartment. When I'd criss-crossed the district on foot after my arrival in Vienna, these buildings and their layout reminded me of the post-WWII council housing estate Granny Pinner had moved to soon after I was born. War and bombs, followed by widowhood and yet another economic downturn certainly did have a distinctive way with them.

For some reason, Michael had decided to give me a lesson about the underprivileged of Vienna. Maybe he assumed I was some spoilt English toff who saw Vienna as nothing more than beautiful buildings, parks and palaces, fancy shops and plush cafés? If that was the case, he hadn't listened to a word I'd ever said.

A few minutes later, we arrived at our destination: a hospital complex housing several specialist units, including a psychiatric one. What on earth…?

Michael checked with the security guard at the gate who confirmed that, even though the clinics were closed for the weekend, we could enter the grounds. We drove slowly up the drive, passing a number of attractive buildings until Michael stopped at a small parking area. 'Let's get out and walk.'

The weather was much friskier than in the town centre, and when I opened the car door I stepped into strong gusts of icy wind. Threatening black clouds were racing across the sky. I wasn't dressed for walking, let alone walking through the hilly grounds on a dreary late-winter's day. Michael offered me a jacket, which helped a little.

I still wasn't certain what the place had to do with a church. A few moments passed before he said, 'I haven't been here for decades.'

After a short walk he told me in a tired voice that we were at Am Spiegelgrund where almost 800 children had been murdered during the Nazi era. The sinister connection between Steinhof, the municipal neurological and psychiatric complex of old, and the Am Spiegelgrund children's clinic housed within it suddenly fell into place. A few months earlier I had accidentally come across the gruesome details but had imagined the institution to be located more to the south of the city.

Suddenly I was annoyed. Michael knew that the Holocaust had infiltrated every aspect of my life in Vienna and that I needed a break – yet, of all places, he had brought me here! But I said nothing.

Knowing how deeply I could be affected by such things, I had only reluctantly accompanied my mother to Terezin on what I had believed was her first pilgrimage in memory of the aunts Camilla and Clara and other relatives. I had felt physical pain because of my grief. It was only after her death that I learned by chance that she had already paid her respects some years earlier. I imagine our trip was her way of saying a last goodbye while also teaching me about the unspeakable without having to say too much herself.

We were driven there by our cousin Luděk, my mother's childhood playmate in Popovice. He had remained stoney-faced but in control throughout, though his wife, Zdenka, suffered a panic attack. 'I think she must have some Jewish ancestry to have reacted that way,' my mother said. Some years later the same thing happened to my cousin Sarah.

When I had visited the Holocaust exhibition at London's Imperial War Museum with a group from the Second Generation Network, I couldn't stop shaking until it was over – and I wasn't the only one. The commemorative event I attended at Mauthausen concentration camp as part of the Austrian schoolchildren's 'Letters to the Stars' project was one of the most difficult days of my life, made worse by being reminded of a truth so often consigned to oblivion by wilful amnesia. 'Of course they knew what was going on,' one of my indignant hosts, whose family hailed from Mauthausen, had scoffed. 'If the kids misbehaved, the mothers used to point to the smoke coming out of the chimneys and threaten them with the same fate!' Back in the safety of my hotel room in Vienna, my stomach turned itself inside out.

Now I was at a hospital where some of the most innocent and vulnerable of human beings had been subjected to unfathomable cruelty by those whose oath of duty was supposed to ensure that they did no harm.

Apart from hundreds of children, several thousand adult patients were either sent to be murdered at other locations or suffered cruel deaths at Steinhof during the secret Nazi T4 Programme,[198] a depravity

---

198 The T4 Programme started in Germany and Austria in October 1939 with the murder by lethal injection or starvation of children at birth and up to the age of three who were deemed mentally and physically 'unfit to live'. The scope was soon widened to include institutionalised youths up to age 17 and then expanded

euphemistically described as 'euthanasia'.

It is more than likely that every single one of the perpetrators will have been a baptised Christian. If one were to indulge in the lazy, self-serving logic that has been applied for millennia to 'the Jews', then surely – and for this alone – every Christian must be a sadistic psychopath?

Steinhof is now on the map as a prime example of Otto Wagner's Secession architectural genius and as a holistic mental-health heritage sight. As attractive as the complex was, my state of mind was too fragile, and I hated being there.

'Ah, here it is!' Michael said. Ahead of us was a smaller building with a few tables and chairs scattered across its terrace. Inside, I realised that we were in the foyer of a theatre, to the right of which was a café.

The only person in the cold and dimly lit dining room was a woman behind the food counter. 'We're not open yet. You'll have to wait ten minutes or so if you want coffee.'

Michael and I returned outside where he gestured to one of the tables. 'Shall we sit here?'

I wanted to say *You must be joking! It's far too cold and I'm freezing!* but I simply muttered, 'No thanks,' and continued walking. I felt as if I were becoming disconnected from myself. How could I have explained that?

Then suddenly something gave my energy a jump start. Beyond the terrace was an expanse of wintergreen, and jutting out from it was a mass of thigh-high cylindrical steel-and-opaque-glass *stelai* positioned in precise rows. White crosses and war cemeteries immediately sprang to mind, and Michael confirmed that we were indeed looking down on a memorial garden to the victims of Am Spiegelgrund.

The *stelai* were not illuminated by natural or artificial light and looked as snuffed out as the lives they commemorated, the lives of many hundreds of innocent children who, for reasons of physical deformity or cognitive deficiencies, were deemed unworthy to live and deserving of unspeakable cruelty.

I stood in silence, concentrating on my breathing in an attempt to banish thoughts and feelings that might get the better of me. Michael

---

to include anybody judged, according to the outcome of lengthy questionnaires, as unfit to 'contribute' to the viability of Germanic superiority. As the numbers of those caught in the net increased, the victims were poisoned en masse by carbon monoxide exhaust fumes directed into the interior of mobile killing wagons, and in locked, fume-filled 'communal shower rooms'. That was only the overture to what was to come: Operation Reinhardt within the literal Final Solution to the Jewish Question.

and I were silent for what seemed like many minutes until I was suddenly struck by an unusual stillness. 'So peaceful,' I said quietly.

As we continued walking through the grounds, I found myself spontaneously telling Michael about my mother's breakdown during which my father, frustrated and fearful of her vulnerability because of echoes from his own childhood, had wounded her to the core. 'Your whole damned family is completely mad!' he had yelled, alluding to my aunt Elsa's breakdown a few years earlier.

Michael was not familiar with Elsa's story, so I told him how she had suffered a breakdown not long after the birth of her youngest child, my cousin Sarah. Perhaps tellingly, her disintegration also coincided with our move to Munich. When neither a stay with us in Munich in the summer of 1959 (when she was not the aunt I had once known) nor electric shock treatment and pharmaceuticals succeeded in raising her out of a state of almost complete withdrawal, her husband (who had already found solace elsewhere) divorced her and gained custody of their two tiny daughters who went to live with his mother. Yet again, Elsa had to leave the family home and stay with friends until she could function by herself. To his credit, at the end of his life her ex-husband asked to be forgiven for not having understood or considered anything beyond his own needs and wellbeing. He also recognised the impact of his actions upon his daughters.[199] In his defence, and as Elsa later wrote to my mother in Munich during her own implosion, neither of them had ever been able to talk about their losses and silent suffering.

'Being forced to leave Hove as an enemy alien just a year after we came to England was a great tragedy for Elsa,' Dawa reflected not long before her own death.

Finally we returned full circle to Michael's car. 'We'll drive up,' he said.

I had forgotten about the church, which was said to be the crowning glory of Otto Wagner's sprawling hillside complex. Known as St. Leopold's Church, its golden dome gleamed like an otherworldly beacon of light. So that was what my eagle's-eye view from the distant heights of Schönbrunn's

---

199 Elsa's ex-husband was very young at the time; he was fundamentally a good man and maintained a co-operative and friendly relationship with her to the end of his life. He provided her with legal advice in contractual matters and even underwrote hire-purchase agreements for my mother at a time when single women were unable to obtain credit – including for our TV after we returned to England. He was generous with his time when I needed legal advice in my early adulthood. When our son was recuperating from a serious illness, he and his wife hosted us at their home in the countryside so that he might spend time with their ponies.

Gloriette had been teasing me with for the last few months![200]

The building was beautiful in its tranquil yet opulent simplicity. The main door was not open for services. 'Let's see if we can go in,' Michael said quietly as he walked on ahead. He disappeared round the side of the building but quickly returned. 'It's closed.'

So far nothing had worked out as intended, and he was clearly fed up. 'We'll go to Café Dommayer, then.' I was pleased; I was freezing and barely functioning.

Dommayer is a congenial establishment in Hietzing that I knew quite well. The previous summer, when its gardens were in bloom, I went there once in a while for a coffee and to find a shady spot to read. It was certainly more congenial than the authentic coffee house Michael had shown me!

Michael brought up the subject of his monumental professional challenges. 'It's all very well knowing what's wrong, but how do you fix it?' We were talking of this and that and 'if I were emperor', when I said, 'If I had anything to do with it, people wouldn't get the vote until they're forty-five. After all, what do most really know about life before then?'

I wasn't entirely joking, although I had wanted to bring up Austria's Green Party's push to reduce the national voting age to sixteen. Michael didn't say anything; his mind had wandered elsewhere and the topic seemed to have nowhere to go.

Suspicions of cynical political intentions aside, it would have been interesting to explore the complex matter of informed choice versus ignorance and an emotional response to deliberately stoked biases, whether these are conscious or not: propaganda.

I once fell into that trap in the late 1960s when I joined a schoolfriend on a CND[201] march. Only sixteen, still very naïve and unaware that the movement was calling for *uni*lateral disarmament, I was happy to do my bit towards making our world a safer place. It didn't take me long to smell a rat. A few minutes into the coach journey to the starting point of the march, it became apparent that (like my friend's parents) all of my fellow travellers were readers of the *Morning Star*, a socialist daily newspaper with a communist agenda and, it later turned out, partly funded at the time by

---

200 A colonnaded viewing monument on the crest of Schönbrunn Hill that now houses a café. Overlooking the rear of Schönbrunn palace and its formal, central gardens, the Gloriette also provides a view over many of Vienna's rooftops. I had noticed the incongruent golden dome amongst the distant trees, often playing a guessing game.
201 Campaign for Nuclear Disarmament.

the government of the Soviet Union. That friend joined the Foreign Office after leaving school and we soon lost touch. But I have always wondered…

I brought up the subject of Vienna's ancient flood plain and its larger island, Unterer Werd, that today houses the city's 2nd District of Leopoldstadt. Into the eighteenth century, the ancient plain's topography of islets and waterways between today's Danube Canal and the main river to the east is said to have rendered life there an intermittently soggy affair. Michael didn't wait to hear me out and described the taming of the main river with its many and ever-changing offshoots into its present-day fixed course.

I'd had a hunch about the possible Viennese background of some of my Jewish ancestors. As far as I'd been able to establish by cross-referencing the genealogy research I'd commissioned in Prague with some of the seventeenth-century administrative records of Kojetin, our Löwenthal branch must have joined that small Moravian town's centuries-old Jewish community during the first half of the 1700s. Perhaps some of my ancestors had been amongst those expelled from Unterer Werd[202] – and from Austria altogether – in 1669 and 1670? Had some continued to wander abroad from one Jewish community to another, perhaps splintering and settling along the way before some of a later generation were granted official permission to settle in Kojetin, only to return full circle after Jewish emancipation and legal freedom of movement were granted in 1849?

***

In the months following my arrival in Vienna, after several hours glued to a microfilm machine at the IKG or steeped in an archive elsewhere, I used to wind down towards late afternoon with a slow stroll through the streets of the old town. Along the way I'd buy a tub of ice-cream before crossing the Marienbrücke (bridge) to the eastern bank of the Danube Canal, just a short distance from where Oma used to live. There I descended the steep steps onto the embankment with its many benches facing the old city.

Relaxing in the warmth of late afternoon had helped me disengage from tragedy and anger and re-engage with the present, a present interspersed with moments from the past when I used to lean on Oma's windowsill as the sun went down behind the roofs of the old town, and the sounds of the bustling city gave way to the mellow summer evenings I had never forgotten. I also hoped to coax to the fore seemingly lost memories that I

---

[202] For a brief overview of the relocation of the Vienna's Jews from the walled city to the district of Unterer Werd see Appendix 3.

knew must still be there.

THE PRESSURE KEEPS MOUNTING

My stepmother, Anna, was almost incoherent when she phoned me. My father's condition had deteriorated and she was afraid that this time it really was going to be the end. Could things possibly get any worse?

Truth be told, I could sense my faint stirrings of anger with my father. I had visited him more frequently after his stroke, knowing that Anna and he relied on me to bring him out of his silence and even make him laugh – but he had left my brothers and me when we still needed him.

Of course I would go to my father if he really were dying, but my brothers also had to see him. There was so much unfinished business and they needed the opportunity to say good-bye; if I dropped everything and rushed to Germany, they would continue to delay.

I phoned my brother Robert. 'I'm not going – you and Martin will have to do it!'

I refused for the moment to leave Vienna; if my father were still alive by the time my brothers returned to England, I would go to him immediately. Meanwhile, and with considerable trepidation, I was waiting for a BBC film crew that was due to arrive in two days' time. They probably wouldn't have been too happy to have their carefully planned schedule disrupted, though I could have cancelled them if I had to. Intuition told me that my father would wait.

I could barely believe what I had let myself in for. When I first responded to the BBC documentary team's enquiry through the Second Generation Network, I was merely curious, then I had realised that perhaps I did have something to contribute. If I could also tell the story of Heinrich Gertler, others might be affected enough reflect on the nature of supposed charity and altruism.

Perhaps I could tell the story of the innocent children who had paid the ultimate price for the intransigence of faithless rabbis who had prayed on parental fears of eternal damnation if their children were not sent to orthodox Jewish foster homes? However, I was also feeling uneasy that the issue of cross-generational trauma might be represented as a Jewish Holocaust experience alone, which it is not.

On the other hand, Vanessa Engle's trilogy of documentaries was about British Jews, and the episode, *Next Generation*, was applicable to me. Vanessa wanted my story and assured me that her film would address my concern that the 'next-generation issue' was not an exclusively Jewish phenomenon. I had eventually agreed to participate and now I had to deal with it.

***

'Since they've agreed to let us into the building and film in the entrance hall, do you think there'd be a chance we could go up to the second floor and film outside my grandmother's front door?' I asked.

'I suppose I could always ask. What number is it?'

'Fourteen.' There was a momentary silence before the BBC's local fixer said: 'Oh! I don't believe it! That's where the owner of the building lives!'

A few days later I was climbing Oma's staircase with a film crew in tow. In spite of having dreaded the moment, I felt perfectly calm with pinpoint focus, even though that morning's interview had wrung me dry. I had been surprised by how deeply affected I felt when telling the story of SS Sturmbannführer Erich Deppner. I had never spoken about his effect on my mother and our lives before now, but as soon as I did the palpitations went into overdrive. I felt so anxious that I ended up cutting corners in order to get the subject over and done with. Afterwards, I had no memory of what I'd said.

Herr Dr. M., the owner of the building, had agreed to come to Vienna from his other home in nearby Baden. When I rang the bell by the familiar, tall double door, he opened it wide. As we stood in the spacious hallway where first my grandfather's and then his successor's clients used to wait, one half of me was introducing myself and thanking him for his generosity while the other half was searching for the past. In forty years not much had obviously changed; the apartment even smelled almost the same.

Herr Dr. M. ushered us through another set of double doors to his spacious sitting room. Oma had rented the room to a fellow solicitor, Dr. B., and his imposing wooden desk in its centre had left a lasting impression.

Motioning to the left and the right, Herr Dr. M. told us to film wherever we liked. Through the open door to the left I could see into the room where Oma and I used to lean by the window. Through the door to the right there were more doors to more rooms that I hadn't known about. Either I'd had no concept of its size when I was younger or I was seeing two apartments that had since been knocked into one.

I was barely listening to the conversation around me because I was so disorientated. It didn't feel as if this was where Oma used to live, where I'd visited as a child; it had little – if anything – to do with my experience.

I returned to the entrance hall from where I entered 'our' wing from a more familiar direction. Memories of delicious salami and Wieners, fresh crusty rye bread, Goulash and Sauerkraut, Gugelhupf, Strudel, Povidl dumplings and large 'Heferl' (mugs) of coffee and buttermilk came flooding back as I walked past the small galley kitchen and adjacent dining nook where I had once pulled holes in Oma's apple-strudel pastry.

I walked through to what used to be the lodgers' room to reach the room I had loved so much. The large bed where Oma had died was long gone; in its place stood a gleaming grand piano. Looking around, I imagined how it used to be; I remembered the herb sweets in the wardrobe in which I'd first made material acquaintance with Grandfather, the aunts Camilla and Clara, and even Great-grandmother Antonia. The wardrobe was now gone and I could see into the room next door: Herr Dr. M.'s sitting room.

As I stood by the window and looked across the Danube Canal to the Franz-Josef Kai on the west bank, I reflected on how bitterly cold Vienna had been the last time I'd been in the apartment. I recalled those letters that, some thirty years after we'd found them in a box beneath that very window, had so disturbed something deep within, setting me on a course that had brought me full circle.

Then I recalled a small, almost transparent piece of yellow paper I had recently discovered in my mother's collection of memorabilia.

Vienna April 17th 1945

CONFIRMATION NO

Comrades Dr. Oskar Löwenthal and Vinzenz Maly have been allocated the apartment of fugitive N.S.D.A.P member name: Wolf Karl, address: Vienna II, Obere Donaustr. 57/14. The apartment and furnishings are currently at their disposal.

The Mayor of the II District

I. A. Bauer

I hadn't known that. Only a week or so earlier, my grandparents and the Malys together with tens of thousands of fellow inhabitants had been blasted out of their homes during the final battle for Vienna. They had probably resigned themselves to living in cellars for the foreseeable future.

In one of the few buildings left standing in Obere Donaustrasse, Karl Wolf, a Nazi whose parent organisation had sanctioned the 'legalised' theft of Jewish homes, businesses and properties seemed to have recognised that his self-serving game was over.

I wondered if Herr Dr. M. had any idea how focused and quietly ruthless a film crew on a tight and fixed schedule could be. He didn't get the opportunity to show me the documents he'd brought relating to my grandfather's eventual signing of the leasehold. What a poignant moment that must have been.

However, when he told me that the building had once belonged to his parents and that after Oma's death he had taken over 'our' apartment, I felt a twinge of irritation. The miserable circumstances my mother and Elsa had found themselves in had been an opportunity for someone else to strike gold in a city where leasehold homes were traditionally passed down the generations. My irritation was not directed toward Herr Dr. M. personally; he just happened to be in the right place at the right time. It was those who deliberately ruined it for my mother's family and others like them who made me angry.

A SHORT REPRIEVE

The use of mobile phones was not permitted in the library of the DOEW. I had placed mine beside me on the reading table while I spoke with their senior archivist who, I had been informed, had the reputation of a ferocious rottweiler. I could see why as she took on the role of drill-sergeant with a young man whom I suspected might have been doing Zivildienst (civilian service) in lieu of national military service.[203]

'Of course, that doesn't mean we wouldn't defend ourselves in the case of attack,' a conscientious objector once said to me. How exactly? I had wondered.

My impatience with that get-out clause, which renders the individual useless in defence of his own or anybody else in an emergency, did tend to get the better of me. If conscription is the law of a genuinely democratically elected government, why not learn the essentials of defence just in case – perhaps with caveats – especially in a country where wings have been clipped to a stump by its declaration of perpetual neutrality? But do not expect others to place themselves in danger or lay down their own lives for you and yours if there is a sudden attack!

Like so much else, it is another complex subject, not least because Adolf

---

203 Austrian conscientious objectors are able to undertake 'civilian service' in lieu of military training. Within the scheme they can apply for a placement at the DOEW in Vienna and in Holocaust archives and memorial museums abroad.

Hitler first secretly broke the post WWI Treaty of Versailles after coming to power before openly flaunting his massive re-armament programme and his contempt for the hamstringing treaty itself. He simply knew in his gut that nobody would do anything about it.

Whatever the true circumstances of the young man at the DOEW, the archivist was nothing but gracious and generous towards me – although when my phone caught her eye, I quickly explained myself rather than wait for her to pull rank. 'I'm sorry, it's set on vibrate. My father is dying.'

My brothers had said their goodbyes to our father and returned to England. A few hours later I boarded the night train to go to him. Five days later he was dead. It was the 31st of March 2007.

My mother used to dread the confrontation with the losses woven into the tapestry of the month of March and was always relieved when April, with its less sustained litany of death, finally arrived. Now it seemed that it was my turn too.

VIENNA, APRIL 2007

LAYERS UPON LAYERS OF GRIEF

Was it unkind of me to leave Frankfurt so soon after my father died? Perhaps. But I simply had to leave, for myself.

My stepmother Anna had wanted me to stay with her; quite understandably she was terrified of being alone after more than forty years of marriage and dreaded the sudden lack of purpose after my father's death.

Before his stroke Anna had already spent years trying to persuade the once-entrepreneurial bon vivant who had become lost to debilitating chronic fatigue that he had so much to be grateful for and that life really was worth living.

She was exhausted and broken after four years of solitary physical and emotional slog that had been preceded by several years of living on the knife-edge of a vicious circle of inner frustrations, blood-sugar disarray and diagnoses of chronic 'diseases' that were medicated with several daily cocktails of pills. While the medications did more harm than good, reductionist thinking and Big Pharma had yet another field day at my father's expense.

Anna was weary after years of disturbed nights, during which his insomnia and anxieties of doom and gloom meant that she eventually had to remain awake to reassure him that all was well.

It was heartbreaking to watch her terror but while I had wanted to give her the hug she so desperately needed, I could not. The last time I had done that to let her know that I really did care and appreciated her lonely and unseen struggle, she had frozen and pulled away. There was nothing else I could do to help her beyond remaining calm and kind and letting her be.

My own nerves were in shreds, too. While I was concerned for Anna, her restlessness and unceasing chatter eventually left me with little choice but to leave as soon as I could. In the past I might have coped, but my head was already too full; had I stayed, I might have snapped when she was at her most vulnerable. I had my own grief to contend with and no longer had the strength to prop up anybody else.

I reminded myself that Anna had friends and neighbours, my father's toxic medications had been removed by her GP who was on full alert, and my stepsister Sybille lived less than an hour's drive away and paid her daily visits. She could stay with her mother for a while.

When I had left Vienna, the weather was still unpleasantly cold and damp; when I returned winter had yielded to the gentle warmth of spring, offering me a perfect excuse to take my fraying nerves and the cacophony of tangled emotions to a sun-drenched bench in my favourite 'secret' garden at Schönbrunn. Armed with take-away cups of black coffee and an impulse purchase of a packet of cigarettes to help ground me, I sat there for many hours, feeling sad as I pondered my father's shattered dreams, all the conflict and hurt and their insidious aftermath, much of which could have been avoided – if only…

I sat there reflecting upon the father I loved very much and whose suffering had pained me deeply; I felt saddened that, in truth and for the most part, I had already grieved his loss long ago. He had made every effort to provide for us children and our mother in the best way he knew how, and only ever treated me with affection, kindness and generosity – but I hadn't really known him.

When my mother, Robert and I returned to England in 1965, he remained in Germany with Anna and their child. We saw him only once or twice a year - fleeting business trips to England, or when he stopped by briefly during his annual vacations.

On the rare occasions when Robert and I spent a week or so with him in Germany during school holidays - long before the days of cheap phone calls, let alone real-time video links - I felt like a visitor on the edge of another family, watching my stepsister relate to him with an ease and familiarity that seemed to increase as mine diminished.

Four years after we returned to England, our father tried to re-enter the English workplace. While lodging with a friend in London, he took a mundane job to cover his immediate commitments, hoping to find something more fitting and eventually bring Anna and Sybille over. But he had been away for too long: his considerable experience in Germany carried no weight and he no longer seemed to belong.

I had loved it when he came to stay some weekends but it also reminded me of what had already been lost. Then it was taken away all over again. Anna later admitted she had been delighted when she persuaded him to give up and return to Frankfurt.

The following summer, my father rented a villa on the Italian Adriatic. On previous visits, when Robert and I had stayed, he and Anna had always been at work; but this time he wanted the family holiday to include both me and Robert (our older brother was at university, absorbed in his own world) and, for a few days, Dawa – who, after a critical illness that had nearly killed her a year earlier – had returned to her self-assured, charismatic form.

All appeared to be going well, although Anna was noticeably tense and more irritable than usual with Sybille whom, much to my father's dismay, she often seemed to treat as an enemy. In Italy, more than ever.

'For heaven's sake, leave her alone,' he'd pleaded.

'Don't interfere, she's not your daughter!' I saw the bullet pierce his heart.

With hindsight I can understand her anxiety, even though it was unnecessary. While my mother still loved my father, she had let go; and, like my father, all she wanted was for everybody to make the best of the situation and to be at ease with one another.

Unfortunately, after my mother left Italy Anna's discomfort exploded into an outburst of resentment and suspicion, followed by strident demands for her and Sybille's supremacy. Our shocked father couldn't reason with her no matter how much he tried. Robert and I were once more confined to the periphery while the three of them went on a boat trip with friends. We didn't show our dismay but our father, who until then had been so alive, was deeply affected and noticeably withdrew as he realised the depressing truth: that there was no silver lining in this particularly dark cloud. Not much later he was diagnosed with diabetes.

After I married, my father and I enjoyed family visits but the moments when we were truly alone were too few to bridge the distance between us. Something precious remained lost.

The first days of wallowing at Schönbrunn were grim. Attempts to lose myself in a book or uplifting music on my iPod were short lived. I grieved not only for my mother, my brothers and myself, but also for my father, a fundamentally kind and honourable man, brimming with creative potential, whose life had been eroded by too many years of stress and disarray.

About a year after the holiday in Italy, my father was further challenged. As a foreigner in Germany during the early 1970's, another sudden ousting by new company bosses left him not only in shock but also in fear of not being able to meet his financial responsibilities. Already vulnerable, he shut down.

My father was more fortunate than the previous generation. Had a friend not unexpectedly arrived to find him sitting inert in a corner, staring into space - and had that friend not explained to Anna that her husband needed understanding and help instead of disdain and impatience - he might, like her own father, never have risen again.

After he began therapy, my father came to blame his parents' misdeeds for his psychological struggles. 'My father was useless,' he once told me contemptuously during our only adult conversation when we were alone for more than just an hour or so. 'I knew I wouldn't feel anything when my mother died – and I didn't.'

I was stunned and deeply saddened for my grandparents by the destructive effects of mediocre psychotherapy that had disempowered my father instead of empowering him.

As often happened, it was my mother who offered a more compassionate perspective: the suppressed traumas of WWI and the early death of his mother while he was stationed far away in the Balkans had had a catastrophic effect upon my young grandfather.[204] Later, when sudden demands for the repayment of a business loan pulled the rug from beneath him, he suffered a mental and physical breakdown that deprived his young son of any meaningful paternal presence. His mother, who still had no

---

204 During the German night-time bombings of WW2, my father only narrowly escaped physical harm by jumping down a burning staircase in his underpants. I have no doubt that the repressed trauma of that event compounded by his epigenetic inheritance had also contributed to his psychological and physical fragility in later life.

understanding of the trauma her husband had endured out of sight, had to find solutions in what was still a man's world within a difficult economic climate while running their hardware store alone. It was not much different for Anna's parents.

Later, when my father recognised that his relationship with Anna had been a misjudgement, he could not tell her, because he understood her past and really cared. Ultimately, he was trapped, and it slowly destroyed him. There was no remedy for losing both family and *heimat*.

The early years of his retirement were filled with extensive foreign travel, yet that did nothing to improve his psychological state. When I asked whether he would like to return to England he'd replied, 'I would if I could afford it.'

To compound matters, a series of traumatic events - beyond his control, yet endured in silence - led to the gradual crumbling of his physical health beneath a carefully maintained public façade of bonhomie. 'I'm very good at pretending,' he once told me. He might just as well have said, 'Men have to pretend to be something they are not.'

It was only after his stroke, when there was nothing to distract him from himself, that my father started to recognise his own unconscious reflexes within his relationship with my mother and the misadventures that had befallen his parents. Had he known to do so earlier, perhaps he might have gained enough understanding to forgive not only them but also himself. How different his life might have been.

'I'm not interested in the past,' he once said during his more defensive days.

I had thought, *What a pity: without understanding the past you can never hope to understand the present, let alone avoid repeating the same mistakes in the future.* Perhaps I should have spoken out, but I still felt too young to tell my father what, in a perfect world, he ought to have been teaching me. Yet nobody had taught him either.

A few months before he died he made up for lost time. 'Don't you ever do anything stupid!' he warned me.

***

My father's dying days were profoundly difficult. 'It's all so complicated,' he lamented, watching with amazement his life unfolding in his mind's eye. 'It's all going backwards coming forward.' I reassured him that nothing was complicated any more. 'Oh, thank you!' he said, yet four days after he was expected to breathe his last he still could not let go.

'Sometimes they can't leave because they are so concerned for the person closest to them who might not be able to cope with being left behind. They often wait until they are out of the room and then slip away,' the terminal patient carer had told us.

I had already given my father the freedom to do what was right for himself, but even so I left leave his room on several occasions in the vain hope that he might let go before I returned.

Then, when my father and I were alone on the morning of the fifth day, I somehow knew what was required of me. Gently cupping his face in both hands, I whispered in his ear and felt his tense body relax. His laboured breaths slowed, becoming peaceful and rhythmic. I stroked his brow, kissed his cheek and watched the furrows on his forehead melt away.

Within minutes my father had moved into a state of deep relaxation. He opened his eyes for the first time since he'd said, 'Oh, thank you,' and slowly looked around.

As his eyes met mine and his lips formed a gentle kiss, they emanated a depth of love that was far beyond anything words could express. A tear gently slid from the corner of each eye and he released his final breath.

Without a doubt, my father had experienced the ecstasy of self-transcendence; he had returned Home.

'Your father must have died a very good death!' The carer, who had arrived within minutes to prepare his body for its last journey to the Goethe Institute of Medical Research, seemed pleased to announce. She even took a photograph: 'You will want it as a reminder.'

He knew that I loved him. No longer burdened by his own resistance, or by another person's fears, he felt the freedom to let go and accept whatever would come naturally. His body gave out just short of his eighty-second birthday; his life force spent, he sank into stillness, too weary to fight another day.

THE PRESSURE KEEEPS MOUNTING

It was Good Friday, and I'd had my fill of caffeine and cigarettes, yet I still needed time out and returned to my garden at Schönbrunn, which was crowded with locals enjoying the sunny public holiday.

I stopped pretending to read. As I lifted my head, I saw a smartly dressed man walking past me, disappearing through the exit at the far end of the garden. A short while later I raised my head again and caught the same man looking intently at me as he passed by. He quickly averted his gaze. What on earth was going on?

A few minutes later, he was back. As he came closer, I looked him straight in the eyes, hoping embarrassment would make him go away. But after a while, I sensed his presence again, even though I couldn't see him. I remembered the path on the other side of the hedge behind my bench and turned around. There he was, peering at me through the twigs. 'Bloody hell, he must be deranged!' I thought.

There were quite a few people nearby, but I was now having horrendous palpitations and felt sufficiently intimidated to scoop up my belongings and speed-walk out of the garden until I found an empty bench on the opposite side of the park.

Although I told myself that he was gone, that sense of unease returned. I saw him again in the distance, scanning the crowd and I immediately dived down a narrow pathway and left the palace grounds.

The following afternoon he was back again. After moving several times, I felt so unnerved by this game of hide and seek that I gave up and returned to my apartment. Pacing back and forth between my front door and the sitting-room window eventually calmed me, and I sat down to listen to one of my father's CDs that I'd brought with me.

It was guitar music by Tárrega, including *Recuerdos de la Alhambra* that my friend Martin had played so beautifully during my mother's funeral. She had loved that piece and I had chosen it because it seemed to evoke the essence of her longing for what had been lost.

Reflecting first on my mother's funeral and then on my parents' lives sent me to my laptop. As my fingers flew over the keyboard, I didn't have to stop to think because the writing flowed. Some 5,000 words later I had a potted history of elements in my parents' lives, the psychological undercurrents and the other influences that had brought me to where I was that day.

I continued scanning my memories and heard some of my mother's and Oma's apparently insignificant throwaway lines. I heard some of Granny Pinner's asides about my English grandfather, who had died suddenly a few weeks before my birth. I heard my mother's comments about the state of her in-laws' dysfunctional relationship ('I thought I was joining a really happy family!'), and a snatched exchange with my father on the same theme.

I remembered the contents of hundreds of family letters and started to collate the new insights of the past few months, the facts I'd uncovered and the additional knowledge I'd acquired as I'd researched the Jewish experience following Hitler's rise to power. I saw centuries of history and my mother's place in them, and I saw my family enmeshed in a dynamic, multi-dimensional matrix of cause and effect.

I was reminded of an extraordinary event many years earlier when I had received a priceless wake-up call that, at the time, I had not recognised.

BUSHEY, ENGLAND, 2000

A LONG OVERDUE CONVERSATION

'Tante Clara told Elsa the Löwenthals were Sephardi Jews through the male line... They used to be called Pereira or de Pereira ... from Amsterdam.'[205]

'Really? That means they were from Spain or Portugal!'

'Yes, that's right. When Elsa travelled through Spain with Luda[206] and Zdena[207] she had the overwhelming feeling she'd been there before, especially in Granada and Seville. Somewhere along the way there's said to have been a connection with the Henriquez clan – Sybil Beddington was a Henriquez – but who knows?'

'Damn religion!' I had scoffed as our conversation moved on to the Spanish Inquisition.

'Yes, darling, but at least the Shema really does make perfect sense if you understand the meaning behind the words.'

'You know the Shema?'

'Of course.'

'Do you know it in Hebrew?'

'Of course!' My mother immediately recited what I later learned were the first few lines of the central prayer in Judaism in Hebrew! 'Have you read Spinoza?' she continued. 'You really should, darling, you'd appreciate it. He was a Sephardi Jew, too.'

There was a short pause before she added, with a faint flick of an eyebrow that seemed to speak volumes, 'He was excommunicated, you know.'

With that, our short exchange came to an end relegating any more profound thoughts to the back of my mind because I was too busy projecting ahead to my next university assignment: a critique of a chapter in Susan Sondheim's book *Illness as Metaphor*.

---

205 What she meant was that at some point there had been the first of ongoing intermarriage within the Ashkenazi community.
206 Cousin Luděk's nickname.
207 Zdenka's nickname.

Ironically, major surgery had interrupted my studies and I had struggled to find the energy and the concentration to produce a coherent piece of work. Then, just hours before the deadline, all had fallen into place during the quiet hours of the night. Later, it occurred to me that the Jewish custom of the Sabbath break from work and 'doing' might have a much deeper meaning.

THE METAPHYSICAL

Unfortunately, by the time I followed my mother's advice to read Spinoza it was already too late. Once again, I was left with another of those conversations I regret never having had, though it was quite pleasing to note that we and Spinoza seemed to have more in common than just the Jewish-Iberian connection.

For the first time during that conversation with my mother I glimpsed the depths of her private inner world. We had little opportunity to discuss the more profound aspects of our existence at any length.

'Father once called me "*mein kleines Dummerl*" (my little Silly Billy). I know he didn't mean to be hurtful ... he was probably referring to my inclination for clowning around and mimicking ... but I don't suppose he will ever have known how that affected me.'

She had only made it into an academically less challenging Hauptschule (an ordinary secondary school), whereas Elsa had attended grammar school and always considered herself the clever one. My mother also felt that Elsa had never expected her to amount to much. She laughed. 'Even though in later life I often knew things while everybody else was still busy scratching their heads!'

My mother read widely and quietly cultivated her inner world for pleasure; she had felt no need for intellectually competitive sparring matches to prove her worth. Intelligent as she undoubtedly was, she lived her life through her heart and intuition rather than her logical mind.

Because of the endless round of coughs, colds and migraines she had suffered, particularly during that last year in Vienna, it is not surprising that there was concern she might fail the medical examination that was essential for a child to secure a seat on the Kindertransport.

Neither my mother's nervous system nor her confidence in her intellectual abilities ever fully recovered, and she retreated unless she felt completely safe. However, after entering a less pedantic educational establishment in England that still taught its pupils *how* to think instead of *what* to think and to memorise, she started to relax and do well enough.[208]

As she buried her head in the sand to survive the pain of separation and loss, her sense of fun and her artistic and empathic gifts found an appreciative audience in Dresden House, and later with the often badly wounded soldiers and airmen she befriended as a Red Cross volunteer.

While preserving her comfort zone often made my mother appear aloof, or sometimes prevented her from speaking out, she never lost sight of our common humanity; she never knowingly inflicted pain on another person or undermined their sense of dignity.

'Father never shouted. One look was enough and then he'd encourage us to reflect upon our behaviour by explaining calmly why it had been unacceptable. The worst thing I could ever imagine was to disappoint him… When Mother was upset or angry about somebody's behaviour he'd say "*Na schau, Marie…*" (Now look, Marie…) then he'd help her see things from another perspective. She always calmed down and all was well again.'

That was unlike his elder brother, Arthur, who learned to keep his council in the face of Ida's infamous histrionics. He was frequently forced to go behind her back and do what he considered right for himself or others. Unfortunately that created a vicious circle in which Ida's exceptionally keen senses meant she eventually never entirely trusted him, so he had to be ever more duplicitous!

I don't understand why he permits himself to be terrorised by Ida's outbursts… You are, of course, absolved of all blame… She is very sick and by nature not the gentlest of people, Grandfather wrote to Toni in February 1940 after an exceptionally vicious outburst from Ida had caused Toni to lose his patience, offload his carefully guarded frustrations and find a new address.

London 7th February 1940

My dear sisters

…As for me, I am becoming used to managing by myself. I must confess that just sitting around on my own day in and day out is beginning to get to me. So, I was quite grateful when a mouse turned up one evening and, quite shamelessly, looked for some crumbs on the carpet and immediately ate them up. Now I often put a little piece of cheese rind out at night so that she's not forced to make the awkward climb up into the rubbish bin where she makes a noise rustling around (which wakes me up, so I have

---

[208] Elsa, who had always done well at school in Vienna, wrote home full of enthusiasm for this new way of doing things.

had to put the bin on top of the wardrobe).

Then, after a series of amusing cartoons depicting his very modest new lodgings, the mouse and daily domestic routines, Toni added:

> *I think by now you will have some idea that I am doing quite well. For the sake of appearances, I apologised to Aunt the day before yesterday for my 'coarse behaviour' (I had threatened to kill her and gave her a couple of additional names) so that at least the last remnants of a bad conscience on my part have been expunged. For what might be going on in her conscience, I am not concerned. And, of course, to provide relief for Uncle (the poor man can't run away).*

There was more to Ida's volatility than was immediately apparent. She may well have developed paranoid bipolar disorder, but she had also experienced a nomadic and obsessive artist's life without ever enjoying much – if any – autonomy over her own. She struggled to be recognised as anything other than an attractive appendage whose job, beyond keeping the hearth warm while her husband pursued his passions, was to make small talk with the wives in polite society.

When her husband's interest in archaeology took them south to explore ancient civilisations, she had established a new home in what since 1882 had been British occupied Egypt. Arthur found the dry climate much kinder to his lungs, which had been compromised by years of exposure to fine dust particles during his gemstone and crystal engraving activities. I daresay his smoking habit was not of much help either!

In Cairo he was happily employed with commissions and other interests while Ida played second fiddle once again. Then, on a working trip to Berlin on the eve of WWI, they unexpectedly found themselves trapped on the wrong side of the political divide.

I'm not certain why they didn't return to Vienna; perhaps it was because Arthur had begun to receive commissions to depict the top echelons of German military, political and imperial life, including the Kaiser.[209] He was a quiet humanitarian with no interest in the tribalism born of political or religious dogma; no doubt a major consideration will have been to use his artistic passions to keep a roof over their heads and to put food on the table.

Much of his work took him away from Berlin for extended periods, but <u>Ida was left alone</u> in a strange city to cope with the fallout of struggling

---

[209] It was said that in order for Arthur, a commoner, to spend time in close proximity to the Kaiser he was bestowed the honorific of 'professor'.

to pay the rent and any other essential living expenses. Some of Arthur's letters held at the Bode Museum in Berlin testify that squeezing payment out his patrons to cover his lodging costs alone proved to be a continuum of the always vulnerable court Jew's well-trodden path of time-consuming and cloyingly diplomatic letter writing. All that a powerless and anxious Ida could do was to wait as she made do as best she could.

After the war ended, any ideas of returning to Cairo to live, or to retrieve their possessions, were blocked by the Egyptian anti-British revolution of 1919. Arthur and Ida returned to Vienna, only to decide that the glove no longer fitted. They went back to Berlin, now the capital of the fledgling post-imperial Weimar Republic, which had developed into a flourishing centre for freedom in the arts, sciences and intellectual thought.

Those halcyon days did not last long. The punitive economic terms of the Treaty of Versailles, the ripple effects of America's Great Depression, and the Weimar Republic's stock market crash of 1929 caused the German economy to implode and led to a violent battle between political activists who forcefully evangelised opposing and extreme ideologies. The more extreme of these took the form of Adolf Hitler's anti-Jewish National Socialist Workers' Party (NSDAP/Nazi).

NSDAP activists had long bullied easier targets; after 1932, when the NSDAP had become the largest political party in parliament, their courage had grown. Ida witnessed the intimidation and thuggery that accompanied Hitler's ascent from party leader to chancellor[210] and then to dictator under the auspices of the Enabling Act of 23rd March 1933.[211] With it, Arthur and Ida's enjoyable life in Berlin fell apart.

Yet again they packed their bags, left their home and started all over again in England. Arthur set about forging wider connections that, until Britain started inching ever closer to declaring war on Germany five years later, served him relatively well.

But what of Ida? For a fragile refugee in her late middle years who spoke little English, life was already challenging enough. Soon she became her own worst enemy as her uncompromising intellect succeeded in alienating just about every woman with whom she might have forged a social circle.

Not everybody was quite so easily intimidated, although they were not particularly useful for learning English. 'She is like a hedgehog. They always prickle but have a very warm heart,' came the helpful aside from

---

210   Via a coalition with another nationalist party.
211   Now Hitler could enact any law without having to answer to anybody. No matter what his agenda, it was 'legal'.

their hostess during one of Toni's private visits with his uncle and aunt to the Czech ambassador's home.

Unable to communicate effectively and made fearful by the increase in antisemitic propaganda in the British popular press, Ida was eventually so consumed with fear and paranoia that she isolated herself when Arthur was not there to help her. While he continued to receive commissions in high places that took him away from home, remuneration was slow to arrive. Anxiety resulting from financial insecurity in a not particularly welcoming environment, coupled with the threat of a Nazi invasion, and spending many nights in the London Underground while the Nazi air-force blitz bombed London and destroyed houses in their street and damaged their own home, pushed her towards the edge.

Ida, highly intelligent and scholarly, always probing deeper and spoiling for a match but also acutely insightful, never did find the social support she was in need of.

As for Arthur, he once wrote to Toni: *I have been very fortunate to have found an understanding soul and a true companion, even though one's sisters might not see it that way.*

Despite the many difficulties Ida caused him during their fifty or so years together, touchingly, he cared for her until there was nothing he could do for her. Ida died in a mental hospital on 30th January 1958 and was buried in Canwick Road Old Cemetery in Lincoln. The formal inscription on her headstone reads: Rosa Catharina Josepha Loewenthal 1881-1958 Requiescat in Pace. A small flower vase at the foot end bears the name 'Ida'.[212]

LOVE THY NEIGHBOUR

Grandfather continued to carry out his responsibilities to my mother and Elsa as best he could from afar after they arrived in England.

Vienna, January 1940

I am happy to see from your letters that you are enjoying good relationships with all those around you, especially your fellow pupils, and I take for granted, without the need to make a special point of it, that you also treat all your fellow human beings with love.

---

212   Arthur was a Grecophile. In Greek mythology Ida was one of the two nurses who looked after the infant Zeus when his mother hid him for his safety on Mount Ida.

Then, as if to remind his daughters of their mother's example, he added:

Children, I cannot begin to tell you what a good mother you have! It probably isn't necessary either because, of course, you know her yourselves. Towards Grandmother and the aunts she is goodness and kindness personified and how good she is towards me, you also know that best of all.

I never saw or heard my mother treat another person with anything less than civility and kindness. When she expressed gratitude, even for the smallest gesture, it was heartfelt – not obsequious. She was a complex human being who, like all of us, had her thoughtless moments and blind spots but, as they became apparent, she was honest enough to admit to them. Was she human enough to dislike the personality traits of certain people? Yes. Did she hate them? No. Was she unpleasant in return? No.

'Why should I be nasty? I like being pleasant towards to people.'

Quite simply, she was far too sensitive and gentle (but by no means insipid) to deliberately hurt another person.

Understandably she was angry with those who had orchestrated or played a direct role in the Holocaust, but her anger came more from sorrow. She knew it would be self-defeating to allow herself to be eaten up by bitterness or to let a sense of victimhood override her sense of identity.

My mother's inclination to assume the best in others sometimes came at a considerable cost and, on one particularly memorable occasion, it was hard for me when she refused to participate in whatever it was I was attempting to offload. Her refusal to collaborate with my anger brought out the worst in me. A couple of times, her optimism and good humour merely served to make me more aware of my own unhappiness at the time.

In Vienna I forced myself to recognise and acknowledge what I had done and the guilt I now felt. Then something extraordinary happened: although my eyes were closed, I seemed to see my mother in front of me. She rested for a short while as she smiled before once more vaporising into the ether. I was not afraid; on the contrary, I somehow knew that all was well. Even so, I cried buckets.

'Darling, if there really is life after death I will definitely make every effort to let you know!' she had once said, and she was obviously not joking. She once confided that her father had appeared by her bedside in England when she was wide awake and had yet to learn that he had died.

During that conversation she had also told me of a near-death experience a few months after we buried Oma. Dawa was critically ill following major abdominal surgery and she swore that she'd been propelled down that much-reported tunnel, at the end of which she had seen her parents, the aunts Clara and Camilla and other close relatives waiting to welcome her. Overjoyed, and about to give herself up to them, she was reminded that her children were still too young and her job was not yet done.

She came back and somehow found the strength to sweep her arm across the bedside cabinet to attract the attention of nurses. I remembered the phone call from a panicked ward sister insisting I rush to the hospital to say goodbye before it was too late.

My mother's will to live had already been extraordinary; this same will also saved her from dying of MRSA-induced sepsis.

BACK IN CAFE SCHOTTENRING

It was Easter Monday and I had a lunchtime meeting with Dr. Vogel at Café Schottenring. I had brought along some photographs of my mother and Elsa as young women. As if there had not already been so many unexpected revelations, it transpired that Dr. Vogel had met them both during their visit following Grandfather's death in 1947. With the passing of so much time, he was no longer certain which one was which; for my part, and without telling him who was who, I was curious to know which sister he and Hans had had a crush on.

He looked from one photograph to the other and back again before pointing at my mother. 'That's her. We took them both swimming at the Gänseheufel ... We tried so hard to persuade them to stay ... with hindsight, they did the right thing not to. They[213] are as antisemitic as ever, just more circumspect about it.'

Yes, I have noticed, I thought to myself but said nothing. Why rub salt into the wound?

Suddenly Dr. Vogel had a vague memory of Elsa wearing a US army uniform but couldn't recall why.

***

Within weeks of the war ending and the implementation of the Allied occupation zones of administration, Elsa and a number of other German-speaking refugees successfully applied for a relatively well-paid position of translator and censor with the American army's civilian division in the US occupied zone. Apart from offering them a chance to earn a living, it also helped them return legally within easier reach of their former homes.

213   Dr. Vogel was referring to the Austrians in general; I was referring to the some of the immediate post-war generation.

Although mail could still take many months to filter through (if it did at all), my mother had heard from her parents via the Red Cross. Not only were they still alive but she had their new address in Obere Donaustrasse.

Elsa took up her post in Frankfurt in the summer of 1945 armed with a secret plan and a small supply of tinned food and coffee passed on by Toni. Luckily, within a short time she was assigned to Esslingen, closer to the Austrian border.

During her Christmas and New Year break in December 1945, Elsa hitched lifts with army vehicles into US-occupied Upper Austria. From there she smuggled herself across the Russian zone of occupation and into the Russian administered Second District of Vienna.

> *The two days during which Elschen was here,* Grandfather wrote to Toni on 3rd February 1946, *were, as you will easily be able to imagine, the most beautiful for your mother and me for many years … let me take the opportunity to thank you wholeheartedly for the thoughtful gifts; the coffee was especially delightful… Yet after seven years of dreaming those two days were too short for me to re-establish our connection of old, most especially now that she has become quite 'independent'.*[214]

For Elsa, the return home was difficult. She was delighted and relieved to see her parents after so many years but appalled by the destruction she encountered on her travels through France, Germany and Austria. She was also deeply disturbed by the trauma she had absorbed from the prisoner-of-war correspondence it was her job to read and censor.[215]

Grandfather, who believed that all work should be done with elevating mindfulness, wrote to Toni: *Elschen is a little weak and I don't think she is happy in her job. I hope it won't be too long before she comes home.*

Her unsanctioned escapade had filled her with contradictory emotions. Her father had said farewell to his still dependent and rather conservative fifteen-year-old daughter and opened the door to a worldly, beautiful and glamorous young woman – with red nail polish and lipstick! After seven years filled with the grey of deprivation, he – forever the mentor – had not been able to resist his duty.

To complicate matters further, having spent her teenage years in England

---
214 'independent' was written in English.
215 Some of the prisoners who were conscripted in a last ditch effort to fend off the Allies were young teenagers. Some were only 12 years old or even younger. Yet they were fortunate: the Soviet Union dragged their heels for many years during which they used their POWs as forced labour under gruelling conditions. Many perished and many families never knew what had happened to them.

with little adult guidance, Elsa had fallen under the influence of avant-gardists with their contempt for the moral standards of a conservative bourgeoisie.

A few years earlier, and with remarkable insight, she had confided in her diary: *A weak person like me needs a god.* Now she had found one. Still confused as to who she really was, she left Vienna feeling criticised and contemptuous of her father's staid conservatism. She also left with a profound sense of loss.

Being fined a sizeable chunk of her monthly salary when she returned to Esslingen did not boost her morale.[216] Perhaps if her employers had also been aware of the American cigarettes she occasionally enclosed before taping up the letters and meagre German prisoner-of-war parcels sent from home, she might have been discharged!

Meanwhile back in England in the spring of 1946, my mother had started her third year of nurse's training at Great Ormond Street Children's Hospital. With leave limited, exorbitant travel costs, the chaos in bomb-ravaged continental Europe and her uncertain legal status, it was decided that it would be safer if she visited Aunt Paula in Sweden rather than trying to see her parents. Her visit home would have to wait until her next annual leave.

Dawa travelled to Stockholm in July 1946, after which Aunt Paula reported back to Vienna:

Stockholm 16th August 1946

My dear ones,
It is now already 3 weeks since Mickele left me, leaving behind a great void. Her presence was of great help in overcoming the traumatic experience with Frieda. All in all, I experienced much joy with the child who has developed well in all respects. She is not only pretty but also intelligent and, despite her youth, possessed of an enviable self-confidence. Before I met her I was somewhat anxious that constantly being together with a young girl would be somewhat tiring for me, but after a few days she felt so at ease that she wanted her freedom to explore by herself.[217] *We then met up for lunch and then drove somewhere or other into Stockholm's beautiful surroundings ... I am enclosing a small photograph that Adele*

---
216 Elsa sent most of her salary to Toni in England, partly to save it but also to support him in finding his feet in civvy street.
217 Dawa told me that she knew Aunt Paula was afraid she might have been bored, but that was not the case. She thoroughly enjoyed her visit.

took of Micky and me on her balcony.[218]

Elsa returned to Vienna once more in January 1947, shortly before leaving her job with the Americans. I don't know whether or not she had permission but on 10th of February 1947 Aunt Paula wrote to Toni in England where, in recognition of his wartime military service, he had just been bestowed with naturalisation:

> My dear Toni,
> ...Only today I learnt from Vienna that last month Elsa paid your parents a three-day visit. This time your father is full of praise and says that he has much to be forgiven. I cannot express in words how happy I am that harmony has been restored. Now your mother and father are longingly awaiting Miki's visit that she is planning for April/May. I, too, have been invited for the same period but I shall defer any journey until conditions have improved; I must use my holiday to regain my strength for another year's work, and Vienna is not exactly a suitable environment for that. To be honest, I dread coming face to face with Vienna; I do believe that at every step I will be confronted by ghosts.
> I regularly read the 'Wiener Kurier', a newspaper published by the American forces of occupation and that is, of course, politically completely colourless. But I can gain an overview of prevailing conditions and thank our maker that I don't have to live there. What must your parents have suffered that, despite the desolate circumstances, they are so content and optimistic. I can also imagine quite well that the aforementioned applies only to your father, and that your mother who has to concern herself with everyday housekeeping matters is far from content.

Nothing worked out as planned. One month later, on 10th April 1947 and before leaving her office when she finished work, Aunt Paula once again sat down at her typewriter:

> My dear Toni,
> It is a deeply sad event that causes me to write to you. As you have probably already heard from your dear mother or from Elsa, your father, my beloved brother, passed away on 7th March after a short illness. If, contrary to expectations, you have not received any closer information, Uncle Arthur will pass your mother's letter on to you, in which she describes his illness in detail. No matter how deeply I feel the loss of my brother, I am only too aware that for your dear, good mother who remained so loyal

---

218 I still have it.

to him through all the wicked years, this will be an infinitely harder blow. My heart is breaking at the thought that her children were not able to be at her side in these dark hours because, as she told me, her telegram to Elsa[219] was so delayed that she was unable to be present at the funeral. Now, the pressing question is, how will your mother move into the future. You did at one time express the idea of bringing your parents over to England, and now that you have found your own place the best solution might be for her to live with you and run the household for you. It goes without saying that, if I had my own home, I would invite her to live under my roof but, unfortunately, my own circumstances in this regard are somewhat tenuous.[220] Of course, I realise it will not be that easy for your mother to adjust to completely strange circumstances, but any discomforts would be outweighed by being reunited with her children, most especially since she longed for them almost to the point of making herself ill. It is a great tragedy that your father was only able to enjoy his newly returned freedom and human dignity for such a short period of time. His letters breathed such a contentment with his existence, and he was so grateful that he could feel free again so that it would not have been too much to ask that he be granted a few more years to walk upon this earth.

Having to inform Arthur was a difficult task for me and I am deeply concerned that this tragic news might undermine his already poor health.[221] But in the long run it would not have been possible to conceal the death of his brother from him. He would have had to be informed sooner or later.

I hope, dear Toni, that despite the prevailing conditions in your country, your new business venture is moving forward and that it will be possible for you to look after your mother. Please write soon, with warmest greetings, your Aunt Paula

How is Mickele doing? Please give her my love. It is of greatest comfort to me that Elserl was at home not long before Father's death and that he had experienced such great joy. Give my love to her too.

Two months later, my mother and Elsa arrived at Vienna's Westbahnhof

---

219 Elsa was in Paris learning French.
220 As was once common for single women without a family and with modest means, Paula was a sub-tenant in another person's home.
221 The strain of his exacting work in Lincoln on behalf of the war effort at the Diamond Works/Industrial Cutting Tools Ltd, the suffering and deaths of his siblings, compounded by a dearth of post-war commissions through which to earn a living, caused Arthur to sink into near suicidal depression.

just as they had left: together, by train. This time, they did not travel through Germany but via France and Switzerland.[222] They had neither citizenship of any kind nor passports; instead, they carried official leave-to-travel documents issued to adult refugees under the auspices of the 'London Agreement' of 15 October 1946.

They knew that they had been deprived of their Austrian citizenship after the Anschluss, but during their visit they discovered that their right to live in Austria as subordinate subjects had also been revoked two days after their flight to England. With no real choice, my mother returned to England to complete her nurse's training in 1948 before immediately marrying the adventurous young Englishman she'd met the previous summer during her return sea voyage from Sweden: my father.

'Why did you marry him?' I asked her.

'Because he was head over heels in love with me... He was such a nice young man ... and I was fed up with not having a nationality and a passport.'

'Didn't you love him?'

'Yes, of course I did. But I wasn't needy of him.'

Elsa, still single, was torn about where to settle after so many years in England. She was keeping abreast of job opportunities in an all-round depleted Vienna through regular deliveries of the Austrian *Arbeiter Zeitung* (*Worker's Newspaper*). In August 1951 she wrote to her mother: *I am determined as ever to come to Vienna but first I must sort out the issue of my nationality.*

***

Back in the present at Café Schottenring, Dr. Vogel was studying another more recent photograph. 'Such strong men,' he offered, pointing to my brothers who were pictured strolling beside our mother. A tender smile crossed his face. 'Tell me about her life.'

I told him as much as I could about my mother's experiences in England before we moved to Germany and after our return to England. When I told him about her experiences in Munich and her eventual breakdown, his eyes began to glisten and the rims turned slightly pink. Something had clearly touched him.

I explained that my mother did not bring up her children to be bilingual but, having lived and attended school in Germany for seven years, I could understand and speak the language. Had I not been granted that German experience and learned to read old German Sütterling script, none of my

---

222 Dawa's journey cost 7x her monthly salary.

translation work and dives into old family documents, books, newspapers and journals would have been possible.

'The universe certainly works in many mysterious ways!' I laughed. It was a relief to discover that I could still laugh, even though what I had learnt about humankind's darker side was no laughing matter.

VIENNA, MAY 2007

THE LEARNING CURVE CONTINUES

Various welcome visitors – and problems with my laptop – interrupted my work. My laptop had been malfunctioning for some time and finally expired after innumerable DIY repairs, leaving me with an anxiety level that pushed the boundaries of the Richter scale. Alex kindly lent me his old laptop so I could at least make contact with the outside world via Skype – and then I discovered that my own laptop was still insured under an extended warranty agreement.

I woke up one morning feeling absolutely marvellous! The tourist season was revving up so that 'we' locals who enjoyed the late-afternoon sunshine at Schönbrunn were once again competing for a space on park benches with the foreign visitors who were arriving by the coachload.

I eventually sat on a bench in the sun by Neptune's Fountain. At first I hesitated: the bench could be seen from quite a distance, not such a good thing if THE STALKER was on the prowl! Even so, I claimed a place at the far end from a man who had his nose buried in a book. I pulled out a book and started reading – but not for long.

'Excuse me, are you English?'

Oh, for heaven's sake, not another weirdo?

'Yes, I am.' *Perhaps if I keep it monosyllabic, he'll get the message?*

'I thought you might be, I noticed you were reading an English book.'

'Yes, it is.'

An hour later I had learnt quite a lot about Peter and the painfully confusing aftermath of discovering that his late father had been a young Jewish refugee from Vienna whose whole family had been murdered in the Holocaust. With very little idea of how to go about it, Peter had arrived on his first visit a few days earlier in the hope of at least beginning the process of discovering more about who his father – and who he himself – was.

As we said goodbye, Peter suggested I might join him and his host, an expat American called Chris, for dinner in the old town. I was far too hungry to wait such a long time to eat so I agreed to meet with them for an after-dinner drink.

I spent an interesting evening chatting with two complete strangers over a leisurely glass or two of chilled Grüner Veltliner. Little could I have guessed that I was about to embark upon yet another stretch of that fascinating learning curve called life!

THE TUMBLE BACKWARDS DOWN THE HILL

Three days later, exactly four weeks to the day since my father had died, I was lying in bed staring into space. I had finally been stopped in my tracks.

That carefree vitality and inner freedom of the past couple of weeks had gone. I was working on my laptop feeling perfectly at ease, when suddenly the tell-tale pain I recalled from several years ago arose from my solar plexus. It advanced with sickening intensity into my chest, spreading and tightening like a crushing vice into my neck, my jaw and down both arms until it reached my fingertips.

I knew from experience that there would be at least twenty minutes of absolute torture. Despite multiple tests after the last two episodes, the doctors had found nothing wrong with my heart: 'Just one of those things.' But it occurred to me that maybe the third time I might not be quite so lucky. Breathe...

I am not prone to panicking but this time I called Don on Skype and he stayed on-line while I summoned an ambulance. I willed it to get to me quickly; I needed to let them in but I'd broken into a cold sweat, started shaking and my legs were weak.

The paramedics seemed to arrive remarkably quickly and I was able to open my front door and press the remote for the main entrance below.

They asked if I had eaten breakfast (I had) before checking my pulse and blood pressure. 'I wish mine were as good as that!' One paramedic was doing his best to reassure me that I was not about to die.

He and his partner decided it might be wise to get me to hospital. I heard the word 'Panikattacke' (panic attack), which irritated me because it told me nothing. I hadn't been feeling in the slightest bit stressed, let alone panicked.

I was taken to a neurological unit. Once at the hospital, a nurse attached me to an electrocardiogram and some other monitoring devices. At the same time another nurse struggled repeatedly to insert a needle into my barely detectable veins. Eventually she struck lucky and, visibly relieved, drew several phials of blood.

The first nurse asked me innumerable health and administrative questions and I slurred my answers. When the paperwork was completed, they hooked me up to a drip and kept me in A&E for observation until they were satisfied that I was stable enough to be moved to the day ward. Once I'd been transferred to my bed, curiosity kicked in. 'What's in the drip?'

'Vitamin C and lots of other stuff.'

'Excuse me, do you have some tissues you could give me?' I wasn't thinking of anything in particular, yet tears were soaking my hair and trickling into my ears. Then I remembered my mother back in Munich, Oma, my great-grandmother Josepha, so much unacknowledged sadness.

It was almost 6pm and I'd been lying in hospital since well before lunchtime. While my mind and my energy might have zoned out, my bladder had not. Although I was still woozy I made it to the bathroom and back. The nurse who accompanied told me that there was a bed on the main ward if I wanted to stay the night, but if I felt strong enough they thought it was safe for me to rest at home.

All I really wanted was to get back inside my own four walls, lie in my bed and sleep for as long as I pleased. I phoned Don about my discharge and signed the pieces of paper that were placed in front of me, took the envelope with my test results and a note to the GP I did not have, and headed for the exit.

As soon as I got outside, I realised that I had no idea where I was! Where was the tram stop? I was carrying only a small amount of change so a taxi was out of the question, and credit cards were not yet king. I went back to the admissions desk to ask for directions.

The nurse and duty officer who had said goodbye to me a few minutes before looked concerned. '*Sind Sie ganz allein? Ist alles in Ordnung?*'[223]

In fact, I was spaced out and moving in slow motion. It took me less than a minute to reach the exit again but the instructions for finding the road beyond the hospital grounds had already vanished into thin air. I was as clueless as before but what was the point of panicking? *To hell with it, just put one foot in front of the other and allow yourself to be taken to wherever. You're not about to fall off the end of the earth!*

How I found my way back to the apartment is a mystery. I vaguely remembered reaching a tram stop and thinking, '*It looks as if it's going*

---

223   Are you all on your own? Is everything all right?

towards town so just get on and see what happens'.

The next morning I opened the envelope and read the discharge notes: in the event of recurrence, seek immediate medical attention. Oh.

Five days after my 'panic attack' I was still taking it easy. I did go to an afternoon barbecue but ended up leaving early because I simply ran out of steam. Curiously, one of the guests brought up the subject of 'men behaving badly' that gave me the opportunity to get the subject of 'the stalker' out of my head – except I was told quite firmly to report him to the police.

Although he had come quite close at times, he had not approached me directly or followed me beyond the park gates. I had no wish to cause any more difficulty for someone who was clearly going through a tricky patch; just one look at his posture and trudging gait was enough to know that. Besides, I had seen a teenage girl run up to him and plant an affectionate kiss on his cheek, after which they had strolled off chatting amiably like the father and daughter I was certain they were.

He wasn't a dangerous pervert, just an unhappy man looking for an opportunity to speak to me because subconsciously he sensed I was empathetic. Unfortunately I no longer had the energy or the inclination to become the focus of a needy man! Much as it vexed me, I had little choice but to find another venue for my only stress-relieving pleasure in life.

Frederick was kind. He and his family had visited us in England once, and Don and I had spent an evening with him and his wife during a visit to Vienna. Now, having received a call from Don, he immediately offered me a spare bed if I felt uneasy being alone at home. Although I was grateful, the logistics would have added to my woes so I declined. Instead I took up his offer to meet for coffee if I needed a little company. It was pleasant sitting and chatting while the sweet coffee perked me up, but by the time I arrived back at the apartment I could barely make it through my front door.

A few days later I was motivated enough to spend a couple hours at the IKG studying some microfilmed files, but by the time I left every cell in my body seemed to be screaming.

After a good night's sleep I woke up feeling considerably better, which was just as well, because my new acquaintance Chris came over and I needed to concentrate. Chris was, amongst other things, a professional astrologer and the old curiosity to expand my understanding of the multiple facets of our existence got the better of me. He had moved to Vienna because he'd felt like it; he was a free spirit following his inclinations. What his wider story was, I didn't know, but as time went by it turned out to be very educational.

One of my friends back in London thought I was mad to invite a stranger into my home but if I'd detected any threat, I would have insisted on meeting in a public place – or probably not at all.

Having introduced his analysis with the rather ominous announcement, 'It's very difficult being you,' there was a lot of technical stuff about planets in houses, double Leo (or was it triple?) conjunctions, sextiles, squares, and trines that went way over my head. However, I was pleased to hear that certain influences could be responsible for what my mother liked to sum up as 'You're far too sensitive for your own good' and Don liked to joke 'You're definitely an alien!'

When Chris pointed to two areas of my chart relating to parental influences, he surprised me with an accurate assessment of my mother's deepest fears and my father's distance in my life. As for the future, he said there would be more ebbs, flows and challenges but things would eventually come together. Thankfully there were no specific predictions to test my credulity or pin my hopes on. Neither did I ask for them.

We spent some time weaving a colourful conversational tapestry with threads of astrology, philosophy, religion, history and politics, and I found myself enjoying an unaccustomed open exchange of ideas. We enjoyed ourselves so much that we agreed to meet again in a couple of days time.

We had arranged to meet for coffee at the Albertina Museum, but as I was leaving St. Stephen's Square underground station my mind went blank. What was I doing? Where was I going? Now what? Ah yes, this is Stephansplatz and we are supposed to be meeting at the Albertina. Where the heck was the Albertina? How did I get there from here?

No matter how much I searched inside my head, there was nothing. I tried not to panic, breathed deeply and waited a few moments. Still nothing. What now? I took out my out mobile. What was his name? It was no good, I couldn't think clearly. I put my glasses on but I could barely see. I blinked several times to try and clear the veil that had descended from nowhere, and little by little the dark object in the hand that no longer seemed to be a part of me came back into enough focus for me to scroll down the address list. I was halfway through the alphabet and beginning to panic again. Then I found him.

'I'm afraid you're going to have to come and get me. I've completely blanked. I have no idea where to go. I'm sorry but I've lost the plot a bit.'

Chris seemed to take this in his stride, though he was a little wary until it was clear that I was otherwise compos mentis. He suggested we go for a beer instead, so we wandered deeper into the medieval old town. The walk re-balanced me; better still, the next two hours flew by as I found myself engaging with a polymath who, apart from Don, was the most respectful male conversation partner I had ever experienced.

VIENNA, JULY 2007

MY MOTHER KEEPS HER PROMISE

Unfortunately, that relatively quiet period after my 'panic attack' was the calm before the storm. The neurons in my brain seemed to be firing simultaneously as they connected all manner of dots at breakneck speed. The chatter in my head reached such a crescendo that I became an uncharacteristically impulsive correspondent, shooting off e-mails with my every thought or new insight to whosoever fitted the bill or at least to whom I imagined fitted the bill. Worse, I found myself becoming noticeably angry.

A six-week break in England helped calm things down for a while, but catching up with friends and a round-trip to Frankfurt for a family gathering in memory of my father left me vulnerable.

One morning, as I lay in bed staring at the modernist triptych hanging above my desk and listening to the traffic building up outside, I suddenly become aware of somebody breathing behind the right side of my head. As the sound came closer, I recognised the evocative scent of Dawa's perfume before feeling the warmth of her breath in my ear. She rested her chin on my right shoulder and gently pressed her left cheek against mine.

Her other-worldly essence filled me with a feeling I had not experienced since an event in my hallway several years earlier, when my consciousness had spontaneously expanded to within a sublime white light. It was infinite and eternal; it was me, I was it. I was complete. The bliss of pure, cosmic consciousness was beyond words.

When my awareness returned to the hallway, I experienced several minutes of heaven on earth that set me on yet another trajectory of searching.

Now, in Vienna, my mother had a life-changing message for me: she was telling me to step out of a specific, destructive footprint.

Vienna's summer season of cultural offerings was in full swing and I went to several events, some on my own and some with Chris, the wandering mystic. Uplifting music and song, educational documentaries, films, good food and happy people – what more could I ask for? Then Don flew in for my birthday and we enjoyed holidaying for a few short days.

But the undercurrent of feeling disconnected exhausted me, and it was both deeply confusing and isolating for Don. No matter what, I had always been a consistently supportive member of our team; now I no longer had the energy or the inclination to cater for someone else's needs when I was crumbling away within.

I had yet to recognise history repeating itself.

Vienna, August 2007

Everyday life continued, though I felt so tired and out of sorts that I just wanted to sleep and blank out the world. Not that I could do that; I still had so much work to complete that I renewed my rental contract.

My brother Martin visited with his foster child and, especially for the boy's sake, I was as engaged as I could be even though it was tough. Tougher still was saying goodbye on the platform at the Westbahnhof before they left for Munich. I had to leave as fast as I could, which was no doubt very confusing for my brother, but how could I have explained in a few words the turmoil that was raging within me?

Vienna, November 2007

SINKING FAST/STONES OF REMEMBRANCE

I went back to Cornwall for a couple of weeks' respite from work, then returned to Vienna. The next two months were busy with research, functions and events in Vienna and London, including a car journey from the UK to Vienna with Don, then back to Frankfurt a few days later to keep him company. I returned by train. How I did it, I don't know; perhaps it was the pleasure of catching up with loved ones that kept me going, though my final return from London to Vienna was a sixteen-hour journey from hell and pretty much finished me off.

My cousin Sarah was due to visit in a few days' time, to be followed a week later by a friend from university. Poor Sarah: what a disappointing time she must have had because I was useless. Joan also had to amuse herself and her first visit to Vienna must also have been deeply disappointing; thankfully she appreciated how ill I had become because she understood the biochemistry of my physiology – although I doubt she could ever have appreciated the root cause of it.

I received an e-mail from Elisabeth Ben-David Hindler, the mover and shaker behind the 'Stones of Remembrance' project in Vienna. We had met a while back to discuss the wording for the remembrance stones for the aunts Camilla and Clara, as well as the other seventeen inhabitants of Schweidlgasse 13 who were deported to concentration camps and murdered. I would have preferred to commemorate each individual separately but I wasn't certain I could raise the necessary funds, so we had reached a compromise: eight named stones with a ninth stone representing all 19 victims. In the event, my cousins and brothers agreed to share the cost.

There was an attachment to her e-mail. A member of the public living close to Schweidlgasse 13 had heard about the 'Stones of Remembrance' via the homepage of the 'Letters to the Stars' project and wished to sponsor the commemoration of one of his former neighbours.

Elisabeth wondered whether I wanted to contact the would-be sponsor because she knew that I had information about some of the other victims who were deported during the 1942 summer purge to render Vienna 'Judenrein'.

After contacting him, we agreed to meet so that I could tell him as much as I could about those who might have nobody left to remember them. Doing my best to remain detached, I typed out a list of victims from which the sponsor could choose who to commemorate.

> **Johann Weinberger**. Born 13th February 1874. Deported to Terezin 14th July 1942. Died 4th April 1944.[224]
>
> **Reisel Königsberg**. Born 10th August 1909. Deported to Maly Trostenets 31st August 1942. Died 4th September 1942.[225]
>
> **Ruth Königsberg**. Reisel's daughter. Born 12th May 1933. Deported to Maly Trostenets on 31st August 1942. Died 4th September 1942.[226]

My eyes began to sting and I felt an enormous pressure on my chest. It was so painful that I should have stopped but I had to go on, get it over

---

[224] Murdered upon arrival.
[225] Murdered upon arrival.
[226] Murdered upon arrival.

and done with. After several deep breaths I continued transferring my handwritten notes into the laptop.

    Benjamin Weinbach. Born 2nd November 1874. Deported to Terezin 14th July 1942. Died 1st July 1943.
    Karoline Weinbach. Born 7th August 1877. Deported to Terezin 14th July 1942. Died 5th May 1943.

Then it was Heinrich's turn. I had been avoiding him but now I had to do it.

    Heinrich Gertler. Born 7th July 1922. Deported to Lodz ghetto 15th October 1941. Location and date of death unknown.

We had arranged to meet at a café on the Mariahilfer Strasse, a modern place that I wouldn't normally have chosen to frequent – though the atmosphere was pleasant enough. The young man was a mature student, perhaps in his late twenties, and we chatted easily before he asked me about my family's story. After a brief outline, we moved on to the other victims. As I'd expected, he was particularly touched by the spectre of Heinrich Gertler and I was sure he would become his sponsor. With a sardonic smile he told me that he'd written to the present owner of Schweidlgasse 13 to ask whether she, too, would contribute to the 'Stones'. 'She's quite a well-known member of the FPÖ.'[227]

A sharp jolt passed through my body. That's the trouble with Vienna: I am always left wondering who acquired what from whom and by which means.

JANUARY 2008

ANTON LUCAS née LÖWENTHAL

I returned to Vienna after a much-needed Christmas break. When I first arrived home in England, I was too drained to check my e-mails and when I finally did, there appeared to be hundreds of them.

    I started deleting one seemingly irrelevant message after another. I'd already consigned one particular message to the trash bin before the words in the header registered: *Anton Lucas.*

    Picked up your request for information on Anton Lucas while browsing through Parachute Battalion sites. I was taken Prisoner of

---

227   Right-wing Austrian Freedom Party.

War with an Anton Lucas who was badly wounded in the leg. We were members of the 6th Airborne Armoured Reconnaissance Regt. which had crossed the Rhine and were advancing across Germany. Should this be the Anton Lucas that you are enquiring about I will gladly pass on any information that I have about Anton.

Gerry J.

It was well over a year since I'd written my second-hand account of Toni's wartime experience, and more than two years since I'd placed my online enquiry with the 6th Airborne Parachute Regiment. A few days later Gerry sent me an account of how Toni had been wounded.

On 4th April – the fateful day – we had progressed to an area west of Minden and passed through a small village named Holzhausen. Leading the way were two tanks of B Squadron, we (C Squadron) followed behind with the Mortar Troop and then behind us came the Machine gun troop. What no one had seen was a battery of twelve 88mm anti-aircraft guns positioned in a field alongside the road. They were alerted by the sound of the tanks and depressed the barrels of those guns that could be used to fire at us. By this time the tanks had gone out of their view but we were right alongside them and they blasted away at us at point blank range. The vehicles in front of us were burning in the middle of the road and we could not get past and likewise the Bren Gun Carriers that Anton would have been in. I landed in the ditch nearer the guns and realised that I was sitting below our jeep and trailer which carried about half a ton of mortar bombs. Obviously I had to move and ran back and across the road towards the Machine Gun Troop carriers. As I approached the first one it was hit by a shell and I am not sure if this was when Anton was wounded. At the carrier I found a Corporal Parker lying on the ground very badly wounded in the back and back of the head. With help we dragged him into the ditch behind the carrier and that is when I saw Anton sitting in the ditch with a leg wound, which at that time appeared to be in the area of the knee. We administered what morphine we had to the wounded and after a while realised that everyone else had gone and that I was on my own with the wounded men. Shortly after that a German patrol came out from the gun site and rounded us up. We carried the wounded up to the gun site and from there we carried them over some fields to what I believe was the school in a small village named Stemmer. That was the last time that I saw Anton because I was moved on very quickly as a POW.

If Gerry J. was ignorant of what happened next, the universe proved itself kinder still.

'When Gerry called from Canada and asked me whether I had known Anton Lucas, I said: "Did I know him? He very nearly got me killed!"'

When we spoke on the phone, Tom B. sounded almost as excited as I was to learn the extraordinary story in which death had tried numerous times to take my uncle but ultimately been left empty-handed.

'Anton and I became friends while serving in the 6th Airborne RAC. I didn't take part in the D-Day operations[228] because I was still in training, but we served together in the Ardennes during the Battle of the Bulge.

'I remember being in a farmhouse by the river Maas, near Venlo – it was my nineteenth birthday and of course there were no presents. Anton, being the gifted artist that he was, did a pencil portrait of me and gave it to me. It was a very kind gesture and I still have it.

'Anton liked to talk about politics – he was, well, somewhat Communist inclined. We had some quite interesting arguments and he used to call me ... capitalist.[229]

'On that day, 4th April 1945, we were ambushed at Holzhausen and fired upon by German and Italian anti-aircraft guns. The entire squadron was wiped out ... Anton was badly injured in the leg but was patched up.

'I and three others managed to get away and eventually met up with the back-up infantry of the 22nd Independent Parachute Company. We returned to the area of the ambush and knocked out the Germans and Italians – there were about thirty of us and about 180 or so of them.

'Anton had a serious leg wound, shrapnel around the knee area. If he'd had proper treatment straight away, it might have been saved, I don't know... We loaded him and the other wounded onto a three-ton wagon that was to take them about twenty miles further back to meet our advancing troops. I had a German water bottle in my hand and Anton asked for a swig – and it turned out to be Schnapps. He took a few more gulps and was probably quite inebriated after that!

'Anton asked me whether I would go with him, so I asked the sergeant for permission. He agreed but then suddenly changed his mind when he realised I was the only machine gunner left. So I didn't go with Anton and

---

228   Toni did; he landed in a glider.
229   Toni, still very young and a former arts and crafts student who had left grammar school early, had been impressed by some academically highly educated, left-wing fellow internees on the Isle of Man. The Soviet Union's quashing of the Hungarian Uprising in 1956 tempered his beliefs.

it was the last time I saw him.

'I later found out that the wagon was attacked about three miles down the road by a group of Waffen SS. They killed everybody and left Anton lying for dead by the side of the road. There were some houses nearby and Anton wrote that he had been taken in by German civilians who handed him over to the British troops when they arrived...

'Anton always said he was Czech, but he didn't talk much about things. He was a very quiet man, deeply intelligent with a wonderful dry sense of humour. In fact, he later sent me a long and extremely witty letter with a series of very funny cartoons depicting the fitting of his prosthesis. There were four pages but the most important ones, to me anyway, were the first two with the drawings. Unfortunately, they have gone missing.

'We corresponded for a while – I think he was setting up a textile design and weaving business – but we lost touch. We got side-tracked by life, I suppose, though I did try to find him in the sixties. I checked out electoral registers but no luck. It's such a pity to learn that he had at one time lived only about forty miles from me.

'A number of years ago I saw an article in *Pegasus*, the parachute regiment journal, by Walter S, one of the German troops firing the anti-aircraft guns at us. He had written a book. He, Gerry and I have remained in contact ever since. He was only a young lad then, seventeen. The story is from the German perspective, somewhat different from ours...'

A short while after that phone call, Tom B. told me that Walter S. had a hazy recollection of some of his fellow prisoners of war, a group of Waffen SS officers. They had boasted about the success of their day's work just prior to their own capture. Thankfully, and unbeknownst to them, they had not finished the job.

Back in England, Toni had been reported missing in action. Whether or not Elsa was then informed of his survival and imminent return, I don't know, but she spent several days waiting at a London mainline train station as wounded soldiers were brought home from the battle front. It marked the beginning of a life-long smoking habit.

As for Dawa, not only did she suffer the news of her brother's misadventures but the Battle for Vienna was raging and her fiancé had just been killed. I cannot begin to imagine what her inner world must have felt like.

COMPASSION VERSUS DUTY

Reflecting later on my mother's state of being when I was young, I recalled her words during our walk through 'her' Vienna seven years earlier: 'I think much of my spirit drowned in the Channel…'

Small wonder she became angry with herself for shovelling the snow or keeping her husband company back in Munich when all she had wanted was to fall into bed and sleep. Anna, on the other hand, had no need for such qualms.

Back in her Dresden House days, Dawa had rarely put a foot wrong when it really mattered – until the day she bumped into her former legal guardian in Great Ormond Street Hospital.

As chairman of the nursing committee of the Middlesex Hospital, Reginald Beddington was there to attend a meeting. He and my mother had not spoken for quite a while. Excited to share her good news that she'd recently become engaged to my father, she blurted it out – but instead of congratulating her 'Uncle Reggie' turned on his heel and walked away. Shocked by what she perceived to be rejection, she didn't go after him. Apart from receiving Christmas cards in response to hers, she never heard from him again.

Beddington's philanthropy had its origins in the conditioned belief that he must act according to The Book: a mitzvah, an ethical command to help those who are not in a position to help themselves. He had acted with the best of intentions out of a sense of duty. There is no doubt that Reginald Beddington became fond of Elsa and Dawa, whom he had publicly once called 'my two little daughters', yet eventually he lost control of them – and he didn't like it.

'I was over twenty-one and I didn't understand that he still expected me to ask his permission,'[230] Dawa told me. 'A few months before I'd phoned Beardie to let her know I'd be coming home to Dresden House for my leave and she'd said, "Oh, but Micky dear, I've cleared your room." I only discovered years later that Uncle Reggie hadn't given up support for me. But I'd let him down… He'd never been a true father figure, but he obviously had certain expectations of me. He had already written to Father complaining about how ungrateful Elsa had been in leaving university… I was young and still so thoughtless … it was such a tragic misunderstanding.'

But who had really been thoughtless? The last time they'd met, Dawa

---

230 Until 1969, the age of majority in UK was twenty-one.

was twenty-one years old and Reginald Beddington's legal guardianship[231] had already ended three years earlier in accordance with the terms of all guardianships of the Jewish child refugees: once they had completed their school education or apprenticeships they were supposed to move to a third country. The magnitude of WW2 had complicated what had once seemed a relatively simply way forward that had been designed to calm anti-Semitic biases and fears of stolen jobs.

Dawa completed her secondary education in the summer of 1944. Unlike Elsa, she was not interested in higher academic education, while moving to another country or even going back home was now out of the question. Under the Guardianship (Refugee Children) Act, 1944 she – along with over two hundred other child refugees who had no parent in the UK – was immediately placed under the official guardianship of Lord Gorell. The Act enabled those child refugees to remain in Britain legally, but the guardianship itself was devoid of any personal connection.

In February 1945, Dawa moved into trainee nurse's quarters at Great Ormond Street Hospital for Sick Children in London. Clearly, she had not understood that, legalities now completed, she could no longer call Dresden House her home.

She was stateless and, to all intents and purposes, homeless. Her father was dead and her mother far away. She was no longer a minor privileged with the rights of a child and she couldn't travel abroad without an official 'stateless' document and financial assistance.

While Dawa was in training, whether at Great Ormond Street Hospital in London or their campuses in Hemel Hempstead to the north and Tadworth to the south, she lived in student nurses' quarters. Her trainee salary was negligible, while (in those days) her anticipated salary as a soon-to-be qualified but low-ranking children's nurse was also going to be meagre. What would happen to her then?

Additionally, the man who had once been her legal guardian had not spelt out his continued personal support.

Like Elsa, Dawa had been ignored by Arthur for years because he had no idea how to relate to a teenage girl. Also like Elsa, my mother had been ignored by the egocentric Ida who had become almost unhinged by her

---

[231] In reality, the Board of Governors of Dresden House were Elsa's and Dawa's legal guardians. As chair of the Board, Reginald Beddington assumed personal responsibility for directing the girls' welfare, while all decisions pertaining to financial expenses, and whatever further education and apprenticeships they might wish to pursue also had to be passed by the board.

fears for her own safety; worse still, they had not adored her sufficiently. My mother had felt cast adrift in a post-war no-man's land where, more than ever, the security she needed continued to depend upon the conditional goodwill of others.

FEBRUARY 2008

DISINTEGRATION

Because of the psychological baggage I was carrying, I was still not well. The exhaustion and physical pain were almost unbearable, made worse by sudden bouts of out-of-control energy that surged through my body leaving me feeling wired as if my fingers had become stuck in an electric socket.

Sleep, other than fitful dozing, continued to elude me. On the rare occasions I *did* sleep, I had terrible nightmares; once I even woke myself with my own blood-curdling screams.

My moods were no longer swinging from one extreme to the other, however; I was calmer, though very low and very anxious. I was suffering numerous physical complaints, from joint pain to skin problems, multiple infections and the re-emergence an inherited auto-immune 'condition'; too much stress had exhausted my adrenal glands and distorted my endocrine and enteric nervous systems to such an extent that they could no longer do their job. Inner tensions had also impaired my breathing when I forgot to pay attention to it.

The stress of worrying about not remembering exacerbated my problems. No matter what I read or heard, the words almost instantly disappeared into the ether; written *aide memoirs* became a time consuming necessity. During a conversation I sometimes had to stop because I lost my train of thought or the natural flow of German; I groped for words and ended up saying, 'Do you mind if I speak in English?'

I forgot how to spell; I forgot the rules of grammar and left words and even parts of sentences out without noticing . Nosebleeds, clumsiness and choking on food became part of daily life; just about everything I had known to be 'me' seemed to be disintegrating.

The ecosystem of my mind-body-spirit was desperately out of balance, disrupted by addressing the traumas of the past. 'Well, Susan Sondheim,' I thought, 'How about this vicious circle as a metaphor?'

Additionally I had Aunt Clara's last words from Terezin concentration camp whispering in my ear, as if urging me to bear witness on her behalf and to ensure that my Jewish ancestors, whose lives are imprinted on my own existence and who have contributed to shaping who I am, were not consigned to oblivion.

Poor Clara, feeling so helpless and alone and painfully aware of her life's impending end, couldn't help herself. Could she have imagined that her anguished farewell would reverberate down the generations so powerfully?

There was no magic bullet; putting myself back together would not be easy – but I was open to it. My mother had experienced similar distress forty-five years earlier. Once, having fled the city's noise to the silence in Munich's iconic Frauenkirche,[232] she had heard a clear voice say, 'Camilla, nobody can help you but you.' Whose voice had it been? She never said. Perhaps she had not known. Curiously, she had sought sanctuary in the church after an out-of-body experience while waiting at a near-by tram stop. As she'd looked down from above she had been deeply shocked by her bedraggled appearance. Had her higher self spoken to her?

My mother entered into a covenant with herself in that church, promising to leave misery behind and to be happy again. It took her some years to regain her physical, mental and emotional strength, but she gradually noticed that the oppressive clouds that had closed in around her were lifting.

'Darling, it's mind over matter. If I can do it, so can anybody.' Her worst memories and feelings, borne out of the loss and grief caused by the Holocaust, were banished once again and gradually she succeeded in rebuilding herself from within.

Beneath her sensitivity, my mother had a very solid core; now I was happy to let her strength be my companion as I determined to regain full health in all spheres of my existence. I hoped that after I'd packed up and left Vienna in a few weeks' time I would get the physical and mental rest I so badly needed.

BENDING UNSUSPECTING MINDS

As often happened I was running late and by the time I stepped onto the street, the No 10 tram was already approaching. There should have had plenty of time for me to catch it providing I walked quickly – but that was the problem. I couldn't increase my speed beyond slow motion. Before I knew it, the tram had caught up and thundered past me.

---

[232] Catholic church in the city centre.

In better days I would have sprinted to catch it but this time I couldn't find the energy, nor did I seem to care. I continued walking slowly towards the stop to wait for at least ten minutes for the next tram. I didn't even have the energy to be annoyed.

As I waited, a replay of a scene suddenly appeared in my mind's eye: expressionless Jews being herded '*SCHNELL!! SCHNELL!!*' (Quick!! Quick!!) to the edge of their own mass grave before being shot in the back of the neck by their SS Sondereinsatz executioners. They crumpled forward into the pit like so many inanimate ragdolls. A man was recalling, a little perplexed, possibly even contemptuous, how they all went quietly 'like lambs to the slaughter'. The children didn't even cry. I preferred to think of the adults as facing death with heroic stoicism and dignity while protecting the children from distress. That is love.

I was reminded of Uncle Toni in June 1940. Like all German and Austrian Jews who had fled the Nazi regime, he knew about the reality of the euphemism 'internment for reasons of national security', and he had been terrified by the rumours of his own impending internment on the Isle of Man. After several anxious months of near destitution,[233] loneliness and deepening depression, he had finally stopped resisting the idea.

> *My dear Elsa,*
> *Thank you very much for your nice letter, unfortunately I have lots of time on my hands and since I'm also in the mood for it, I shall reply straight away. As it is, it's quite possible that this will be my last letter from here. All Austrians and Germans in Class C are going to be interned. However, I am no longer filled with the horror as I used to be with that thought. Since I don't have any work anyway, I'm just pleased that I shall no longer have to struggle with the day-to-day problems of living. I did go and try to get registered with the Pioneer Corps this morning, but the doors have already been closed.*

Suddenly my apathy vanished and I was completely focused. How many times over the years had I heard the question: 'How could the Holocaust have happened in such an educated and cultured country?' I was reminded of Elsa's enthusiastic observation about her new school in England where

---

233 To avoid the Blitz bombings London's textile industry had relocated from London; Elsa and Dawa tried to help Toni out by selling scarves that he knitted, but it wasn't enough to live on. When he could no longer find any work to pay for his rent and food Toni was assisted with small donations from the Jewish Refugee Committee.

she was taught *how* to think by reflecting upon a question instead of being told *what* to think and memorising it: self-cultivation towards a higher expression of consciousness[234] versus unquestioned acceptance of a perceived higher authority's words.

The theories as to how the Holocaust became possible are endless. While it is worth remembering that other minorities were targeted to rid the German Reich and its conquered territories of the 'racially inferior' and 'socially undesirable', what happened to the Jews in the Holocaust was nothing new.

Neither was the myriad of excuses for hating and persecuting Jews anything new. The over-generalisations or downright false accusations were nothing new; the ease with which envy of professional and economic success were whipped up was nothing new – except that Nazi ideology employed the race card to tap into a deeply ingrained Christian church-induced and subsequently often politically or commercially expedient vilification of 'the Jews'.[235]

Creating a sense of superiority by firing up the crowd with emotive rhetoric to divide and rule is nothing new either. Since the beginning of time every leader on a mission has grasped the psychology of the crowd in order to motivate others and garner their support.

There was nothing new about the Holocaust apart from the co-ordinated Germany and Austria-wide attacks of Kristallnacht and the pre-meditated industrial scale of the violence, theft, disenfranchisement, psychological and physical torture and murder at a time when the effects of the three-hundred-year-old 'age of reason' and the advent of universal education should have already consigned such prejudice and barbarity to the Dark Ages.[236]

Unfortunately, the bias underpinning Jew hatred is immune to reason; it is a piece of junk[237] DNA that cannot be erased by reason or willpower alone. Meaningful history lessons or a miraculous moment of mass enlightenment aside, as with any bias it also requires the process of an honest and all-too-often uncomfortable dive into one's own psychological hinterland. I suspect only the revelation of our inner Truth followed by

---

234 What Albert Einstein is said to have called 'the happiest thought of my life'.
235 For a brief historical outline of the Christian Church induced Jew hatred see Appendix 7.
236 For an outline of the growth of anti-Semitism in Vienna and Hitler's rise to power, see Appendix 8.
237 How arrogant that term is!

consciously sticking to it can begin the process of re-balancing deep-seated individual and collective disharmony.[238]

As I waited at the tram stop, I noticed a large advertising hoarding across the road. I cringed as I remembered the one it had replaced, the memory of which refused to go away.

As is often the case in contemporary advertising, the imagery of the sales pitch was infantile. The poster was promoting mobile phone cards called 'Kläxchen'; the combination of the umlaut over the 'a' and the diminution 'chen' gave a connotation of something small but also tiny, sweet, cute. The visual was a cartoon bee, but within another context it could easily have been one of the seven dwarfs, Mecki the hedgehog, Bambi the fawn, the Mainzelmännchen dwarfs or innumerable other cartoon cuties that have proliferated in common culture.

From what I can recall that style of advertising had already been common currency in both Austria and Germany. By employing infantile motifs and bright colours, the advertisers aimed to infiltrate the unsuspecting inner world of a mass audience within a competitive market.

As Goebbels wrote in his diary on 15th December 1940, the greatest enemy of any kind of propaganda is rationalism. Every single one of us can be manipulated unless we know how to stand back, peel away the layers and honestly examine our emotions, biases and true motivation.

I recalled sitting at a newspaper library workstation in 2004 scouring the microfilmed pages of the *Berliner Tageblatt* as I searched for the article about Uncle Arthur's Dionysus Cup[239] and any others about him and his work.

Soon my attention was drawn to other, more sinister news items. By the time I had read my way through every available edition of the newspaper between January 1931 and mid-1933, it had become impossible not to notice a pattern of increasing thuggery being orchestrated against Germany's 'the Jews' and Jewish-owned establishments until they were almost erased from public life after Hitler's accession to power in January 1933.

It was also impossible not to notice a pattern of carefully managed intimidation of non-Jews – including newspaper editors – who might be tempted to continue to express (or permit the expression of) disapproval. I was left wondering how many other Germans with much to lose were

---

238 For my own experience of 'revelation' see Appendix 9.
239 After a radical clear-out of my office, it has gone missing; I can only assume that the folded piece of paper was disposed of by mistake.

called to heel; I also asked myself whether I would have had the courage to raise my head above the parapet if I had not been a Jew.

Maria K., whom Dawa got to know in Munich, never claimed to have raised her head above any parapet in defence of another's humanity; on the contrary, she had been an enthusiastic card-carrying member of the Nazi party. When my mother found that out some thirty-five years after first meeting her, it was a terrible shock but she had tempered that shock with reason. After all, heaven help anybody who wanted a job and a reasonably quiet life who was not prepared to at least pretend to conform!

Unfortunately, as her sister told me after Dawa's death, Maria had been a genuinely enthusiastic supporter of the Nazi party because Hitler had given ordinary Germans a renewed sense of pride and hope for the future.

If Maria and others like her in her working-class community believed they were benefitting from a new structure that promised ongoing improvements to their lives, perhaps it is understandable that they might have been grateful after the destructiveness of WWI and the years of deprivation and insecurity that followed.

Maria was a few years older than Dawa and I don't know if she was a member of the League of German Girls in the Hitler Youth[240] before it became mandatory in 1939, but when she became a willing paid-up member of the Nazi party (which was not mandatory but often advisable) she must have been fully aware of its dehumanising, antisemitic propaganda. Blaming the Jews for every ill had already been all-pervasive for many years. It was akin to learning the times tables and the rules of grammar: ongoing repetition.

Could Maria have known that Jews who had not succeeded in emigrating from Germany and its annexed territories would be rounded up, used as slave labour until they dropped dead of disease, starvation and exhaustion, or been deported to death factories and murdered? Of course not. Had she known, would she have cared? I cannot know. Neither do I know if she intimidated Jews or came to their defence. She would have had to be very principled and brave to do the latter, whether openly or secretly.

Maria could be good fun, very kind and very generous, but from my experience of her in adult life she never showed any signs of critical thinking or an ability to relate to the world around her with some degree of objective reasoning. She loved and despised fiercely according to the

---

240 The female arm of the Hitler Youth.

wind. She was one of Hitler's 'ignorant workers' who, he had observed, could be easily swayed by emotional rhetoric and propaganda. And she was a Catholic. Her sources of information were limited and the soil of her roots was tainted; quite simply, she knew nothing better.

My tram had still not come. I felt exhausted, miserable and cold, so I slowly returned to the apartment where I sat down at my desk in an attempt to order my constantly weaving thoughts as best I could.

MARCH 2008

SAYING FAREWELL

At the end of February, I suddenly felt that my research was done. That spark of curiosity that had often helped me to set aside exhaustion and given me a purpose seemed to have been snuffed out.

Almost immediately, the chatter in my head was subdued. Perhaps penetrating the inadequate inner worlds of Hitler and Goebbels through their hubristic writings had become too much for me to deal with, or perhaps I had simply learned enough for now.

It was just as well because Don was flying over to help me pack and freight my belongings back to England, after which I would return the keys to my landlord's parents. It turned out that they were Christian refugees from the Ayatollah's fundamentalist regime in Iran and passionate participants in interfaith dialogue.

'You must speak up more! And when you do you will be surprised at how many there are just like us!' I was tempted to say. 'But I don't do religion.' Instead I bit my tongue.

I knew that it would be a wrench to leave both the apartment and Vienna. My exploration of the past, however difficult, had brought me a renewed sense of ease with my mother's birthplace and helped me recognise its influence on me.

In the final weeks before Don arrived, I felt a little better. The flamenco classes I'd recently joined lifted my spirits and gave fewer opportunities for my mind to wander into less hospitable territory.

I had released myself from my self-imposed work timetable that, until recently, had included reading Adolf Hitler's *Mein Kampf* and Josef Goebbels' wartime diaries. Though mostly odious, they taught me a great deal. It was also the case that I couldn't help feeling compassion when I stopped to contemplate the two wounded little boys lurking beneath the hubristic psyche of their adult selves. It explains so much, yet excuses nothing.

My new freedom and the arrival of spring also tempted me back to Schönbrunn for the first time since the previous September. During mid-morning strolls under brilliant blue skies with my neighbour, Angi, I rediscovered the pleasure of stimulating, open-minded conversation.

Angi had once lived in Hove, just two streets away from Dresden House, but her German family background and psychological hinterland also bore an uncanny resemblance to my own, although from the other side of the fence: 'My grandfather once said that the Jews are to blame for everything.'

Chris, the wandering mystic, had already left town for new adventures, but there were other friendly acquaintances to say goodbye to. I had appreciated Alex and Frederick's occasional company (and Alex's delicious cooking) more than they probably realised. Then there was Liesl, the driving force behind the Stones of Remembrance project, who had understood the difficulties I experienced in exploring the past. I had just completed an article she'd requested for possible publication in a district newspaper about the importance I attached to commemorating not only the aunts Camilla and Clara but also the other Holocaust victims who were sent to their deaths from Schweidlgasse 13.

I struggled to find words that might touch the reader; in truth, part of me was not ready to share my private thoughts with the public, but I didn't want to blandly regurgitate a litany of facts and dates. When I finally sat down at my laptop, I was moved to write about the pebble and the ripples in the pond, the reverberations of which had brought me back to their source and the Stones of Remembrance.

By the time I'd finished, one of the many ripples had brought me unexpected clarity. I was now certain that the loving bond between Oma and my mother, especially when we were all together in Vienna, had given me a sense of wellbeing like no other. It was the subconscious search for that feeling that had been exerting its influence on me ever since the day that Oma had died almost forty years earlier.

It must have been much the same for my mother, who was always slightly different in Vienna. In spite of everything that had happened there, Vienna was the only place where she'd known unconditional love and a sense of security. When she returned to the city, she seemed to grow a little taller, become a little more decisive and confident. Quite simply, my mother was whole again because she was home – and it was the same for me.

I said good-bye to Etti.[241] She was physically, mentally and emotionally overwhelmed by the task of transcribing and bringing to publication her father's manuscript in which he described his incarceration in Dachau and Buchenwald concentration camps.

He had been Austria's first sports journalist but, unfortunately for him, a Jewish one. Two weeks after his arrest immediately after the Anschluss, he and 150 other 'prominent undesirables' were sent on the first transport from Vienna to Dachau. Six months later he was transferred to Buchenwald until his wife's heroic efforts eventually resulted in his release in November 1938. He was expelled from the country; once in England, he wrote an account of the atrocities perpetrated on himself and his fellow prisoners so as to give a voice to those who had either already lost their own or had been left behind and silenced.

When his wife joined him a few months later, she recorded the struggles of the gentile spouse of a Jew and her battle to secure her husband's release and passage to safety. Difficult though her experience had been, she was also fortunate in some ways because gentile spouses who stayed at their partners' sides for the duration of Nazi rule (most of them women) had to endure their suffering in silence. For many it remains an unacknowledged suffering that, as with Oma and Dr. Vogel's mother, blighted all that had been good in their lives.

Etti's parents' hopes were dashed when no British publisher would accept their manuscripts: '*Atrocity propaganda ... such things are not possible in a civilised Europe*'. Now, seventy years later, Maximilian and Emilie Reich were having their say through their elderly daughter's work. A signed copy of the recently published book *Zweier Zeugen Mund* (*Two Witnesses' Testimony*) was now sitting on my bookshelf, though I am afraid I was no longer strong enough to participate in any more suffering.

In July 1946, one year after war's end, Etti's father enjoyed a bittersweet victory when he received a telegram from the Austrian National Press Association asking him to return to Vienna to help rebuild the country's newspaper industry.

---

241 The lady I met at Frederick's home and who later gave a talk at ESRA where I met Dr. Vogel.

CONSCIOUS LIVING

<u>Paula Löwenthal to Toni</u>, Stockholm, 21st December 1945

I deal with the newspaper over breakfast, even though it does not exactly help put me in a joyful mood. But one really shouldn't bury one's head in the sand, satisfied in the knowledge that we in Sweden are enjoying (undeserved) good fortune. No, whatever you might say, it's no pleasure being a contemporary and I do believe that I would be exercised by the events in this 'the best of all possible worlds' (Leibniz?), even were I an entirely unaffected witness sitting on one cloud or another. The only thing that might unite humanity would perhaps be an attack by the inhabitants of a neighbouring planet, and even then one can assume that, after having repelled the enemy, the old envies and discords would re-ignite themselves. And yet, in an age when technical achievements have succeeded in bridging time and space, it would seem only perfectly natural to no longer have to feel oneself to be English, French or Russian but simply a citizen of the world. Sadly, I doubt that even the up-coming generation will come to experience this ideal state of being.

***

'Do you feel Jewish?' Vanessa Engle, the BBC documentary maker, had asked me during our interview a year earlier.

'If you can tell me what it means to be Jewish, maybe I can give you an answer. Is it a religion? Is it a race? Is it a culture?'

It had not been her job to provide an answer, but would she have been able to? To this day I have yet to meet a Jew who has come anywhere close to providing a satisfactory answer, even though the construct of being a Jew remains the epicentre of their identity, irrespective of their place of birth and nationality, their national consciousness, their observance of ritual and taboos or lack of it.

Certainly I had remained pretty nonplussed as to what my mother's label '*I am Jewish*', which had been so stimulated by her childhood, might actually have meant. She was brought up in a family environment in which 'being Jewish' was not regarded as a race or a culture expressed through often mechanical practices in daily life.

What had led her to insist that Judaism was her ethical, spiritual and psychological home? What had made her *feel* Jewish, in spite of having been an integrated Austrian national from birth, the child of a mixed marriage and later a loyal British citizen? And what exactly did my mother mean when she described the Pfeffergasse Löwenthals as the embodiment of the best of Judaism?

'I've become a JewBud!' an English friend nervously laughed several months earlier when he announced his defection from occasional lip-service to certain orthodox Jewish conventions in favour of a heartfelt commitment to Nichiren Buddhism. He had converted – and he had remained a Jew.

Perhaps my irritation was simply an emotional response out of respect for my grandfather's integrity that I had come to realise had its roots in the ethical teachings of Moses and the exhortation of the Shema. As it was, I found myself re-energised to find that elusive golden nugget buried deep beneath the many sectarian expressions of what is known as the 'Jewish religion'.

I wanted to understand why the Mosaic ethos, once so dear to my grandfather and his family, had nothing to offer my Jewish friend who had felt compelled to find another framework in which to make his inner and outer worlds a better place.

'The Bible is so full of aggression and threats of punishment,' the JewBud had complained.

It was a fascinating exploration as I surfed the internet for anything relating to the deeper inner workings of Judaism. I intuitively opened books to pages that revealed a new nugget that helped me in my quest. What's more, during my last visit home I'd been fascinated by the Christian Bible's Old Testament.

In my earlier efforts to discover what it really means to be a Jew rather than religiously Jewish, nobody had suggested it might be more useful to forget about the limiting identifications of ethnicity and religious practices and just read the Old Testament instead. Even if they had, back then it might have been a step too far: my mind had been firmly closed by the clumsy teaching of religious education I had endured at school and the superficiality of so much I had heard since.

Yet my JewBud friend triggered an unexpected response that sent me on a renewed quest to discover what lay at the heart of Judaism.

I didn't read the Old Testament in its entirety, nor did I understand everything I did read, but I sensed that at the core of the rich blend of history, 'the moral of the story', literalisms and hyperbole to make admonitions stick (and allowing for mistranslations of nuances), Torah represented a metaphor for loving kindness towards all that is. I knew another journey of learning lay ahead.

'Why are you here?' one of Erwin's sons had asked when I first arrived in Vienna. Without stopping to think, I had answered, 'To exorcise demons.' Would I have come if I had known how hard it would be? Had it been worth it? The truth is that, even with hindsight, I would not change a thing: my entire life had merely been a preparation for 'now'.

The freedom I enjoyed while living in Vienna on my own gave me the opportunity to read widely, to remember much of what I had forgotten and to lift the veil of forgetfulness shrouding unresolved ancestral trauma that had continued to affect me.

I had been privileged to speak at length with two men who had known my grandfather and could tell me about that remarkable man. While he may not have been perfect, I was more than grateful for that reconnection to such a beacon of light.

My archival research had helped to return pieces to a puzzle. The genealogy report from Prague had given me plenty to reflect upon as I explored the male Löwenthal line going back to my four-times great-grandfather, David Kohen Levindal.[242]

Apart from seeing my mother's and Elsa's names on a couple of Kindertransport lists, the post-Anschluss IKG archives revealed nothing about them or their family's circumstances either before or after the girls' flight to England. Naturally I was a little disappointed to have nothing to show for my efforts, but I suspected that there was little I could have discovered that I did not already know – but had yet to recognise.

As time went by, I also began to wonder whether Grandfather and the aunts had chosen not to avail themselves of assistance that others needed more. Oma had gone back to work to support the entire household. I also found evidence that she was left a small bequest by one of her gentile employers who must have known of her circumstances.

The privilege of studying the copious files relating to every aspect of the Kindertransport undoubtedly helped me to infiltrate my mother's traumatised psyche and that of all Austria's Jewish families. In many ways it brought me much closer to an indefinable part of me that had been concealed behind a silence that not only protected my mother from herself but also protected her children from their past.

That learning curve was steep and painful, as was the one that resulted from my examination of numerous other files. They gave me great insight

---

242   He also signed himself 'Levintar'.

into almost every facet of Jewish Vienna from immediately after the Anschluss until the last months of 1944, when all remaining Jews corralled in Vienna and not protected by an Aryan spouse or parent, or hidden by a member of the resistance, were transported to be murdered. Much of what I had read distressed me beyond words and moved me at the very core of my being.

Yet even where there was such darkness there was so much enlivening light. It was deeply inspiring to witness the extraordinary and tireless determination to uphold the Jewish community's individual and collective dignity and wellbeing under the most dangerous and complex of circumstances. It was an object lesson for all communities, if not the entire world, never to remain inert in your helplessness. Do something constructive to help yourselves and others; one step leads to another and then another. You may not always reach your desired destination but you will know you have done everything in your power – and we are all much more powerful than we realise.

As I was sitting in my armchair reflecting upon my imminent return to England, my eyes rested on a book that Michael had recommended a while back: Arthur Schoppenhauer's *The World as Will and Representation*. The breadth of the discourse had made my heart sing, though his bleakness and pessimism had not, and I can't imagine I would ever have chosen to spend much time in his company. Still, I couldn't help smiling as I remembered his contempt for those who take another's ideas and make them their own without critically reviewing them and thinking things through for themselves.

Suddenly my thoughts turned to *Ethics* written by the seventeenth-century Jewish philosopher Baruch Spinoza. I determined to re-read his magnum opus once I was back home in England.

EPILOGUE

I am glad that Chris, the wandering mystic, did not offer any clues about my future beyond 'some more ups and downs'. I am even more than glad that I did not ask for them because I would probably have died of fright instead of always looking ahead to better possibilities. The troughs have been many and deeply challenging but I kept to my promise and have done well.

There have also been spontaneous, perception-changing mystical peaks. While I have *owned* them all, it has taken many chance encounters with mystics and teachers of the esoteric to begin to put into context what I had not previously read or heard about. It has been, and continues to be, a deeply illuminating adventure of remembering what has been forgotten.

I did re-visit Spinoza's *Ethics*. Much has been written about what the intellectually prodigious young Torah-Talmud student did or did not say and do that provoked the accusation of heretical thoughts and dastardly deeds which he refused to recant. They led to his excommunication from his fledgling Sephardi Jewish community of Amsterdam for whose religious teachings of the time he had had no patience.

From my own experience I am able to claim that Spinoza did not 'get it all right'. However, could it be that after having been cast back into the desert where he was able to pursue his sovereign right to think and speak freely and to investigate other philosophies he had, in his maturity and in his own way, returned full circle to reveal Torah without the stories? Could it be that with a subconscious glance over his shoulder to the still carefully guarded inner dimension of Torah, Kabbalah, and with an intuitive glance ahead to quantum science and the theory of quantum entanglement as it is evolving, he had – in effect – ended up paying homage to the Shema, a précis of the interdependent geometry of cosmic/natural law: the microcosm within the macrocosm?[243]

Oh Tante Clara, is this what that whisper was really all about: diligently applying oneself to the task of tipping the scales of probability from shadow to light?

Now there's some food for thought!

---

[243] For a brief outline of Spinoza's concept of God see appendix 10.

APPENDICES

APPENDIX 1

DORIS

Aunt Doris was born in England to a British Jewish mother and a Romanian Jewish father. Until the law changed in 1948, British women who married a foreign national automatically lost their citizenship and had to assume that of the husband. However, any children they bore in Britain were automatically British.

When Doris was three years old her parents moved with her to Romania, where her brother Martin was born. It was a decision that proved disastrous. From the outset of declaring war on Germany in September 1939, the British government had made plans to evacuate its citizens from Germany and other immediately affected countries; evacuations from other foreign countries continued as the war progressed.

On 23 November 1940, Romania formally aligned itself with Nazi Germany. In early 1941, Doris, a British citizen, was ordered by the British consulate in Bucharest to evacuate to Istanbul, Turkey. She left behind her parents, her brother, and her fiancé. From Istanbul, she made her own way to Haifa, a port city in the then British Mandate of Palestine, where she hoped to remain safe - and somehow advocate on behalf of her family and fiancé. She was twenty years old, alone, and had negligible funds. Her official status fell under the heading 'Destitute and/or Distressed British Subjects'.

In Haifa, Doris soon became unwell and struggled to find permanent work to support herself. Fearing that she might become a financial liability to the government of the Mandate of Palestine, officials considered writing to her relatives in England to ask them to cover her travel expenses. Doris eventually secured a permanent position with the military authorities.

Meanwhile, the Jews of Romania were being violently persecuted, murdered or stripped of civic rights and forced into labour battalions. The violence reached a climax between 28th June and 6th July 1941 when – with the tacit agreement of Romania's Jew hating, fascist dictator Marshall

Ion Antonescu[244] - over 10,000 Jews were massacred in the Iași[245] pogrom. It was a foretaste of what was to come.[246]

Then, in December of that year, in Haifa and still under pressure to return to Britain, Doris learned that her parents, brother, and fiancé had joined hundreds of other refugees in the Romanian port of Constanța, where they boarded a ship called the Struma. In reality, it was a decrepit cattle barge, barely seaworthy, with room for at most 150 people. In the event, more than 760 refugees, including over 100 children, were crammed on board. Each family had paid an exorbitant price for a 'ticket', but for Jews in Romania, facing the tightening grip of persecution and murder, it seemed their last chance to escape.

The Struma never delivered them to safety. After its second-hand, faulty engine failed, it was towed to Istanbul and kept in quarantine. For more than two months, the refugees were trapped on board—in freezing, fetid cabins, with little food, one toilet, and no way forward. Turkey, wary of upsetting either Britain or Germany, refused them entry. Britain, dogmatically determined to enforce its immigration quotas in Palestine, would not relent. A final plea to at least save the children was denied. Doris' desperate appeal, on bended knees in the High Commissioner's office, proved futile.

On 23 February 1942, Turkish authorities towed the Struma back out to sea and cast it adrift. The next day, it was torpedoed by a Soviet submarine. Some 500 refugees died instantly in the blast; the rest succumbed to wounds, exposure, or exhaustion in the icy waters. Rescue came too late. Of the 769 passengers, only one survived.

Doris received the news that her parents, brother, and future husband - whom she had been waiting for - were dead, while the British authorities now wanted her gone. After much to-ing and fro-ing, they loaned her the money for her passage to England, but once there, she struggled to support herself and repay the debt. She was pursued for years for repayment, until it was eventually written off.

Doris' life became a testament to resilience - but also to endurance in the face of the long shadow cast across her soul.

---

244 'I give the mob complete license to massacre (the Jews). I will withdraw to my fortress, and after the slaughter, I will restore order.' Session of the Council of Ministers, 15th 1941. Source: Yad Vashem. 'The Role of Ion Antonescu in the Planning and Implementation of Antisemitic and Anti-Roma Policies of the Romanian State'.
245 A city in the east of Romania.
246 Between 380,000-400,000 Jews were murdered in territories under Antonescu's war-time leadership, including Western Ukraine

APPENDIX 2

THE VONDRAS

When Oma was born on the industrial outskirts of Prague, the city was the capital of the Kingdom of Bohemia, a crownland within the wider Czech territories subject to Austria-Hungary's imperial and royal rule from Vienna. Bloody revolutions and wars, devolutions and the union of provinces gave rise to the independent Republic of Czechoslovakia in 1918, before – after more recent separations – giving way to what is now Czechia, the Czech Republic.

At the time of Marie's birth her father Vojtek, like his father Jakub before him, was described in official documents as *Arbeiter* (worker), which suggests they were both unskilled in any specific trade. In fact they were part of the remnants of a feudal system that, in one guise or another, had existed in Christian Europe for centuries and had only recently come to a legally enforced end.

Historically, the peasantry of what had become (after centuries of violent religious infighting between spin-offs of the Hussite[247] reform

---

[247] Named after Jan Hus. Born into poverty in Bohemia c 1369, became a Catholic priest, theologian and philosopher; master, dean and, for a short period, rector of Charles University in Prague. Hus challenged prevailing Christian Church dogma, religious practices, and the infallibility of the pope. Instead, he saw the scriptures as a personal journey of discovery and not to be dictated by a self-appointed authority. He also challenged the corruption within the institution itself and the granting by secular rulers of vast tracts of Bohemian land to the Church that levied heavy taxes upon the population for its own benefit. The lifestyle of the higher clergy had become anything but humble and meek; from the very top down, the institution of the Christian Church was beset by nepotism. Hus also challenged the selling of higher clerical offices and other important roles to members of the secular elite, and the selling of indulgences that were said to guarantee the purchaser entry to heaven; profit from the latter were divided between the Church and secular ruler. In 1414 Hus was called to appear before an ecumenical council at Constance and promised freedom of passage irrespective of the outcome of the hearing. However, when he arrived in November of that year he was kept in confinement. Eight months later, after three appearances before the Council during which he refused to recant, he was denounced as a heretic. In the spirit of 'no blood on our hands' the Church Council

movement and pro-Roman Catholic Church crusaders) a predominantly Protestant Bohemia had enjoyed relative autonomy as subject tenants. That ended after the victory by a confederation of Catholic armies supporting Holy Roman Emperor Ferdinand II at the battle of Bílá Hora[248] on 8th November 1620, followed by the gruesome, symbolism-laden[249] executions in Prague town square on 16th June 1621 and the subsequent imposition of Catholicism as the only permitted religion in Bohemia in 1624.[250]

The mass exodus of the majority of Protestant landowners, the educated towns people and their vast entourages of highly skilled artisans who refused to convert was followed by the take-over of their estates[251] and properties by Catholics of German descent. Consequently, generations of Bohemia's uneducated peasants were tethered to pieces of land in return for providing labour, produce, services and conscripted fighting forces for their overlords who supplied the troops for the Catholic empire's armies. The peasants had no autonomy over their personal destinies.

In England, where feudalism had arrived in the eleventh century with Roman Catholic and territorially ambitious William the Conqueror, the system had gradually declined until it was completely eradicated by the Tenures Abolition Act of 1660. In France it took just over another hundred years before the revolution in 1789 gave rise to a decree abolishing the feudal system that finally granted civil liberty and (in theory) equality to all its citizens.

The arch-elitist Frederick the Great of Prussia's somewhat lame efforts to end serfdom in his domain remained unsatisfactory during his lifetime, while Catherine the Great of Russia continued to drag her heels. No matter what she is reported to have thought in more educated and

---

handed Hus over to the civic authorities who condemned him to the usual earthly punishment for heresy: he was burned alive at the stake on 6th July 1415.

248   White Mountain, a short distance from Prague.

249   For example, Jan Jesensky, polymath extraordinaire, philosopher, rector of Prague's Charles University and skilled public speaker had his tongue cut out before he was decapitated.

250   The imposition of Catholicism went against Emperor Rudolf II's politically expedient Letter of Majesty (1609) that was supposed to ensure religious freedom in Bohemia. The Catholic victory at Bílá Hora marked the escalation of the Catholic v Protestant conflict across Europe. Known as the Thirty Years' War, between 4-8 million people are estimated to have perished due to battle casualties, famine and disease. The conflict ended in 1648 after a series of agreements known collectively as the Treaty of Westphalia.

251   Apart from the manor house complex, the rural estates generally included several villages.

enlightened terms, there were too many landowning princes and nobles on whose financial, political and military support the imperial power base depended and who it was necessary to keep on side.

The Vienna-born and based Holy Roman Empire's Empress Maria Theresa did tinker around the edges to start the process of removing the shackles of mass ignorance within the empire, but it was only upon the succession of her son Joseph II in 1765 that matters really began to move in a more liberal direction.

Reportedly with half an eye on the economic benefits of expanding the taxation system directly to the population at large, instead of relying upon income-generating landowners who tended to be creative in avoiding tax, Joseph is also reputed to have been a more sensitive individual than most in his position. Apparently disturbed by the plight of the peasants he had observed during his travels, he is said to have been deeply impressed by the writings of thinkers such as Voltaire and attempted to tread completely new ground with his 1781 Serfdom Patent.

The more enlightened autocrat Holy Roman Emperor Joseph II may have envisaged a different way of doing things, but the failure of those with vested interests to implement his policies in their entirety during his lifetime is said to have left him feeling disappointed and unappreciated.

It took another fifty years and several more local skirmishes before the 1848–9 full-blown anti-monarchist uprisings across the now renamed Austrian Empire eventually frightened the landed elite into making concessions. Even in Bohemia, where the peasantry had continued to be subjected to the most steadfast of feudalism, the land-owning nobility finally capitulated to unstoppable forces, while rethinking and implementing strategies for their own survival within a new order. Absolutism and feudalism were finally dead.

Whether serf or free citizen, Vojtek was still obliged to submit to conscription into the Austrian Royal Imperial Cavalry. After serving time helping foil the Muslim Ottoman Empire's latest attempt to conquer central Europe and impose Islam (of which he was very proud) he returned home from Bosnia and married.

The couple's rural environment held little promise of moving beyond the lowest rung of the newly available socio-economic ladder. Moving to an urban industrial environment with greater opportunity for regular paid work must have been perceived as a better prospect.

APPENDIX 3

THE RELOCATION OF VIENNA'S JEWS FROM THE WALLED CITY TO UNTERER WERD 1624

Following another round of demands by vocal members of Vienna's Catholic inhabitants Ferdinand II decided instead that they relocate to a designated area beyond the walled city within the district of Unterer Werd (Lower Werd) on the eastern bank of the Danube Canal. There, they were assured the emperor's protection 'forever' and permitted to cross the canal toll-free to continue running their businesses in town. In return, the Jewish community had to pay considerable sums of money each year in taxes to the city coffers and even more in tributes each year into the imperial treasury as protection money.[252] It was tough, but still they thrived.

After Ferdinand II's death in February 1637, Vienna's city council once again pressured his successor Ferdinand III to expel the Jews from Unterer Werd – and preferably from the whole of Austria. He declined; instead, they were denied free entry to the city, putting considerable financial stress on the poorer Jews. Nonetheless, social interactions between Unterer Werd's Jews and loyal Viennese Christian friends continued within the ghetto.

As with the Eastern European Shtetl Jews their marginalisation also caused many to turn inward. Over the subsequent three decades, intellectual and spiritual life flourished as the cream of Europe's rabbinic community, including Kabbalists, and philosophical thinkers (not always Jews) found their way to Unterer Werd to teach, learn and grow. For those who had less appreciation that internalising the subtle esoteric concepts of Kabbalah was a life-long commitment to individual exponential

---

[252] The Catholic ruling elite relied heavily upon loans provided by wealthy Jews because Christians were not permitted to lend money to another Christian for interest. Jews could. They were useful – but always vulnerable to the often destructive whims of their clients and patrons, as well as the mischief making of a general population conditioned by anti-Jew indoctrination. Christianity as a whole has since grown up, and while anti-Jew biases - whether acknowledged or not - still exist, Jews are free citizens in the Western world.

expansion of consciousness, their messianic fervour also grew. You create what you imagine, therefore freedom was just around the corner.[253] They were mistaken.

The ghetto had originally consisted of 15 dwellings; it eventually grew to 132 houses and two synagogues, the 'Old Synagogue' and the later the 'New Synagogue'.

---

[253] At the time a messianic movement lead by the false messiah Sabbatai Zevi was gaining momentum across Jewish communities and no doubt contributed the messianic fervour.

APPENDIX 4

The Expulsion of the Jews from Vienna 1669–70 by Holy Roman Emperor Leopold I

On 12th May 1665 the skilfully dismembered body of a woman was found submerged in a watering hole for horses by the periphery of the now walled ghetto at Unterer Werd. Her body parts had been placed in a sack and weighed down with a rock. To identify the corpse, Vienna's magistrate ordered her decapitated head be put on public display inside a glass box. A Christian woman recognised the deceased and claimed to have watched her entering the Jewish ghetto three weeks earlier, never to return.

When the dead woman's husband denied any culpability in her death, he was accused of having arranged her murder with a Jew; this he also denied, though he did admit to common theft together with stealing from a church. For this, he was strangled and burned.

With the crime unsolved, the finger of accusation remained pointed at the Jews. Several were arrested and questioned then released, while up to 300 musketeers were called in to protect the ghetto from threats of violence by the lesser elements of Vienna's Christian population.

The perpetrator was never found but the event provided the catalyst for mass anti-Jew hysteria amongst the Viennese incited by smear campaigns and hate propaganda in news outlets, popular songs and other artforms. At the same time, the city authorities heaped additional painful financial demands upon, and proscriptions against, the Jews in the ghetto.

Emperor Leopold I was an exceptionally devout Catholic who, until the death of his older brother Ferdinand IV in 1664, had been preparing enthusiastically for a clerical career under the tutelage of Jesuit priests known for their anti-Jew sentiments.[254] Despite that religious indoctrination, Leopold initially resisted calls for their eviction and confirmed all charters granted to Vienna's Jews by his father Ferdinand III.

---

254 The Jesuits worked on the now well accepted principle 'give me a child until the age of seven and I will show you the man'.

Following a fire in February 1668 at Vienna's imperial residence, the Hofburg, which was falsely blamed on 'the Jews', and after the death of his first child with his wife Margarita Teresa[255] that she blamed on the presence of 'the Jews', as well as being under immense pressure from openly Jew-hating Bishop Leopold Kollonitsch, Emperor Leopold I finally ordered the eviction of all Jews from Vienna and Lower Austria – and vowed to never let them back in again.

Vienna's Jews were forced to sell their houses at a large loss, and their eviction took place in two stages: the poorer members (the majority) were evicted in 1669 and the remainder in 1670. Neither appeals to reason followed by appeals to compassion by Jewish community leaders (the wealthiest and closest to the imperial court), nor interventions by the Catholic former Queen Christina of Sweden, who was now residing in Rome, could change Leopold's mind.[256]

Within less than ten years, after the economic pinch had become too painful, the first two 'privileged' Court Jews[257] and their large retinues were granted permission to reside in Vienna – for which they were charged a large initial fee followed by an annual tax. By 1700 the number of incoming privileged families had increased to ten, and continued to increase.

In the meantime, Unterer Werd had been renamed Leopoldstadt. The New Synagogue had been knocked down and the Leopoldskirche

---

255 Catholic educated and Jew hating daughter of Philip IV of Spain.
256 Although the expulsions must have been deeply traumatic for all concerned, in a sense they were fortunate. An almost year-long anti-Jew pogrom across Austria, known as the Vienna Gesera (Vienna Edict 1420), culminated in an attempt by Duke Albert V of Austria to convert all the wealthier Jews now rounded up and detained in Vienna through torture. Rather than convert, several hundred who had been imprisoned in their synagogue committed suicide. On March 12th 1421, the remaining 92 men and 120 women held captive were condemned to death and immediately delivered to a meadow beyond the city walls where they were publicly executed by burning that same day. The University of Vienna later used the stones of the destroyed synagogue to build a new faculty. The episode became known in Jewish history as 'Ir ha-Damim', the City of Blood. Today there is a plaque on a building close to the former synagogue that includes the statement 'Today, Christianity acknowledges its responsibility for the persecution of Jews and understands its shortcomings.' Its presence stands in deliberate opposition to another plaque, dating from the fifteenth century and still affixed to a building in the same square - today's Judenplatz - that chillingly commemorates the killings of the 'Hebrew Dogs'.
257 Samuel Oppenheimer, followed later by Samson Wertheimer, were both highly educated and wealthy Jews who were mainly active as military suppliers and mediators in procuring international loans for the emperor.

(Leopold's Church, consecrated in August 1670) built upon its foundations. In 1675 the remains of the Old Synagogue were used to build St Margaret's Church.[258]

---

258   See Appendix 4; Major source: Kaufmann, 1889. *Die letzte Vertreibung der Juden aus Wien und Niederösterreich.* ISBN/EAN 9783743405851. (*The Last Expulsion of the Jews from Vienna and Lower Austria.*)

APPENDIX 5

An Overview of the History of the Löwenthal Family and their Name

By the time my great-grandfather Samuel was born in 1837 in the small Moravian town of Kojetin, Jews had been living there for almost 700 years.

From cross-referencing the genealogical research I had commissioned in Prague with a number of documents that reached back over the last 300 years, it appears that our Löwenthal male line arrived in Kojetin sometime during the eighteenth century. Perhaps, and this can only be an educated guess, this was as a result of the expulsion of Jews first from Prague and then from Bohemia as a whole by command of Holy Roman Empress Maria Theresa in 1744. Certainly, the first Löwenthal I have been able to trace is my four-times great-grandfather who, until German surnames became mandatory in 1784, was known as David Kohn. He, his son and a third Löwenthal were designated community representatives responsible, amongst other things, for appointing rabbis from further afield.[259]

The spelling of names back then seems to have been somewhat fluid. Transformations, most likely due to local pronunciation and script conventions, took place so that what began with Levindal graduated along the way to Lewenthal, Lebenthal, Lebentall and to Loewenthal, until finally settling with its latest spelling of Löwenthal: Valley of the Lions. Using Levi as the root, and perhaps alluding to Israelite inner strength and longevity as represented by the emblematic Lion of Judah, Löwenthal became the rather grand sounding Germanisation of the Hebrew name.

Classical Jewish historiography has it that the name Kohn signifies descent from the sons of Aharon HaKohen (Aaron the Priest) who, as the elder brother of Moses, was the first high priest to be appointed 3,500 years ago from within the tribe of Levi. Traditionally the Levites are claimed to have been the source of teachers, prophets and spiritual healers to the Hebrew people as a whole. In Vienna's Municipal Archives I discovered

---

[259] A fellow researcher in Israel sent me a copy of a letter in which the authors requested the services of Rabbi Perles; it was signed by three Levindals.

that Gideon, one of Great-grandfather Samuel's older twin brothers, was a 'teacher of the Jewish religion'. A rabbi.

It is also the case that after the wider publication of secretive Jewish mystical texts in the eighteenth century some highly advanced Torah Jews adopted the additional designation of a Kohn/Kohen.

I had assumed the Hebrew script on the Löwenthal gravestone to be a direct representation of the German inscription. Several years later I asked around for a translation – which proved to be more of a challenge than I had imagined. The words revealed not only that 'The loving and kind in life are not separated in death' but also that Rav[260] Gideon had been preceded in high standing by his father Rav Isaac who, for bureaucratic reasons, I had only known as Wolf. Is it possible that Gideon could have been the mere tip of an historical iceberg?

After delving deeper into Rav Gideon's additional Hebrew designation of 'the Rabbi Gedaliah', I also started to grasp more of what my mother had alluded to when speaking of the characters of the Pfeffergasse Löwenthals, Gideon's son Karl and daughters Rosalie and Cäzilie.

> *'Gedaliah was a wise man, gentle and modest. He zealously began to encourage the people to cultivate the fields and vineyards, and thus lay the foundation of security. Under the wise administration of Gedaliah, the Jewish community began to prosper. Its fame began to spread abroad. Many Jews who had fled to places of safety in neighbouring lands during the war of destruction were attracted by the news of the revival of the Jewish community in Judah. They came to Gedaliah in Mizpah and were warmly welcomed by him.*
>
> *'The Jewish governor exhorted his brethren to remain loyal to the king of Babylonia and promised them peace and security. His advice was well taken. The Babylonian garrison stationed in the land did not molest them; on the contrary, it offered them protection against unfriendly neighbours. The young Jewish commonwealth was well on its way to recovery when it was suddenly struck by a cowardly deed of treachery and bloodshed.'*[261]

Gedaliah is said to have been warned that jealous rivals within his administration were plotting against him. He refused to believe it and did not take action. He was murdered along with others loyal to him.

---

260   Rav also means rabbi, though not necessarily one with a religious congregation; can also denote a man with greater expertise in Jewish law and/or a personal guide in spiritual matters.

261   Source: www.chabad.org

APPENDIX 6

Generalplan Ost and Lebensraum/Living Space

There was more to Hitler's 'Blitzkrieg'[262] invasion of Poland and his subsequent betrayal of Stalin: in his diary entry of 1st October 1942, Josef Goebbels reported on the Führer's current conviction that Germany no longer required any foreign colonies[263] beyond perhaps a small one for the supply of pepper.

Instead Germany must penetrate into the east, where the fertility of the soil would provide everything necessary for expanding Germany's 'Lebensraum' (living space) for the sake of the nation's self-sufficient future. It was *this* project that must now be pushed through.

That same day, Goebbels also reported on a speech given by his Führer in Berlin in which he expressed himself with 'exceptional sharpness and aggression' towards the Jews whom he had threatened with annihilation within the Reich.

On their drive back to the Chancellery, the two men continued to discuss the 'Jewish problem,' during which Hitler agreed with Goebbels's radical views on eliminating the Jews from the Reich, particularly those in Berlin. Goebbels reports that Hitler said he did not care how this was carried out, provided it was done with the agreement of Albert Speer, the Minister for Armaments and War Production, so that armaments output would not be adversely affected. Goebbels further noted that Hitler's approval gave him renewed courage to withstand any opposition, especially from the Ministry of the Interior

Even before war was declared in 1939, Heinrich Himmler had been engaged in preliminary feasibility discussions on how to turn the already

---

262   Lightning attack/sudden and unexpected. Compared with warfare of the last few centuries, when battles were arranged then fought until there was a clear winning party, Blitzkrieg represented the apex of dishonourableness. Perhaps it was throwback to the tactics employed by ancient Germanic tribes who were infamous for their 'guerilla' attacks.
263   All lost to the Treaty of Versailles.

long-standing idea of 'Lebensraum' into reality. A more detailed and expanded version of the various options, put forward under the umbrella term *Generalplan Ost* (Masterplan for the East), is believed to have been devised sometime between 1941 and1942 on the confident assumption that the prevailing war against the Allies to the west and the recent invasion of the Soviet Union to the east would end in Germany's speedy victory and territorial enrichment.

After what was presented as extensive academic research and analysis,[264] an increasingly grandiose *Generalplan Ost* set out a systematic, twenty-five-year post-war programme of ethnic cleansing in the territories that were expected soon to be conquered in the east. Beyond already occupied Poland, these were envisaged to include large parts of the western Soviet Union, Belarus, Ukraine, and the Baltic states of Lithuania, Estonia, and Latvia. In parallel, ten million 'racially pure' Germans, together with those classified as ethnically German under a convoluted system of criteria, were to replace the so-called 'inferior' populations in an ambitious colonisation project that was planned down to the smallest detail.

At the time the total population within these territories amounted to some 45 million. Of those, between five to six million were Jews; they were to be rendered extinct by immediate, conveyor-belt mass murder.

Those of mixed origin arising from more recent German migrations (the wider history of Germanic peoples migrating eastwards extends back many centuries) were to be 'Germanised' by indoctrination. Some 31 million men, women and children, deemed to be racially Slavic or of mixed race but too ethnically Slavic, were to be killed or expelled to die of cold, malnutrition and disease in Siberia.

The remainder of those deemed 'racially inferior', including tens of thousands of Roma and Sinti, were to be either murdered outright or enslaved into hard labour such as on infrastructure construction projects across the new German area of Lebensraum settlement.

The bottom line for anybody who was not of supposedly superior Aryan origin was eventual extermination by pre-meditated means.

By the time of Germany's defeat and unconditional surrender to the Allies in May 1945, the Nazi regime had massacred millions of Eastern European Jews, millions of Soviet prisoners of war, hundreds of thousands of Roma and Sinti, and an estimated two to three million Polish civilians of Slavic origin.

---

264 So-called scientific verification of their theories was most important to the Nazi regime because it provided apparent authoritative justification for their actions.

To her lasting regret, my mother never knew whether Zygmunt's family survived

APPENDIX 7

A BRIEF HISTORICAL OUTLINE OF CHRISTIAN CHURCH INDUCED JEW HATRED

The Holocaust perpetrated by the Nazi regime against Jews did not arise in isolation but drew on centuries of hostility – religious, cultural and political - that took root in late antiquity and deepened over time.

At the First Council of Nicaea[265] in 325 CE, Roman emperor and recent Christian convert Constantine the Great convened the first ecumenical council of bishops to consolidate opposing schools of Christian thought and establish Christianity as a legal religion[266] within the Roman empire.

Like Constantine, the bishops were largely of pagan ancestry, heirs to a polytheistic culture in which countless forces were anthropomorphised and their images worshipped as gods. They neither shared the Israelite consciousness of monotheism nor could they have grasped the Biblical command forbidding idol worship – least of all the worship of another human being, however enlightened an example of humanity he might have been.

After lengthy and often heated debates that were intended to settle the matter of the nature of Jesus the council resolved - though not unanimously - that he was the only begotten Son of God and the unique manifestation of His presence on earth. Disputes over his nature continued at subsequent council meetings with ever greater complexity of concept and language until the Decree of Thessalonica in 380 CE fixed the Nicene Creed as the empire's one true faith. With it, not only was religious diversity extinguished, but freedom of thought itself was shackled: dissent became treason against both God and emperor.

The triumph of Nicene Christianity also marked a turning point for Jews within the Roman empire. No longer simply one faith among many,

---

265 Today Iznic in Turkey.
266 The once pagan Roman empire had originally persecuted Christians who preached a single God.

Judaism became defined in official doctrine as a stubborn rejection of divine truth. Early Christian Fathers – from John Chrysostom's vitriolic sermons against Jews to Augustine's teaching that Jews were to be kept in a state of humiliation as 'witness' to Christian truth – laid theologically justified foundations for contempt. Imperial edicts followed, restricting Jewish worship, forbidding new synagogues, and branding Jews as outsiders within their own lands. The accusation of Jewish deicide also began to take firmer hold until collective guilt became a staple of searing Christian preaching.

Over the centuries, these theological judgements hardened into cultural prejudice, legal disabilities, forced conversations, and outbreaks of violence. By the Middle Ages, Jews were vilified as Christ-killers, excluded from most occupations, and periodically massacred.

Within the territory that had once been the Western Roman Empire, this ongoing vilification helped lay the groundwork for the first massacre of thousands of German Jews by an unofficial faction of the First Crusade in 1096. While some senior clerics attempted to intervene and protect the local Jews, their efforts were mostly unsuccessful.

From then on, the fate of surviving Jews, their descendants, and Jews across Christian Europe became ever more tenuous as the ongoing collusion of superstition, ignorance, cynical interests, and false accusations - both petty and heinous [267] - conspired against their physical safety and material welfare. That hatred also evolved into a potent political instrument. The murder, violence and cruelty perpetrated over the centuries by Christians upon Jews in Europe alone makes for horrific reading.

Before 380 CE, the Roman world had thrived on diverse faiths and free thought; the Decree of Thessalonica shattered that liberty, enforcing Nicene Christianity as the sole creed and shackling minds to orthodoxy for the next thirteen hundred years.[268] One can only imagine that this development would have moved Abraham, Moses and Jesus to profound sorrow.

It was not until forty years after the Holocaust, following long and intense discussions at the Second Vatican Council in 1965, that the Roman Catholic Church formally renounced the accusation that all Jews, alive at the time of the crucifixion and living in the present, could be held

---

267 The Blood Libel accusation being one of the most infamous and persistent – and deadly – lies.
268 Until the emergence of the Age of Enlightenment/Age of Reason in the 17th century.

responsible for the death of Jesus Christ. Yet the damage is not easily undone; anti-Jew bias, layered with unacknowledged survival and success envy, remains a deep-seated prejudice that can be easily triggered.

APPENDIX 8

AN OUTLINE OF THE GROWTH OF ANTI-SEMITISM IN VIENNA AND HITLER'S RISE TO POWER

In his manifesto *Mein Kampf*, Adolf Hitler claimed that during his days as an itinerant labourer in Vienna he had observed that the average worker lacked any nuance of understanding and could easily be swayed in one direction or another depending upon the emotional intensity of the argument presented to them. They were not educated enough to be capable of autonomous critical thinking.

Hitler wrote that the electorate should not be confused by multiple issues: select one issue that resonates and use it to manipulate support. As Dr. Karl Lueger, founder of the Austrian Christian Social Party and subsequently mayor of Vienna (1897-1910) had already learned, Jew baiting provided an excellent means of getting ahead in politics: the sport of the rabble.'

Lueger needed an overwhelming popular vote to finally gain Emperor Franz Josef's endorsement after four previous failed attempts,[269] so he had deliberately targeted the less educated elements of Vienna's petit bourgeoisie. He knew that they (if they did not already) would easily accept that 'the Jews' were to blame for their own ills.

What neither the rabble nor the predominantly Catholic petit bourgeoisie will have known was that, unlike the University of Vienna's highly active and fanatically anti-Semitic Burschenschaften, Lueger was more of a political opportunist. He is said to have privately confessed to holding no malice towards Vienna's Jews while also recognising that the city could not do without them as they were the 'only ones who always feel like being active'.

Yet Lueger, primed by the anti-Jew political landscape in Berlin led by

---

269 Apart from being concerned with his antisemitic posturing, Lueger's background was not of the social class historically associated with political power. Emperor Fanz Josef only relented after the personal intervention of Pope Leo XIII

the Lutheran theologian Adolf Stoecker,[270] and riding on the coat tails of the Burschenschaften, unwittingly paved the way for a less-balanced Adolf Hitler to continue where he had left off.

By a twist of fate, Adolf Hitler found himself in Vienna during the final years of Lueger's term as mayor. Naive and provincially minded, he had originally come to the Austro-Hungarian capital to pursue his ambition of becoming an accredited artist at the Academy of Arts.

He did pass some elements of the preliminary tests but ultimately failed in two attempts to be considered for admission to the Academy on the grounds that his work revealed a lack of soul. His skill with a paintbrush also having been judged to point more towards the inanimate, he was advised to apply to the Academy's school of architecture – provided he completed his final grammar school exams.

His past came back to haunt him: his resentment towards most of his grammar school teachers of the academic subjects for whose uninspiring delivery, lack of any deep knowledge and autocratic behaviour he had felt zero respect. His disdain had caused him to not bother much when it came to his school exams, particularly his finals. At least, that was his story. Wherever the truth may lie, he left his grammar school with insufficient academic qualifications, which barred him from higher education, including at the Academy of Arts. He remained in the capital for a few weeks before going home to Linz on learning of his mother's serious illness. She died soon afterwards.

Hitler chose not to catch up on missed academic qualifications. Instead, he returned to Vienna. He was grief stricken, alone and lost, and emotionally labile. Contemporary reports tell us that by nature he needed tidiness, cleanliness and order yet now, with too much time on his hands, he adopted an indolent lifestyle made possible by some savings and a small orphan's pension. That gave him time to pursue his passion for eclectic reading - anything that resonated with his inner world: orderliness, clarity, a sense of superiority, and an early inclination toward Germanic nationalism.

In the cultural melting pot of Vienna, Hitler also noticed Jews from diverse walks of life whose presence began to make an impression on him.

Then Hitler ran out of money. With no earthly skills or qualifications, he attempted to earn a living by selling his paintings. While he did sell some, it was not enough and the rapid decline in his circumstances

---

[270] Stoecker was also chaplain to Emperor Wilhelm I and founder of the Christian Social Party in opposition to the Social Democratic Workers' Party.

was humiliating. Destitute and homeless, increasingly bedraggled and depressed, he sometimes begged for money while sleeping in shelters or even in the streets. Finally, he found some reliable protection from the elements in a hostel for the homeless while earning a meagre income through casual labour.

The hostel the young Hitler frequented was located in the district of Leopoldstadt where he found himself living within a greater concentration of Jews, including destitute Eastern European Orthodox refugees - many fleeing pogroms and still wearing their traditional sidelocks and black kaftans. They tended to gather here, where the familiar culture and community offered a greater sense of safety and belonging. At this stage, however, Hitler's understanding of Jewish resilience and achievement was limited, and his perceptions were shaped more by visible difference and social prejudice than by any nuanced view of their experience or capabilities.

Leopoldstadt was also home to many other foreign-speaking economic migrants from the outreaches of the empire who were pursuing an envisioned upwardly mobile trajectory. Predominantly of Slavic peasant origin, poorly educated and not always fit for polite society.[271] Germanic attitudes had long looked down on Slavs, yet the Slavs had not faced the centuries of Christian church-driven hostility and existential threats that Jewish communities had endured. However, they also presented Hitler with a challenge to his own narrow, provincial sense of order and that difference provided a useful stepping stone for his later political career.

Immersed in Vienna's swirl of nationalist and antisemitic and anti-Slav rhetoric and electioneering tactics of Mayor Karl Lueger, he also absorbed the lessons of political electioneering by fixating on difference.

By all accounts, Lueger was no fanatic but neither was he a political socialist, despite his record for championing the lives of the underprivileged first through his legal activities and later as Vienna's mayor, when he raised the bar in health, education, social welfare and public amenities.

Hitler's own political activities began in Munich, where he soon became involved with inciting mob violence against various Bavarian political groups that were vying for power within post-WWI political chaos. These included Marxists of one hue or another who wanted to install a Soviet-style regime in Bavaria in opposition to the Weimar Republic that was

---

271 In Mein Kampf Hitler claims to have watched parliamentary debates from the public gallery and wrote about his contempt for what he judged to be the uncivilised behaviour of the Slavic representatives who might have had little or no knowledge of the rules of Germanic polite society.

based in Berlin. This culminated in the famous 'Beer Hall Putsch' when Hitler, high with excitement, declared the Bavarian government deposed.

However, after two days of violence the Bavarian government succeeded in regaining control. Hitler was arrested two days later, charged with treason, subjected to a court trial and sentenced to five years' incarceration in Landsberg prison, though he was released after only nine months during which he created his memoir and manifesto *Mein Kampf*.

After that he decided to take the legal route to reach the pinnacle of political power to restore Germany's greatness and, to his mind, Germanic superiority. The autocrat who imposed laws to suit his own purposes was now well in the making. He also remembered Karl Lueger. The rest is history.

Hitler also proved to be an extremely shrewd operator where his personal financial enrichment was concerned and he died a very wealthy man. In the first instance, he made millions of Reichsmarks from the sales of more than 12,000,000 copies of *Mein Kampf*. As well as straightforward sales, every marrying couple had to receive a gift copy – and the local civic authority was ordered to foot the bill. Hitler also received two generous salaries as leader of the Nazi party and as Chancellor.

Hitler is believed to have profited handsomely via an arrangement that ensured his personal photographer and friend retained sole copyright on all images of himself that decorated streets and public buildings (a diktat that was rigorously enforced), as well as the walls of private citizens 'doing the right thing'.

Unlike ordinary Germans, whose welfare he claimed to hold so dear to his heart, he never paid any income tax because he ensured that he became exempt, nor was he beyond dipping his bucket into party funds and 'accepting' donations from corporations in order to amass his property portfolio, art collections and other luxuries in life that remained concealed from public view.

Unlike Lueger, Hitler cannot have had any interest whatsoever in 'the little people'. Everything he did and said points towards one end: his own self-aggrandisement. 'Without you I am nothing.' he told the crowd, having cajoled, flattered and hypnotised it. Perhaps he also understood the importance of the 'critical mass'? If he did, by the time this would-be emperor in socialist clothing committed suicide he knew the scales had definitely tipped out of his favour!

Whether deliberate or out of ignorance, from what I have read of

Hitler's rationale and presentation of historical and cultural 'facts' in *Mein Kampf*, they are as un-nuanced and biased as a toddler's temper tantrum.

Dietrich Eckart, a German nationalist and Hitler's surrogate father as well as his mentor in thought, belief, performance, and much else that contributed to the cult of Adolf Hitler, is said to have instilled in his eager protégé the idea that he was the Aryan Messiah. If Hitler came to believe in—and radiate—the conviction of a divinely ordained mission, why would those suffering material hardship and psychological privation not look to him as their saviour from both real and imagined injustice?

Did those Germans who fell under the spell of Nazi propaganda and Hitler's antisemitic diatribes ever realise how cynically they were manipulated? It is something Hitler's Reich Minister of Propaganda, Joseph Goebbels, understood only too well when, in a diary entry on 13th January 1942, he mocked a British propaganda leaflet drop over Germany, pronouncing them to be pathetic. He posited that the British were not good psychologists because they were mostly Jewish and had proved it with the fact that they were useless when they themselves were confronted with good psychologists; that a nation was only defenceless against the Jews once they had lost their anti-Semitic instinct which, he wrote, could not be said of the German people.

In an earlier diary entry on 12th December 1940 that seems to reflect a needy ménage à trois Goebbels reported that the Führer had just given a superlative speech before a crowd of workers at an armament factory where not a single dignitary had been present; that the workers had been wild with enthusiasm as the Führer gave a beautifully sculpted speech reinforcing his determination to continue fighting because of his belief in the German people who would bring about victory; the Führer had given thanks to the workers and peasants; it had been an incomparable speech because the Führer spoke as one of the people; the applause had been deafening because the Führer was always at his best when speaking to the workers; Hitler was so thrilled with his speech and couldn't wait for the next opportunity to speak before the workers because they were his real audience - because he knew them more intimately.

Then Goebbels added: 'Intelligence is not as intelligent as it thinks it is.'

APPENDIX 9

REVELATION

THE TEACHINGS BEGIN

I have never taken any perception-altering drugs, but after the spontaneous experience in my hallway of cosmic unity consciousness[272] followed by the experience of heaven on earth, I was desperate to know how to recapture that lightness of pure being in fully conscious, everyday life because, quite evidently, it was possible.

There followed days and then weeks of frustrated inner questioning and longing until, defeated, I eventually gave up. All I could do was hold on to the memory and treasure it, knowing I had been touched no matter how fleetingly by something very special, even if it seemed beyond the realm of everyday possibility.

In keeping with a fundamental truth in life, as soon as I stopped fixating on something that was not about to happen unless I completely let go and allowed for providence to take its course, something extraordinary did happen.

One seemingly ordinary day, I was packing my supermarket purchases as they came off the check-out conveyor belt when an irresistible force compelled me to look up. My eyes instantly homed in on a woman several counters away who was also busy packing her shopping. At that moment that elusive sensation of heaven on earth overcame me, echoed with the recognition that *'we are related because you are me and I am you, we are One'*, not as in 'the same' but as 'of the One'. Then I looked around and knew it was true for everyone.

The experience lasted for only a few moments before it waned and, in a state of wonderment, I steered my shopping trolley past the woman and out of the supermarket.

I had asked a question, but only when I let go and let it flow did an

---

272 In theological terms it might be described as a meeting with the 'Father'.

infinitely higher state of consciousness respond. It was the wake-up call that I did not fully appreciate because it did not tell me how to maintain that profound inner peace. It was only when I hit rock bottom in Vienna that I was moved to ask another question.

The answer came over time: conscious living and honest inner reflection with compassion for myself and for all and everything. I am sovereign and can choose to transmute the disharmony held within. Unlike my father's meeting with the 'Divine', I didn't die back then in my hallway, only the accumulation of shadows across my soul did - for a short while.

APPENDIX 10

BARUCH SPINOZA'S CONCEPT OF GOD AS PRESENTED IN ETHICS

While the philosopher Arthur Schopenhauer postulated that human love is an illusion and merely a selfish means to a selfish end, Spinoza theorised that true love transcends the material: it is spiritual; it is harmony; it is completion.

Spinoza posited that God was not (as is still widely believed) an invisible anthropomorphic being sitting in judgement, rewarding and punishing according to his whims. Instead, Nature is God, God is Nature; Nature/God is a self-organising intelligence[273] of infinite possibilities limited only by our thoughts and those limitations are a result of ignorance. Everything we perceive as the material world is an extension of Nature/God within Nature/God;[274] all in Nature/God is of one interconnected and interdependent energetically pulsating substance endowed with the symmetry of divine consciousness in action. It is an infinite field of energy that exists in harmony with itself before the interference caused by mankind's ignorance, disharmonious thoughts, words and deeds.

Spinoza suggested that everything an individual observes, judges and reacts to is based upon preconceived ideas.[275] However, as sovereign human beings who have been endowed with the capacity to think and to question, we are also endowed with the power of reason and conscious choice. We have the choice to cultivate a tranquil mind through learning and honest introspection that results in changes of perception, diminishing impulsiveness and reactivity – and less disharmony caused by the limiting thoughts that lead to disharmonious words and actions and their counter reactions.

---
273   Sometimes also termed 'the Divine', 'the pure mind', 'the primordial mind'.
274   In the consciousness/spiritual communities and in Jewish Kabbalah also termed 'a spark of the Divine'.
275   For example: a vulcanic eruption, an earthquake, a germ or virus, or those we don't resonate with or plain don't like, etc., are not inherently bad.

Spinoza rationalised the importance of taking responsibility for our emotions, arguing that they reflect our internal state and preconceived ideas, rather than the external events themselves. He also emphasised forgiveness of self and of others as a prerequisite for a tranquil mind and of true self-empowerment, even though that forgiveness does not preclude appropriate legal punishment and rehabilitation according to the scales of justice of an orderly, civilised society.

Spinoza rationalised the sovereign right of individual self-defence and the right of a civil society's governing body to take self-defensive action against those who seek to do it harm.

He suggested that our greatest blessedness comes from expanding our understanding of God/Nature and the unity and interconnectedness of God/Nature: a tranquil mind, accompanied by the understanding that our actions have consequences for the whole, promotes empathy and compassion.

Is it possible that Spinoza was also paying homage to the spiritual purpose of the annual forty-nine day period of the Counting of the Omer, a conscious engagement with character refinement for the benefit of one's self and of humanity as a whole?[276]

I cannot know whether Spinoza achieved the ideal state of tranquillity he so cherished. Contemporaries describe him as a magnanimous man of calm demeanour and warmth, yet it is also the case that his correspondence in late life reveals a subtle undercurrent of forgivable bitterness.

---

276   The Counting of the Omer is a systematic Jewish practice of individual inner refinement. There are multiple on-line explanatory resources available to the curious reader.

Acknowledgements

Bringing Clara's Whisper to completion has been a long and often deeply challenging journey, yet synchronicity has been my companion throughout. Without each person I encountered along the way, none of it would have been possible. I am eternally grateful to every single one of you, whether named directly or indirectly within the narrative. You not only assisted me selflessly in my quest but taught me so much.

I would like to express my everlasting gratitude to my husband, Don, who allowed me the freedom to do what I needed to do and supported me generously in so many ways. You are no longer with us in the physical world, but I know you continue to support and help me from beyond the veil. With all my heart, thank you for everything, including your wicked sense of humour!

I also thank my son, Zascha, my daughter-in-law, Jennie, and my beautiful granddaughters, Athena and Thebe, for their forbearance over so many years. I love you so much.

Tim Clark, you encouraged and gently supported me from the very beginning, when Clara's Whisper had barely been conceived. At times when I felt tempted to give up, your quiet words of wisdom and encouragement helped me to keep going. Thank you - I am so very grateful to you. I love you dearly.

Dorothy Chitty, your words of encouragement and wisdom have been priceless - our conversations and laughs no less so! Thank you, Dorothy. With love and gratitude.

I must also thank my editor, Karen Holmes. You have not only been more generous with your time than I could have imagined but you also saved the reader from going down too many rabbit holes! Thank you, Karen. I love you.

Finally, heartfelt thanks to Catherine Cousins and 2QT Publishing Services for doing all the work to bring Clara's Whisper into book form!

www.ingramcontent.com/pod-product-compliance
Lightning Source LLC
Chambersburg PA
CBHW031233290426
44109CB00012B/272